FORLORN HOPE OF FREEDOM

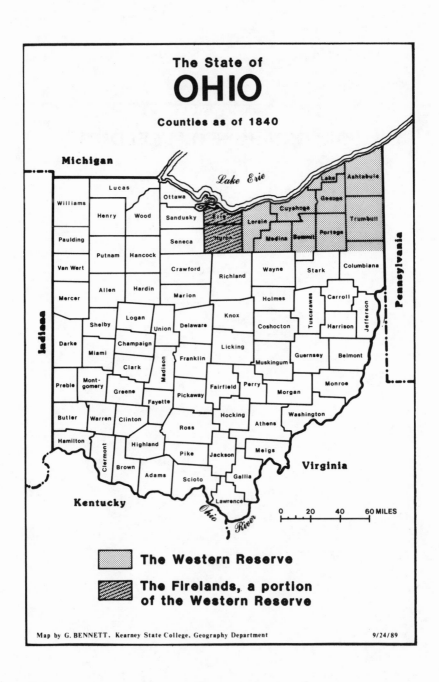

The State of
OHIO
Counties as of 1840

FORLORN HOPE OF FREEDOM

The Liberty Party
in the Old Northwest, 1838–1848

Vernon L. Volpe

THE KENT STATE UNIVERSITY PRESS
Kent, Ohio, and London, England

F
484.3
V65
1990

© 1990 by The Kent State University Press, Kent, Ohio 44242
All rights reserved
Library of Congress Catalog Card Number 89-24411
ISBN 0-87338-408-3
Manufactured in the United States of America

Library of Congress Cataloging-in-Publication Data

Volpe, Vernon L.
   Forlorn hope of freedom : the Liberty Party in the Old
Northwest, 1838–1848 / Vernon L. Volpe.
      p.   cm.
   Includes bibliographical references.
   ISBN 0-87338-408-3 ∞
   1. Northwest, Old—Politics and government.   2. Ohio—Politics and govern-
ment—1787–1865.   3. Liberty Party (U.S.)   4. Slavery—United States—Anti-
slavery movements.   I. Title.
F484.3.V65   1990   89-24411
973.7′114′0977—dc20   CIP

British Library Cataloging-in-Publication data are available.

To

Lewis Volpe
Hawaiian Air Depot, Hickam Field
1942–1945

and

Evelyn Bomati Volpe
War Department, United States Navy
1943–1945

"We are verily guilty concerning our brother—
therefore, is this distress come upon us."

Motto of *The Philanthropist,* 1836

CONTENTS

ACKNOWLEDGMENTS

James A. Rawley guided this project from its inception as a doctoral dissertation at the University of Nebraska–Lincoln. His scholarship and professional example also provided essential inspiration. Benjamin Rader, Jack Sosin, and Edward Homze served as members of the reading committee. Frederick J. Blue of Youngstown State University first suggested the Liberty party as a possible topic and then offered much encouragement and advice in the ensuing years. I also benefited from his considerable knowledge of Salmon P. Chase's career. Stanley Harrold of South Carolina State College read the entire manuscript and provided numerous incisive comments based on his study of Gamaliel Bailey. Two readers for Kent State University Press also made valuable contributions. No doubt this work would have been much improved had I accepted these scholars' suggestions more consistently.

The Department of History, University of Nebraska–Lincoln, provided important financial support, including a summer Heitzman grant. The staffs of the Ohio Historical Society, Western Reserve Historical Society, Rutherford B. Hayes Library, Lake County (Ohio) Historical Society, Mahoning County Historical Society, Sutliff Museum of the Warren Public Library, Indiana State Library, Indiana State Historical Society, Illinois State Historical Library, Chicago Historical Society, Bentley Historical Library, and the Detroit Public Library assisted in the quest for obscure Liberty party materials. The interlibrary loan staffs at the University of

Acknowledgments

Nebraska and at Kearney State College also aided this search. My colleagues in the Department of History, Kearney State College, provided additional help and encouragement.

This book is dedicated to my parents, who made my professional career possible. My wife, Laurel, and our two sons, Vernon and Nicholas, made the sacrifices seem easier and worth the effort.

INTRODUCTION

FORLORN HOPE OF FREEDOM

America's first political party devoted to black liberty and equal justice found few friends. Beginning in 1840 the Liberty party struggled against the determined hostility of the major parties, only to be buried by the resistance and apathy of the overwhelming majority of Northern voters. In 1840 just 903 of over 270,000 Ohioans supported Liberty candidate James G. Birney for the nation's highest office. Just 3.3 percent of free-state voters cast a third party presidential ballot in 1844. Spurned by most antebellum voters, the abolition party was finally forced to rely on a relatively limited segment of American Protestantism. Because religious radicals and seceders would provide the Liberty movement's most dedicated core, the third party faithful's predominately religious orientation is crucial to judging Liberty's political record, including the party's demise in 1848.

Historians have long debated why a small but significant minority of free-state voters began to cast their ballots against slavery and the South through such third parties as Liberty. Examination of Liberty party voting holds special interest; the third party was the closest America ever came to having an abolitionist party in politics. The Liberty party also represented evangelical America's first organized (but ultimately unsuccessful) effort to build a party based primarily on devotion to religious principles. Despite Liberty's limited political effectiveness, the tiny third party committed to equal justice can continue to inspire those seeking a fundamental social or moral reformation of American society.

Pious abolitionists in the small Ohio community of Hartford banded together in 1845 to elect the entire local Liberty ticket.[1] Analysis of township voting records reveals that third party strength in the Old Northwest was indeed concentrated among particular communities of believers such as those in Hartford. Northwestern Liberty voters were typically members of separatist religious groups who denounced slaveholding as grievous sin while resenting the biblical arguments Southerners used to justify their "peculiar institution." Voting for the abolition third party was often the political equivalent of religious "comeouterism."[2] Pious Christians traditionally escaped moral contamination by withdrawing from unholy institutions; the commitment of religiously minded abolitionists to the Liberty party signified their refusal to be implicated in sin by supporting the proslavery parties. Not only were the major parties corrupt by nature—forcing men to bend their wills to the lash of party discipline—but they also served the interests of Southern holders of slaves and Northerners of impure motives. By casting a Liberty ballot, concerned Christians separated themselves from the sins they thought infected much of antebellum America.

Having been more comfortable studying economic conditions or political alignments, historians have devoted less energy to understanding antebellum denominational disputes. As a result the ramifications of the slavery controversy within the major religious bodies have yet to be fully appreciated.[3] Secular-oriented scholars who often consider religious faith to be shaped by more fundamental social or economic conflicts have consequently neglected the sectarian origins of the Liberty party.

When the churches rejected the abolitionist critique of slaveholding, pious abolitionists were left with difficult choices.[4] While some remained with their churches, others denounced the national church bodies as slavery-corrupted institutions. Some of these evangelical abolitionists thereupon withdrew to form new abolition sects and to ratify this religious decision by supporting the Liberty party at the polls. Many third party voters believed (with some justice) that they had been denied their religious fellowship by the aggressive actions of slavery's defenders. In the Northwest this sentiment was strongest among "Wesleyan" Methodists, Free Will Baptists, Anti-Slavery Quakers, many Congregationalists, and certain Presbyterians. For these people the Liberty party was primarily the anguished revenge of religiously minded abolitionists who had been forced out of their church societies at least partly at the South's behest. This experience convinced third party voters that sin corrupted much of American society, symbolized most by the greed and lust of the slaveholder.

The concentration of the third party vote in certain northwestern townships also demonstrates the influence the fading but still compelling force of community exerted in antebellum America. Liberty voters were not simply scattered across the northwestern countryside. Centered in small, sometimes stagnant, self-conscious village communities, the Liberty party often drew the bulk of its strength from members of one local religious body. More than any other factor, identification with a particular church community motivated individuals to cast Liberty party ballots. In a symbolic yet meaningful way, the commitment to Liberty helped reaffirm and unify the community while further insulating it from society's woes.

Despite clear evidence of the religious origins of the third party movement, the once-fashionable theory of economic determinism continues to mar the history of the Liberty party. In the year of the Great Crash, Julian P. Bretz presented a flawed economic analysis of the abolition party's political appeal. Gilbert Hobbs Barnes quickly and convincingly disputed this approach in his seminal study of the religious roots of the abolitionist impulse. More recently, however, even Richard H. Sewell, who capably defends the Liberty party's idealism from Bretz's "materialistic reasoning," concedes "there can be no doubt that Liberty strategists found in appeals to the white man's pocketbook an effective weapon in the war against slavery."[5]

A contemporary version of the economic approach relates abolitionism to the modernization of Northern society, contending that evangelical reform served the interests and reflected the attitudes of the nascent urban middle class.[6] Yet evidence on the northwestern Liberty party challenges the mounting scholarly consensus that antislavery activity grew from fundamental social conflict between a dynamic North and a stagnant South. Most Liberty communities were not experiencing the profound social and economic changes of the industrializing North. Unlike the developing commercial and manufacturing centers, Liberty towns remained religiously based colonies or "covenanted" communities whose social consensus had not yet been torn away by cultural and economic pressures. Moreover, Liberty villagers denounced the free North's corruption nearly as often as they condemned the sin of the slave South.[7]

These communities were in effect Liberty sanctuaries, both for the occasional fugitive slave and for those who sought separation from a society they saw debased about them. Third party communities were remarkably free of what they considered were corrupting bonds, both with slavery and the "modern" society of the North. They showed little interest in the economic issues stressed by party politicians based in the growing cities and towns. Liberty churches were or became congregational in form and were independent of slaveholding members and hierarchical controls. Thus separated, third party voters cared little to retain political alliances either with the South or with political forces in the North. Liberty party abolitionists were free to denounce what they considered was the sin of slavery because they were indeed so independent of those economic, political, or religious ties that induced others to adopt a more moderate or accommodating position.

Motivated by devotional concerns, religiously minded abolitionists invigorated the Liberty movement and proved its most faithful followers. However, they also confined the party to a tiny minority when only a united effort could offset the tremendous power slavery had gained in the nation's political and religious councils. Pious third party members were extremely critical of those church members and church bodies who condoned the sin of slaveholding. Partly for this reason, Liberty advocates failed to convince others of the essential evil of slavery or the sinfulness of Northern society; most free-state voters remained committed to their national churches as well as the major political parties. At the same time the religious motivations and sectarian loyalties of the Liberty faithful encouraged endless internal debate over the party's primary mission, thus adding to Liberty's troubles.

Religiously minded third party voters were preoccupied with affairs within their church communities. Their political activities in the Liberty party were circumscribed by sometimes specific religious concerns, though they always insisted, in the words of Hartford's Reverend John Keep, "there must be freedom in the Church before there can be freedom in the State."[8] Pious party voters largely resisted the efforts of their politically minded leaders to broaden the Liberty appeal by diminishing its abolitionist message. Facing powerful political opponents and distracted by religious and ideological quarrels, Liberty followers thus fell victim to the efforts of politicians eager to form a free-soil coalition for the 1848 campaign.

Local voting returns reveal that northwestern third party votes came primarily from members of abolitionist religious groups, which were often located in small communities surrounded by unsettling social changes. To evaluate Liberty's role properly, emphasis must be redirected from political to religious channels. The third party was not just another political organization with conventional partisan goals; those who voted for the tiny abolition party were intent on entirely different objectives. To fail to recognize that Liberty voters might not have distinguished political from religious concerns is seriously to misunderstand those who believed that God's hand (and Lucifer's) still intervened in the affairs of man.[9]

Liberty voters were seldom interested in the normal affairs of party, nor was it their only goal to achieve justice for America's blacks, though this would be their Zion. Religiously minded abolitionists sought first to reform their churches of the sin of slavery and thereby speed the process of political and social reformation that would include more than freeing the slaves. It would also free themselves and their nation of the oppression of sin and avoid the divine retribution they were convinced would be swift and terrible and just should God's word remain unheeded.[10]

"There never was a party composed of truer or nobler spirits" was how Salmon P. Chase eulogized the Liberty party only a year after its death in 1848. Aside from the posthumous honor he granted it, Chase did not mourn the passing of the abolition third party. Being at odds with party members and regretting their political and religious sectarianism, Chase helped to engineer the free-territory defection of 1848 that ensured Liberty's demise. The Ohio Free Soil and later Republican leader hoped that a new antislavery coalition could more effectively battle the Slave Power, for he always understood the party he called "that forlorn hope of Freedom" could never achieve its dream of emancipation and equal rights for America's blacks.[11]

Seldom conceding Chase's kind, if somewhat belated, remembrance of Liberty, historians too have spared little grief for the ill-fated abolition party. Gilbert Hobbs Barnes, the leading advocate of the evangelical origins of the antislavery movement, considered those who formed the Liberty party "the most pathetic residue of antislavery organization." Many have seconded his judgment that the party's goal of turning the antislavery religious crusade into a political one was doomed from the start. According to Aileen Kraditor, the Liberty party "was conceived in frustration and self delusion, acted out a farce, and died by betrayal."[12] Basic research on the Liberty party has advanced little since Theodore Clarke Smith's history of the northwestern party was published in the last years of the nineteenth century. Moreover, studies on the abolition party typically have been limited to conventional political questions, leaving other aspects of the third party movement unexplored.[13]

At first glance the Liberty party record seems to merit such disdain. Having gained only meager popular support, the abolition party never came close to achieving its nearly utopian goals. The party made such a poor showing that even some of its most devoted supporters abandoned it before it was finally overwhelmed in the Free Soil coalition. Deserved perhaps was the lament of third party editor Gamaliel Bailey: "God help the poor slave, if he is doomed to wait for his freedom, till the Liberty party has literally become the majority party of the country." Before the abolition party was founded, Bailey had warned it might never overcome "the common prejudice against color" and the inclination of "many leading politicians in the free states to please the South."[14] Most historians would agree with his reasons for Liberty's failure to achieve political legitimacy. Another factor less appreciated by scholars and one that will be stressed by this study was how the Liberty party's narrow sectarianism necessarily limited its political appeal. Nonetheless, Liberty advocates, including Bailey, never denied the importance of what he called the "powerful *indirect* influence of a steadfast minority." Despite their weakness at the polls, third party voters remained committed to the duty of a righteous minority to regenerate politics and society. Liberty's "indirect influence" on antebellum politics, while admittedly elusive, has not been systematically studied.[15] A more complete understanding of politics in the 1840s requires a better appreciation of the role played by the tiny though sometimes troublesome third party.

There is no denying that the northwestern Liberty party held little real political power. While Ohio was evenly balanced between the major parties, from 1828 to 1852 only frontier hero William Henry Harrison was able to loosen the Democracy's grasp on the electoral votes of Indiana, Illinois, and Michigan. The relative strength of the Democratic party in these three northwestern states effectively limited the third party's political impact to weakening still further the Whig party, Liberty's prime contender for antislavery support.[16]

It is misleading, however, to consider the Liberty party's influence only on the state level. Often overlooked is that the abolition party's strength was concentrated in particular regions of the northwestern states. In 1846, for example, the Liberty party received just over 5 percent of the total Illinois vote, yet, in the northern counties of Lake, De Kalb, and Kendall, the third party replaced the Whigs as the Democrats' chief rival.[17] Indeed, in some localities such as Hartford, Ohio, or New Garden, Indiana, support for the "third party" often reached a majority. In Ohio, moreover, the major political parties were so closely matched that even a small number of third party voters could mean the difference between victory and defeat. The entrance of the Liberty party into the confusing swirl of northwestern party politics was certain to catch the watchful eye of wary political managers.

Pious abolitionists founded the Liberty party in response to the frustrations they faced in seeking to maintain their convictions in a party system hostile to abolitionism. In fact, the rise of the third party encouraged politicians in both sections to escalate their attacks on those who held unwelcome views on abolition and racial justice. In an era before legal restraints and countless informal hindrances prevented concerned citizens from mounting third party protests easily, the major political parties often resorted to less savory methods to blunt third party challenges.[18]

Democrats and most Whigs abused Liberty without regret, finding that antiabolitionism pleased many of their voters. The sometimes savage antiabolitionism practiced by northwestern Democrats would hinder Liberty efforts to lure antislavery Whigs. Only political circumstances induced some Northern Whigs to treat the third party initially with more caution. By 1844, however, Whigs abandoned forbearance and employed political trickery against the abolition party. When this too failed to stem the Liberty defection, some Whigs thought their opposition to Texas annexation and a war to spread slavery to the southwest would lure third party support. Despite their best and worst efforts, Whigs could not discourage Liberty party independence; party politicians and organizations could neither appreciate nor cope with such an uncommon party effort. Liberty's resolve to reform American morality by renouncing national sins proved to be hopelessly out of place in the antebellum party system.

Minor parties have often been studied by an approach suggested by the work of John Hicks. Admitting third parties have found little success in America's two-party system, Hicks argued that at least they have seen their principles triumph eventually, even when the party itself has long since died.[19] Whatever validity this approach might hold for most minor parties, it is doubtful it fits the sometimes despised Liberty party. Unlike other third parties, Liberty failed to sting before it died, and no major party ever preempted its fundamental principle of human equality. Emancipation did not come about peacefully through national repentence, as Liberty advocates hoped, but from a terrible war they had feared but were powerless to prevent. No worthy successor to Liberty ever arose to achieve its dream of equal justice for America's blacks. Rather than clearing the way for another party to carry its standard of liberty, the third party's dismal performance might have discredited its radical goals forever.[20]

Having said this, however, one must admit that the Liberty party might still have exerted important influence in a sadly ironic way. Third party supporters might have indirectly hastened the judgment day they foretold by provoking worried Southern political leaders to take rash action meant to protect slavery from the menace of abolitionism. Though Liberty advocates sought to prevent the approaching war, only the blood of America's young finally washed away the sin of slavery from the South.

Despite the Liberty party's evident ineffectiveness, scholars often consider the first antislavery party the forerunner of the Free Soil and Republican parties. Typically, the Liberty party has been treated as part of a larger growing Northern majority against slavery and the South.[21] The assumption of logical progression from Liberty to Free Soil is reflected in the common practice of studying the two parties together and considering both as the vanguard of Republicanism. On the surface this approach might seem justified, but it risks serious distortion by viewing the party from the perspective of events yet to occur, particularly the coming of civil war.[22] Sharing basic antipathy to slavery, the Liberty, Free Soil, and Republican parties each represented unique constituencies and each chose different paths to achieve slavery's fall. Above all, the tendency to connect Liberty with Republican victory should be avoided; the political repudiation of the Liberty party proved beyond all doubt an abolitionist party could never achieve popular approval, particularly in the states along the north bank of the Ohio River.[23]

Many historians nonetheless echo Joshua Leavitt's 1848 rallying cry that the abolition party was "not dead, but translated" into the Free Soil movement. Dwight Dumond, for example, argued that the Free Soil party was not simply the absorption of the third party, but "it was an expansion of the Liberty party under a new name." From Liberty to Free Soil, Dumond insisted, "no one abandoned their principles." The guiding idea behind works such as Theodore Smith's was to show how antislavery agitation through the Liberty and Free Soil parties laid the groundwork for the Republican "uprising of 1854."[24]

Not all historians consider the Republican party the rightful heir to Liberty (Louis Filler for one replied to Leavitt's claim by insisting that the Liberty party was indeed "dead" by 1848), but the approach dominates the scholarship of the Liberty party. The only capable modern survey of the Liberty party is contained in Richard Sewell's general study of antislavery politics, *Ballots for Freedom*. Sewell believed that historians had exaggerated the decline of moral principle in the political antislavery movement after the fall of Liberty. Admitting some lowering of abolitionist principle was inevitable in the emerging Republican coalition, Sewell countered that, given the racism of the age and the demands of majoritarian politics, antislavery leaders remained remarkably committed to achieving a measure of black civil rights. He thus concluded it was correct to view "the Republican triumph of 1860 as the culmination of efforts begun twenty years earlier by a small but dedicated band of Liberty party pioneers."[25]

One unfortunate result of this historiographical tradition is that the Liberty party has rarely been studied on its own terms. Because it has usually been viewed in light of subsequent events, the party has been held partly responsible both for the Republicans' later political success and for nineteenth-century America's failure to achieve racial justice. Some of the more durable misconceptions could be avoided by distinguishing the Liberty movement from other forms of abolitionism. Only those generalizations that can apply to those who actually cast Liberty ballots should be used to define the abolition third party movement. Despite considerable scholarly debate over the Liberty party, few have attempted to use local voting returns to examine the character of the third party in Ohio and the Old Northwest.[26] By concentrating on the thoughts and motivations of those few who did break their party ties to stand for Liberty, this study seeks to advance understanding of the abolition party movement.

The area north and west of the Ohio River had been denied to slavery and by the 1840s had emerged as a region crucial to the contest between the free and slave states. Being third among all the states in population, Ohio dominated society and politics in the Old Northwest. In 1840 Ohio cast more electoral votes than Indiana, Illinois, and Michigan combined. Only New York and Pennsylvania cast more presidential ballots than the Buckeye State. Ohio was evenly balanced between Whigs and Democrats, so the growth of a disruptive third party only increased the state's uncertain political fate.[27] Due in large part to the Liberty party's political weakness in Indiana, Illinois, and Michigan, the fate of the third party in Ohio tends to overshadow events in the other northwestern states. Ohio's political preeminence is reflected in this study.

Ohio was also the northwestern state with the longest history of antislavery activity. Abolitionism and religious intensity were especially strong in Ohio's northeastern counties, a region known as the Western Reserve. Together the Western Reserve counties cast about one-third of all Liberty votes in the state. This center of northwestern abolitionism witnessed desperate political contests between Whigs and Liberty advocates competing for the allegiance of potential third party voters. Whig success in Ohio and the nation was often dependent on the result in these predominantely Whiggish Reserve counties. Special attention is devoted to the fortunes of the Liberty party in this strategic and revealing region.

Given Ohio's political importance, scholars have assumed that the Ohio third party also dominated the northwestern Liberty movement. Several key party leaders lived in Cincinnati, the Northwest's leading commercial and cultural center. The Queen City was also home to the most important Liberty paper in the Northwest, Gamaliel Bailey's *Philanthropist*. Moreover, several Ohio regions supported (at one time or another) a third party press; other northwestern states were usually limited to just one Liberty journal. Historians naturally have come to rely on these relatively extensive primary sources for Ohio.

Exclusive attention to Ohio, however, has distorted the history of the Liberty party. The remaining northwestern states, including Wisconsin, which finally achieved statehood in 1848, add vital insight into the religious roots of the third party movement. The Michigan *Signal of Liberty,* Indiana *Free Labor Advocate,* Chicago *Western Citizen,* and Wisconsin *American Freeman* are third party documents worthy of scholarly attention. By neglecting the Liberty party record in the other northwestern states, historians have overlooked especially the contributions communities of believers made to the third party effort. Thus, an important part of the troubled history of the first party devoted to ending the nation's torment over black bondage was lost.

Scholarship on the northwestern Liberty party has long been hampered by a view, now outdated, that was always weak in documentary evidence. Repeating somewhat carelessly the contentions of Joseph Rayback, historians have commonly considered the northwestern Liberty party distinct from its northeastern relative. Scholars assumed that Cincinnati party leaders Salmon P. Chase and Gamaliel Bailey inspired a "western" Liberty party that was more practical and less imbued with abolitionist fanaticism than its eastern counterpart. As expedients, westerners supposedly were less committed to the goal of racial equality and much more willing than easterners to barter principles for political success. Opposed to these western coalitionists were eastern purists who insisted on strict adherence to abolitionist ideology and independent organization. Demonstrating its debt to Turnerian sectionalism (an approach long questioned even by frontier historians), the traditional interpretation closes with the practical men of the West routing their stubborn eastern antagonists in the Free Soil fusion of 1848.[28]

Actually, the Old Northwest was divided against itself. In their efforts to broaden the political appeal of the Liberty Party, Chase and Bailey encountered nearly as much opposition in the Northwest as they did from northeastern leaders. Being hardly a cohesive movement, the northwestern third party (like the northeastern) was torn by diverse views about its antislavery program as well as its political strategy. Most westerners were not eager coalitionists; indeed, unlike other third parties from Free-Soilers to Populists, the northwestern Liberty party seldom cooperated or fused with elements from the major parties.

Almost from the founding of the Liberty party, tensions grew between the Cincinnati leadership and the party faithful. Although the most vocal challenges to Cincinnati's leadership came from outside Ohio's borders, enough opposition developed within the state to cast doubt on the common concept of a purposeful and united Ohio Liberty party. Perhaps this internal conflict was inevitable among such dedicated advocates of religious and ideological purity. A party founded on the principle of Protestantism was itself likely to experience separatism and schism in the end.

A further source of division within the northwestern Liberty party was the often serious cultural differences between the Ohio River area and the Lake region of the Northwest. True, the lower portion of the Old Northwest contained more than a few dedicated opponents of slavery, but these antislavery pioneers faced overwhelming hostility from their antiabolitionist neighbors.[29] The Lake region proved more hospitable to antislavery activity, and, as a result, Liberty advocates there were more adamant about the party's independent position as well as its abolitionist message.

Differences between the two regions sometimes could be demonstrated quite dramatically. Mobs along the Ohio River threatened abolitionist editors in Cincinnati and killed another along the Mississippi in Alton, Illinois. Blacks were seldom welcomed in the southern half of the region (Cincinnati had tried to expel its black population in 1829), while northern Ohio's Oberlin College opened its doors to black students.[30] What opposition existed to the discriminatory Black Laws of the region was concentrated in the northern counties. In the 1850s angry crowds once again roamed northwestern streets, but this time they were residents of the Lake region seeking to protect blacks from possible capture under the controversial new Fugitive Slave Law.[31] Disagreement and dissension among Liberty advocates might have been predicted in such a large and diverse region as the Northwest. If not actually dead by 1848, the northwestern Liberty party was by then at least in critical condition with bleak prospects for survival.

From 1810 to 1850 the northwestern states were among the fastest growing in the nation.[32] Improvements in transportation brought more and more settlers who added to the region's already diverse cultural landscape. Ohio in particular provided a symbolic battleground between those of Northern, Southern, and European origins who settled within its borders. Economic development and social fluidity especially troubled those concerned with moral imperatives and religious tradition. Some northwestern citizens connected with certain churches found reassurance in God's promise of racial harmony; others focused their confusion and suspicion on racial minorities who were themselves victims of antebellum America's uncontrollable economic and territorial expansion. As northwesterners sought to restrain forces beyond their grasp, racial prejudice and Christian brotherhood developed simultaneously in the same region. Emerging from common origins, the two sentiments grew in opposition; neither prevailed in the end.

1

The Northwestern Impulse

"*Race prejudice* seems stronger in those states that have abolished slavery than in those where it still exists, and nowhere is it more intolerant than in those states where slavery was never known." In this often-quoted passage, French traveler Alexis de Tocqueville was inaccurate in at least one respect. Despite the straightforward language of the antislavery provision of the Northwest Ordinance, black servitude continued to exist in the region in various forms. Support for the slave system of labor was strong enough in Illinois to gain considerable support in 1824 for a constitutional convention that might have made the land of Lincoln virtually a slave state.[1] Tocqueville doubted whites and blacks would ever live "on a footing of equality" in the United States because it was "not possible for a whole people to rise . . . above itself."

Tocqueville thought it ironic that in the slave states "less trouble is taken to keep the Negro apart" than in the free states. In the North the "tyranny of laws" and social intolerance combined to perform similar functions of racial control as the South's system of bondage. Ohio, Indiana, and Illinois each had enacted Black Laws meant to insure not only white supremacy but also to prevent the awful consequences of what Tocqueville referred to as whites and blacks being "confounded together." In no northwestern state did blacks hold the right to vote, and all but Wisconsin passed draconian laws designed to prevent black immigration. Although they were seldom enforced, these exclusionary provisions nonetheless testified to white society's determination to curtail an undesired population.[2]

Historians have followed the famous Frenchman in viewing the Old Northwest as "the region most firmly committed to white supremacy."³ Why the Northwest was a particularly racist region is not as well understood. The northwestern states were home to relatively few blacks, yet antagonism toward blacks was not limited to those Southern in origin. The Black Laws received support from all elements of northwestern society, although those of New England origins frequently opposed the discriminatory codes.

Noted historian Eric Foner has suggested that the Northwest's greater degree of opportunity and social mobility paradoxically provoked white fears about the status of free blacks in their midst.⁴ Social and economic competition did in fact exist between whites and blacks, yet the extent of opportunity in the Northwest can be exaggerated. Moreover, does Foner's approach suggest that less opportunity existed in the areas of Yankee settlement in which the black codes were often unpopular? Indeed, the Black Laws received their greatest support in the Ohio River region, the oldest area of settlement which was quickly being surpassed by the more dynamic Lake region. Perhaps more than any other issue, the Black Laws symbolized the growing cultural gap between those who settled the southern counties and those primarily of Yankee sentiment developing the Lake counties to the north.

Whatever the origins, the Northwest's antiblack sentiments and laws significantly shaped the political abolition movement there. While it stood for black freedom, the northwestern Liberty party was necessarily a lilywhite political organization. Ever since Theodore Smith's influential study of northwestern antislavery politics, historians have attempted to trace the rise of Republicanism to the growth of the Liberty and Free Soil parties in the Northwest. Even Smith, however, finally admitted (in the very last line of his last appendix) that the "anti-negro feeling" of the region meant that "philanthropy could not hope, unaided, to build up a party."⁵ Advocates of Liberty certainly faced difficult times ahead trying to persuade the great majority of northwestern voters to accept the abolitionist message of freedom and equal justice for blacks, slave or free.

Northwestern hostility toward blacks was rooted partly in the profound social and economic changes sweeping the region. Roads, canals, steamboats, and railroads promoted economic expansion as well as cultural diversity. With its first permanent white settlement laid in 1788, Ohio had become by 1840 the nation's third most populous state and its leading producer of wheat. In 1850 Ohio would pace the nation in the production of corn and wool and in the number of horses and milk cows. Cincinnati trailed only the great seaports as a center of population and commerce. By

1860 Chicago had grown from a frontier outpost to a thriving commercial center and, appropriately, the scene for the Republican national convention that year. In 1844 Indiana cast as many electoral votes as Massachusetts and more than any Southern state except Virginia, Tennessee, and Kentucky.[6]

This rapid growth was fostered by a diverse group of peoples who streamed into the Northwest. The earliest white settlers came primarily from Virginia and Kentucky, but emigrants from Pennsylvania and the Middle States soon joined them. New Englanders, who were among the earliest of settlers, arrived in larger numbers after Ohio achieved statehood in 1803. Added to these native migrants after 1825 came more and more European immigrants, primarily German and Irish laborers who built the region's canals and railroads. A less welcome strain of population also came from the South. Freed or fugitive slaves entered the Northwest in relatively small numbers but enough to arouse the displeasure of much of white society.[7]

The population of the Old Northwest then was a collection of various cultural groups drawn from the cities of Europe and the East, the farms of New England, and the hills and slave cabins of the upper South. These diverse peoples encountered each other in the society of the Northwest, but each tended to settle in separate and homogeneous farming communities. Even those who ventured to the more heterogeneous market and manufacturing centers often clustered in familiar groups within the city.

Economic development brought new disturbances to the Northwest's cultural setting. Many northwesterners, who felt buffeted by confusing social change—their heretofore independent and homogeneous communities increasingly being invaded by persons of all description—sought at least to control the influx of even more strange and feared blacks. Although they had little influence over the other forces shaping their society, northwestern voters could register their disapproval of blacks entering their communities unwelcomed. Northwestern political leaders proved only too willing to accommodate the racial fears of the region's voters.

The Northwest's varied cultural and religious groups often looked upon their neighbors as strangers and sometimes as mortal enemies. Historians in the tradition of Frederick Jackson Turner have portrayed the sectional contest as one between North and South for the allegiance of the Old Northwest.[8] More than a conflict between free and slave states, the antebellum political struggle was one that raged within the northwestern states themselves for political supremacy and cultural superiority. The institution of slavery and the rights of free blacks often became merely another point

3

of contention between rival cultural and religious groups battling over matters of infinitely greater importance to them.[9]

In its early years the Old Northwest was dominated by transplanted Southerners who settled the hills and river valleys of the southern half of the region. Whether friendly to slavery or not, men of Southern origin dominated the social and political culture of the Northwest until about 1830. With new waves of settlers, however, political power started to drift north. Still, settlers to the south maintained their Southern outlook, preferring presidential candidates such as Henry Clay and Zachary Taylor, or Andrew Jackson and James K. Polk. They had little use for the meddlesome Yankees settling to the north.[10]

Among these same Southerners, however, were some who had no special hatred for blacks and who had even risked social displeasure to oppose slavery while in the South. Like the harried runaway slave, some white Southerners also fled their native land to escape the institution of slavery. These white refugees usually came from North Carolina or eastern Tennessee, where hostility to slavery had once been strong. Finding themselves a hopeless minority in the South's increasingly hostile slave society, many of these antislavery Southerners migrated north, sometimes as a body, to the free states of Ohio or Indiana. Some were Quakers such as Charles Osborn and Levi Coffin, who eventually settled in eastern Indiana. Scotch-Irish Presbyterians were well represented by Reverend John Rankin, who became pastor of a Ripley, Ohio, church and there helped black fugitives from across the river.[11] This virtually forced emigration strengthened the group solidarity of migrants whose religious bonds had been reinforced by common hostility to slavery. Like other émigrés, these antislavery Southerners, once having settled in their adopted land, sought one day to redeem their fallen homeland of the defects that had caused their flight.

Among the most conspicuous of emigrants to the Northwest were those of New England origins. Whether arriving directly from New England itself or being once-removed from Yankee colonies in western New York, these Yankee offspring maintained close cultural ties with old New England. Easily the heaviest concentration of New Englanders was in the Lake region of the Northwest, including northern Illinois and the Connecticut Western Reserve of northeastern Ohio. Lacking the Southern leaven of sister northwestern states, Michigan and Wisconsin were even stronger areas of Yankee culture.[12] Due to swamps, bad reputation, and land speculators, northwestern Ohio and northern Indiana attracted fewer New Englanders and thus were much weaker in abolitionist strength.[13]

Most New England settlers arrived in the Northwest in single family groups but quickly reestablished contact with friends and relations from their home region. Other Yankees came in timeworn Puritan tradition, as a group of dedicated pilgrims anxious to build a new Christian commonwealth in the wilderness. Religious colonies such as Oberlin in Ohio and Princeton and Geneseo in Illinois, founded sometimes with formal covenants, were planted by Yankees eager to found a new society and "to consider the betterment of their growing families." Religion often unified and governed these communities; in Tallmadge, Ohio, for example, only church members could buy land. Although they were not yet awakened to the evils of slavery, these tiny puritan commonwealths in the wilderness insisted on respect to the traditional New England virtues of sobriety, schooling, and the Sabbath.[14]

Many of the transplanted New Englanders had been Congregationalists, but soon found it difficult to support independent churches in struggling northwestern communities. To save their flock from irreligion, Presbyterians and Congregationalists had agreed in 1801 to a Plan of Union allowing members of the two denominations west of the Hudson to form united churches. As a result, most churches in western New York and northern Ohio were a combination of Congregational and Presbyterian forms. For almost thirty years this arrangement produced satisfactory results and seemed to advance the goal of Christian unity. By the middle 1830s, however, those of Congregational heritage regretted this alliance with Presbyterianism and sought to reestablish the church of their fathers.[15] Congregationalists thereupon selected the slavery issue as a fitting one to help distinguish their church from that of the Presbyterians.

As they filtered into the northern region and challenged the south for political power, New Englanders inflamed the southerners' pride with their characteristic Yankee cultural imperialism. Remembering the achievements of their New England homeland, Yankees found the essentially Southern culture of the lower Northwest deficient in nearly every way. Eventually, as New Englanders sought to refashion northwestern society in the manner of their own covenanted communities, they sought common goals and cooperated politically in order to win control of state and local government.[16] The Lake region naturally looked east to New England and New York for social and political guidance; few transplanted Yankees were impressed with the leadership provided by residents of the Ohio River region.

The northern and southern sections of the Northwest typically struggled over political office and patronage and disagreed over issues such as improvement projects and others more cultural in nature. Probably the cleanest break came over the civil rights of blacks; support for repeal of the Black Laws was centered in the northern counties, while black exclusion found even greater favor in the Southern counties. Southern Illinois was especially noted for its antiblack sentiments and support for the Democracy. Indiana politicians knew the "enterprising Yankee" of northern Indiana despised the "sluggish and inanimate North Carolinian, Virginian, and Kentuckian in the Southern part of the State," and that the Southerner looked upon the other as "a fanatic and a fool."[17] Southern Indiana too was a stronghold of "hoosier" customs and Democratic loyalties.

This internal contest between north and south also influenced many abolitionists from the Lake region, who thought they saw the "Slave Power" entrenched within their own states. Antislavery men knew abolition and support for black rights found their greatest enemies among the southern counties. Despite the presence of Southern-bred abolitionists such as John Rankin and James G. Birney, many assumed those of Southern origins were by nature proslavery. Illinois and Indiana included the largest proportion of Southerners and thus were considered the most proslavery and antiblack of all. George Washington Julian, an Indiana Free Soil and Republican politician, later testified that the people of Indiana "hate the Negro with a perfect, if not a supreme hatred." Only with extreme caution did abolitionists venture into the inhospitable "dark portions" of the Northwest, which were peopled by those of Southern birth given up as hopelessly racist and antiabolitionist.[18] Jacksonville was one Illinois town where this conflict of cultures was especially intense. Being the home to Illinois College and an outpost of Yankee culture, here settlers from the South met New Englanders face to face. The result, according to one observer, was a "collision between two antagonistic civilizations," the one born "of slavery and the other of freedom." Holding different views of Christianity and society, these hostile cultures confronted another they considered their "mortal foe."[19]

Throughout the Northwest Yankees and Sons of the South disagreed over nearly every question of social and political consequence—especially black slavery, which stood as the most important symbolic issue separating the two cultures. As a result, abolitionism was particularly strong among what historians term the Yankee "evangelical subculture."[20] With important exceptions, particularly among Quaker and Presbyterian emigrants from Southern states, Liberty party strength would be concentrated in northwestern areas strongly identified with New England culture. Yankee evangelicals considered slavery the most detestable element of the Southern culture they disliked so much. By focusing on this sore point, abolitionists gained what they considered a critical moral advantage over their opponents, northern and southern alike.

Even so, scarce Liberty party votes could hardly be representative of such a large ethnoreligious group as Yankees or evangelicals. Those of New England origin did not always support the Liberty party, and not all third party voters were Yankees. Few evangelicals engaged in antislavery work; fewer still embraced political abolitionism, much less the struggling Liberty party. Abolitionists and other evangelicals, who shared similar origins, parted company when dealing with the disturbing problem of a church corrupted by slaveholding and racial intolerance. Beginning in the 1830s, a few communities anxious to preserve their cultural identity and sense of community embraced a religious and antislavery tradition that helped set them apart from other northwestern cultural groups. By 1840 these church communities began to testify against the sin of slavery by deserting the so-called corrupt political parties and supporting instead the separatist Liberty party.

"We are verily guilty concerning our brother . . . therefore is this distress come upon us," proclaimed the motto of the *Philanthropist* in 1836, as the abolitionist press began its long and turbulent history in Cincinnati. Unable to edit an abolitionist journal in the South safely, James G. Birney had decided to aim printed broadsides at the peculiar institution from across the churning Ohio River. Birney, the son of a Kentucky slaveholder, had progressed under the prodding of Theodore Dwight Weld from being an agent for the American Colonization Society to a dedicated abolitionist who demonstrated his faith by freeing his own slaves. After bravely facing antiabolitionist mobs and invigorating the Ohio antislavery movement, Birney reluctantly went east to become a corresponding secretary of the American Anti-Slavery Society. Before leaving Ohio, however, he began to point the antislavery movement toward more direct political action. His leadership was awarded the dubious honor in 1840 and again in 1844 of being the Liberty party's presidential candidate.[21]

After Birney's departure the *Philanthropist* passed into the capable hands of Dr. Gamaliel Bailey, a New Jersey–born physician who had taken part in the famous debates at Lane Seminary near Cincinnati. With Bailey as its editor, the Cincinnati press remained the leading abolitionist paper in the Northwest, for over ten years managing to survive the two most dangerous threats to an abolitionist press: angry antiabolitionist mobs and unpaid subscriptions.[22] In 1840, after some initial hesitation, the *Philanthropist* became the leading voice of the northwestern Liberty party, although some resisted Bailey's claim to speak for the entire "western movement."

The year of the founding of the *Philanthropist* is a useful one to date the beginning of organized abolitionist efforts in Ohio and the Northwest. The first annual state convention of the Ohio Anti-Slavery Society (formed the previous year) also took place in the spring of 1836.[23] Northwestern abolitionists had been quite active for several years but had lacked central direction and continuity. Birney's leadership and the *Philanthropist* gave Ohio abolitionism the guidance it needed. The movement had never lacked for enthusiasm and dedication to the cause, particularly since 1834 when a spellbinding evangelist began a revival of antislavery religion that included immediate abolitionism as its central tenet.

According to its most influential historians, the antislavery movement was "prompted by an impulse religious in character and evangelical in spirit." Gilbert Barnes and Dwight Dumond sought the abolitionist impulse in the Great Revival begun in western New York in the 1820s under the influence of the great Presbyterian-Congregationalist evangelist, Charles Grandison Finney. Finney was most famous for his innovative "new measures," which his opponents saw as a serious freewill assault on their remaining Calvinistic traditions.[24] As Finney sought souls more than converts to abolitionism, inspiration for the antislavery crusade came more from his leading disciple, Theodore Dwight Weld.

Weld, a remarkable preacher, has been given the most credit for introducing Finney's evangelical crusade and the antislavery impulse into the Old Northwest. After engaging in the dispute at Lane Seminary over the discussion of immediate abolition, Weld and his handpicked followers tramped Ohio to spread God's antislavery word. Indeed, Weld and his disciples preached the abolitionist gospel so successfully that Barnes and Dumond claimed that the area of Weld's agency in Ohio, western Pennsylvania, and New York "and the regional chart of antislavery societies in the West of 1837 coincide."[25]

Theodore Weld was partly responsible for the conversion to his brand of evangelical abolitionism of James G. Birney, antislavery Whig congressman Joshua Giddings, many of the students and faculty of Lane Seminary and Western Reserve College (in Hudson), and uncounted others. Despite Weld's impressive achievements, it is true no one person can be held responsible for the conditions that underlay the northwestern antislavery movement. In fact, closer examination of Weld's Ohio travels reveals more important considerations than his own preeminence as an antislavery revivalist.

Finney's theology and new measures stressed that an individual must recognize man's sinful nature but then accept responsibility for his own salvation. Evangelical preachers encouraged their followers to open their hearts to God's saving grace. Once having experienced this dramatic change of heart, the converted individual was expected to praise God by serving others. Performing acts of "disinterested benevolence," such as helping the slave, would improve society while demonstrating the power of God's word. This was Weld's appealing message, but, rather than merely awakening the conscience of pious individuals, the young evangelist stirred the hearts and convictions of entire communities of believers to the new doctrines. Not surprisingly, this occurred most often in communities where hostility to slavery was already present and where those of New England origins were ready to receive the evangelical message.

The great antislavery preacher himself testified to this fact. Barnes stressed the antiabolitionist violence Weld faced as the "most mobbed man in America," but even Weld was not foolhardy enough to wander into areas where he might face more than brickbats and taunts. The antislavery preacher selected those places in which the abolition cause had at least a few friends who could protect him from antiabolitionist fury. Weld later advised Birney that if he could not establish his press in Cincinnati, he should do so in the Hillsboro area whose "strong Abolition Influence" would act as his "body guard."[26] Often, in the familiar manner of itinerant evangelists, Weld sought the pulpit of a supportive local preacher. Not surprisingly, he traced his journey through those areas where friends of the slave were already well established.

In 1834 Weld began his Ohio campaign appropriately enough in the Ohio River town of Ripley, the home of the Reverend John Rankin. Rankin, an old friend of the slave who had fled the South, had continued his assault on slavery from his Presbyterian pulpit, penning an influential early antislavery work, *Letters on American Slavery*. Leaving Ripley, Weld continued on to West Union, where the Reverend Dyer Burgess had long been preaching and writing for the cause of the slave. Weld described Burgess as "the oldest Abolitionist and Anti Colonizationist of whom I have any knowledge." From West Union, Weld proceeded north to Greenfield, the home of Samuel Crothers, another antislavery Presbyterian minister. Now within the vicinity of the Paint Valley Anti-Slavery Society, the largest and one of the oldest societies in the Northwest, Weld admitted he saw no reason to form new antislavery meetings in this well-tilled field.[27]

For the first third of his journey Weld was within the bounds of the Chillicothe Presbytery, the only ecclesiastical organization in Ohio that had formally denounced slavery as a sin. Rankin, Burgess, and Crothers were the leading antislavery spirits within this presbytery, and in years to come they continued to lead the antislavery religious sentiments of their flock. While they welcomed Weld's abolitionist message, these Presbyterians of primarily Southern stock did not embrace his new school theology; thus, many of them remained conservative in theology even while far exceeding others in abolitionism.[28]

Weld again traveled a well-blazed antislavery path along the National Road in eastern Ohio. At Mount Pleasant and St. Clairsville, Charles Osborn and Benjamin Lundy had led a Quaker movement against slavery since at least 1815. Here Osborn had published his *Philanthropist* and for a time Lundy issued his *Genius of Universal Emancipation;* they had also formed the antislavery Union Humane Society. As with the Presbyterians of southwestern Ohio, Weld succeeded in reawakening the long dormant antislavery sentiment of these pious Quakers. The evangelist also found some response among those of New England origins who had settled in the bustling towns along the National Road.[29]

Weld's greatest achievement undoubtedly came on Ohio's Western Reserve, whose New England offspring had not yet arisen to the evils of slavery. A cultural region resembling New York's "burned-over" district, the Reserve also knew repeated waves of religious excitement, and thus its transplanted Yankees welcomed Weld's antislavery message. Once Oberlin College received the remainder of the Lane Rebels, the Lorain community became the fountainhead of abolitionism on the Western Reserve, the most important area of antislavery sentiment in Ohio and perhaps in the entire Northwest.[30]

Weld's chief contributions then were to revitalize the antislavery convictions of those who had traditionally opposed the South's system of bondage and to serve as the messenger of the abolitionist gospel to the Western Reserve. In northern Ohio, however, the importance of his mission went beyond the beginning of antislavery organization. Even before Weld's arrival, religious upheaval and new doctrines had begun to unsettle the Reserve churches.[31] As another agent of eastern religious doctrines, Weld heightened the turmoil among those who always understood that along with his abolitionism went the new measures and outlook of the Finney school of revivalism. As time went on, more and more of the Reserve faithful pondered the proper position they should adopt toward slavery. Some sought to prod their churches on to greater denunciation of slaveholders, while others considered more forceful steps to deal with the problem of a slavery-corrupted church.

Antislavery messengers such as Theodore Weld found their greatest response among farming communities. Weld himself shunned the cities and doubted their promise as fertile ground for antislavery action; he advised his followers to "let the great cities *alone,* they must be burned down by *back fires.*"[32] Partly as a self-fulfilling prophecy, then, abolitionism was usually confined to rural villages in the Northwest. When the abolition gospel came to the growing commercial centers, it was typically carried by preachers or agents who usually plowed country fields and who found support among the transplanted sons of rural New England or the Northwest. For such communities as Reverend John Rankin's, the abolitionist commitment reaffirmed the community bond that once had been based on opposition to slavery. For the Western Reserve Yankee colonies it established an emotional link with the mother region and helped distinguish transplanted New Englanders from other cultural groups streaming into the Northwest.

Thus the Ohio Anti-Slavery Society Convention of 1836 marked the coming together of the older Southern Presbyterian and Quaker antislavery traditions with the relatively recent Yankee abolitionism sparked by Weld. To many contemporaries and later historians this "modern abolitionism" represented something radically different from the gradualism of earlier antislavery advocates. Surely there was greater urgency in the appeals of Theodore Weld and William Lloyd Garrison, but the dividing line between gradual and immediate abolitionism should not be drawn too boldly.

The distinction between old and new abolition certainly escaped John Rankin, whose antislavery career bridged both eras. In 1839 Rankin told a convention of his peers in the American Anti-Slavery Society, "The doctrine of immediate emancipation is said to be new, but societies were formed all over the country twenty years ago, and many members of these societies advocated the same doctrine." Benjamin Lundy, mentor to William Lloyd Garrison, also resented the strict distinction being made between gradual and modern abolition, suggesting that considerable continuity indeed existed between the older antislavery movement and the abolitionist crusade of the 1830s.[33]

Defenders of Garrison and proponents of Weld have in this respect combined to make the early 1830s a virtual fault line between the doctrine of immediatism and the gradualism of earlier years. But William Birney (who naturally protected his father's claims) insisted that modern abolition was created neither by Garrison nor Weld but had evolved over a longer period of time with vital Southern roots.[34] Considering the long history of antislavery sentiment in southern Ohio, the work of such pioneers as Lundy and Charles Osborn, and the role of Southerners such as Rankin and Birney, the younger Birney's approach is the best way to view the development of northwestern abolitionism, particularly in Ohio. Yet there is no doubt that the doctrine of immediatism and Weld's new measures invigorated northwestern abolitionism and propelled it down a path leading to eventual political protest. As he traveled from Ripley to Hudson, Weld reawakened Presbyterian and Quaker antislavery sentiments and helped to join their abolitionist traditions with the Yankee impulse he had done much to create.

By 1836 Ohio's one hundred and twenty antislavery societies claimed an estimated membership of ten thousand persons. In 1838 these numbers had grown to roughly three hundred local societies with some 25,000 members. The great bulk of these were found on the Western Reserve, with east central and southwestern Ohio providing the rest. Although the antislavery impulse soon spread to other northwestern states, Ohio remained the strongest toehold abolitionism gained in the region. Even so, abolitionists represented only about one in sixty of the state's population.[35]

In the other northwestern states abolitionism grew more fitfully. Generally, the Ohio pattern was repeated throughout the region, but the national society's financial problems and internal tribulations meant that antislavery agitation further to the west would be largely left up to those states. Perhaps this was as it should be; as they accepted the limits of federal power over slavery in the South, abolitionists also left the antislavery cause in local and state hands. After the panic of 1837 dried up the sources of abolitionist funds and the national society split wide open in 1839 and 1840, the expansion of the antislavery movement was left to the vigor and resources of local and state societies.[36] As a result, in the remaining northwestern states the local antislavery societies usually functioned mainly as shadow organizations of abolitionist church groups.

Quakers played a prominent role in early antislavery efforts both in eastern Indiana and in Michigan. New Englanders tended to skirt the Wabash country, so Quakers living in Indiana's Whitewater Valley dominated the state's antislavery movement from the beginning. Many of them, such as Levi Coffin and Charles Osborn, were antislavery veterans from the South;

in some cases abolitionism found support among Friends whose entire meetings had migrated from the slave South. Indiana abolitionists formed a state society in September 1838, but the movement languished until antislavery agent Arnold Buffum began his work in the eastern part of the state. Buffum found encouragement from his fellow Quakers, particularly in the small community of New Garden. There he founded an abolition press, the *Protectionist.* Later another antislavery Friend, Benjamin Stanton, also edited a New Garden abolition journal, the *Free Labor Advocate,* named for a favorite Quaker program of abstaining from the products of slave labor.[37]

Quakers also dominated the early antislavery movement in Michigan, but as that state's New England element was stronger than in Indiana, members of other denominations were also active. In September 1836 the Quakers of Lenawee and the Presbyterians of Detroit helped organize a state antislavery society at Ann Arbor. The Michigan society adopted a constitution recognizing that states alone had the constitutional power to abolish slavery. Still, Michigan abolitionists promised to work "directly to the extinction of slavery and the slave trade in the District of Columbia and the Territories" and to operate "elsewhere by moral influence." These efforts would be within constitutional limits, but they nonetheless sought the "entire abolition of slavery" and the elevation of their "colored brethren" to their "proper rank as MEN."[38]

Yankee abolitionists were even more important in Illinois, which attracted fewer antislavery Southerners than either Ohio or Indiana. As a result the southern part of the state was virtually barren of abolitionists, except for a rather obscure religious body called the "Friends of Humanity." Methodists led by Peter Cartwright had also opposed making Illinois a slave state in 1824, but their antislavery fervor waned over the years. By 1836, however, the antislavery impulse quickened at Alton and Quincy as Yankee Presbyterians and Congregationalists came to dominate Illinois abolitionism. That year the Illinois Congregational Association denounced slavery as a "heinous sin" and called for its immediate removal. By 1844 the state association resolved not to accept members who did not regard slaveholding as sin.[39] In Alton, Reverend Elijah Lovejoy included antislavery material in his Presbyterian *Observer* to the outrage of antiabolitionists there and across the river in Missouri. Lovejoy was joined by the Reverend Edward Beecher, president of Illinois College, an outpost of Yankee culture on the frontier. Farther to the north the impulse was strong in Putnam County and also in Knox, where Reverend George Washington Gale's struggling Knox Manual Labor Institute was just getting off the ground.

Gale had been Finney's mentor in New York and was now transplanting his religious and educational colony to the Illinois prairies. In the years ahead Galesburg provided an important source of Liberty party strength.[40]

The inspiration for the Illinois State Anti-Slavery Society formed at Upper Alton in October 1837 came primarily from Lovejoy and Beecher. Both were motivated by the antiabolitionism they had encountered as well as the "violent proceedings of the General Assembly of the Presbyterian Church in 1837."[41] Lovejoy and Beecher had witnessed the actions of this assembly when old-school Northerners closed ranks with almost the entire South to exscind four Northern synods where Finney's new measures and Weld's abolitionism were strongest. Reacting to these circumstances, the state society proclaimed "no human authority can in any case whatever controll or interfere with the rights of conscience."[42] Illinois abolitionists would be deeply stung by Lovejoy's death at the hands of an antiabolitionist mob in November 1837.

Illinois abolitionism struggled to regain its momentum until 1839 when the Quaker antislavery veteran Benjamin Lundy arrived in Putnam County to publish his *Genius of Universal Emancipation*. When Lundy died suddenly, antislavery advocates arranged for Zebina Eastman, Lundy's assistant, and Hooper Warren, who had taken part in the antislavery struggle of 1824, to edit the *Genius of Liberty*. By 1842 the direction of Illinois abolitionism had migrated to Chicago where Zebina Eastman edited a Liberty journal, the *Western Citizen*. Moving from Alton to Galesburg and later to Chicago, the Illinois antislavery crusade became closely associated with New England culture in general and, eventually, Congregationalism in particular.[43]

The early antislavery crusade was meant to fulfill primarily moral or religious objectives. In 1834 the Western Reserve Anti-Slavery Society pronounced that the "great principles of antislavery" were identical with "the principles of God's moral government." The Quaker *Free Labor Advocate* expressed "the self evident truth" that slavery was a sin against God. Their Quaker press offered the pious further counsel that "to him that knoweth to do good, and doeth it not to him it is a sin." Studies of other states would no doubt agree with a Michigan case study that found most abolitionist leaders were "actively and intensely religious" and were typically products of the Great Revival.[44]

Initially, the antislavery movement demanded only that slaveholders recognize their guilt and renounce the sin of slavery. Next abolitionists attempted to persuade Northerners of their complicity in the sin of oppression through their states' unjust Black Laws and the federal government's connection to slavery. By 1836 abolitionists were petitioning their representatives to abolish the slave trade and slavery itself in the District of Columbia, where they believed Congress had full power to act. Beyond these efforts, abolitionists had few goals, and some of the most prescient began to realize the limitations of their appeals to the moral sensibilities of the people. The primary achievement of their crusade to this date had been to reawaken and unite communities of like-minded Christians to the sin of slavery. Even so, abolitionists found little success in persuading the rest of the church of its responsibility for slavery's curse.

In the middle 1830s a severe antiabolitionist reaction in the towns and in Congress produced new antislavery converts concerned with the danger the Slave Power posed to the liberties of Northern whites. Still, prospects for the future were uncertain, and committed abolitionists ranged from the heights of religious ecstasy to the depths of apocalyptic despair. A good representative was James Birney, who was quite pessimistic about persuading Northern freemen, much less Southern slaveholders, of the need for immediate repentance. To Birney progress was discouragingly slow, and he warned, "God will avenge himself of a Nation like this."[45]

2

OUTRAGES AGAINST LIBERTY

The years 1837 to 1839 further frustrated pious abolitionists who worried about American immorality. First the panic of 1837 financially humbled the antislavery movement, as it did much of the nation. In Philadelphia the Presbyterian General Assembly precipitated a complete division of the church by expelling three synods in western New York and the Synod of Western Reserve, the very synods where Finney's revivalism and Weld's abolitionism were strongest. Most tragic of all, an angry antiabolitionist mob killed Elijah Lovejoy in Alton, snuffing out the life of an important antislavery leader and crippling Illinois abolitionism for a time.

Responding to these almost simultaneous setbacks, abolitionists began to consider carrying their crusade into politics, experimenting in the 1838 Ohio and Michigan state elections by supporting candidates considered friendly to the cause. Only after discovering that the nation's parties and political leaders would not tolerate their unorthodox views on religion and racial justice did pious abolitionists grudgingly accept the necessity of separating from the corrupt political system. As the Lovejoy incident and other outrages showed, sermons and strictures failed to move the moral sense of the American people. Perhaps righteous political protest would have greater impact.

To pious abolitionists the panic of 1837 revealed the reckless course their nation seemed to be following. Many persons, if not actually wiped out, at least faced the possibility of financial ruin and did some serious soul searching. Ohio lawyer Joshua Giddings for one renounced selfish aims and committed himself to more benevolent work, including freedom for the black slave.[1] Although the panic converted few to abolitionism, many people were shaken by its implications. Some of them concluded this was but the first of many plagues to be suffered by a corrupt society that condoned such sins as slaveholding. The panic only intensified abolitionists' resolve to purify their churches and society of the taint of slavery before it was too late. Not only was Southern society unholy, but, to many antislavery churchmen, Northern society desperately needed cleansing as well.

Understandably, abolitionists sought to make the public turmoil over the panic serve antislavery ends; they would have been poor propagandists for their cause had they not attempted to blame the nation's ills on slavery. The national society created a committee to decide "how far the present commercial distress of the country is to be attributed to the existence of slavery." The intention was to take tactical advantage of the financial situation that in other ways severely damaged the abolition campaign. Weakened and unable to raise funds, the national society entered a period of decline and reorganization. The state societies lacked the necessary organizational skill, much less the financial resources, to replace this loss. To see some good come out of the panic, abolitionists determined to focus public attention on slavery's financial sins alongside its moral ones.[2]

Without lessening their moral condemnation of slavery, abolitionists argued the nation's financial troubles could also be traced to the South's system of bondage. The panic only confirmed abolitionists' judgment that slavery was an immoral and inefficient institution supported only by Northern complacency and capital. To convince others of slavery's moral evils, abolitionists used the panic to contrast the virtuous free-laboring North with the extravagant and indolent slave South. This approach was calculated to appeal to a culture that made little distinction between moral and economic questions. By demonstrating slavery's inherent flaws and inefficiencies, abolitionists believed they went far toward revealing the institution's essential sinfulness as well.[3]

In the northwestern states the panic brought to a sudden end countless overblown schemes for internal improvements. Some of the more elaborate and visionary projects were undertaken by the states, but many communities were also victims of wild economic dreams and foolish speculation. The collapse of these plans dashed the hopes of many people, thereby producing severe social and political strain. Some abolitionists had not been immune to the prospect of economic advance and, like others, sought scapegoats when their dreams turned to disappointment.[4]

In the rural villages where the antislavery gospel already had been preached the panic further discredited the social and economic leadership of the cities and towns, which were just consolidating their hold on the surrounding countryside. Ohio's Western Reserve was one northwestern region that witnessed many improvement schemes, including harbor improvements and a proposed railroad from Lake Erie to the Ohio River. Even some abolitionists were enlisted to support such projects.[5] Differences over the proposed route of canals or railroads set community against community, and these contests were often reflected in election results as well. Political leaders had used such community hopes for advancement to bind local voters to their policies and their party. Once the improvement schemes vanished, however, the party politicians based in the towns had little to offer country voters, whose attentions were diverted more than ever to moral and religious concerns. Partly as a result of the economic panic, then, antislavery villages were further separated from the control of political managers in league with the forces of the town.

The year 1837 also brought to culmination the inner turmoil that had been troubling the nation's Presbyterians. Along with serious theological differences, slavery helped to divide their church into competing Old School and New School wings. Dissension within Presbyterianism had been developing over inclusion of Congregationalists under the Plan of Union, authority over missionary activities, and especially the doctrinal innovations followed by such evangelists as Charles G. Finney. A further divisive force was the new doctrine of immediate abolitionism common among Finney's and Weld's followers in the synods of western New York and the Western Reserve in Ohio. Abolitionists in Ohio and Illinois, as well as in New York, had managed to bring their churches, presbyteries, and synods to denounce the sin of slavery and to call on the church to reform itself of the evil.[6]

Presbyterian abolitionists hoped to persuade the General Assembly to reaffirm its 1818 declaration that slavery was "utterly inconsistent with the law of God." In 1836, however, the assembly refused the minority protest of Ohio antislavery preacher James H. Dickey, who proclaimed slavery a heinous sin. Instead, the national body ruled that the discussion of slavery tended "to distract and divide our churches," and that it was "not expedient to take any further order in relation to this subject."[7]

In May 1837 the Old School faction secured a working majority within the General Assembly in Philadelphia by uniting impressive Southern strength with important support among Northern Presbyterians as well. Against the protests of the New School group, the Old School alliance abrogated the Plan of Union and then exscinded the Synod of Western Reserve and three western New York synods (Utica, Geneva, and Genesee). This action by the Old School produced a complete disruption of the church as the New School objected and proceeded to form the "Constitutional" Presbyterian Church. This New School organization included some Southerners but was primarily a Northern denomination supported mostly by those of Yankee background, including of course the four exscinded synods.[8]

In the ensuing months the division of the Presbyterian assembly forced synods, presbyteries, and churches throughout the nation to choose up sides and adhere to one group or the other. This meant all Presbyterians must identify themselves as either Old School or New School. Such bitter religious controversy only intensified group loyalties while producing prolonged agony, especially within individual churches where a minority (according to Old School ruling) could announce itself the rightful church body.

Historians have disagreed over the role the slavery issue played in the Presbyterian division. Some have argued with considerable effect that the division would not have been possible without the controversy stirred up by slavery and abolitionism. These scholars contend the Presbyterian was the first great Protestant denomination rent asunder as the entire nation would later be by slavery. While conceding that slavery played a contributing role, most scholars argue instead that the primary cause of the division lay in theological differences. The division did not occur along North-South lines, much less abolitionist-proslavery ones. Much of the abolitionist protest before the assembly was Old School in sympathy. For example, James H. Dickey of the Chillicothe Presbytery announced, "I hate New Schoolism—and I hate slavery," and he remained with the Old School, even while admitting it was dominated by "pro-slavery views."[9] Most abolitionists went with the New School, but it hardly became an abolition body. Indeed, in the years ahead abolitionists grew dissatisfied with the New School's toleration of slavery and were again forced to separate from their religious society.

The importance of slavery to the Presbyterian schism has typically been viewed from the perspective of the national assembly; less attention has been given to the ensuing divisions on lower church levels, where differences over slavery were often more apparent. Naturally, the exscinded Western Reserve churches reacted with confusion and uncertainty. Their leaders advised the churches to "remain undisturbed" and to "retain their present organization." (Supporters of the Plan of Union evidently hoped to prevent

19

a rush to congregational organization.) Their expulson by the Old School did not intimidate Reserve Presbyterians, however; the Presbyterian *Observer* reiterated that "slavery is a sin and . . . the pulpit is the proper place to say so."[10]

The reaction in Illinois to the division of the Presbyterian church provides further insight into slavery's role in religious affairs. Elijah Lovejoy and Edward Beecher had attended the 1837 assembly that began the process of schism. By December discord emerged at the meeting of the Synod of Illinois in Springfield. The majority considered the division of the church a "great evil" that ought to be prevented. Responding to a memorial from Alton Presbytery, the synod ruled slavery a "heinous sin in the sight of God," regretted its finding "refuge in the bosom of the Christian church," and contended that it should be a disciplinable offense.[11]

The following August Schuyler Presbytery saw a more serious split. After defeating an attempt by the Old School group to endorse the "reform" measures of the national assembly, the New School majority found the "exscinding act" null and void by a margin of 18–10. Many antislavery activists were prominent in the New School group. The Reverend George W. Gale, leader of the Galesburg colony, served as moderator; other participants included William Holyoke and John J. Mitre, both of whom were later active in Liberty party councils.[12]

Shortly after the Schuyler meeting, the Synod of Illinois gathered in Peoria to complete the division of the church. While the Old School minority withdrew to form a new synod, the remaining New School majority went on to condemn slavery. It was not surprising—given that Edward Beecher was present—that the synod first lamented the death of Lovejoy, Beecher's friend and a member of the synod, while it abhorred the "corrupt public sentiment" that left the antislavery editor "to the mercy of an infuriated and unprincipled mob." Next the group adopted a committee report proclaiming slavery "an invasion and violation of the laws of God" that deserved warning and rebuke. The synod noted that in many churches "the cause of the slave is nobly pleaded," but it recommended that ministers preach at least one sermon in the coming year "on the subject of the immorality of slavery." Again present were many antislavery advocates of New England heritage, particularly from the Gale community. Taking a still stronger stand in 1840, the synod of Illinois determined to exclude "for ever all slaveholders from our pulpits and our communion."[13]

The division of the Presbyterian church in Illinois might have occurred primarily over theological differences, but slavery was integral to the entire controversy. The Old School objected to including Congregationalists

20

under the Plan of Union and to the "gross errors in doctrine and disorders in practice" found among the exscinded synods. The division proceeded generally along cultural lines, with New Englanders and those of Southern origins often found on opposing sides, while the slavery issue served as a further divisive issue between the two groups. As a result, the Illinois Old School was reduced to about thirty ministers and fifty churches. By breaking with the New School, the Old School weakened both sides but rid itself of those in error on the Confession of Faith and abolitionism.[14]

Many New School adherents were convinced that the slavery controversy had indeed disrupted their church. Even the moderate Lyman Beecher insisted " 'twas slavery that did it." Naturally, abolitionists were even more sure they had been cast out of their church by an alliance of Southern apologists for slavery and their Northern conservative allies. Alvan Stewart of Oneida Presbytery believed the synods had been expelled "solely on account of slavery," while fellow New Yorker Gerrit Smith scolded the Presbyterian leadership for succumbing to slavery's power. Within their religious councils and congregations, many of slavery's opponents had witnessed what they called "an unholy alliance between *ultra-orthodoxy,* and *anti-abolition.*"[15]

In several important ways the Presbyterian schism contributed to the eventual formation of the Liberty party. Many of the early exponents of political abolitionism, including Stewart, Smith, and James G. Birney, were members of the Presbyterian church. Some belonged to the exscinded synods of western New York and the Western Reserve. In their abolitionist activities, particularly in their developing political roles, these religiously minded abolitionists responded to what they considered an aggressive and unrepentant proslavery majority that held sway in their religious bodies as much as in Congress.

Abolitionism challenged many elements of the antebellum status quo and thus inevitably invited a severe reaction from opponents. The antislavery message not only seemed to threaten white supremacy, but abolitionists' methods also could undermine the status of groups who traditionally wielded power in American society. Their severe rebukes of the colonization movement, which included indictments of the socially and politically prominent, earned abolitionists the enmity of many powerful foes. River towns would not tolerate abolition agitation, which many feared would endanger Southern trade. Politicians found attacks on abolitionists gratified their voters more than sympathy for the slave. Antiabolitionist politics also held the enormous advantage of "pleasing the South" in national campaigns. By the middle 1830s, then, a strong antiabolitionist reaction developed that throttled the drive to end slavery. Just as abolitionists eventually sought political remedies, their opponents also used political methods, and with considerably more success.[16]

Historians often argue that the frequently violent antiabolitionist reaction actually advanced the antislavery cause by winning new supporters concerned with Northern civil liberties. Contemporaries, including those not friendly to abolition, believed the reaction in Congress and elsewhere only produced more abolitionists, or at least opponents of antiabolitionist oppression. Abolitionists were certainly aware that the violence directed against them won new supporters, and they were quick to exploit this advantage. Theodore Weld believed his opponents "mobbed *up* the cause vastly more than I could have *lectured it up.*"[17] The public disorder and disregard of civil liberties engendered by opponents indeed won the antislavery cause new and valuable friends, chiefly John Quincy Adams in Congress and Salmon P. Chase in Ohio, but it should be admitted that in the end antiabolitionism proved the more formidable force.

Before the rise of immediate abolitionism, colonization of freed blacks was the favorite benevolent solution to America's racial dilemma. The growth of abolitionism in the 1830s, however, often resulted in the division of the social leadership of many communities. While most of the elite remained colonizationists or at least opponents of abolitionism, a few did join the new abolition societies. To the social elite, division within their own ranks was unsettling and dangerous. Sometimes the hidden tension surfaced at such occasions as the Ashtabula Fourth of July celebration in 1835. Community leaders customarily offered toasts in the spirit of the celebration, but in this case a leading member of the Ashtabula Colonization Society rebuked those who had joined the abolitionist society. Horace Wilder lifted his glass to "*The Rights of the States.* Their protection from encroachment [by abolitionists] is essential to the perpetuity of the Union." The colonization society continued to represent the community elite, but it did suffer some embarrassing defections, including antislavery Congressman Joshua Giddings, O. H. Fitch, the editor of the *Sentinel,* and other local notables.[18]

Many communities witnessed two almost simultaneous events in the middle 1830s: the visit of an antislavery lecturer and an antiabolitionist meeting expressing community rejection of such "misguided and fanatical men." Typically, these gatherings attracted local leaders who denounced the abolitionists for meddling in the South's "internal domestic affairs," warned of the dangers of amalgamation, and pronounced that the abolitionist doctrine was "alarming in its consequences, as tending directly to a civil war and a dissolution of this Union." Traveling abolitionist preachers were thus marked as "enemies to the peace and harmony of the community" and the well-being of the Union.[19]

Perhaps the most serious antiabolitionist activity occurred against the freedom of the press. The *Philanthropist* withstood the fury of several Cincinnati mobs, but the *Observer* of Alton, Illinois, and its editor were not so fortunate. Presbyterian minister Elijah P. Lovejoy had infuriated citizens of Missouri and Illinois with his extreme anti-Catholicism and his developing abolitionist views. Finally, in 1837 the editor's stubbornness and the formation of the Illinois Anti-Slavery Society in the town so angered the antiabolitionist element that it decided Lovejoy would not be permitted to edit an antislavery journal there. It was in a final confrontation between the mob and the besieged defenders of the press that a member of the mob and Lovejoy himself were shot dead.[20]

Along with many Northerners, abolitionists considered Lovejoy's murder a serious "outrage on liberty," one that portended more ominous events. Antislavery societies roundly condemned the "ferocious and wicked spirit of misrule, the barbarian outrage against all order and government" that the incident seemed to expose. Abolitionists in Putnam, Ohio, believed the outrage revealed the "reckless spirit of insubordination which characterizes our country at the present time." Another Ohio society warned that "prompt and decisive action" was needed to protect "civil and religious liberties" from the "spirit of insubordination and mobism." Some thought a political response was called for, and they sounded the tocsin for all good citizens to "relinquish party attachments" in order to secure constitutional safeguards and the "equal rights of all."[21]

Many agreed with the Ashtabula Anti-Slavery Society that the spirit of mobs was "most dangerous to the Commonwealth." Besides recognizing Lovejoy to be the "first victim whom the Juggernaut of slavery had crushed at the North," abolitionists believed his murder was representative of society's more profound woes. They insisted mobs only acted at the behest of so-called gentlemen of property and standing. The Cincinnati *Philanthropist* charged that mobs attacked abolitionists at the orders of "politicians who had something to hope [for] from the favor of the south," saying, "It is to the editors of a venal press, to the expectations of office, in the shape of congressmen, judges, postmasters & c., that we are to look for the cause of these frequent and shameful outrages."[22]

In a similar way, Ripley abolitionists claimed mobs were the "deliberate workings" of a "few wealthy aristocrats combined with some Orleans traders and principal mechanics who are interested in trade with slaveholders."

In other words, abolitionists charged the nation's liberties were under attack by those corrupted by selfish interests, either office or material advantage. It was this fundamental moral decay of American society that abolitionists found most disturbing; Northern society was implicated in sin just as much as the South.[23]

To bring the total reformation abolitionists were convinced was necessary they first had to win over society's leading classes. Thus, in his protest of the Lovejoy murder, Edward Beecher appealed to the better instincts of the "wise and good" of society, whom he held ultimately responsible for the Alton tragedy. Only when the friends of religion and good order were once again united, Beecher believed, could American society heal its corruption and escape "the impending judgments of God."[24]

In May 1838, as Presbyterians convened in Philadelphia to complete the division of their church, an antiabolitionist mob in the same city set aflame Liberty Hall, a temple to free discussion erected with abolitionist funds.[25] Contemporaries understood the relationship between such simultaneous episodes. The cumulative effects of such events as the panic of 1837, the Presbyterian schism, and the antiabolitionist reaction that ended in Lovejoy's death must be considered when examining the decision of many abolitionists to pursue political goals. Too often, historians consider the growth of political abolition to have been an inevitable development. On the contrary, abolitionists embraced political action only because they had exhausted all other avenues and were left with few alternatives. More than ever, they felt separated from society's leading political and religious institutions. To religiously minded abolitionists, particularly those connected with Presbyterianism, the nation's churches appeared to be in the hands of slaveholders and their apologists in the North. The Lovejoy and similar antiabolitionist incidents persuaded others that American society lacked the moral fiber to withstand the challenge to law and liberty posed by the Slave Power; the nation's political leaders too seemed under slavery's spell. To protest this lamentable situation through righteous religious and political action was the only course left to a dedicated Christian. Holding apocalyptic visions of America's violent future, pious abolitionists were unwilling to wait for unregenerate politicians to condemn slavery's curse.[26]

Abolitionists (including Garrisonians) never abjured political activity; the petition campaign of the middle 1830s demonstrated their resolve to prod Congress to take action against slavery. Still, only the most visionary among them foresaw the eventual organization of a separate political party. Most pious abolitionists considered party politics a foul game best avoided by those committed to moral and religious action. Many northwestern abolitionists joined those to the east by insisting the abolition enterprise should not abandon its religious mission to adopt tarnished political tools. Nearly every abolition society that discussed some sort of political action first made an obligatory declaration "deprecating" the formation of an independent party.[27] For now at least, an abolition party was out of the question.

By 1838 many abolitionists were nonetheless willing to undertake more aggressive political activity in order to register their moral disapproval of slavery and the society that tolerated the sin. Leadership on this score came primarily from New York abolitionists led by Alvan Stewart, William Goodell, and Gerrit Smith, who had grown impatient with the limited gains made thus far. In 1837 the national leadership advised abolitionists to reject those "who will not sustain the freedom of speech, freedom of the press, the right of petition" and who did not support abolition in the federal district and in the territories. In May 1838 the parent society recommended that abolitionists interrogate candidates and vote "irrespective of party" only for those endorsing "the principles of universal liberty." The executive committee urged members to proceed with their motto being: "Form alliances with no political party, but enstamp our principles upon all."[28]

Thus in the 1838 state elections the decided policy of abolitionists was to throw whatever political influence they possessed to those candidates considered friendly to the cause of the slave and equal rights. Leading abolitionists hoped to demonstrate they held the balance of power in several states and could exploit this advantage to advance the cause. This essentially pressure group political strategy was put to its greatest test in the important states of Ohio and New York.

Abolitionist strategy devised in the East, however, was not always appropriate to the northwestern states. The national leadership included relatively few westerners (and those, such as James Birney and Elizur Wright, who were from the West, soon adopted an eastern outlook) and thus was not always attuned to the situation in the northwestern states. Massachusetts abolitionists, for example, suggested scattering votes in the 1838 election, a tactic somewhat sensible in New England but useless in the Northwest where candidates did not require a majority of all votes cast.[29] The balance-of-power strategy proved equally irrelevant in the Northwest.

Ohio abolitionists remembered their own bitter experiences with anti-abolitionist violence and were especially frustrated with the denial of their right to petition and other civil liberties. While he was editor of the *Philanthropist* and a leader of the Ohio Anti-Slavery Society, James G. Birney had faced antiabolitionist mobs and thus advocated greater political responsibility on the part of abolitionists. Before leaving Ohio for the East, he urged fellow abolitionists to bring political pressure to bear against those who upheld slavery and particularly against those who condoned mob violence. Birney was primarily concerned with reforming the Christian churches on slavery, but he also insisted that "with the political action of political men, and the holy action of religious men there is . . . no inconsistency that is irreconcilable."[30]

Because the questioning tactic seemed to avoid the pitfalls of an abolition party, it encountered only limited resistance, usually among supporters of Garrison or clergymen who feared losing their moral influence.[31] As editor Bailey of the *Philanthropist* warmly supported the parent society's political plans (for the moment at least), the influential Cincinnati antislavery journal encouraged Ohio abolitionists to act "intelligently, consistently and unitedly" at the polls. Following the national society's lead, late in May the Ohio Anti-Slavery Society endorsed the "propriety and great importance of questioning candidates for office." Throughout Ohio, particularly on the Western Reserve, abolitionists formed committees to interrogate local candidates for Congress and the state legislature. Questioning was also pursued in Michigan, where abolitionist organization had advanced far enough to undertake such action.[32]

From the outset abolitionists to the east considered the Ohio contest more important for its impact on the New York campaign. New York abolitionists hoped to rebuke Whig gubernatorial candidate William H. Seward for his evasive replies to their inquiries. The Democratic replies were virtually insulting, prompting abolitionists to support Luther Bradish, the Whig candidate for lieutenant governor. New York abolitionists hoped that Bradish would poll more votes than Seward and thus demonstrate their political influence. As Ohio voters went to the polls first, abolitionists looked to the Buckeye State to prove political abolition's power and to encourage New Yorkers toward greater efforts.[33]

Before the Ohio campaign was over, however, it took on an importance all its own. At first this was due to the *Philanthropist*'s efforts to win abolitionist support for Democratic legislative candidates to reelect Thomas Morris to the United States Senate. While he was in the Senate, Morris had opposed Texas annexation and protected the right of petition.[34] Editor Bailey's endorsement of the antislavery Democrat probably gained him few votes, but it did help ensure that the controversial senator would be deposed by the Ohio Democracy and thus become an early abolition political martyr.

More important was the election eve surrender of an Ohio abolitionist,

John B. Mahan, to Kentucky authorities by the Whig governor, Joseph Vance. Mahan was a Brown County Methodist preacher charged with aiding fugitive slaves. Proclaiming the surrender of an Ohio citizen to a slave-holding state to be "as great an outrage as the murder of Lovejoy," editor Bailey urged abolitionists to help defeat Governor Vance and the Whigs in the ensuing election.[35] To return Morris and rebuke Vance, Bailey thus encouraged Ohio antislavery voters, who were primarily Whig partisans, to demonstrate their political independence by voting against Whig candidates.

Ohio Democrats swept to a statewide victory in October to the Whig's disgust. Wilson Shannon reversed a six-thousand votes Whig majority (in 1836) to unseat the hapless Vance by over 5,700 votes. Democrats also won control of both houses of the state legislature and overturned a Whig majority in the Ohio congressional delegation.[36] Bailey claimed credit for the Whig debacle, insisting abolitionists not only defeated Vance but other unfriendly candidates as well. To eastern abolition leaders he crowed, "you see . . . what our Western boys can do." Overjoyed by the apparent success of his efforts, Bailey was convinced abolitionist political tactics had produced results, and he predicted "what has been done this year in comparatively few counties, Abolitionists next year may do throughout the state."[37] Eastern abolitionist papers, including the *Emancipator* and the *Liberator,* thereupon seized on the Ohio results to encourage New York abolitionists soon to go to the polls.[38]

Whig editors in areas where the antislavery movement was weak, who were eager to attribute their defeat to abolitionism, followed the *Ohio State Journal* in blaming their losses on the activities of the abolitionists. The Whig state press complained that the abolitionists indeed held the "balance of political power in a number of the counties of the State" and helped give the legislature to the Democrats. Some Whig editors warned that the new element of political abolitionism endangered not only the Union but also the Whig party: "We are not yet ruined, but we are on the very brink, staring danger in the face."[39]

Historians have been too quick to accept the claim of some Whigs that abolitionists were primarily responsible for the apparently surprising Whig defeat.[40] In fact, the Democratic state paper dismissed Whig complaints as "ridiculous." The *Ohio Statesman* noted that Vance's total surpassed any other on the ticket and argued that, since few in the state knew anything of the Mahan incident, it hardly cost the Whig governor "a single vote." Several Whig papers, especially on the Western Reserve, did not attribute their defeat to abolitionism. Even those Whig sheets that did blame abolition

27

voters also mentioned other factors, especially Whig lethargy and banking issues that favored the Democrats.[41]

One of the most influential Whig journals in the state, the *Cincinnati Gazette,* printed an article recalling that Whigs actually increased their vote total over 1836, although Democrats polled even more. The *Gazette* credited the Democratic margin of victory to the "cry against Banks." The *Gazette* conceded that in a few counties the Mahan case might have been important, yet Democrats made their greatest gains in counties where abolitionists were few but "hostility to banks" was strong. The parties were so closely balanced in Ohio, the *Gazette* reasoned, that the result could well depend on "vigilance" (or party turnout).[42]

No substantial evidence has ever been presented to show that Ohio abolitionists abandoned their primarily Whig loyalties for the doubtful policy of supporting Democratic candidates. Abolitionists on the Western Reserve were little tempted to vote for the Democracy, considered on the Reserve to be merely a federal officeholder's party. Unlike the Democrats, many Whig candidates were friendly to abolitionists and had returned favorable replies to their questions.[43] Although Reserve abolitionists disapproved of Bailey's support of the Democrats, Whig managers nonetheless took care to prevent any abolitionist defections, and their efforts were rewarded.[44]

Close examination of the election results, both on the county and the township level, discounts the view that abolitionists decided the 1838 contest by deserting the Whigs. The Whig decline was general throughout the state, including those counties where virtually no abolitionists lived. Indeed, Whigs tended to hold their own in counties where abolitionism was especially strong. In Ashtabula County, perhaps the banner abolition county in the state, Vance actually improved over his 1836 total and even ran slightly ahead of the abolition favorite for Congress, Joshua Giddings, then president of the Jefferson Anti-Slavery Society. Abolitionist voters could have had little impact on those legislative seats that changed hands, since so few lived in these areas. In Brown (Mahan's home county), Mahan's captor, Governor Vance, gained slightly over his 1836 total. Township returns where abolitionism was strong suggest most abolitionists ignored Bailey's electioneering pleas and voted in 1838 as they had always voted.[45]

Without examining the voting returns, historians have erred in relying on the statements of Whig editors eager to place responsibility for their drubbing at the feet of the abolitionists. Nineteenth-century party editors were not in the business of providing dispassionate, objective analyses of election results. Rather, their main task was to console the party faithful and explain how hallowed political principles could lose to the political cant of unscrupulous opponents. No sooner were the votes of one race counted than party managers must look to the next election. In 1838 many Whig editors not only blamed abolitionists for their defeat but used this charge to motivate party supporters to prevent the catastrophe from happening again.[46]

Following the 1838 elections Ohio Democrats took immediate steps to repudiate their supposed coalition partners. The Democratic *Statesman* dismissed the questions of an "abolition nigger committee," instead charging that Whigs and abolitionists had consummated a political marriage aiming to turn "the whole slave population of the South loose upon us." With the opening of the legislature, Democrats used their majority control in the lower house to pass resolutions presented by antiabolitionist representative Daniel Flood. The resolves declared Congress had no power over slavery in the states and denounced abolition schemes as "wild, delusive and fanatical." Democrats also opposed repeal of the Black Laws and granting blacks and mulattoes the right to petition the legislature, actions they said that would only place blacks on a par with whites and invite "the black population of other states to emigrate" to Ohio. The Mahan case ended with an ironic twist as Democrats passed a stringent fugitive slave law at Kentucky's request. Throughout the session Democrats proved to be bitter enemies of abolition, while Reserve Whigs showed they generally deserved the support abolitionists had given them in the last election.[47]

Bailey's policy in the 1838 campaign received its greatest rebuke when Democrats deliberately repudiated Thomas Morris due to his antislavery sentiments. Not only was Morris passed over for reelection to the Senate, but in his place Democrats selected Benjamin Tappan, a Van Buren Democrat known to hold safe views on the slavery issue.[48] (Ironically, Tappan was a brother of Arthur and Lewis Tappan, two leading New York abolitionists.) The Democratic state convention then declared Morris a "rotten branch that should be lopped off" and proceeded to weed him and other abolitionists out of the party. As a parting gesture, Morris delivered a stirring reply to Henry Clay in the Senate, a performance that won him the gratitude of abolitionists and second place on the Liberty party ticket in 1844.[49]

As Whig papers took pleasure in the abolitionists being "gulled" by the Democrats, abolitionists were further dismayed when Senator Tappan refused to present their petitions to the Senate. This forced the *Philanthropist* to admit that the new Democratic senator "manifested a decided opposition to the designs and proceedings of the Abolitionists." Some tried to put the best face on the situation, but there was little doubt the 1838 election and its aftermath dealt a devastating blow to abolitionist political strategy in the northwestern states. Moreover, editor Bailey's role in the 1838 Ohio contest demonstrated that even abolition's most dedicated leaders failed to appreciate that conventional political issues and arguments left most pious abolitionists unmoved. Only deeply emotional church controversies would finally induce many abolitionist voters to cut their ties with what some considered the confining "bands of political party."[50]

The 1838 contest marked the emergence of political abolitionism as a controversial element in northwestern politics. Many observers spurned careful analysis of the election results and convinced themselves abolition voters had indeed played a critical role in the Whig defeat. While Reserve Whigs hastened to reforge their links with local abolitionists, others used the apparent strength of antislavery sentiment to help replace Henry Clay with northwestern favorite son William Henry Harrison on the 1840 ticket.[51]

More importantly, antiabolitionism also entered northwestern politics with full force following 1838. In contests to come both parties exploited popular fears of abolition, but antiabolitionism proved especially strong in Democratic ranks. To counter Whig tactics in the coming presidential campaign, Democrats took full advantage of the apparently Whiggish roots of abolitionism. As they became targets of unscrupulous political attacks by the major parties, abolition voters were officially welcomed into the rough-and-tumble world of northwestern politics.

By demonstrating that the questioning tactic and the balance of power strategy were not effective, the outcome of the 1838 state elections created even greater momentum, especially in New York, for the formation of an independent abolition party in 1840. Once the polls closed, abolitionists had no control over the representatives they helped elect. In some cases those who returned favorable replies simply ignored their pledges once safely in office.[52] Even more significant, abolitionism proved too weak to wield much political power. In New York the abolitionist endorsement may have cost Bradish more votes than it gained him. According to the *Journal of Commerce,* abolitionists failed to demonstrate their political influence "unless in the defeat of the candidates to which they gave their preference."[53] Events in Ohio soon showed antiabolitionism to be more popular and thus more politically powerful than either sympathy for the slave or concern for equal rights.

Following the 1838 election worried Whigs on the Western Reserve worked hard to keep abolitionist voters in line. This was especially important to Joshua Giddings and Benjamin Wade, who depended on abolitionist support to counter their conservative opponents.[54] In the 1839 campaign, however, Wade discovered that an abolitionist endorsement could do more harm than good. As part of a conciliatory strategy, Whigs gave Ashtabula abolitionists a prominent place in local conventions prior to the 1839 canvass. In return, abolitionists seemed willing to work within Whig ranks to achieve their political goals. Angry antiabolition Whigs bolted the party, however, to support Democrats instead. In the strongest Whig county in the state, Wade fell in defeat to the antiabolitionist Whig-Democratic alliance.

From the outset the political course of abolitionists dominated the 1839 campaign in Ashtabula and Geauga counties. The 1838 Whig defeat exacerbated lingering local tensions; early the next year antiabolitionist meetings were held in Geauga's Batavia and Mentor townships. These local gatherings denounced abolitionists as a "class of fanatics and disjointed politicians" and insisted that their efforts be "promptly stopped." Reserve abolitionists were not dissuaded by such veiled threats. Instead, they responded to a pledge by New York abolitionists to support no candidate not in favor of immediate abolition, by themselves resolving to refuse any man "not heartily opposed to Slavery." Antiabolitionists were just as determined and sought to proscribe abolitionists by expelling them from Whig ranks. Caught directly in the middle, Giddings delivered a Fourth of July plea for unity but failed to bring the warring Whig factions together.[55]

Fearing the worst, the *Painesville Telegraph* warned that divisions among Whigs only played into Democratic hands. The Whig press urged there be no proscription of the abolitionists, which had already occurred in some townships. Geauga Whigs defended their ticket despite the fact that it contained no abolitionists and included some hostile candidates. When Geauga Whig representatives to the senatorial convention refused to meet with the Ashtabula delegates, abolitionists interpreted this as a refusal to support Benjamin Wade for reelection to the state senate.[56]

Responding to the threat of proscription and the unfavorable Whig ticket, Geauga abolitionists decided to support their own candidates. Wade won their endorsement, but the Whig candidates for representative were replaced by two who were more friendly to abolition. This experiment with independent political abolition was avoided in Ashtabula where abolitionists had been given a prominent part in the county convention, and several friendly candidates were included on the Whig ticket.

The "Anti-Whig" nominations incensed Geauga Whigs who charged abolition voters were in league with the Democrats.[57] Ashtabula antiabolitionist Whigs were even more upset by the prominent role abolitionists played in their local party. In retaliation, hundreds of Whigs took the drastic action of uniting with Democrats on an "amalgamation" ticket aimed at defeating Wade and other antislavery candidates. Antiabolitionist Whigs thus proved more willing to desert their party than abolitionists had a year earlier.

The shocking result in the two banner Whig counties was that Wade's Democratic rival was selected senator and Democrats were swept into office in Ashtabula as well. Abolition voters provided the core of Wade's support (his percentage of the vote correlated at +.53 with that of the Geauga antislavery ticket), but they were too few to overcome the antiabolitionist alliance.[58] In Geauga Wade was the only Whig candidate not elected. Wade lost Ashtabula by nearly one hundred and fifty ballots; the previous year Whigs had swept the county by over thirteen hundred votes.

In a public ceremony early the next year Ashtabula Whigs (including Wade) took steps to reestablish party unity, but the proscription of abolitionists continued as the 1840 campaign approached. Giddings was again caught in the center of the controversy and was careful to avoid being gored by it as Wade had been. Wade was defeated partly by local causes, but most of all the episode revealed the depth of antiabolitionist feeling even in Whig strongholds where antislavery sentiment was also strong.[59] Abolitionist political activity only invited an even stronger antiabolitionist response—a dilemma abolitionists confronted as they considered organizing politically to achieve their primarily religious or humanitarian objectives.

The 1839 Geauga antislavery ticket was one of the first independent abolition tickets in the nation. In the same year Jackson County, Michigan, abolitionists also made independent local nominations, although their action was repudiated by the state society's executive committee. Both tickets provided an opportunity to test the appeal of an independent antislavery party, but both proved premature. Considering the repudiation Western Reserve voters gave an independent antislavery slate in 1839, it was hard to see how abolitionists could be more successful on the state or national level, where abolition voters were not only rare but resented.[60]

Due primarily to their religious commitment, or what one historian has termed the "martyr spirit," some abolitionists (primarily in New York) refused to read the political handwriting and persisted in organizing an abolitionist party. Memories of the 1839 debacle only worsened relations between Whigs and abolitionists, and, more than ever, northern Ohio abolitionists were alienated from the Whig party establishment that ruled the Reserve. A determined minority thereupon came to the firm conclusion that the impossible situation demanded formation of an independent party.

By 1840 political abolitionists were left with few choices. In Geauga they had been deliberately proscribed by the largely unprovoked hostility of local antiabolitionists. As many as three hundred Geauga Whigs (and even more in Ashtabula) deserted Wade, a popular candidate who was not even an abolitionist. In Ashtabula County Whig leaders had attempted to maintain abolitionists' loyalty by allowing them to take part in party affairs. Even as abolitionists welcomed this sensible policy, however, antiabolition Whigs refused to cooperate and instead amalgamated with the despised Reserve Democratic party. Political abolitionism simply stood little chance of success, inside or outside the parties.

In 1838 and again in 1839 political activity produced only disaster for northwestern abolitionism. Abolitionists, who had been spurned by Democrats and proscribed by antiabolitionist Whigs in their strongest region, understandably approached further political activity with extreme caution. Recent events convinced even Bailey's *Philanthropist* that "the Van Buren party is, distinctively, the slavery party." Although Whiggery also proved hostile to abolition, many abolitionists chose to consider the nomination of William Henry Harrison a concession to their political influence. Wary abolitionists did not want to risk another Democratic victory. With this troubled history behind them, northwestern abolitionists looked askance at the drive for an abolition political party that came from the East.[61]

3

1840: A PREMATURE BIRTH

Presbyterian preacher Lyman Beecher claimed abolitionists were the "offspring of the Oneida denunciatory revivals," and it is not too much to say that the abolition party was born in the same region of western New York that bred countless other movements for social and religious reform. What support an independent party gained in 1840 was concentrated in this "burned-over" region of New York where a few years earlier (in 1837–38) three new school synods had been expelled from the Presbyterian church, partly because of the "modern" abolitionism that flourished there. Although the Northwest held similar regions where religious enthusiasm was also intense, a party dedicated to liberty initially won little support west of New York.[1] The abolition party, which was resisted strenuously at first, was eventually most welcomed in those northwestern areas where the Yankee children of western New York and the grandchildren of New England itself had settled.

Torn by dissension for several years, the American Anti-Slavery Society disintegrated completely in 1839–40. Dispute centered on the role of women in the movement and on the political duties of abolitionists, but the division also reflected fundamental differences between the supporters of William Lloyd Garrison and church-oriented abolitionists who rejected Garrison's perfectionist, nonresistant, and anticlerical views. The anti-Garrisonians, whose leadership was based in New York, seceded from the old society and formed a new "American and Foreign" antislavery organization. Many of these church-oriented abolitionists (with the important exceptions of Theodore Weld and Lewis Tappan) soon were providing the core of support for the emerging abolition political party.[2]

As the national society broke into warring wings, a few leading abolitionists convinced of the need for more aggressive political action gathered support for an independent abolition party. At first they found few followers even in western New York, but determined men such as Alvan Stewart, James Birney, Gerrit Smith, and Elizur Wright were not easily discouraged. Most persistent was New York's Myron Holley, a former Anti-Mason with unorthodox religious views. Holley was spurred to action by Henry Clay's February 1839 Senate speech vilifying the abolitionists and imploring them to halt in their "mad and fatal course." Other abolitionists were equally angered by the actions of antislavery Whigs in Congress.[3]

In a series of antislavery conventions in New York Holley struggled to create an independent abolition party. Late in 1839 he turned west seeking northwestern support, but a Cleveland convention rebuffed his efforts. Returning to New York, Holley found some success when a Warsaw convention nominated Birney for president and Francis LeMoyne for vice president. Disappointment soon followed, however, when LeMoyne refused the nomination and Birney also held back, waiting for a greater show of support. After gaining Gerrit Smith's approval, Holley finally persuaded an Albany convention on April 1, 1840, to name Birney and Thomas Earle, a Pennsylvania Democratic abolitionist, to an independent abolition ticket. Holley's was a narrow victory (the final tally was forty-four in favor and thirty-three opposed and included many abstentions), demonstrating that even in New York abolitionists were badly divided over political abolition. The Northwest did not have a single delegate at Albany, although Levi Sutliff of Ohio wrote a letter of support.[4]

The new third party, which had been born of internal dissension and founded over the protests of many abolitionists who accepted the need for political action, faced hard times simply gaining acceptance from fellow abolitionists. Most seriously, the abolition ticket encountered stiff opposition from antislavery Whigs and virtually a complete lack of support in the northwestern states. Many religiously minded abolitionists feared sordid political calculations would destroy the purity of their holy crusade. Moreover, the Whig nomination of William Henry Harrison encouraged many evangelicals to try converting the Whig party into an agent of moral reform.[5] Pious abolitionists thus hesitated to embrace the new third party, though in time they rallied to its separatist banner.

Nowhere was resistance to an independent party more pronounced than among Ohio abolitionists led by Gamaliel Bailey of the *Philanthropist*. In the Northwest the new party faced not only the hostility of Whig partisans and Garrisonian critics, but it also had to survive personal and ideological disputes between eastern political abolitionists and an able core of anti-slavery leaders centered in Cincinnati. Moreover, northwestern Whigs and Democrats did their best to gain political advantages at the expense of the abolition party, further hindering its growth. Eventually, third party ballots were distributed and a small number were cast in the Northwest in 1840, but only after a long and revealing debate exposed serious differences among abolitionists and foreshadowed the eventual demise of Liberty as well.

"So they have done the deed?" Gamaliel Bailey rhetorically asked the nominee of the Albany convention. "I am sorry—deeply sorry." The Cincinnati editor had long opposed a separate abolition party and now feared the Birney nomination would only create "an irretrievable breach in our ranks." It would be "political suicide for you to accept," he advised Birney; "you are now merely an altar on which a few men will offer up their votes." More ominously, Bailey predicted "nearly the whole body of Western Abolitionists" would deprecate the "premature movement." In the months ahead he helped to fulfill this prophecy by working "tooth and nail" against the independent nominations. The influential Ohio editor pronounced the Albany convention a failure and advanced every argument conceivable against the expediency of an abolition party.[6]

Bailey's hostility was a serious blow to whatever hopes the abolition ticket had in 1840. His Cincinnati antislavery press, which Birney had founded, was the mouthpiece not only of the Ohio Anti-Slavery Society but, for the moment, of the Indiana and Illinois state societies as well. Bailey did not create northwestern opposition to an abolition party, but his reluctance to support the Birney nomination until relatively late in the campaign handicapped the already crippled political abolition movement there.[7]

Bailey's reflexive opposition to an independent party might have been rooted in his religious connections. He was a member of the Methodist Protestant church, which earned criticism from Garrisonians and other abolitionists for tolerating slaveholders in its Southern conference. In 1838 Bailey remarked he would as much regret seeing abolitionists "drawing off" from their parties as see them "leaving the churches of which they are members to build up a separate anti-slavery church." The Methodist Protestant editor advised that reformation of a church or a party could not be accomplished by schism but would progress only "so long as the reformers

36

continue *within* it.*" Secession from a church or a political party, even on righteous grounds, Bailey reasoned, would only produce division and weaken the influence of the departing reformers. He accepted that "right voting" and "strict discipline in the church" must bring slavery's fall, but he warned that party organization might "cut us off from all hope of any efficient alliance with the church."[8] (Several years later Bailey did withdraw from his church due to its position on slavery.)

The political setbacks Ohio abolition experienced in 1838 and 1839 did not shake the editor's conviction. Neither the "results of political action last fall" nor the "late disgraceful acts" of the legislature were said to have dispirited the Ohio Anti-Slavery Society convention of 1839. Bailey opposed both Gerrit Smith's suggestion for an abolitionist political oath (similar to the temperance pledge) and the resolution of an Albany gathering to vote only for supporters of immediate abolition. Most Ohio societies also rejected the Albany proposal and, except for the abortive antislavery ticket in Geauga County, followed the policy of questioning candidates in the 1839 campaign. Bailey's cautious policy now earned him the ridicule of Joshua Leavitt's *Emancipator* for "advising abolitionists to take up with a mere favorable answer to two or three incidental questions."[9]

In November 1839 the Cleveland antislavery convention lent substance to Bailey's view that northwestern abolitionists "as a body" were opposed to a separate party. Some 360 Ohioans were among the four hundred delegates who rejected Myron Holley's resolutions suggesting the formation of a new political party.[10] Feeling confident that he was sustained by most Ohio abolitionists, Bailey thus determined to block any attempt to form an abolition party at the upcoming state antislavery convention.

As it turned out, supporters of independent nominations were few at the Massillon convention in May 1840 and declined to make an effort. Bailey, who was firmly in control as a member of the business committee, guided the convention to endorse his view that the present antislavery organization was "primarily a *moral* one" and it would "view with disapprobation any attempts made to convert *it* into a political party."[11] The Cincinnati editor thus derailed third party efforts by insisting that any new political organization would have to be independent of the antislavery society.

Abolitionists on both sides of the party issue advanced arguments based on principle as well as expediency to justify their respective positions. Opponents complained that a political party would call their motives into question and subject their religious campaign to the designs of political adventurers. Bailey echoed these fears, but his opposition was also based on more specific concerns, not the least being his often-stated desire to avoid division within abolitionist ranks. Ohio abolitionism included Quakers, Covenanters, and others opposed by tradition to political activity. He also doubted an abolition party could ever overcome prejudice against blacks and the practice of free state politicians to curry favor with the South. Editor Bailey likewise could not forget the disasters Ohio abolition had witnessed in the 1838 state election and Ben Wade's defeat in 1839.[12]

Beyond this, Bailey had serious political and constitutional reservations about the proposed "radical change" in the antislavery movement. He doubted the expediency of independent nominations in 1840 (believing rash action had brought Wade's defeat the previous year) and for a time recommended William Henry Harrison to fellow abolitionists, which again earned him Leavitt's suspicion.[13] Moreover, he maintained that antislavery societies could not undertake political action because he believed that abolition could not be achieved constitutionally through federal interference in the Southern states. To win Bailey's support, a party based on opposition to slavery would require a nonabolitionist platform instead.

Editor Bailey opposed an abolition party because he suspected its major sponsors, especially Alvan Stewart, held a faulty view of the antislavery movement's constitutional doctrine. When it was first organized, the American Anti-Slavery Society included in its charter a clause acknowledging that the federal government had no power to abolish slavery in the Southern states. Some abolitionists later regretted this critical concession granted to slavery and sought to redefine their constitutional position. In 1838 Stewart argued his view of the antislavery nature of the Constitution before the national society. Eventually, Stewart would win greater approval from abolitionists, but his proposal to strike the concession from the society's constitution fell short of the required two-thirds majority. Then, a few months later, the New York advocate of constitutional abolition emerged as a leading proponent of an abolition party.[14]

Bailey wondered how any honest person could consider "so dangerous a heresy" as Stewart's constitutional position, and he resolved to prevent its acceptance in Ohio. Shortly before the next meeting of the state society, Bailey exposed the "total fallacy" of Stewart's assumptions in a long article in the *Philanthropist*.[15] Stewart's so-called novel construction of the Fifth Amendment to extend due process protection to black slaves, Bailey argued, was not supported by the historical record and ran counter to the framers' intentions. The editor's constitutional exegesis had its intended effect. The state convention reaffirmed its position that "Congress by the

Federal Constitution has no right to legislate for the abolition of slavery in the States." No doubt Bailey was disappointed, however, when within a few years the Illinois and Indiana state societies removed the concession from their constitutions, an action that Michigan abolitionists had taken in 1838.[16]

Believing that abolitionists' political activities should "be measured by our constitutional responsibilities," Bailey at first opposed an independent party in large measure because of his suspicion that its formation was merely part of a greater effort to alter abolitionism's constitutional position. The border state editor envisioned instead a broad-based "Liberal" party that would forswear "meddling with slavery in the states" but nonetheless would work to "wipe out from the nation the foul blot of slavery." Bailey's party would end "the encroachments of the slaveholding power" and eradicate slavery, but it would pursue its aims "always within the limits of the federal constitution." When Bailey reluctantly swung to the third party's support in July 1840, his constitutional opinions remained unchanged. The same group of Ohio abolitionists—primarily from the southwestern corner of the state—that finally approved the Birney ticket in September 1840 also ratified Bailey's view that slavery could indeed be abolished, but not through direct interference in the Southern states.[17]

Bailey's opinions are often considered representative of political abolitionism in the entire Northwest, but the Cincinnati editor's insistence on strict constructionism was not always followed by fellow northwestern abolitionists. In 1839, for example, the Ohio Anti-Slavery Society had adopted resolutions opposed by Bailey. The editor, against some opposition, strove to engraft his constitutional opinions onto the growing Ohio Liberty party. When Salmon P. Chase joined the third party in 1841, he added his voice to Bailey's by advocating "divorcing" the national government from all connections with slavery rather than directly interfering with the Southern institution.[18] Even as they struggled to establish the Liberty party, abolitionists found themselves disagreeing over fundamental ideological issues that would later contribute to the party's dissolution.

Gamaliel Bailey was far from alone in opposing abolition nominations in 1840. Nearly every major Ohio antislavery leader, including John Rankin, Leicester King, Edward Wade (and his brother Benjamin), Thomas E. Thomas, Jonathan Blanchard, and Salmon P. Chase, resisted abolition politics that year. In Michigan the editor of the *Freeman* regretted that his state had sent no delegates to Albany in order to discuss the "expediency" of the abolition nominations. Indiana and Illinois abolitionists were especially unprepared to handle the responsibility of forming a new third party. Most northwestern Whig abolitionists simply refused to enter the third party tent, preferring Harrison's Log Cabin instead.[19]

Across Ohio antislavery societies registered their disapproval of the abolition nominations, many out of fear of what they called "the overweening influence of party." Yet conversely, the chief challenge facing the new party in 1840 and throughout the decade was to persuade hesitant abolitionists to leave their party loyalties behind and cast an abolition ballot instead. Most abolitionists were Whig partisans for whom casting aside party faith was "like plucking out the right eye."[20] Their experiences with the trammels of party—both with politicians eager to please the South and among fellow abolitionists—convinced third party supporters of the evils of party loyalty, which they likened to the spirit of slavery.

Ohio's Whig abolitionists were not eager to desert their party for an uncertain third party movement. The abolition party had been founded on the conviction that the major parties were equally subservient to slavery, but Whigs rejected this view when they recalled how they had been "bamboozled" by the Democrats in 1838 and 1839. The Reverend John Rankin recalled that since 1838 Ohio had a legislature "that would disgrace Turkey." The *Philanthropist* agreed that the "profigacy of the leaders of the reigning party in this state [the Democrats] is equalled only by the stupid apathy with which the people regard their acts." As early as 1838 Bailey announced that "no consistent, honest-hearted abolitionist" could vote for Martin Van Buren, who had "libelled the character of abolitionists, apologized for mobs, and avowed himself the protector of slavery." Bailey insisted that the New York Democrat, "*the* Northern man with Southern principles," was "entirely subservient to the slaveholding interest."[21] Because it caused so many Whig abolitionists to hesitate, the strength of anti-abolitionism among northern Democrats proved one of Liberty's most formidable obstacles.

The leading Whig candidate, Henry Clay, however, was considered no better. The Kentucky slaveholder and "Great Compromiser with Slavery" had forever alienated most abolitionists by his speech of February 1839. Abolitionists were thus relieved when Whigs passed over Clay in favor of northwestern hero William Henry Harrison. Many believed this choice was a concession to antislavery sentiment, thinking the Old General "less offensive to abolitionists." Among abolitionists Harrison had no greater defender than editor Bailey, who considered him "emphatically the candidate of the Free states." Because he was convinced that Whig policy was a conciliation to the abolitionists, Bailey believed "decisive action" should be postponed until after the 1840 canvass when a third party would perhaps be more expedient. Even after the Albany nominations, the editor continued to rest his hopes on the old hero of Tippecanoe.[22]

Many northwestern abolitionists were thus convinced that a vote cast for Harrison would advance the cause more than a vote for Birney. Even the Ohio Anti-Slavery Society forsook a neutral course when in June 1840 its executive committee reported that the Ohio General Assembly belonged "to that party [Democrats], whose uniform policy is to conciliate the South, by extreme measures against abolitionism." In its very first campaign, the abolition political party confronted the challenge it would face for the rest of its existence. To win antislavery voters, third party abolitionists would have to show that a Liberty party ballot would aid the cause of the slave, not elect hostile Democrats and by misdirection serve the cause of the Slave Power instead.[23]

The abolition nominations also faced serious opposition among Western Reserve abolitionists, who had cast Whig ballots even in 1838 and 1839. The *Painesville Telegraph* and the *Ashtabula Sentinel* reflected Reserve opposition to slavery and "Southern dictation," but, not surprisingly, both Whig papers opposed the abolition ticket. A further hindrance to the third party was that many Reserve Whigs championed antislavery causes, especially Joshua Giddings and Benjamin Wade, who supported Harrison strenuously during the campaign. To hold antislavery voters in line, Ohio Whigs also dispatched party leaders Thomas Corwin and Thomas Ewing to the Reserve.[24] No doubt many abolitionists were distracted by the excitement of the Log Cabin campaign. Because the third party made no nominations other than for president in 1840, most antislavery voters continued to carry Whig ballots to the polls without bothering to scratch Harrison's name from the head of the ticket.

Ashtabula abolitionists joined other Reserve antislavery societies in resisting the formation of an independent party. In 1840 Ashtabula County cast both the largest Whig majority and the highest number (97) of third party ballots in Ohio. Friends of the third party faced serious obstacles in the opposition of the *Sentinel* and the respect Giddings had earned among area abolitionists. The small number of third party advocates were led by Flavel Sutliff, who was a law partner of Giddings and also one of the antislavery Whig candidates defeated in the antiabolitionist-Democratic alliance of 1839. In Trumbull Sutliff was joined by his brother Levi of Warren and George Hezlep, a member of the Gustavus Congregational church, whose minister, Benjamin Fenn, advocated an abolition party. By 1844 their church had adopted formal resolutions denouncing slavery as sin and calling for righteous political action. Hezlep and the Sutliffs rejected Bailey's advice to keep political abolition separate from the antislavery societies, and in February 1840 they sought the county society's support for a third party. The majority, however, dismissed the minority report, repudiating both political parties (and, by implication, Giddings and other friendly Whigs), and instead resolved that an abolition party was "unwise, inexpedient, and wholly unnecessary."[25]

After again meeting defeat in May, Ashtabula third party advocates took greater care to gather their friends for the next meeting in September. This time they gained the further advantage of the presence of Joshua Leavitt, who was then in Ohio seeking support for the abolition party. Leavitt won few converts, however, and third party supporters suffered still another setback. In October the citizens of Austinburg, an abolition stronghold, were treated to a two-day public debate between third party advocates and antislavery Whigs led by Joshua Giddings. As most Whigs in attendance determined to remain with their party, third party supporters gathered later to plan a convention after the close of the present campaign. Even when the excitement of the 1840 contest faded, the Ashtabula county society refused to endorse independent nominations. Finally, in September 1841, third party advocates went ahead and nominated a local slate of abolition candidates.[26]

Beginning in 1840, third party advocates had difficulty answering the critical question posed by other antislavery supporters. How could voting for a weak third party advance their cause without contributing to a Democratic victory? Many potential antislavery voters, most often Whig partisans, failed to see the logic in the Liberty position. Why not send Joshua Giddings or John Quincy Adams to Congress to plead the cause of the slave? Because so many could defend this sensible position, the few who did break party ranks to support Liberty were not motivated by conventional political considerations but, typically, by paramount religious ones.

Independent nominations won at least some support in 1840, oftentimes from those who testified to their religious motivations. In April the Bellefontaine (Ohio) Anti-Slavery Society resolved to "come out" from the corrupt political parties so that they "may get rid of the unclean thing, and escape its plagues." Reverend Dyer Burgess, an antislavery veteran from Adams County, voiced the frustrations of many abolitionists virtually disenfranchised by the major parties' nominations. Burgess explained that his desire for an independent ticket was "not merely [so] the world may see that some will vote right, but that God may see that I vote right." Augustus Wattles, a former Lane Rebel now working among Mercer County blacks, offered the realistic advice that voting for Birney was little different than the old abolitionist tactic of scattering votes: "it is simply agreeing before hand upon whom our scattering votes shall be concentrated." Wattles had no illusions that third party advocates could elect their ticket, but they could do something of equal importance—"show that we value our principles more than money or party."[27] For many disaffected church-oriented abolitionists, supporting the new abolition party became literally an act of faith.

The debate among northwestern abolitionists over the wisdom of an abolition party revealed lasting divisions, which became more important later in the third party's history. Probably most northwestern abolitionists first opposed the new party, but, even as they did, their respective positions were already emerging. Some, led by Bailey and Salmon Chase, approached third party politics from a primarily political perspective, concerned most with the party's realistic prospect of achieving conventional political goals. Others, particularly clergymen, were more interested in how moral and religious ends could best be advanced by righteous political action. Although, eventually, they would make the third party cause their own, many church members and much of the clergy hesitated to support the new party in its first campaign.

Religiously minded abolitionists were still badly divided over third party action in 1840, prompting Gerrit Smith to complain that "political and ecclesiastical sectarianism is the giant foe of our cause." Reverend John Rankin (but not his son) joined fellow Ohio Presbyterian ministers Jonathan Blanchard and James Gilliland in publicly opposing independent nominations. Although several members of the Galesburg community helped organize the Illinois Liberty party, the Reverend George W. Gale was not found in third party ranks in 1840. Yet Dyer Burgess, who was, like Rankin, a member of the Chillicothe Presbytery, and the Reverend John Cross of Illinois favored Birney. Despite these differences among individual preachers, most antislavery clergy evidently opposed the new party. Gerrit Smith noted that "a considerable proportion of the abolition ministers of the gospel" opposed substituting political action for their favored "work of moral suasion." Theodore Foster believed clergymen feared that, as the antislavery cause took a political direction, they would be excluded from the movement's "connection and control." Foster also suggested that ministers might have feared the "censure of their ecclesiastical brethren and churches," especially those who disapproved of "the mingling of ecclesiastics in the primary meetings and nominations of the people."[28]

Presbyterian minister Thomas E. Thomas encountered the popular prejudice against political ministers (particularly when they ran counter to church members' own opinions and party loyalties), when he attended the Hamilton convention that finally granted its meager support to Birney and Earle. Thomas actually led the fight against independent nominations, but he did take part in renouncing both parties for their "abject subservience to the slaveholding interest." Even this limited action was taken "in direct opposition to the sentiments of a large majority of his church and congregation, and nearly all his intimate friends in Hamilton."[29]

The Reverends John Rankin and Jonathan Blanchard preferred Harrison over Van Buren (as did Bailey and most abolitionists), but they were concerned less with typical political considerations than with the moral burden the individual voter assumed for helping to elect so-called proslavery candidates (meaning Van Buren Democrats). Believing third party ballots would only serve those hostile to abolition, Rankin insisted there was "no sacrifice of principle in so voting as to keep out of power the more dangerous party." Considering the new party's poor chances, Blanchard reasoned, "how much *moral* influence will a defeated political Abolition party exert in favor of their principles?"[30]

Rankin and Blanchard were two of many northwestern abolitionists who joined other evangelicals in supporting "Harrison and Reform." Even Oberlin abolitionists opposed the third party at first, agreeing with the Cleveland convention of 1839 that it would be "highly injurious to the cause." Many Oberlin residents believed the Whigs to be "the party of order and progress" and considered it as important "to be Whigs as to be Christians." Once Harrison's position on slavery was clear, however, few Oberlin abolitionists could continue to support him. Finally, in late July 1840, the *Oberlin Evangelist* admitted both parties were essentially proslavery and recommended that its readers support Birney and Earle instead. Although in 1840 Oberlin remained divided over political abolition, by 1842 the colony was providing the bulk of Russia township's more than 50 percent support for the abolition party. By comparison, the Presbyterian *Cincinnati Observer* continued to doubt its expediency, reflecting the mounting division among Presbyterians and Congregationalists over the necessity of a third party.[31]

Others were equally motivated by religious and benevolent convictions, but their political calculations were less influenced by purely moral or religious concerns. Bailey advised, for example, that this was not an abstract issue but one that depended on circumstances: "Let our common sense decide the question, independently of ingenious abstractions, supposed impracticabilities, imaginary evils." As they turned to independent action, politically minded abolitionists showed less concern with slaveholding in the church than with the political and economic power of slaveholders. These abolition leaders began to advance pragmatic arguments for the third party rather than rely on exclusively moral or religious appeals. Although this represented a significant shift in antislavery emphasis, it must be remembered that such growing attacks on the political power of slavery were delivered to conventions of already committed abolitionists—such as the September Hamilton convention and the Akron convention in December—where the most pressing issue was the switch to political abolition (and the arguments frequently failed to persuade hesitant pious abolitionists).[32]

The appeals of politically minded third party leaders were meant primarily to convince other abolitionists of slavery's sins requiring solutions beyond the moral ones. As part of his effort to win over hesitant abolitionists, Joshua Leavitt thus presented his political and financial indictment of Southern society to the Hamilton convention in September 1840. Eastern abolitionists were in dire need of northwestern support for their political strategy, and Leavitt was convinced that a program of free trade appealing to the region's desire for grain markets would "give us the West." Following Leavitt's 1840 tour, leaders concerned with the political aspects of the abolition movement continued to apply his arguments against those who preferred that abolitionism remain a moral crusade. While religiously minded advocates stressed the corruption of the slaveholding church, those who were more political preferred to concentrate on slavery as the cause of "hard times" in the North as well.[33]

Whether they were moved by slavery's religious or its political and economic sins, third party voters shared disaffection from the nation's two political parties. Some had actually been proscribed by the parties for their antislavery views, while others simply could not stomach their political representatives' servility to an institution they considered sinful and illegitimate in God's eyes. Most attempted to work first within normal political channels but soon discovered this would be impossible. If their consciences would not permit the compromises necessary for effective political action, neither would antiabolitionist foes allow them any significant role in the delicately balanced sectional party system.[34] As both political parties repudiated their antislavery elements to please their antiabolitionist allies, abolitionists understandably developed an enduring abhorrence of party loyalty, which fettered the individual conscience as much as slavery did the soul of the slave. Third party abolitionists were often perversely opposed to the nature of party itself, but, nevertheless, they were brought to a last desperate step by the unwavering hostility of their antiabolitionist and Southern opponents, not solely by their antiparty inclinations.

The scattered and disorganized efforts of third party supporters found little success through June 1840, and, thus, the abolition party cause gained a much needed boost when Bailey publicly reversed himself in midsummer and slowly turned to the support of Birney and Earle. The Albany nominations had placed the editor in an awkward position. On the one hand, a straightforward third party stand could sow division among Whigs, Garrisonians, and other nonpolitical abolitionists within the Ohio antislavery movement. Yet, on the other, Bailey's endorsement of Harrison placed him at the mercy of the general's political managers. By late June it was clear Whigs valued their Southern alliances more than their supposed arrangement with Bailey's abolitionists. During the campaign summer, Harrison thus took deliberate steps to repudiate his hopeful abolitionist supporters. Bailey in turn charged him with "dishonest duplicity," complaining that Harrison and his friends first cultivated the impression that the general was "a very good anti-slavery man," then were only too eager to show "the South that they are hostile to abolition, and friendly to its institutions."[35]

Bailey's first response to Harrison's duplicitous course was pique; he announced his intention of withdrawing from the conflict and leaving Harrison Whigs "to the alliance you have courted." The editor had little to offer abolitionists but his earlier lame advice that they withhold their votes or do what was no better or worse and vote for Birney. Finally, in mid-July, Bailey joined a call for an antislavery convention at Hamilton to decide the political course of Ohio abolitionists. Some of them in Harrison County and in northern Ohio already had begun to select third party electors.[36]

On September 1 some one hundred and seventy abolitionists, primarily from southwestern Ohio, debated whether both parties deserved abolitionists' scorn and if they should thereupon support the Albany ticket. With the opening of the Hamilton convention, tension surfaced between supporters and opponents of an abolition party, but Dyer Burgess took the edge off with his remark that slavery—"the great Anaconda party"—was actually the "third party." This time Bailey advocated independent nominations against the arguments of Whigs such as James H. Purdy of the *Xenia Free Press* and reluctant religious leaders such as Thomas E. Thomas and James Gilliland. Joshua Leavitt lent his support to the Birney forces by detailing the "connection of slavery with the financial embarrassments of the country." The supporters of Birney and Earle won a narrow 57–54 victory on the critical question. The slim margin and the slight attendance put third party advocates on the defensive, but a small success was all they could have hoped to accomplish this year.[37]

The Birney and Earle ticket began to win wider support from Ohio abolitionists with Bailey's somewhat lukewarm endorsement (he claimed support for Birney "was no sin and will do no harm"). A Knox County antislavery meeting ruled it was not consistent for abolitionists to vote for either Harrison or Van Buren, while an Akron convention endorsed Birney and suggested a Freeman's party to nominate other candidates as well. Portage County abolitionists refused to approve the Whig candidate for state representative and nominated a man of their own.

Although the third party won some support from Whig abolitionists (for example, Q. F. Atkins of Cleveland and General J. H. Paine of Painesville), Bailey knew relatively few would abandon their party to cast an abolition ballot.[38] His fears were realized when Edward Wade, a leading Reserve abolitionist, requested his name be removed as a third party elector (to be replaced by Atkins). In Belmont County Eli Nichols predicted only one abolitionist in twenty would support Birney, and his guess that only forty abolition ballots would be cast in Belmont was six too high.[39]

These dire forecasts proved accurate as the Birney ticket polled just 903 of over 270,000 Ohio ballots cast in 1840, or only about 0.3 percent of the total. Nineteen Ohio counties cast no Birney ballots, and seventeen others counted fewer than five. The great majority of Ohio abolitionists themselves repudiated the third party ticket; only about one in ten could have supported Birney and Earle. In Geauga County an independent antislavery ticket polled some five hundred votes in 1839, and just fourteen in 1840. One Reserve abolitionist complained that "more than 5/6th of the third party men could not screw up their courage to vote."[40]

The abolition party was no more successful in the other northwestern states. As in Ohio, "the bands of political party" proved the greatest obstacle to an independent party. Indiana Whigs managed to blunt the third party drive and no Birney ballots were cast in the state in 1840. In Michigan the *Freeman* helped form an electoral ticket at Jackson, while Calhoun County abolitionists also prepared a slate of candidates. Gerrit Smith had hoped Michigan abolitionists would give Birney and Earle one to two thousand votes. The 321 ballots the abolition ticket actually polled fell far short but was proportionally (0.7 percent) the highest among the northwestern states.[41] The following year Michigan third party advocates launched the Ann Arbor *Signal of Liberty* (edited by Theodore Foster and the Reverend Guy Beckley) and entered local campaigns. Nonetheless, the

Michigan third party's political influence remained slim, primarily due to the Democracy's strength in the Wolverine State.

The Liberty party was nearly stillborn in Illinois as well. Lovejoy's murder left political abolitionists without a press to organize a statewide campaign. Third party supporters then failed to win the support of the state antislavery society meeting in Princeton in August. Advocates of independent nominations, including some members of the Galesburg colony, thus organized separately and selected a Birney electoral ticket. Still it was Adams, not Knox County, which cast the bulk of Illinois's 159 Birney ballots in 1840. The Illinois abolition party lacked any organization in its first year; as they went to vote, two Illinois College third party supporters (the only two) found no poll had been opened for Birney, and election officials acted surprised when handed a third party ballot.[42] Unlike the major political parties, the abolition political organization made virtually no campaign efforts in an election famous for its innovative electioneering techniques.

At first Bailey claimed that the abolitionists' "vigorous political demonstrations" induced Whigs to nominate candidates "not particularly exceptionable to abolitionists," but, when the magnitude of the defeat was known, he admitted "we do not think politicians hereafter will have much occasion to fear the abolitionists."[43] Bailey's tortuous course in 1840 revealed how Harrison's nomination had confused and divided abolitionists, although these bitter memories faded with time. Eventually, the 1840 campaign and its aftermath helped some abolitionists embrace the new party by demonstrating what third party advocates had always maintained: both political parties refused to renounce slavery, although they hardly hesitated in denouncing the institution's critics.

Despite the new party's meager popular support, party politicians did not ignore the abolitionist political organization, and while they were unconcerned with the motivations of the third party faithful, they cared about the traditional political implications. In pivotal states such as Ohio, a relatively small number of votes could separate party victory from defeat. Perhaps more important than the scarce third party ballots cast in the beginning, was that no one knew for certain how large the Liberty defection would ultimately grow. Whigs were the most wary, for the third party carried the potential to ruin their hopes. On the other hand, Democrats realized that this new party could help overcome their own problems caused by internal disputes. Beyond this, the abolition party allowed both Whigs and Democrats to prod their voters to put down the abolitionist menace to racial and social relations, the Union, and most of all, their own party.

From its inception abolitionism produced heated public debate; such controversy only intensified once abolitionists organized as a political force. Even before the 1840 Birney nomination, party politicians scrambled to denounce political abolitionism. The loyalty of the South not only hung in the balance, but also countless Northern voters similarly motivated by hostility to abolitionism. Actually, the Log Cabin campaign of 1840, viewed by many scholars as lacking substance or significance, stimulated vigorous antiabolitionism among the major parties. Both parties claimed their opponents were tainted with abolition sympathies, but Democrats proved especially eager to exploit popular disapproval of abolitionism.

By the late 1830s few abolitionists doubted the Democrats' hostility to abolition and its advocates. The editor of the *Philanthropist* claimed no party was "guilty of such infamous servility, such outrageous anti-abolition violence" as the Van Buren party. Democratic antiabolitionism further dissuaded many antislavery voters from supporting the third party. Some Oberlin abolitionists no doubt hesitated to support Birney in 1840 because of the realization that third party ballots would only rebound to the benefit of antiabolition Democrats. Democrats, led by Samuel Medary, the Democratic state printer, threatened to repeal the charter of that "hot bed of abolitionism" where "whites and blacks were placed on the same level."[44]

For many years historians failed to credit abolitionists' complaints against the Democrats; the role antiabolitionism played in the Log Cabin campaign thus has not been fully appreciated. Customarily, the election has been viewed as a nonsensical one in which Whig politicians rode to victory by exploiting the voters' folly. Progressive historians thought the Whigs represented only the economic and cultural elite, while they regarded the Democracy as the "party of the people" rather than the party of slavery. Recently, scholars have changed course, casting the Democrats as both antiabolitionist and proslavery.[45]

Attacking abolitionists was no doubt helpful in luring Southern support, but Democrats used antiabolitionism in the free states as well. Seeking to bind nonevangelical voters to their party, Democrats combined antiabolitionism with denunciation of Whig "Native Americanism," charging that the "Federalists" sought to restrict the freedom and suffrage of the foreign-born.[46] Whigs, on the other hand, reminded their voters how the abolition party criticized the evangelical churches as the bulwarks of slavery. Party politicians clearly sensed that questions involving race and slavery were emotional issues to many of their followers, but they understood voters viewed these issues through the prism of their religious or ethnic concerns.

Ohio Democrats seized the antiabolitionist initiative in January 1840. Their state convention pronounced political abolitionism "but ancient federalism, under a new guise," whose aim was not the overthrow of slavery but "the overthrow of democracy." The Democratic state address claimed that abolitionists formed a Whig faction more odious than any other, as they combined "religious fanaticism with political zeal." Just as serious, Democrats warned, was that abolitionists intended to fill Ohio and other free states "with an ignorant, degraded race of men . . . and to confer upon them the same rights, civil, political and social, as are enjoyed by ourselves." And General Harrison, Democrats cried, was "the favorite candidate of this party!"[47]

The state Democratic party went on to pledge not to interfere in the domestic institutions of the states and to promise "no sound democrat" would have anything to do with abolition societies. The convention took definite steps to ensure this policy by instructing each delegate to approve the antiabolition resolutions or to have their names published as in opposition to party resolves. The restraining lash of party discipline was what Democrats offered antiabolitionist voters over their silent Whig opponents.[48]

Ohio Democrats were in an excellent position to wage an antiabolition campaign. In the past eighteen months they had "chopped off the rotten branch" of antislavery Democrats led by Thomas Morris, sent a senator to Washington who refused to present abolition petitions, adopted House resolves against abolition and race mixture, and passed a more severe fugitive slave provision. In 1839 Democrats had exploited antiabolitionism by recalling that the ten votes opposed to the fugitive slave bill were all Whigs, while Democrats had united to pass the measure at Kentucky's request. Democrats denounced Whig Congressman Joshua Giddings as a "rank abolitionist" who "loves niggers but hates his own color." In 1840 the Whig nomination of Thomas Corwin for governor over Elisha Whittlesey, a leading member of the state colonization society, was marked "as much an abolition triumph as the nomination of General Harrison, at Harrisburg."[49]

Most dramatically, Democrats charged that "federal abolition Whigs" favored mixing of the races. Tailoring their racist appeal to lure foreign-born voters, Democrats insisted that Harrison wanted to place German and Irish immigrants "on a level with Negroes and Mulattoes!" Under large black letters the *Ohio Statesman* claimed Whig candidate Corwin favored granting blacks the right to vote and to testify against white men. To prove that abolitionism and "Whig negroism" went "cheek by jowl together," the Democratic state press reported a "beautiful spectacle" took place at a Whig celebration at Ft. Meigs. "Large NEGROES" attended wearing *"whig badges on their hats"* and drank "HARD CIDER, OUT OF THE GOURD WHICH WAS SUSPENDED FROM THE BARREL!!!"[50]

The nomination of Birney and Earle at Albany did not deter Democrats from smearing Whiggery as a stalking-horse for abolitionism. Democrats quickly realized that the abolition nominations could work to their benefit. A forgery was prepared for circulation in the South to prove the Democratic charge that Harrison was the abolition candidate. The forgery purported to show that three notorious abolitionists (Arthur Tappan, Joshua Leavitt, and H. Dresser) were replacing Birney's name with that of General Harrison on the masthead of the *Emancipator*. The abolition leaders were made to recommend that New York abolitionists support Harrison, whereas to vote for Birney "only insures the election of Mr. Van Buren . . . whose views on the subject of slavery are so entirely hostile to our own."[51] Apparently, such an endorsement of the Whig ticket was all Democrats needed to frighten antiabolitionist voters.

Whigs, who were hardly friendly to abolitionism, reluctantly followed a somewhat different path than their Democratic opponents.[52] Being sometimes reliant on antislavery support, many free-state Whigs had to be content with doubting the expediency of an abolition party. The Whig economic program stirred little interest among third party voters, who insisted slavery was the leading impediment to national prosperity. Whig partisans, unappreciative of Liberty's sectarian roots, found normal political arguments strangely ineffective in luring third party voters to the Whig banner. By 1844 some Whigs, who were restrained from attacking abolitionists as Democrats were not, resorted to campaign trickery to deal with the growing Liberty menace to their party.

To forestall further abolitionist defections, Whig editors in 1840 depicted the abolition party as at best a futile gesture and at worst a foul trick hatched by Van Buren Democrats to trap sincere but misguided abolition Whigs. Nineteenth-century party politicians customarily dealt with third party challenges by denouncing their leaders (not necessarily their followers) as "a gang of mercenary, corrupt scamps, whose only object is office." Log Cabin Whigs were no exception. The *Ohio State Journal* charged the third party was organized by Gerrit Smith and "a host of political gamblers," whose object was not to promote antislavery goals, but "to throw a firebrand amongst the Northern Whigs." The Whig state journal went so far as to charge the Birney tickets were actually printed at the office of its Democratic opponent, the *Ohio Statesman*. Northwestern Whig editors tried to convince antislavery voters that the third party was favored by few abolitionists and was actually "a device to help Mr. Van Buren." The

Detroit Advertiser insisted third party advocates were merely "loco focos in disguise."[53]

Actually, Whigs did not need to stoop to such low campaign tactics. Many abolitionists were themselves fighting the third party they feared would only help their Democratic enemies. The antislavery Whig editors of the *Painesville Telegraph, Ashtabula Sentinel,* and *Xenia Free Press* offered more reasoned arguments against an abolition party, and in 1840, at least, the great majority of abolitionists concurred.[54]

The contest on the Western Reserve was vital to all Ohio Whigs; to overcome Democratic margins in other parts of the state, Whigs required huge majorities in the Reserve counties. Minor defections or low turnouts were of little danger to Reserve candidates, but either could bring Whig defeat on the state level. Party leaders took the precaution of sending prominent Whigs Thomas Corwin and Thomas Ewing to the Reserve, but the real battle was waged by Joshua Giddings and Benjamin Wade. With their help Reserve abolitionists turned back the third party drive that received only minor support during the campaign summer. Many Reserve Whigs were thought to be hostile to slavery, while in some cases Whig conventions nominated candidates friendly to the abolition cause. The result was a Harrison victory across the Reserve, even though this was the center of third party voting strength.[55]

Democratic fears about their prospects proved all too accurate; an elaborate campaign strategy and a final attempt to win antiabolitionist support through fakery could not overcome the tremendous appeal of Tippecanoe and Tyler to a majority of northwestern voters. Harrison swept to victory in the nation, carrying Ohio, Indiana, and Michigan into the Whig column as well. That Van Buren went down to defeat, however, did not mean the Democratic strategy was also beaten. Indeed, Democratic efforts during the campaign had compelled Whigs to act quickly to prevent potential political damage.

Whigs had to take great care to reassure Southerners and others of Harrison's nonabolitionism, while not directly repudiating their badly needed antislavery supporters. Deemed to be a friend to freedom, the Old Hero was also portrayed as a "devoted lover of the Union" and a "rigid and unbending champion of the rights of the several States." Whigs were caught in this dilemma and at first relied on the timeworn policy of saying as little as possible while allowing antislavery voters to believe they held Harrison's favor. The Democratic antiabolitionist attack, however, demanded an abrupt change in strategy; even Old Tippecanoe must pay homage to antiabolitionist dogma. Addressing cheering Whig celebrations in the northwest, Harrison denied any abolitionist sympathies, and once he was safely elected, the general still took care to renounce all ties to abolitionism.[56]

In his inaugural address, Harrison reaffirmed his campaign promise not to interfere in the South's domestic affairs (meaning slavery) over the angry protests of antislavery Whigs. He also denied that Congress held exclusive control over the District of Columbia and thus, by implication, could not abolish slavery there. The Old General instructed his fellow citizens of the American "Confederacy," but by inference singled out abolitionists to forbear from meddling in the concerns of sister states. "Agitation by citizens of one part of the Union of a subject not confided to the General Goverment," Harrison cautioned, produces nothing but "bitterness, alienation, discord, and injury to the very cause which is intended to be advanced."[57] To most abolitionists, it made little difference who finally won the antiabolitionist campaign of 1840.

The abolition third party made only minor progress following the disastrous campaign of 1840. The party was not established on a permanent basis in Indiana and Illinois until 1842, and in Michigan third party advocates were locked in bitter disputes with Whigs over the wisdom of an independent abolition party. Only in Ohio did Liberty party supporters manage to achieve a degree of unity and organization soon after the 1840 election.

Northern Ohio abolitionists finally granted the abolition party their long-awaited endorsement in December 1840. Nearly a thousand citizens (now including Edward Wade) signed a call for an Akron convention, advising that next to the Gospel, righteous political action was the highest form of "moral suasion." With some lingering dissent, the convention deemed it expedient to continue to nominate those "true to the principles of Equal Rights," and it suggested Thomas Morris as a suitable candidate for governor in 1842.[58]

To restore "harmony and confidence" among Ohio abolitionists, third party leaders organized a Columbus state antislavery convention in January 1841. Following editor Bailey's instructions, Liberty supporters overcame the attempt of Whig editor J. H. Purdy to commit abolitionists to nominations only after the major parties had acted. Instead, the delegates affirmed the policy of prior nominations and in effect gave sanction to the Liberty party in Ohio. Relieved at last by the belated victory, Bailey hoped that "the political course of antislavery voters of Ohio . . . is now determined." By June Bailey dropped his earlier objections to local Liberty nominations, and a political convention at Mt. Pleasant determined to offer third party candidates for the state legislature. Although returns for the

1841 election were scattered, the Ohio party managed nearly to triple its poor performance of 1840.[59]

As the furor of the Log Cabin campaign abated, the Liberty party was strengthened by the conversion of some antislavery Whigs who had not resisted the temptation to vote "just this once" for party favorites in 1840. Perhaps a more significant factor was the sudden death of General Harrison and the accession of a Virginia slaveholder to the presidency. An important convert was Samuel Lewis, respected for his service as Ohio's first superintendent of public schools. Lewis, a leading Methodist layman, added his influence to the Ohio third party and became its candidate for governor in 1846.[60]

No Liberty convert was destined to have a greater impact on the Ohio party than Salmon P. Chase, a capable lawyer of New England heritage who won election in 1840 to the Cincinnati city council. Sorrowed by personal tragedies, Chase had turned his considerable talents to the aid of those more unfortunate than he, especially the helpless fugitive slaves often deposited on the banks of the Ohio at Cincinnati. Antiabolitionist mobs and public disorder in the Queen City aroused Chase to greater alarm over the threat the Slave Power posed to civil liberties. Being primarily concerned with legal and constitutional issues, he did not join an antislavery society and remained a loyal Whig in 1840. In July he declined to sign a call for an antislavery convention (probably the Hamilton meeting) due to the "impropriety of the step at the present time." Chase, who was an aspiring Whig politician, thought the political efforts of abolitionists in 1840 were premature and, as a "small movement," stood no chance of success.[61]

Early in the new year Chase addressed a Cincinnati antislavery meeting on congressional powers over slavery in the federal district, but he continued to be close enough to Harrison to advise the new president to "make no allusions to the subject of slavery" in his inaugural address (though Harrison did not follow Chase's advice). Harrison's death and the rise of a slaveholder to the presidency no doubt troubled Chase. Still, he hesitated to cast his lot with the Liberty party until local Whigs proscribed him, apparently for his antislavery views.[62]

Chase considered himself "not technically an abolitionist" but a "decided opponent of Slavery and the Slave Power." He thus rivalled Bailey as an advocate of "the principles of Liberty men as distinguished from abolitionists." Beginning with a Columbus Liberty party convention in December 1841, Chase promoted his favorite doctrine of the "absolute and unqualified divorce" of the national government "from all connection with and responsibility for slavery." Almost immediately, he sought to broaden the party's appeal, attempting to win the support of antislavery Whigs such as Joshua Giddings. He also suggested Birney be replaced on the 1844 ticket by John Quincy Adams, William Seward, or some other more attractive candidate.[63] Even more than Bailey, Chase soon found these efforts placed him at odds with Liberty party members to the east as well as in the Northwest.

Although many religiously minded abolitionists at first shunned the Birney ticket, after the 1840 campaign had passed they became Liberty's most devoted followers. Especially because so few northwesterners approved of the abolition party, those who sought a "Christian party in politics" soon provided the core of support for the struggling third party. The untimely death of Old Tippecanoe in April 1841 finally convinced many wavering pious abolitionists to join the new party. Instead of a northwestern hero, a Southern slaveholder now sat in the White House. Indeed, after Harrison's death slaveholders would occupy the presidential office for the remainder of the decade; both major parties nominated prominent slaveholders to the presidency in 1844.

When presented with such a choice, many pious abolition voters simply refused to accept any more political leaders guilty of holding others in bondage. Moreover, in the next few years the slavery issue produced further dissension in the nation's religious bodies, prompting still more abolitionist defections. As the sin of slavery continued to infect American society, abolitionists concerned about the nation's moral failings steadily adopted the lonely Liberty party to convey their religious convictions to their fellow citizens and to their God.

4

CRUSADERS FOR LIBERTY

Early in 1847 the Female Anti-Slavery Society of Dundee, Illinois, presented its banner to a delegation from Mill Creek in Lake County. Mill Creek abolitionists had cast the largest majority in the state—over 60 percent—for "Lovejoy and Liberty" in the 1846 congressional elections. Speaking for the ladies of Dundee, Reverend Edwin E. Wells congratulated the Mill Creek faithful for making the "condition of the poor slave, a *paramount question* in politics," leaving others to settle "the minor considerations of dollar and cent policy which divide the two great political parties of our nation." Accepting the banner, Reverend W. B. Dodge insisted Mill Creek third party voters were only doing their duty to "God and our country," after finding the Whig and Democratic parties "wanting in regard to the momentous subject of human rights." Dodge explained that Liberty voters sought only to relieve the sufferings of the slave and "to bring the colored man on to the platform of the white man."[1]

Scholars have long debated the nature of political abolitionism. Disciples of Charles Beard have argued that the "economic circumstances of the time" best explain the origins of the Liberty protest. Others deny the role of economic factors, insisting instead that an abolition revival provided the impulse behind the third party crusade. By studying northwestern township voting returns and banner communities, this chapter argues that both approaches are incomplete and flawed. Too often scholars have searched for the Liberty party appeal in individual motivations, either the conscience or the pocketbook. The Mill Creek ceremony suggests not only that religion and religious leaders often did play a prominent role in the third party movement, but, more to the point, it shows that typically a good portion of an entire community, not just a few scattered abolitionists, stood together for Liberty.

Those who consider economic conflict at the root of political competition naturally attribute a third party defection such as Liberty to economic causes. In an influential 1929 article Julian Bretz maintained that the Liberty party fed on the "economic distress which spread over the country following the panic of 1837." The third party was said to promise that a friendly Northern government would open new markets for western grain by securing free trade and repeal of the British Corn Laws. In Bretz's estimation, the abolition party thus helped to create a powerful engine for antislavery action by linking the comparatively weak reed of moral outrage with the North's selfish economic and political concerns.[2]

Despite the persuasiveness of his argument, Bretz failed to demonstrate that Liberty voters had actually responded to such economic considerations. He left unclear how hard times produced third party votes. One might consider, for example, that the Western Reserve Bank, located in a center of Ohio abolitionism, was one northwestern bank that remained solvent during the crisis. The panic brought ruin and uncertainty to many, but comparatively few turned to political abolitionism to solve their problems.[3]

Besides discounting the moral content of abolition's economic arguments, Bretz relied too heavily on the thoughts of politically minded abolitionists who hoped to turn the movement away from moral suasion alone. Bretz cites the partly economic appeals of Joshua Leavitt, but he does not appreciate that Leavitt spoke of slavery's political and financial power to conventions of already committed abolitionists, where third party activists strove to persuade hesitant moral suasionists to accept an independent party. That these arguments were necessary at all suggests that most of the Liberty faithful were not initially motivated by such economic or political issues. Moreover, most voters were not privy to these gatherings and thus knew next to nothing of such goings-on within abolition ranks.

Bretz presented only limited evidence of the appeal of economic issues to northwestern Liberty voters. Some of the politically minded, such as Salmon Chase and Gamaliel Bailey, favored free trade and repeal of the Corn Laws, partly from a desire to emulate eastern and British abolitionist leaders. Free trade won support among some Illinois Liberty partisans, including the editor of the Chicago *Western Citizen*. A few Liberty conventions passed resolutions complaining of the financial and political power of slav-

ery. In 1843 the Liberty national platform included an economic indictment of slavery, but not necessarily at the urging of northwestern third
party voters. Actually, very little is known about rank-and-file opinion on
such economic issues. Whig strategists did not believe, evidently, that free
trade ideas were popular with the Liberty faithful; Whigs tried to win back
third party voters by ridiculing their leaders' free trade notions. Moreover,
even those who did favor free trade never lost sight of the larger issue of
Liberty.[4]

Perhaps as many third party advocates favored the tariff as favored free
trade. Chase and Bailey often aroused the ire of Whiggish Liberty voters by
advocating Locofoco economic views. Eastern Indiana abolitionists led by
Arnold Buffum supported a protective tariff, as their press, *The Protectionist,* made clear. The Columbus Liberty paper, the *Freeman* (formerly a
Whig sheet), promoted a "Home League" to protect the interests of the
nation's laborers and producers, while the Cleveland *Declaration of Independence* included on its masthead the motto "Protection to free Labor."
Liberty leaders had no more success than the major parties in solving the
tariff labyrinth of Pennsylvania, whose abolitionists often favored a high
tariff. Rather inconsistently, proponents of an economic interpretation
have also attributed the Western Reserve antislavery sentiment led by
Whig congressman Joshua Giddings to a desire for a protective tariff.[5]

Few Liberty conventions discussed economic issues while spending hours
debating other matters. Bretz cited a convention that did denounce slavery's financial sins, but it also insisted that "national morality is the highest
object of governmental care, which no question of mere political economy
should ever take precedence." The convention went on to call for "righteous political action," pledged to support no candidate not a "firm and
unwavering friend of Temperance," and reminded its attendees that the
"interests and rights of the free colored population of these United States
should never be considered by us as less important or sacred than our own."
In short, economic questions were not of special significance to most Liberty voters. More common was the sense of a Richmond, Indiana, antislavery meeting that "the true issue before the American people at this time, is
not bank or no bank, tariff or no tariff, but it is slavery or no slavery." An
Illinois abolitionist confessed that Liberty voters could not respond to
issues of the tariff or free trade, "because they have no position. They are
not agreed among themselves, and perhaps never will be. With them it is a
matter of minor interest."[6]

The Bretz argument helps to obscure the vital fact that the Liberty party
failed to present a coherent economic or political program and, partly for

this reason, remained politically weak. Considering its scant public support (just 3.3 percent of the 1844 free state vote), the Liberty party was not very successful in capitalizing on the nation's economic distress. Ironically, some critics have attributed Liberty's political ineffectiveness to moral inflexibility and an inability to accept political realities. Theodore Foster of the *Signal of Liberty* later chided Liberty voters for their stubbornness in refusing to adopt positions on the economic issues of the day, and he attributed this reluctance to the dominance of clergymen in the movement.[7]

Because of his singular attention to a particular group of Liberty leaders, Bretz overvalued the role of economic factors in the movement. He did not consider voting returns even on the county level to determine the actual sources of third party strength. Examination of such data reveals little relationship between Liberty votes and the economic factors Bretz stressed. According to Bretz, the appeal of the northwestern Liberty party was partly related to the region's need for new markets for its surplus grain. Were the Liberty party responding to this agricultural distress, we would thus expect the party to gather support in those areas that produced the most wheat. Yet little correlation existed between wheat production and abolition votes, particularly in Ohio and Indiana. (See table 1.) Simply put, the strongest Liberty counties were not leading wheat-producing areas, while the leading wheat-producing counties were weak in third party support. (See the Ohio rankings in tables 2 and 3.) Counties in which the abolition party was strong often specialized in other products; the Western Reserve, for example, concentrated on dairy products and was well known for its cheese.[8]

The somewhat stronger (but still weak) relationship observed in Michigan and Illinois would most likely disappear when township voting returns, which showed wide variation in Liberty strength, were compared to wheat production within those counties in which production probably varied little. In Ohio's Trumbull County, for example, the third party vote ranged from 30 percent of the total in Hartford township to none in Milton. Yet township wheat production varied only slightly; indeed, one of the stronger Liberty townships (Johnston) was at the bottom of grain production in the county.[9]

While crude economic determinism has gone out of favor, economic factors continue to be considered the basis of the Liberty party appeal. A more sophisticated yet more elusive interpretation relates benevolent religious activity to growing urbanization and industrialization in the North.[10] As new social and economic relationships emerged with capitalistic development, evangelical religion served to rationalize these changes while helping

TABLE 1
Northwestern Wheat Production in 1840 and Liberty Vote in 1844

State	Correlation Coefficient
Indiana	+.02
Ohio	+.05
Illinois	+.28
Michigan	+.30

Sources: Department of State, *Compendium of the Sixth Census* (Washington, D.C.: Thomas Allen, 1841), 274–76, 286–88, 289–300, 322–24. County election returns were taken from the 1844 presidential contest. *Whig Almanac, 1845,* 49–53.

TABLE 2
Leading Ohio Wheat Producing Counties in 1840 and Liberty Vote in 1842

County	Liberty Vote (%)	Liberty Rank
1. Stark	.5	53
2. Wayne	.9	46
3. Fairfield	.2	63
4. Licking	3.0	13
5. Knox	2.4	19
STATE AVERAGE 2.1		TOTAL COUNTIES 79

TABLE 3
Leading Ohio Liberty Counties in 1842 and Wheat Production in 1840

County	Liberty Vote (%)	Wheat Production Rank
1. Ashtabula	11.5	54
2. Lorain	9.5	48
3. Trumbull	6.7	31
4. Geauga	6.4	58
5. Lake	4.9	59
6. Medina	4.7	32
7. Cuyahoga	3.9	53
8. Harrison	3.8	14
9. Summit	3.4	20
10. Columbiana	3.3	8

Sources for Tables 2 and 3: Department of State, *Compendium of the Sixth Census* (Washington, D.C.: Thomas Allen, 1841), 274–76; *Whig Almanac, 1844,* 52.

to smooth over the inherent conflicts that also arose. Moreover, as economic change transformed the North into a modernizing region, Southern slave society seemed increasingly barbarous and thus "unholy." While this approach is perhaps more intellectually satisfying, it follows Bretz in avoiding an examination of voting returns, at least those of the northwestern Liberty party.

If economic forces were indeed critical, we would expect the effect to be either spread somewhat generally throughout the population or, more likely, concentrated in those areas experiencing the most economic and social change. Yet electoral data show that the Liberty appeal was limited to particular regions of the Northwest and even to specific townships. Fully one half of the 1842 Liberty vote in Lorain County, Ohio, for example, came from the single township of Russia, home to the Oberlin colony and college. In Wayne County, Michigan, 61.5 percent of the 1843 third party vote was centered in just two townships (Plymouth and Livonia), which contained just 16.6 percent of the county's voters. In northern Illinois counties, typically, a few townships provided the great bulk of the abolition vote. Such data and the region's settlement patterns immediately suggest a cultural dimension more than an economic one.

Any attempt to attribute the Liberty appeal to dramatic economic change must struggle with the fact that the party drew its strength from relatively small, homogeneous, and stable agricultural communities. Most scholars have stressed the rural origins of revivalistic religion and antislavery sentiment. Ever since Theodore Weld's mission in the 1830s, abolitionism found its greatest response in the agricultural villages of particular regions of the North. Theodore Foster recalled that the "antislavery seed produced the best crops in an agricultural community, in the cities and large towns it was found impossible to gather into the Liberty party any considerable numbers."[11]

Despite the strong rural antecedents of antislavery sentiment, scholars have persisted in attempting to relate the movement to the developing modern, industrial society of the North. According to this view, abolitionism arose in areas of New England tradition that were also experiencing "momentous economic developments." As areas such as northeastern Ohio grew from "a cluster of back-country hamlets and isolated homesteads into mature centers of capitalist agriculture and commercial enterprise," their crossroads villages were in this view transformed into "important commercial and manufacturing centers and into beehives of abolitionism."[12]

If economic change had been the vital factor, we could expect Liberty strength to be relatively great in areas experiencing such development. Yet the voting returns reveal that the "important commercial and manufacturing centers" often lagged far behind their rural neighbors in support for the third party. No connection existed between Liberty strength and centers of manufacturing capital. The amount of capital invested in Ohio counties in 1840 correlated at −.05 with the 1842 Liberty vote. The *increase* in commercial activity from 1844 to 1846 correlated with the 1846 Liberty totals at an equally insignificant +.01. When compared to the surrounding countryside and smaller towns, Ohio's growing manufacturing and commercial centers were not consistently strong sources of third party votes.[13]

The Western Reserve is often used to demonstrate the connection between economic dynamism and reform upheavals, yet even here the Liberty vote in the developing harbor and market towns nearly always lagged behind that of the surrounding country (table 4). Reserve counties led Ohio in third party support, but this strength came most often from the least commercialized areas. The amount of merchants' capital and money at interest held in Reserve counties in 1839 was negatively correlated (−.45) with the 1842 Liberty percentage of the vote. In Ashtabula County the amount of merchants' capital invested and the township Liberty percentages correlated at −.07. In Cuyahoga, too, the third party did not draw its strength from the most prosperous and thus the most commercialized townships. The 1846 township Liberty percentages correlated at −.29 with the average valuation of township lands.[14] These results suggest that rather than drawing strength from areas undergoing rapid economic growth or profound social change, the Liberty party was strongest in areas *not* experiencing such developments. Indeed, the fact that the "transportation revolution" and other forces of modernization had not yet reached these Liberty villages could help account for the community's third party choice.

TABLE 4

Towns on Ohio's Western Reserve and 1844 Liberty Percentage of Total Vote

Towns	Town Liberty Vote (%)	County Liberty Vote (%)
Ravenna	1.0	4.6
Cleveland	3.6	4.9
Akron	3.9	3.6
Warren	4.9	9.1
Ashtabula	5.0	10.7
Painesville	5.6	4.2
Conneaut	7.5	10.7
Youngstown	10.3	9.1

Sources: *Ohio American,* October 28, November 4, 1846; *Ashtabula Sentinel,* November 2, 1844; *Liberty Herald,* October 16, November 6, 1844.

A somewhat more promising approach to discovering the social origins of abolitionism examines the signers of antislavery petitions. John Jentz and Edward Magdol have demonstrated in separate studies that many artisans and small shopkeepers joined the relatively broad antislavery coalition of the urban Northeast. Abolitionists no doubt won support from what they called the "bone and muscle" of society, especially given the predominance of artisans, workers, and shopkeepers in antebellum Northern cities.[15]

Despite its superior methodology, however, the approach that examines antislavery petitions tells us little about the Liberty party in the northwestern states. Signing an antislavery petition, while significant, was not the same as casting a third party ballot. Of the hundreds who signed petitions, few joined the Liberty party. Moreover, searching for the soul of Liberty in rapid economic development seems misplaced for the Northwest, which was, in the 1840s, still primarily an agricultural region lagging behind the Northeast in industrial change. It is quite possible, however, that the Liberty party drew support from farmers, mechanics, and shopkeepers, especially in those villages threatened by the changes transforming nearby cities and towns. Scholars might also consider that the social origins of the northwestern Liberty party might have differed substantially from its eastern counterpart.[16] Certainly, a degree of tension always existed between party members in the two regions.

Liberty strength in certain northwestern communities cannot be directly related to economic variables. A good illustration is provided by eastern Indiana's Wayne County, one of the leading Liberty counties in the state with a third party average of nearly 10 percent. (See table 5.) With the great majority of its citizens casting third party ballots, New Garden township alone cast over one-third of the Liberty party votes in the county. Together, the relatively small townships of New Garden, Perry, and Greene accounted for over 70 percent of Wayne's Liberty vote. New Garden was home to the *Free Labor Advocate* and was the epicenter of the Anti-Slavery Quaker and Wesleyan Methodist secessions in eastern Indiana. By comparison, the third party was much weaker in the market center of Richmond. New Garden's Liberty advocacy thus may have been motivated in part by resentment, or a lack of understanding, toward its more successful neighbor.

Communities such as New Garden (as well as Richmond) challenge the common scholarly assumption that antislavery activity reflected middle-class interests and attitudes.[17] Does it really help that much to say that new Garden promoted middle-class values by voting for the Liberty party?

TABLE 5
Liberty Townships in Wayne County, Indiana, 1845

Township	Total Voters	Liberty Voters	Liberty Vote (%)
New Garden	190	129	67.9
Perry	163	71	43.6
Greene	184	42	22.8
Franklin	156	17	10.9
Clay	147	9	6.1
Wayne (Richmond)	673	32	4.8
Jackson	415	18	4.3
Abington	147	5	3.7
Centre	478	9	1.9
Jefferson	206	1	.5
Washington	335	0	—
Boston	140	0	—
Harrison	133	0	—
	TOTAL 3367	TOTAL 333	AVERAGE 9.9

Source: Report on the 1845 congressional contest, *Free Labor Advocate,* August 16, 1845.

What are we then to think about so many of New Garden's more developed neighbors, such as Richmond, who decisively rejected the third party message? If third party voters are to be included in ambitious theories about antislavery motivation and ideology, then scholars must take into account the actual distribution of Liberty party votes. On the other hand, perhaps the Liberty faithful represented dissenters, or at least a minority wing, within the dominant antislavery movement.

Scholars simply must accept the fact that in the Northwest the Liberty party commitment reflected group loyalty, not simply many acts of individual conscience. In New Garden two of every three voters cast a third party ballot. Liberty party voters shared certain religious beliefs and a strong sense of community, not necessarily the aggressive values of a triumphant capitalist ideology.

Voting records reveal that communities such as Mill Creek, New Garden, or Sycamore in northern Illinois provided the Liberty party's core of support (see table 6). In 1846 Sycamore gave more than 30 percent of its votes for the third party. The town's growth had been stunted by a deficiency of waterpower, but at least one resident was optimistic:

Good religious principles are here enjoyed, and the two leading denominations of the place have each of them in contemplation the erection of a meeting house. . . . The F[ree]. W[ill]. Baptists are also quite numerous in a settlement

64

TABLE 6
Liberty Banner Towns in Illinois, 1846

County	Town	Total Voters	Liberty Voters	Liberty (%)
Lake	Mill Creek	140	93	66.4
	Bristol	177	93	52.5
	Lake	99	51	51.5
	Middlesex	151	76	50.3
Bureau	Lamoille	117	68	58.1
	Dover	69	36	52.2
	Princeton	443	118	26.7
De Kalb	Shabonah	56	29	51.8
	Orange	38	19	50.0
	Worcester	57	27	47.4
	Sycamore	267	92	34.5
Du Page	Warrenville	215	109	50.7

Source: *Western Citizen,* August 11, 25, 1846; February 9, 1847.

a little east of the village, and are warm abolitionists. The "Wesleyans" have also an organization at Brush point. . . . With their unflinching anti-slavery character you are well acquainted.[18]

Communities such as Sycamore indicate third party strength was concentrated in relatively small villages with a strong cultural or religious tradition rather than in areas with specific economic interests or those experiencing fundamental economic or social change.[19] Indeed, an important part of Liberty party motivation must be attributed to growing alienation from Northern society, almost as much as moral outrage over Southern slavery.

Since the work of Gilbert Barnes and Dwight Dumond, historians have been aware of the religious motivations of antislavery advocates, though the role of revivals and appealing preachers as Theodore Weld can be (and has been) overemphasized. Abolitionists often found their way after a revival, but countless revivals were held that did not produce antislavery sentiment or votes for the Liberty party. Many evangelicals, including many Methodists who turned revivals into a sort of ritual, were openly hostile to the third party movement. Southern evangelicals of course failed to enlist in the Liberty party crusade.[20]

The roots of antislavery sentiment lay in religious commitment that was often fanned by the work of itinerant evangelists, but the Liberty party was a much narrower phenomenon, including only those abolitionists who had abandoned pure moral suasion and the regular political parties for a separate political existence. Many abolitionists remained Whig loyalists, often supporting such antislavery insurgents as Joshua Giddings. Although Giddings represented their antislavery principles tolerably well, Liberty voters refused to abandon the independent party. Third party voters were not simply extreme evangelicals; in this case, the ethnocultural methodology and classification scheme lacks the precision needed to explain the Liberty party phenomenon.

Historians in the Barnes and Dumond tradition have suggested that a denominational approach holds more advantage but have offered little in the way of statistical support. Electoral data tend to support their contention that Liberty voting thrived among members of particular religious groups such as Anti-Slavery Quakers, Free Will Baptists, Wesleyan Methodists, Congregationalists, and Free Presbyterians. The northwestern Liberty party drew the bulk of its strength from communities containing large numbers of these religiously minded abolitionists.[21] That a denominational approach deserves further study is supported by the connection between Congregational churches in Ohio counties and their Liberty ranking in the state (table 7).

Ample literary evidence indicates religious concerns were most crucial to many Liberty voters. The editors of the Michigan *Signal of Liberty* concluded that third party votes "have been almost entirely from the class of Philanthropists and of religious men." Theodore Foster recalled that Liberty's friends "were mostly moral and religious men, but little influenced by ambitious views." Zebina Eastman, of the Chicago *Western Citizen,* later wrote that "the anti-slavery movement was largely an emanation of the religious sentiment." According to Eastman, antislavery advocates "were usually professing Christians and largely developed in the line of personal piety and human benevolence." Henry B. Stanton conceded that "those who preached to the wealthy, aristocratic churches of the chief cities" were often antiabolitionist, but he insisted the clergy "of the rural districts" were among the firmest champions of the slave. Even a Reserve Whig paper granted that Liberty supporters were "benevolent, pious men" and that among them were "many teachers in religion, who have passed through a regular course and study of divinity."[22]

The northwestern Liberty party received its greatest support where pious abolitionists persuaded their church communities to take united action against what they considered to be the sin of slavery. These churches, usually of congregational polity, recorded their testimony against slavery and refused to hold fellowship with anyone implicated in the sin. The Reverend Levi Spencer led his Illinois Congregational church in declaring slavery a

TABLE 7
Ohio Congregational Churches and Liberty Rank in 1846

County	Number of Churches	Liberty (%)	Liberty Rank
Lorain	19	18.4	1
Ashtabula	11	12.2	4
Medina	11	11.5	5
Portage	10	4.2	30
Geauga	8	10.1	7
Trumbull	7	7.4	12
Huron	7	9.5	8
Summit	7	11.3	6
Cuyahoga	6	16.8	2
Erie	6	4.6	17
	STATE AVERAGE 4.3		TOTAL 84

Sources: DeBow, *Seventh Census, 1850, Appendix,* 870–71; "Chronological List of the Congregational Churches of Ohio," *Papers of the Ohio Church History Society* 9 (1898): 68–70; *Whig Almanac, 1846,* 51; *Ohio State Journal,* December 12, 1846.

"sin against God and an outrage upon the rights of man" and then in denying their communion table to those who sanctioned property in man.[23] Local voting records show that the third party did indeed draw its strength from such abolitionist church communities.

Precinct voting returns survive from thirteen northern Illinois communities in which churches formally renounced slavery and anyone who upheld it. The thirteen communities cast an average of over 27 percent of their votes for Liberty, far above the state average of about 5 percent. While holding less than 3 percent of all voters in the state, they alone cast over 15 percent of Illinois third party votes. The Princeton colony church declared slavery "manstealing" and gave 27 percent of the town's votes for their leading minister, Liberty Congressional candidate, Owen Lovejoy. Galesburg, home to Reverend George W. Gale's religious colony, cast 60 percent of its votes for the third party.[24]

The Liberty party gained support from a number of religious groups, but, in northern Illinois and on Ohio's Western Reserve, Congregationalism tended to dominate. Illinois abolitionism and Congregationalism were linked as early as 1836 when the Congregational Association of Illinois declared slavery a "heinous sin" and called for its immediate removal. Illinois Congregational churches were often built on firm antislavery foundations; dedication to abolitionist principles was typically a requirement for membership. Their freedom from hierarchical controls and entangling sectional alliances allowed Congregationalists to adopt uncompromising positions against slaveholding and to deny fellowship with any guilty of the sin. Not surprisingly, then, Congregationalism provided the leadership, theological rationale, and base of popular support for the Liberty movement in Illinois.[25]

Owen Lovejoy's Rock River Congregational Association denounced the sin of slavery and called on its followers to "break away from the pro-slavery parties" by carrying their religion to the polls: "Go to the polls in the fear of God, and record your votes in such a manner that you will be willing to have the poll books unrolled at the day of judgment." Congregational voters evidently responded to election sermons such as Lovejoy's plea that "religion and politics have been separated long enough."[26] Township election returns demonstrate a clear connection between communities with Congregational churches and Liberty voting strength. In eight northern Illinois counties, township third party percentages correlated at +.48 with those communities containing Congregational churches. In some cases, abolition votes might be entirely due to Congregational sources. In Fulton County over 87 percent of the entire county 1844 Liberty vote was centered in three communities with Congregational churches once served by Levi Spencer.[27] Bureau County's Congregational churches correlated at +.86 with the township Liberty percentages, while the corresponding figure for Lee County was +.88.

Illinois antislavery sentiment was not limited to Congregationalists. Indeed, the initial organizational work for the state antislavery society had been undertaken by New School Presbyterians Edward Beecher and the soon-to-be-martyred Elijah Lovejoy. Both had witnessed the 1837 Presbyterian Assembly, which had precipitated the formal division of their church. The Presbyterian colony at Galesburg provided early support to the struggling Liberty party.[28]

Illinois synods, presbyteries, and churches continued to express disapproval of slavery through the 1840s, but the issue became entangled in the reassertion of Congregational independence and eventual breakup of the historic Plan of Union. Even in Galesburg slavery became embroiled in a dispute between the moderate Gale and the Congregationalist-Liberty advocate, Jonathan Blanchard. Yankee settlers began to establish independent Congregational churches in Illinois in the mid-1830s. The festering slavery controversy encouraged separation from the New School Assembly (which still contained slaveholders) and the founding of still more independent churches. This religious dispute strained relations among members of the two denominations, while abolitionism and support for the third party added another divisive factor. Levi Spencer said he encountered opposition from Presbyterians "because I have organized some Congregational Ch[urche]s.—and I am too ultra on abolition."[29] For those Congregationalists who had repudiated slavery and the connection with the Presbyterian Assembly, voting for the Liberty party served to affirm this religious decision and to reinforce community identity and solidarity.

The Illinois Liberty party reflected this close connection between political and religious abolition. In 1844 the Lake County third party convention denounced slavery as a sin against God. A LaSalle meeting stated frankly that "our aim and object is to effect the downfall of the pro-slavery principle, both in Church and State." Zebina Eastman, editor of the *Western Citizen,* withdrew from his church for its failure to adopt a more radical position on slavery and then devoted close attention to the progress of the abolition cause in the churches. The state Liberty press often criticized church bodies who sanctioned slavery, but it approved such antislavery secessions as the Wesleyan Methodist movement. In addition, the dominance and aggressiveness of Congregationalists sometimes angered other church members and the few nonreligious Liberty advocates in Illinois.[30]

The Liberty party in Wisconsin Territory often resembled that of northern Illinois. The Rock County Liberty Convention declared in 1845 that political parties were "bound to obey the laws of God" and that those who voted for slaveholding candidates were "living down the gospel and practically denying the authority of God." The Grant County Liberty Convention renounced slavery as "a most heinous sin against God" and called on other Christians to "come out from the ranks" of the proslavery parties. In late 1846 Ichabod Codding, formerly of Maine and soon to be ordained a Congregationalist minister, assumed the editorial duties of the Wisconsin *American Freeman.* Like Stanton of the *Free Labor Advocate,* Codding was devoted to third party principles and independence, believing the party had been "called into existence by the Providence of God." Almost immediately, he stirred controversy by attacking so-called proslavery churches, a tactic opponents likened to Garrisonism. In December the Wisconsin Liberty Association remonstrated against proslavery ministers and churches who used the "gain of robbery and the price of blood to sustain their religious institutions."[31]

Again, as in Illinois, Wisconsin Congregationalists dominated the third party, though other religious groups were well represented. (One party leader was a Universalist.) The slavery issue and third party politics thus entered religious affairs, stimulating controversy in the Wisconsin Presbyterian and Congregationalist Convention. Under Codding's leadership the state Liberty convention denounced the American Sunday School Union, which was then part of a dispute brewing in the Presbyterian and Congregationalist Convention. Even more than third party advocates in other states, those in Wisconsin did not hesitate to advise fellow abolitionists that it was as much their "imperative duty" to withdraw "all connection and fellowship from a pro-slavery church, or pro-slavery missionary organizations" as it was to withdraw from a "pro-slavery political party."[32]

While antislavery sentiment ran deep on Ohio's Western Reserve, only a portion of it was expressed through the Liberty party. Many who had come to accept the sinfulness of slavery during the religious excitement of the 1830s chose to remain with Joshua Giddings and the Whig party, both of whom represented the Presbyterian (or Plan of Union) element on the Reserve.[33] Those who favored the third party were most often members of religious groups who had renounced all connection with slavery and its abettors. Whig antislavery appeals could not satisfy the moral outrage of these abolition sects. Voting for major party candidates identified with antislavery issues (but still connected with proslavery elements) simply could not fulfill the religious requirements of the abolitionist churchmen.

As in northern Illinois, northern Ohio churches formerly declared their opposition to the sin of slaveholding, while denying their pulpit as well as their communion table to those who refused to denounce the sin. Trumbull County township Liberty percentages correlated at +.56 with those communities whose churches had announced their opposition to slavery. When Ashtabula County is added, the third party vote correlated at +.50 with ten townships whose churches denounced the sin of slaveholding.[34]

On the Reserve these religiously minded third party advocates were most frequently Congregationalists affiliated with Oberlin, Free Will Baptists (along with some "Closed Communion" Baptists), and Wesleyan Methodists. Using multiple regression analysis, the 1846 township Liberty percentages correlated at +.53 with those Reserve townships containing Congregational, Free Will Baptist, Wesleyan Methodist, and several other churches that had denounced slavery as sin. Antislavery sentiment had flourished among Reserve Congregationalists and Presbyterians when Theodore Weld and others spread the antislavery gospel there in the 1830s. In 1835 the Western Reserve Synod had declared slavery a sin against God, and the Presbyterian *Observer* added "the pulpit is the proper place to say so." This abolitionist sentiment was a contributing factor in the expulsion of the synod from the Presbyterian Assembly in 1837.[35]

Most Reserve Congregationalists and Presbyterians had been united in churches formed under the Plan of Union. By 1835, however, strain within the alliance increased as some preferred to adopt the "Congregational way." The expulsion of the synod and the continued connection of the New

School Assembly with slavery encouraged many to seek freedom from hierarchical control and the taint of slavery. Some abolitionists learned independent churches might be more easily won over, while friends of Oberlin discovered their doctrines were stoutly opposed by the orthodox Plan of Union establishment. By 1840 the slavery controversy on the Reserve was thus hopelessly entangled with confusing disputes over religious theology and church polity, even before the third party arrived to complicate Reserve religious matters still further.

With its perfectionist theology and abolitionist sentiments, Oberlin was at the center of the religious turmoil. Presbyterians often considered Oberlin followers to be "apostles of disunion," and they blamed the Lorain community for raising "the standard of revolt" in the Ohio churches. In reply, Oberlin Congregationalists denied they were "schismatics," insisting instead that the Reserve churches were originally congregational in form ("after the purest form of the Puritan fathers"), and thus Presbyterians were the "real intruders." Nonetheless, Presbyterians across Ohio expressed alarm with the abolitionist dissenters; in 1843 Professor Calvin Stowe of Lane Seminary addressed the Cincinnati Synod on the sin of schism. Strictures such as these failed to prevent the founding of Congregational churches and the further decline of Presbyterianism on the Reserve.[36]

Rivalry might have been expected from the beginning between Oberlin and the Presbyterian-dominated Western Reserve College at Hudson, which resented the founding of another theological school on the Reserve. Although it had once witnessed the labors of Charles Storrs, Beriah Green, and Elizur Wright, the Hudson school was no longer as advanced on the slavery issue. Reserve Presbyterians continued to denounce slavery as sin, but their stand differed from Congregationalists in two important respects. First, Presbyterians (or supporters of the Plan of Union) denied slavery need be always and everywhere a sin, making a distinction between voluntary and involuntary slaveholding. They also remained "sincerely attached to the General Assembly of the Presbyterian Church." To maintain this connection with what many abolitionists considered a slavery-corrupted institution, Presbyterians adopted a view of individual responsibility and church purity that many Liberty party supporters, particulary Oberlin perfectionists, found abhorrent: "Not every omission of duty in a church destroys its character as a true church, any more than every imperfection in an individual Christian destroys his character as a true believer." In contrast, the Oberlin-led Western Reserve Congregational Association uncompromisingly denounced slavery as a sin against God and proposed "to free the American Church" from the curse. The final break between Oberlin and Reserve Presbyterians came in 1844 when a Plan of Union convention in Cleveland purposively excluded disciples of Oberlin by restricting entry to "orthodox Congregationalists."[37]

Religious disputes between Oberlin and the orthodox were reflected in their respective positions on the legitimacy of third party politics. Oberlin championed Congregationalism and warmly embraced the abolition party, the colony typically giving over 50 percent support to Liberty candidates. The Presbyterian *Observer* called for church unity (or adherence to the Plan of Union) and hardly noticed the third party. Indeed, in 1842 the *Observer* abandoned neutrality by repeating Whig charges that Liberty gubernatorial candidate Leicester King was a heavy gambler.[38]

The Reserve Liberty party thus received its greatest support from those communities with Congregational rather than Presbyterian churches. In Ashtabula, townships with Congregational churches were far more likely to cast Liberty ballots than those whose churches remained with the Presbyterian connection; the 1846 Liberty township percentages correlated at +.33 with townships containing Congregational churches. When other antislavery churches are added, the coefficient of multiple correlation rises to +.64. Ashtabula townships with churches of Presbyterian form correlated at −.22 with the 1846 Liberty vote.[39]

The Austinburg Church, one of the first formed in the state, had a long tradition of religious excitement before it received Oberlin graduate and Weld lieutenant Sereno Streeter to its pulpit. Eventually, the Austinburg Church dissolved its Presbyterian connections and joined the Ashtabula Consociation in denouncing the sin of slavery and calling for separation from proslavery organizations. Austinburg, home to the Oberlin-connected Grand River Institute, recorded 27 percent support for Liberty candidates; members of the church provided local leadership for the third party.[40]

Congregationalists also dominated the Trumbull County Liberty movement. The chairman of the 1844 county Liberty convention served as clerk to a meeting of his Gustavus church, which denounced slavery as sin and declared its refusal to vote for proslavery candidates. The Gustavus minister also opened the county Liberty meeting with appropriate prayer. Several other Trumbull churches formally announced their abhorrence of slavery as well as their unwillingness to be implicated in the sin through either religious or political associations.

Perhaps the strongest third party advocate in Trumbull was Reverend John Keep, Oberlin professor and pastor of the Hartford church. In 1847

Keep drafted the Reserve Liberty convention's report on slavery and the churches. As expected, the report condemned proslavery churches, insisting on the need "to reform the churches, or to separate from them." Keep also advocated independent Congregationalism, writing a small book and lecturing on its advantages. Along with other religiously minded abolitionists who found themselves battling church hierarchies over slavery, Keep believed the churches would not have been "seduced into so close an alliance with Slavery, had they known no ecclesiastical connection but the local church." Favoring "good, old, New England Congregationalism," the Oberlin professor charged that the "churches and professed Christians" who were "sticklers for orthodoxy" were also "defenders of oppression." This "strange combination" between the religiously orthodox and the protectors of slavery (whose aim, he said, was "to resist the searching application of divine truth") not only portended that "Satan is preparing to fight his last battles," but it also implied the moral superiority of Oberlin Congregationalism.[41]

The Hartford pastor's religious outlook assumed the connection between religious and political action, holding that "the religious character of a people is tested by their political acts." Obeying Keep's charge to "pray right . . . and to vote right" to support equal justice, the Hartford church acquired a reputation for taking "quite an advanced position on the subject of slavery." In 1845 Keep's congregation helped to elect the entire township Liberty ticket.[42]

In Cuyahoga County Oberlin student James A. Thome served the Free Congregational Church of Strongsville, while a leader in the church was a county Liberty officer. With 31 percent of its votes in favor of Liberty, Strongsville cast nearly twice the county average for the third party. The Harrisville church in Medina County withdrew from the Presbyterian connection and probably provided the bulk of the town's 27 percent support for the abolition ticket. The pastor of the Litchfield church complained bitterly that Oberlin was responsible for the division of his congregation. This religious schism apparently provided the source of Litchfield's over 32 percent Liberty total. Together these two communities, with only 11 percent of the total county vote, accounted for almost one-third of Medina's third party votes.[43]

While Congregationalism often dominated, the Reserve third party was favored by other religious groups as well. Free Will Baptists, who were of rural New England origins, had traditionally taken an antislavery stand. In 1839 the Free Will Baptist General Conference held in Conneaut, Ohio, promised not to tolerate the sin of slavery, urging other churches also to bear testimony against the unholy institution. The *Western Citizen* credited the Free Will Baptist as "probably the most free of any of the sects from the contamination of slavery." By 1845 the Free Will Baptist connection had pledged "to act on anti-slavery principles at the ballot-box."[44]

Township voting returns from northern Ohio indicate Free Will Baptists practiced their antislavery principles at the polls. Reserve townships with Free Will Baptist churches correlated at +.31 with the township Liberty percentages in 1844 and 1846. In Geauga County the center of Liberty strength was Chester township, where Daniel Branch, formerly of Oberlin, presided over a Free Will Baptist academy. (Free Will Baptists lacked their own theological school; many attended Oberlin instead.) In 1844 Branch served as president of the Chester Liberty Convention.[45]

The Reserve Liberty party gained popular support from still another body of religiously minded abolitionists, the Wesleyan Methodists. After the General Conferences of 1836 and 1840 rejected his antislavery appeals, Orange Scott led an abolitionist secession from the Methodist Episcopal Church. Scott was joined by Daniel Worth and M. R. Hull of eastern Indiana, Robert McMurdy of Ohio, William Sullivan, former editor of the *American Freeman,* and Guy Beckley, editor of the *Signal of Liberty.* As Methodist founder John Wesley had denounced slavery as the "sum of all villianies," abolitionist Methodists named their new abolition sect the "Wesleyan Methodist Connection." The Wesleyan secession was especially strong in eastern Indiana. Along with Anti-Slavery Quakers, Wesleyans provided the force behind the Liberty party effort in the Whitewater Valley. This segment of the movement also spread into southwestern Ohio, providing a good portion of the Liberty votes in this section of the state. The third party was relatively weak in Franklin County, but the votes cast there came primarily from communities of Wesleyan Methodists.[46]

The Wesleyan movement was also felt seriously in northern Ohio. In 1844 Cleveland hosted the First General Conference of the Wesleyan Methodist Connection. A quarterly conference of the church in Greene, Trumbull County, denounced the sin of slavery and affirmed that "we cannot discharge our duty to the slave while connected with a pro-slavery church, any more than we can while connected with a pro-slavery party in politics." The township returns suggest Wesleyan Methodists deserved their reputation as "a very efficient class of Liberty voters."[47]

In southwestern and east central Ohio the Liberty party drew support among Old School Presbyterians often Southern in origin. Chillicothe Presbytery boasted a long history of antislavery sentiment and included veteran abolitionists John Rankin of Ripley and Dyer Burgess of West

Union. In St. Clairsville Presbytery the antislavery impulse was strong in congregations at New Athens, Cadiz, Mt. Pleasant, and Franklin College.[48]

The division of the Presbyterian Assembly in 1837 left these abolition churchmen in a quandary. Some, including John Rankin, went with the New School, declaring their intention to hold no fellowship with any guilty of the sin of slaveholding. Others remained with the Old School but continued their barrage of antislavery petitions. For these the last straw came in 1845 when the Old School Assembly rebuffed their antislavery appeals and pronounced slavery to be "no bar to Christian communion." The St. Clairsville churches thus joined the Free Presbyterian Church founded eventually by Rankin. In Harrison, Brown, and Clermont counties, the Liberty party drew the support of these antislavery religious communities. The Ripley and Sardinia communities provided 60 percent of the third party votes in Brown County. Four such communities cast half of Harrison County's Liberty votes.[49]

Another group that provided a potential base of Liberty support was the Religious Society of Friends. Traditionally, Quakers had taken an advanced antislavery position, but many northwestern Friends avoided the Liberty party. Some supported the Whig party, while others sided with Garrisonian (or nonpolitical) abolition. For example, the Quaker Garrisonian *Anti-Slavery Bugle* of Columbiana, Ohio, was a dedicated opponent of the third party. The Liberty party received support from many antislavery Quakers, especially among a particular group centered in eastern Indiana. A colony of Quakers in Marlborough, Stark County, Ohio, also supported the party, at least for a time.[50]

Indiana's Whitewater Valley was home to many Quakers, including those such as Levi Coffin who had migrated from the South to escape slavery. By the early 1840s the Quaker antislavery consensus was threatened by disputes between moderates who favored a gradual antislavery approach (including colonization) and those who embraced immediate abolitionism. Schism was perhaps inevitable, but the final break came in 1842 as a result of Kentucky slaveholder Henry Clay's visit to Richmond in Wayne County. While on a swing through Indiana, the presidential hopeful unwittingly stepped into a bitter political and religious dispute in the Quaker community. A segment of Indiana friends favoring immediate abolition decided to petition the prominent slaveholder on his visit to Richmond. Not only did Clay brush aside the abolition Quaker petition, but the moderate majority then warmly received him in their meeting house. (Abolitionists were particularly outraged when the Quaker women lined up to kiss the famous slaveholder.) The abolitionist group hardly had time to protest before they found themselves proscribed by the main body. Led by Coffin, Charles Osborn, and Benjamin Stanton of the *Free Labor Advocate,* the abolitionist faction thereupon formed an independent meeting of Anti-Slavery Friends. Centered in New Garden and other rural areas, the "country" Quaker secession spread to western Ohio and as far as Iowa.[51]

Understandably, Anti-Slavery Quakers were dedicated opponents of what they considered the proslavery party in both church and state. The Clay visit demonstrated the quite real connections between politics, religion, and the slavery issue. Charles Osborn called on his fellow Friends who had been "cut off from the communion and fellowship of Society" to register their testimony by refusing to vote for proslavery candidates."[52]

Anti-Slavery Quakers cast their votes for the Liberty party, while criticizing those who remained "in connection with pro-slavery churches or political parties." They never tired of pointing to the apostasy of the "body group" in supporting proslavery (Whig) candidates. There was no firmer advocate of third party ideological and organizational purity than Benjamin Stanton's *Free Labor Advocate.* Stanton was particularly fond of contrasting the virtues of New Garden (and its majority support for Liberty) with the proslavery corruption of the much larger town of Richmond, the center of the main body's strength. These Anti-Slavery Quakers provided perhaps the most important single source of Liberty votes in Indiana. Together six counties (Wayne, Grant, Henry, Union, Hamilton, and Randolph) where the Quaker and Wesleyan secessions were centered cast over half of all the third party votes in the state.[53]

The Liberty party was an unusual antebellum political organization; few of its supporters were absorbed with prospects of party victory. Instead, the party's base represented those communities whose churches had denounced the sin of slavery. The third party organization gave these religiously minded abolitionists the opportunity to remove their political fellowship from those who remained connected with Southern slavery. The primary concern of Liberty advocates such as the Reverends John Rankin and James Dickey was to defend their version of God's word from the Southern biblical defense of slavery. Many antislavery churchmen could recall the long struggle within the South over scriptural authority for slavery. For many Liberty voters the critical event was not the publication of Garrison's *Liberator* in 1831 or even the Lane Debates of 1834. Rather, what bothered religiously motivated third party supporters most was the relative success proslavery apologists in the North and South had in using biblical arguments to justify the institution of slavery. Liberty voters, hardly worried about winning office, sought to purify the Protestant churches of slavery and thereby regenerate all society. When this failed, Liberty advocates had little choice but to "come out" from corrupt religious and political bodies to at least preserve their own purity.[54]

Pious Liberty voters were most concerned with the progress of abolition principles within their own church communities. Many had witnessed first hand what the politicians called "Southern dictation," but they had felt its lash in their religious assemblies as well as in Congress. They also had direct knowledge of the intersectional alliance between apologists for slavery and the religious equivalent of Northern "doughfaces" who cooperated in blunting the abolitionist challenge. For their defiance of the churches Liberty advocates were tarred as religious radicals and disunionists. These experiences taught those such as Wesleyan Methodist-Liberty editor, M. R. Hull, that "Slavery in the Church is worse than slavery in the nation."[55]

Sectional economic and political concerns were of secondary concern to most third party voters. Liberty advocates were intensely critical of the South, but unlike their Free Soil and Republican successors they demanded *national* recognition and repentance of the sin of slavery. Not only Southerners but also Northern church members must accept their complicity in the nation's sins and agree to change their beliefs as well as their behavior.

Third party advocates did not hesitate to condemn much of Northern society. They especially resented the moral indifference of the city, nowhere better demonstrated than in its refusal to accept the antislavery gospel, and the lack of moral responsibility among the leaders of the new economic order. Not only was the Liberty appeal strongest in rural areas, but some Liberty communities were relatively isolated. Modernization had not yet transformed their way of life but seemed to be passing the community by. Support for the separatist third party thus built solidarity while reaffirming older loyalties and values in communities separated from Northern society's most unsettling social changes. For these reasons the third party might be considered the protest of stagnant communities being surpassed by a world they resented but hardly understood. The Liberty party thus did not serve to legitimate the new order but might have represented a fundamentalist reaction to the compromises and complexities of modern life.[56]

Historians, largely unaware of the concentration of the Liberty vote in particular communities, consequently have focused too heavily on the individual sources of the abolitionist commitment. Bertram Wyatt-Brown has suggested that such an approach has largely reached a dead end: "no psychological or attitudinal key will ever be found to unlock the mystery of the abolitionists' motives."[57] Third party voting statistics were not simply an aggregation of disconnected individuals; Liberty voters belonged to church communities or abolition sects whose religious fellowship encouraged independence from proslavery institutions.

Rather than considering the abolitionist commitment an aberration requiring special explanation, scholars should recognize that the force of community in Liberty party voting was representative of social and political behavior more common to antebellum America. Unlike his modern counterpart, the antebellum voter did not enter the polls removed from the gaze and concern of the rest of the community and then cast his ballot in secret. The difference was not just that it was assumed one's position was the business of the rest of the community but that community concerns were what shaped and motivated the individual and dictated what issues were of primary importance to both. When viewed in this light, it becomes clear that the Liberty party represented a political manifestation of other ethnoreligious issues, such as the disruption of the Plan of Union, which were then gripping the peoples of the Northwest.

The divisions of the national church bodies, not fully understood by modern historians, worried contemporaries. After the division of the Methodist church in 1845 the *Western Citizen* warned that the church divisions might presage the division of the states. While welcoming the progress of antislavery sentiment in the churches, the Chicago Liberty press could not applaud such a political separation: "We fear that a division of the States will introduce a process of emancipation which a philanthropist could not look upon with satisfaction." The Reverend John Keep was even more fearful of the "quenchless conflagration" he felt threatened the American nation, which sat "on the crust of a heaving volcano."[58]

These predominately religious concerns motivated the political actions of the Liberty faithful. While other antebellum voters were often moved by cultural or religious matters, Liberty voters were typically alienated from society's leading religious, political, and economic institutions. More than their fellow citizens, third party voters expressed a sense of moral or religious outrage through their independent political connections. In so doing, pious Liberty advocates also warned of the dire consequences should God's directives remain unheeded. While such religious convictions motivated the third party protest, their religious separatism and severe rebukes of proslavery churches ultimately hindered Liberty supporters in winning members of these churches to the third party cause.[59]

Knowing that Liberty party support came primarily from communities of abolitionist believers does not of course tell us why some people belonged to these groups while most did not. Without having detailed records, we will probably never know why certain individuals joined these abolition sects.[60] Recent research suggests that those of lower status embraced antislavery opinions nearly as often as those of middle-class origins studied most often by historians. Indeed, the portrait of a broader antislavery consensus suggested by the work of John Jentz and Edward Magdol certainly is consistent with the strong support the Liberty party enjoyed in certain northwestern communities.

Perhaps the social status of Liberty party voters did not differ that much from their antislavery Whig counterparts; after all, both were simply registering their disapproval of slavery in different ways. Clearly, third party voters were concentrated in certain communities maintaining a strong cultural or religious tradition. But until historians know more about what motivates individuals to accept different versions of religious faith—indeed, until we understand better why religion is important to begin with—we should probably refrain from too much speculation about the social or economic motivations for personal belief.

Clinging to their abolition sects, Liberty advocates proved insensitive to the apparently rational arguments advanced by spokesmen of the major parties. Pious Liberty voters spurned the emphasis politics placed on economic issues; religious devotion prevented them from accepting any candidate implicated in the sin of slavery. Having little concern for party victory or patronage, they professed to be unconcerned with their party's poor standing at the polls. This stubborn and apparently perverse political stance angered and frustrated the leaders of the major parties, who determined to deal with this unusual third party challenge by familiar political means.

5

LIBERTY DEFRAUDED

"Slavery is our misfortune, not our fault," the Southern gentleman scolded his Quaker supplicant, "but whether our misfortune or our fault, it is none of your business." Speaking these words in the fall of 1842, Henry Clay refused the petition of a heretofore unknown Indiana Quaker, Hiram Mendenhall, who requested that the presidential aspirant set free his own slaves. Clay was in Richmond, Indiana, on a swing through the Northwest to gather support for perhaps his last run at the White House in 1844. A Quaker abolition committee planned to petition the prominent slaveholder in the privacy of his hotel room, but a Whig politician, James Rariden, insisted they make a public presentation instead. Clay handled this awkward situation with characteristic aplomb, but his rebuke of Mendenhall further enraged those already hostile to the slaveholding statesman.[1]

In addition to precipitating the division of Indiana Quakers and thereby encouraging Anti-Slavery Friends to support the Liberty party, the Mendenhall episode also portended that Clay would again face difficulty in earning the votes of Whig abolitionists. Protesting the "shameful abuse of Mendenhall," abolition voters were more than ever likely to desert the Kentucky slaveholder. In the words of Carl Schurz, "many thousands of Mendenhalls were to rise up in the campaign of 1844," as the cause of that "humble Quaker" proved the "absorbing question of the time, and the fatal stumbling-block of the great orator's highest ambition."[2]

"Harry of the West" had never been a particularly popular candidate among northwestern Whigs, who preferred one of their own to challenge the Jacksonians for power. In 1840 Clay had been denied his party's nomination, partly due to the growing antislavery sentiment in key Northern states such as Ohio. In 1842 Thomas Corwin's failure to win reelection as Ohio's governor was viewed as another setback for Clay's hopes. The next year's congressional results caused further Whig worry; third party votes helped to defeat two worthy Whigs, Edward S. Hamlin in the Oberlin district and Joseph Ridgway in Columbus.[3] Many Whigs thus believed the famous slaveholder suffered serious handicaps in the Northwest, including the hostility of the abolitionists.[4]

As it turned out, Clay's 1844 defeat at the hands of Democrat James K. Polk further complicated third party independence. More than ever the northwestern Liberty party faced Whig charges that third party ballots only served the opponents of abolition by depleting Whig ranks. Although Liberty advocates countered with evidence that third party votes sprang equally from both parties, the Whig claim was more nearly true and undoubtedly persuaded wavering antislavery Whigs to stand aloof from the abolition party. Yet, even as Whigs encouraged third party voters to "back out of the Liberty movement," pious Liberty voters stood firm in their third party defiance.[5]

Joshua Giddings and other antislavery Whigs could never quite fathom the third party's persistent refusal to support favorable Whig candidates. Whigs believed they had taken all the correct political steps; normally, this would have mollified party dissidents. Whig leaders often failed to recognize that third party supporters responded to religious rather than political imperatives. Unlike those abolitionists who favored Whiggery, Liberty voters' denominational connections encouraged an independent political stand. Most of all, the Liberty faithful refused to endorse a candidate himself guilty of the sin of slaveholding. Being unappreciative of such pious political motives, Whig political leaders interpreted third party defiance as folly or even perfidy; their efforts to lure Liberty support proved misplaced and inadequate.

Whigs found Liberty party independence particularly upsetting. Both movements sought the support of society's respectable and pious elements by claiming to represent the moral conscience of the nation.[6] This Whig concern was especially intense on Ohio's Western Reserve, although in most Reserve counties (with the important exception of Trumbull), Whigs held a more than safe majority. The struggle for political power locally could be intensified by the third party, but beyond this consideration the bitter conflict between Whigs and Liberty supporters suggests they were competing for more than just the political endorsement of Reserve voters. Northern Ohio third party advocates and Whig partisans struggled for the moral sanction of a community in which moral and religious imperatives were believed uppermost. In particular, the political conflict between Whigs and Liberty followers reflected more fundamental religious disputes dividing the citizens and churches of the Reserve. While they polled few votes even here, third party abolitionists presented a serious challenge to the Reserve's social and political elite by questioning the very basis of their leadership.

That Whigs and Liberty advocates both appealed to similar ethnoreligious groups made their competition for votes especially intense. The danger facing the Whigs was not just the defection of a critical part of their electoral coalition but that their efforts to gain political advantage over their Liberty rivals would undermine their claim to moral leadership. Whig chiefs evidently gave little thought to this aspect of the third party challenge. Northwestern Whigs angrily resorted to fraudulent campaign devices, after failing to win third party votes with antislavery professions. Whether or not Liberty voters actually held the political balance, Whig leaders took no chances. Having little concern for the sanity or sanctity of the political process, they prepared to blunt the Liberty challenge with all the means at their disposal. In the end the 1844 campaign and its Mexican War aftermath only confirmed third party fears that the political system was sadly in need of reformation.

William Henry Harrison's untimely death in April 1841 and the accession of Virginia slaveholder John Tyler to the White House disillusioned many abolitionists and intensified the struggle between Whigs and abolition voters, which reached its peak in Ohio's northern counties. Even before Harrison's death, Whigs worried over the progress the third party had made in establishing a press in Cleveland, the *Palladium of Liberty* (and later the *Declaration of Independence*). Whig leaders now became openly critical of the abolition party. Loyal Whigs were warned not to accept a third party nomination, and Ashtabula's Benjamin Wade followed suit. In 1841 Wade rejected the Liberty nomination (while accepting the Whig) for state senator from Ashtabula and Lake counties, repudiating the third party and denying he had ever been a political abolitionist—"so far from it, that I never yet belonged to an abolition Society." In marked contrast to his frustrating 1839 loss to an antiabolition alliance, Wade won easily.[7]

Besides Wade, Joshua Giddings represented the most formidable Whig obstacle to third party success on the Reserve. He was president of the Jefferson Anti-Slavery Society when he entered Congress in 1838, and his efforts in behalf of the right of petition and against Southern dictation earned him great respect. Liberty party leaders thus invited Giddings to join with them so that "all the true friends of Liberty" would be united. Believing the Whig party was "going to pieces," Lewis Tappan suggested Giddings and John Quincy Adams head an abolition party in its place. Not only did Giddings spurn these requests, but in future campaigns he proved Reserve Whiggery's biggest gun in their war against the third party.[8]

Congressman Giddings was determined to pursue antislavery goals within the Whig party; he remained a Clay Whig in 1844, even after Southern Whigs joined with Democrats to censure him in March 1842 for his antislavery agitation. Shaken but determined, Giddings promptly resigned and returned to his Reserve district to stand for reelection in a special spring election. His prospects looked grim at first as conservative Whig opinion even on the Reserve repudiated his action. The Ohio delegation in Congress failed to come to his aid, fearing it would be seen as "an abolition movement & do hurt in Ohio." Seth Gates, a New York abolitionist Whig, thus warned Giddings, "the Lord send you deliverance, for your Whig colleagues wont [*sic*]."[9]

On the Reserve, however, abolitionists united to return their champion to Congress. Bailey's *Philanthropist* called Giddings's censure an "Outrage on Ohio" and hoped he would be unopposed (though Democrats did run a candidate). Local third party leaders led by J. H. Paine promised their support as well and helped the antislavery Whig win an overwhelming victory. Liberty supporters rejoiced at Giddings's triumph; Salmon Chase sent a personal note of congratulations.[10]

Despite third party support for Giddings, his martyrdom and eventual triumph over the Slave Power backfired on the Reserve Liberty party. More than ever Giddings was the Reserve's antislavery favorite; even some Liberty advocates objected to placing a candidate against him in future elections. By August the *Philanthropist* regretted its earlier endorsement of Giddings, criticizing his "connection with one of the pro-slavery parties."[11]

Support for Giddings in 1842 left Liberty voters in an awkward position for the 1843 congressional elections. Although the party nominated Giddings's friend Edward Wade, some Liberty voters refused to repudiate the popular Whig. The *Liberty Herald* insisted that "members of the Liberty party are alone entitled to the votes of liberty men" but hinted that Giddings might win their support anyway since "exceptions are admissible in extreme cases." As a result, Edward Wade ran over one hundred votes behind the rest of the Ashtabula Liberty ticket and trailed in Geauga as well. Still, while admitting Giddings's value to the cause, nearly eight hundred Liberty voters declined to support him due to his Whig connections.[12]

Liberty leaders had unwittingly played into Giddings's hands. Giddings had always been an advocate of conciliation (recalling the proscription controversy of a few years back), but by 1842 he had embarked on a campaign to bring third party voters back into the Whig fold. Indeed, Giddings used his appeal to abolition voters to persuade hesitant Whig brokers to support him rather than a conservative Whig who could not lure third party voters. As part of his effort to win over Liberty voters (as well as hesitant Whigs), Giddings published a series of letters under the pseudonym "Pacificus" in the winter of 1842. In these letters the Whig pacifier combined antislavery appeals with an insistence on the Whig economic policy as part of the Northern rights that suffered at the hands of Southern influence. Like his fellow Whigs, Giddings believed that no argument was stronger than that directed to a "man's pocket."[13]

Despite the mistaken claims of some historians, the economic arguments by Whigs (or that of any others) found little favor among third party voters. In fact, Liberty advocates sought to separate themselves from Giddings by insisting in the *Philanthropist* and *Declaration of Independence* that the true Liberty party did not stand exclusively for Northern rights but looked "to the rights and interests of the whole country." (The *Ashtabula Sentinel* responded that "all Northern rights are so identified with each other, that one cannot be rejected without prejudice to the others.")[14] When they rejected Giddings's and his party's leadership on the slavery issue, Liberty voters also spurned an emphasis on the tariff and other economic issues that Reserve Whig abolitionists continued to support.

Whigs intensified their efforts to attract third party voters in the 1843 congressional contests. Reserve Whigs nominated besides Giddings, two antislavery candidates, Edward S. Hamlin in the Oberlin district and Daniel Tilden in Trumbull. Hamlin's appeal to abolition voters was strong enough to induce a number of Oberlin abolitionists, including college president Asa Mahan, to support the Whig nominee. Even with these Oberlin defectors, Hamlin lost to his Democratic opponent, whose 416-vote margin of victory was less than the 650 votes given to the Liberty candidate.[15]

During the campaign Giddings spoke at Oberlin but concentrated his efforts in the bitterly contested Trumbull district, where a Warren Whig meeting repudiated the third party by name. At a Ravenna (Portage County) gathering, Tilden insisted he was a truehearted abolitionist and deserved Liberty support. As soon as he closed his remarks, his fellow Whigs rushed for the door before Liberty speaker B. F. Hoffman could reply. When Tilden managed a narrow victory, the editor of the *Liberty Herald* complained that Giddings was personally responsible.[16]

Besides the growing conflict on the Western Reserve, the 1842 state results had already deepened Whig concern. Whig Governor Thomas Corwin suffered defeat while the Liberty party increased its 1841 total by at least four times. In 1842 the third party nominated Leicester King for governor, a former Whig state senator from Trumbull County and president of the Ohio Anti-Slavery Society. King might have been chosen by the Whigs some day if Reserve hopefuls had not encountered such resistance in the southern counties. Whig editors could not deny that King was an "estimable and worthy gentleman," but they could denounce him for heading "the most incendiary and most disorganizing party which ever had an existence."[17]

As long as the abolition party won such scant respect at the polls, Whigs paid little attention, but, when King's nomination promised more antislavery defections, Whig partisans were quick to jump to the attack. Their favorite argument was that King votes would actually help Wilson Shannon, the Democratic nominee and no friend to abolition. Whigs warned that voting for Liberty was "nothing less than playing into the hands of Locofocoism. Indeed, we have all along considered the abolitionists as the allies of the destructives." The Whig state press complained that the efforts of their antislavery neighbors appeared as quixotic as "running a tilt at a windmill." Dropping their forbearance to the third party, Whigs insisted the abolitionists' political organization marked them as "not merely eccentric but infatuated, *demented,* insane."[18]

Whigs went on to charge that Democrats favored the acquisition of Texas and planned to gerrymander the state in a "foul scheme of submission to the south." Worried Whigs went so far as to claim that Judge King and Samuel Medary (the Democratic state printer) were sworn allies in a "desperate effort" to prevent Corwin's reelection. Arguing that King supporters were nothing more than "open-mouthed Loco Focos," Whigs urged abolition voters not be taken in by the "designs of these disaffected, ill-used people."[19] From its initial view that third party voters were sincere but misguided, the Whig press had gone far toward the policy adopted in 1844 of using a campaign forgery to "prove" third party leaders were merely Locofoco agents, not serious representatives of a legitimate political position.

Eager to encourage Liberty defections from the Whig fold, Democrats altered their aggressive antiabolitionist position of 1840. Without moderating its racist tone, the *Ohio Statesman* suggested King should have been the

85

Whig candidate and rejoiced at each "slice from the Clay Whigs" the third party managed to carve. The Democratic state paper insisted that a Corwin victory would only deliver the abolitionists to the slaveholder Clay: "sell them like cattle in the market place." The Whig journal noted the Democrats' uncharacteristic "marvellous loving kindness for the Abolitionists" and wondered whether the *Stateman's* desperate alliance with the abolitionists meant it wanted "to play the *Mahan* game over again."[20]

As the Whig *State Journal* suggested, the 1842 Ohio election resembled that of 1838. Again Democrats swept to an off-year election victory with Whigs wailing they had been betrayed by abolitionist voters. Whigs denied accusations they had been done in by their own decision to walk out of the assembly, insisting Democrats triumphed due to unfair apportionment schemes. Beyond this Whigs attributed their loss "directly to the abstraction of votes by the 'Third Party'." Liberty voters did exactly as Whigs had warned and threw "the entire Legislature into the hands of men who will *Gerrymander* the State, and fill Congress with the allies of the slave power."[21]

Bailey's *Philanthropist* just as eagerly accepted responsibility for the Whig defeat. Unlike in 1838, however, these claims now carried at least some substance since the Democratic margin of victory (3,443) was far less than the Liberty total (5,405). Moreover, three of the legislative districts in which third party votes were blamed for Whig defeats were areas of relative abolitionist strength. (See table 8.) In Belmont, for example, the Democratic candidate triumphed by just five votes while the third party polled 171 ballots.[22]

TABLE 8
Whig Ohio Legislative Seats Lost and Liberty Vote in 1842

County	Democratic Margin		Liberty Votes
Lorain ⎫	328	(Sen.)	⎫ 507
Medina ⎭	263	(Rep.)	⎭
Clermont ⎫			⎫
Brown ⎬	1521	(Sen.)	⎬ 230
Clinton ⎭	1510	(4 Reps. avg.)	⎭
Harrison	34	(Rep.)	142
Belmont	5	(Rep.)	171

Sources: Counties listed are those where Whig papers claimed legislative seats were lost to Democrats due to abolition votes. (Returns for Guernsey County were unavailable). *Ohio State Journal,* October 19, 21, 24, 1842. See also *Painesville Telegraph,* November 2, 1842; and *Ashtabula Sentinel,* October 29, 1842. The Liberty totals are those for the candidate for governor.

86

Still, Whig complaints were designed mainly for political effect. In 1844 and 1846 the Liberty vote was much larger, but there were fewer gripes since Whigs managed to win those elections. Contemporaries were none-theless correct in believing that the great bulk of third party supporters were former Whigs. In 1842 Liberty votes came primarily from counties where Harrison had run strong in 1840. (Harrison's county percentages correlated at +.41 with those of King in 1842.) Whigs lost support in several counties where the third party was strong, although Democrats also improved over their 1840 showing in counties with few abolitionists. No doubt Liberty votes contributed to the Whig defeat; in some counties Whig losses were not matched by Democratic gains and can be safely attributed to Liberty defectors. (See table 9.)

Third party supporters were further alienated from the Whig party after the 1842 campaign in which "no method fair or foul was left untried to

TABLE 9
1842 Liberty Vote in Ohio Counties with Whig Decline and No Democratic Gain

County	Whig Loss (%)	Liberty (%)
Brown	1.7	2.8
Carroll	.7	1.8
Clinton[a]	3.1	2.4
Delaware	1.7	2.7
Geauga	3.3	6.4
Guernsey	1.7	1.8
Harrison	3.0	3.8
Highland	1.8	2.1
Lake[a]	6.7	4.9
Licking[a]	2.6	3.0
Logan	3.4	3.3
Lorain	8.3	9.5
Ross	0	1.7
Trumbull[b]	5.5	6.7
Union	.8	2.8

STATE AVERAGE 2.1

Sources: *Whig Almanac, 1843,* 44; *Whig Almanac, 1844,* 52. The Whig decline was figured from 1842 to 1841 rather than the 1840 presidential race as Democrats were bound to gain over their 1840 totals.

[a] Clinton, Lake, and Licking are included since the slight gains Democrats made there did not match the much larger Whig decline and the Liberty share.

[b] The Whig decline in Trumbull is compared to 1840 rather than 1841. The Whigs actually gained slightly in 1842 over 1841, but this was still below their total of 1840. Trumbull was always contested fiercely and the growth of the Liberty vote there cut severely into the Whig percentage.

crush the Liberty party." Some took solace in the belief that they had instead crushed the hopes of Henry Clay in the approaching presidential election. Corwin blamed himself for the Whig defeat but admitted "a strong abolition force" existed against Clay. While they polled just over 2 percent of the total Ohio vote in 1842, third party supporters threw a scare into the plans of Clay's northwestern backers. "Money is power," the editor of the *Ohio State Journal* advised Corwin's "friends in Kentucky," and "without power nothing can be done in this State for the next two years."[23]

The Michigan *Signal of Liberty* also believed the Whigs had few hopes "until the Liberty party shall be destroyed." Whigs "flattered, coaxed and abused" Liberty defectors, while using "every method to induce them to return to the Whig ranks." Third party advocates insisted that the Whigs were "deeply interested in our political destruction, and are actively at work to accomplish it."[24] Michigan Whigs were indeed shaken enough to take a leading role in developing the campaign forgery Whigs were to use in 1844.

The response of party politicians was already fixed before the most important election the Liberty party would engage in. Whigs rightly considered the third party a serious threat, while Democrats welcomed the abolition party as a decided advantage. Both parties worried less over the issues the Liberty party raised than the damage or profit it might hold for their own chances to win election. Their correspondence reveal party politicians unconcerned with the basis of the Liberty protest, since it had so little to do with their own narrow interests in party infighting and disputes over patronage. Party politicians not located in abolition strongholds, unlike Joshua Giddings, made little or no mention of the third party in their private correspondence.[25]

While both parties abused Liberty, Whigs were especially intent on blunting the harm the third party could do to their election hopes. Antiabolition Democrats naturally did little to attract third party support, but Whigs sometimes altered their policies slightly to accommodate the Liberty challenge. In abolition strongholds Whigs at times selected candidates attractive to potential third party voters. More than this, however, Whigs willingly adopted unsavory means to deal with the growing threat.[26] Pious Liberty voters had hoped to encourage a moral reformation through their political independence; instead, they had helped to confuse the scramble for political office and, indirectly, to worsen the corruption of political life they had always found most abhorrent.

Beginning in 1844 slavery's threat to expand to the southwest gave Whigs an ideal opportunity to appeal to antislavery voters. The most pressing

88

issue was the annexation of Texas, on whose back first President Tyler and then Southern and western Democrats sought to ride to the White House. Northern Whigs, however, realized the Texas controversy could help heal their antislavery divisions. In early spring Whigs and Liberty advocates across the North joined together "without distinction of party" to refuse any candidate "not *openly* opposed to the annexation of Texas."[27] Once again the Democratic position on slavery-related issues allowed Whigs to pose as sincere friends of abolition while questioning the wisdom of an abolition party.

The Liberty party had little to do with the greatest advantage handed Whigs in 1844. When Southern Democrats used Texas and the two-thirds rule to nominate Tennessee slaveowner James K. Polk over Martin Van Buren, Whigs with some justice could announce the "Triumph of the Slave Breeding Annexationists" and the "dissolution of the Loco Foco party." Indeed, the Whig view that the Polk nomination represented "a complete triumph of Southern dictation and the advocates of *immediate Annexation,* over the *doughfaces* of the North" squared completely with the *Philanthropist*'s opinion that Polk was a "man of small talents"—his only recommendation being "he is in favor of the immediate annexation of Texas, and it is the mandate of the slaveholders that he be the candidate." "Polk and Texas" also divided Ohio Democrats, many of whom had been diehard Van Buren men. Other northwestern Democrats, especially Lewis Cass men in Michigan, had all along favored Van Buren's rejection and warmly endorsed the annexation of Texas.[28]

At first the Democratic embrace of Texas allowed Whigs to appeal for abolitionist support, but Clay soon fumbled this advantage to prevent more serious Southern defections. During the campaign the Whig candidate issued a series of letters purporting to explain his Texas position but which only further confused the issue. His first letter, the Raleigh letter, joined Van Buren in opposing immediate annexation. While antislavery Whigs breathed a sigh of relief, Democrats nominated the expansionist Polk. When this threatened to undercut Clay's support in the South and in some areas of the Northwest, Clay penned the Alabama letters, expressing his desire to see Texas added to the Union if it could be done without war or dishonor, with the "common consent of the Union" on "just and fair terms." Warned by northwestern Whigs that this promised to undermine his antislavery support, Clay wrote still another letter returning to his stand against immediate annexation. The Great Pacifier's uncharacteristic maladroit handling of this issue probably cost him the election.[29]

Whigs long recalled what a "chilling effect" Clay's letters had on antislavery voters. At first his Raleigh letter placed the third party on the defensive; Whig editors easily defended Clay's Texas policy while complaining of the "marked unfairness and illiberality" Liberty papers exhibited toward Clay. Whigs were hard-pressed once their candidate started to switch positions, however, while Clay's Alabama letters especially embarrassed northern Ohio Whigs. A Cleveland Whig convention had endorsed Clay's opposition to annexation expressed in "the manly, explicit and patriotic" Raleigh letter. With Clay's help, the *Philanthropist* now dismissed his views as "thoroughly Southern" as Polk's. The Liberty party thus stood as the only "antagonistic force to the Slave Power." Unlike the Great Compromiser, it abhorred preserving the balance of power between "Slavery and Liberty." The Liberty party believed instead that "slavery ought to have no power at all."[30]

When the Liberty party nominated the presidential ticket of James G. Birney and Thomas Morris in 1841 and reaffirmed both nominations in 1843, the Texas issue had not been pressing. Few could doubt the abolition party's opposition to more slave territory, however, and, just to make sure, Birney announced he regarded as unconstitutional the annexation of Texas or any foreign territory. In the *Philanthropist* Bailey explained that his opposition was based not on constitutional issues but on the existence of slavery in Texas. (Unlike eastern abolition leaders, Bailey endorsed the occupation of Oregon.) Liberty conventions denounced both Clay and Polk as servile to the Slave Power, while claiming only the third party uncompromisingly opposed annexation.[31]

Angered by third party independence, Whigs especially feared the impact of Clay's tortuous Texas policy on antislavery strongholds such as the Western Reserve. Whig leaders thus dispatched to the Reserve Cassius M. Clay, the candidate's antislavery kinsman. Together Clay, Joshua Giddings, and Benjamin Wade vouched for their candidate's antislavery virtues. With Thomas Corwin, C. M. Clay told Reserve audiences not to fulfill the hopes of Southern slaveholders by "diverting enough from the Whig ticket to secure the election of the Polk ticket." The antislavery Clay made enough progress to worry Democratic and Liberty party leaders alike. Foster of the Michigan *Signal of Liberty* doubted Clay had done much damage, while demonstrating he was a "true Whig" and "mere emissary of Henry."[32]

By then, however, the Whig hopeful had begun to worry over the damage his cousin's efforts might do in the South. C. M. Clay and Ohio Whigs were making much of candidate Clay's supposed antislavery sentiments. "I do not mean to say that Mr. Clay is an emancipationist," his cousin reassured antislavery audiences, "but I believe his feelings are with the cause." As cousin Cassius promised "the great mass of Whigs are or ought to be anti-slavery," Clay's Southern stock plunged accordingly. Finally, candidate Clay repudiated his kinsman's efforts, believing Cassius had been too "sanguine" of his receiving Liberty support anyhow. The candidate's letters renouncing the sentiments professed by Cassius eventually became public and were given full play in Democratic journals, but not in Whig ones.[33]

Giddings was not discouraged by Clay's twisting and turning on the slavery issue. The Reserve Whig admitted "we shall have trouble with the Liberty party I expect," so he welcomed Clay's Raleigh position, which he thought followed the entire doctrine of his Pacificus essays. With some naïveté, Giddings was delighted to hear his favorite "declare my sentiments correct," expecting Clay to maintain "the Constitutional rights of the free as well as the slave States." By July, however, even Giddings began to worry about Clay's stand on the slavery issue.[34]

Following Clay's Alabama letters, Ohio Whigs informed him the "effect in this quarter is not happy." The state Whig committee reminded Clay that in Ohio and New York "the only hope of the Whigs" was in "largely neutralizing the vote that ordinarily would be given for the 3rd party." Responding to these warnings, Clay wrote directly to Giddings, regretting "extremely the state of things which you describe in Ohio." It was especially lamentable, in Clay's words, as "the loss of its Electoral vote will I fear lead to the defeat of the Whig party." Still, Clay could not have let his cousin's claims go unnoticed because that would endanger four Southern states, "a much greater loss than any gain in your quarter." Clay feared that Giddings's "Patriotic efforts to conciliate" the Liberty party would, in any event, prove "vain and fruitless."[35]

Clay, who by this time was frantic over the political mess of his own making, issued his last letter announcing he was "decidedly opposed to the immediate annexation of Texas." Giddings then spelled out "the duty of anti-slavery men in the present crisis," further embittering Liberty partisans who refused to accept the slaveholder Clay. At first third party advocates worried little over Whig efforts to lure Liberty voters, as "they cant [*sic*] make any body believe that Henry Clay is opposed to the extension of Slavery," but their anger grew as Giddings made claims for Clay that were "utterly, notoriously groundless" and that assumed antislavery voters were "either dishonest or foolish." Whigs of the Lake region answered the Liberty challenge by nominating decided abolitionists of the Giddings type. Whatever Clay's position, Reserve Whigs insisted they were "firmly and uncompromisingly" opposed to annexation. Some wavering Whigs might have heeded these appeals, but loyal Liberty voters remained steadfast. An Ashtabula Liberty convention promised to increase its votes, "the labors of J. R. Giddings & Co. notwithstanding."[36]

It was Ohio's uncertain political fate that drew the attention of national party managers anxious to win its large block of electoral votes. This doubt doubled after the October state election. Reversing their 1842 loss, Ohio Whigs managed to elect Mordecai Bartley governor, but by the slimmest of margins. With over 300,000 votes cast, the Whig candidate carried the state by less than thirteen hundred ballots. Over 8,400 third party votes were counted, roughly one thousand more than a year before. These results convinced observers that the "two great parties are so nicely balanced that a straw may decide the fight." Whig committees warned that even "a *single* vote withheld by negligence, or thrown away upon a Third Candidate" would breed regret by aiding those who would extend slavery through a bloody *"unjust and unholy war."* While Democrats hoped third party voters would stand firm, Whigs meant to see that Liberty voters did not stand in their way in the approaching presidential contest.[37]

Fraudulent campaign practices were common to northwestern politics, but Liberty advocates expected to be treated somewhat differently due to what they thought was the righteousness of their cause. Not surprisingly, with Ohio's presidential prize tempting them, party politicians took a markedly different view. To them third party voters were fair game, and each party took steps to insure that their side secured the political advantage. Despite their loss in October, Democrats hoped the third party would help them win Ohio in the presidential contest. Whigs were ever wary and moved to neutralize, as they put it, the Liberty party's influence. Not only did Whigs mount strenuous efforts to induce third party voters to support Clay, but they collaborated in a number of schemes aimed at discrediting the Liberty candidate.[38]

Hoping to reverse Ohio's October verdict, Hamilton County Democrats prepared a secret circular urging Democrats to persuade "the Democratic portion of the Liberty party" to support Polk. In a torch light procession Whigs denounced this plan as proof "of the Design to sell Whig Liberty men to the slave Candidate!" Whigs hoped to convince Liberty voters that their "suicidal policy" was the Democrats' only hope. Yet the third party was also put on guard against the Whigs when, before the state election, the Roorback forgery, which purported to show Polk was a particularly cruel slaveowner, was exposed. Democrats stumbled badly too when a pamphlet designed for circulation in the South was presented as evidence of Democratic intentions to extend slavery and Southern political power through immediate annexation. The discovery lent substance to Cassius M. Clay's charge that the contest was one between "Polk, Texas and Slavery" or "Clay, Union and Liberty." In this climate, the *Philanthropist* warned, "no means will be left untried" by either party to seduce third party members to their support.[39]

A tactical error by Liberty candidate James G. Birney prompted Whigs to concoct one of the more elaborate campaign hoaxes of the nineteenth century. Due to purely local circumstances, Birney was nominated for the Michigan state legislature by a Saginaw Democratic convention. Birney insisted it was never considered a party nomination, but his acceptance allowed Whigs to charge that a foul alliance existed between Democrats and the Liberty party leader. In stark headlines the *Ohio State Journal* announced: "Liberty men of Ohio, who have been seduced from Whig ranks, hear!—The mask thrown off!—James G. Birney nominated for Representative by the Locofocos of Michigan!" Despite Birney's denials Whig journals claimed substantial proof now existed that "Mr. Birney is now fully in the hands of the Locofoco party." With apparently corroborating evidence from the Michigan Whig Central Committee, Whig leaders asked "can *Whig* Abolitionists after this, vote for him?"[40]

Whigs were unwilling to let the matter rest there. Shortly after the story broke, the Michigan Whig committee had dispatched an agent to the Saginaw area to fetch more ammunition. Now on the eve of the presidential election in several states, a forgery was prepared purporting to be from Birney to Jerome B. Garland of Saginaw. In this Garland forgery, Birney was made to admit to the incredibly false statement that "I am now and ever have been, a Democrat of the Jeffersonian School." The Liberty candidate was said to be willing to "forego the agitation of the slavery question" to serve "Democratic men and Democratic measures." Whigs cleverly released the letter to prevent Birney from exposing the forgery before the damage was done; the Liberty leader had just embarked on a Great Lakes steamer at Buffalo and was unaware of the forgery until he docked at Fairport, Ohio. When he was informed of the scheme, Birney quickly denounced it as a "forgery throughout," and third party leader James H. Paine rushed to New York with news of his denial.[41]

Even before Birney was able to refute the forgery personally, Liberty and Democratic papers sought to expose it based on internal evidence. For good measure the *Ohio Statesman* and the *Detroit Free Press* republished Clay's antiabolition speech of February 1839. Even so, the *Ohio State Journal* stood by its Garland statement, discussed at great length the evidence in its support and insisted the affair only confirmed Birney's prior course was to "defeat Mr. Clay, and of course to elect Mr. Polk." Once the election passed, northern Ohio Whigs continued to exploit the incident, claiming Paine's mission to New York had not been to aid the Liberty cause but "really to secure the success of the Locofoco party."[42]

The Garland forgery only added to the already bitter struggle between Whigs and Liberty advocates. Before the forgery was released, the Liberty Central Committee of Cuyahoga had warned of a "new edition" of the Whig scheme to portray Birney as a Democratic puppet. Still, the Garland plot caught Liberty organizers off guard. In Lorain, Oberlin abolitionists worked through the night before the election to distribute circulars with Birney's earlier denials. Although the Garland letter was scattered "thick as leaves" over the county, this quick action might have prevented more serious damage. Lorain was one of the few counties in the state that did not experience a small drop-off of third party votes from the state to the presidential election.[43]

Birney was not so fortunate elsewhere; third party totals fell slightly where the Garland forgery had not been contradicted. Liberty partisans were especially angered by Giddings's cynical use of the Garland letter, which was credited by few confirmed abolitionists. Some claimed the Ashtabula Whig took a leading role in the forgery. Giddings denied these charges but continued to attack the third party and to question Birney's integrity.[44]

Whig use of the Garland forgery was not limited to Ohio. Indiana Whigs made "every exertion" to turn Liberty voters to Clay, making sure the Garland letter was "industriously circulated." The Whig state press published the forgery while the chairman of the Whig central committee circulated several thousand copies. Indianapolis Whigs prevailed upon Calvin Fletcher to distribute the Whig charges to abolitionists in Westfield, Hamilton County. In Illinois correspondents from De Kalb and Kane counties reported the slanders had done Birney "immense injury."[45]

Michigan Whigs were especially frustrated with their poor performance, preferring to blame their failures on the Liberty party. Democrats, meanwhile, moderated their hostility to abolitionism and devoted close attention to developments within Liberty ranks. The *Detroit Free Press* encouraged Liberty voters to resist Whig appeals to support their "slave breeder, slave buyer, slave holder, and slave seller." (Democrats were little concerned, evidently, if abolition voters snubbed their own slaveholder candidate.) The *Free Press* dismissed C. M. Clay as a tool of Henry and observed "there is evidently a want of sincerity on his part on the subject of the abolition of slavery." Such Democratic efforts might have prompted angry

Detroit Whigs to invent the Garland forgery, as Detroit Democrats insisted.[46]

The Garland incident might have cost the Liberty party some votes, but this did Clay little good in Indiana, Illinois, and Michigan. In Ohio few Liberty supporters doubted the Whig hoax injured their party as Clay carried the state with a greater margin than Whigs had won in the October election. The Liberty candidate's son later claimed the Garland forgery caused his father's vote to diminish by at least half, while in Ohio Birney was said to have lost several thousand votes to Clay. The *Philanthropist* also blamed the Liberty decline on "the vile slanders and gross libels which were perpetrated just before the election."[47] It is unlikely that the Garland distortion swayed many loyal Birney followers, but the whole incident might have persuaded undecided antislavery Whigs to stay with Clay. The Garland forgery undoubtedly had some effect; the evidence cited above indicates the third party vote remained firm where the forgery was exposed. Most of all, the affair further embittered relations between Whig and Liberty partisans.

The Ohio Liberty press traced the forgery back to the *Ohio State Journal,* claiming it had been published with the sanction of the Whig state central committee. The Whig *Journal* denied the charge and claimed that, if any forgery was committed, it was done in Michigan and not in Ohio. Eventually, the trail led back to Michigan, where Liberty leaders and Democrats were convinced Detroit Whig chieftains had plotted the whole scheme.[48] Still, it was the stubborn independence of third party voters, motivated by religious devotion and a refusal to support slaveholding candidates, that had induced frustrated Whig leaders to concoct the entire scheme.

Despite their cynical use of the Garland forgery, Whigs did not shrink from blaming Clay's defeat on the abolition party. While Ohio went safely Whig, the third party might have contributed to Clay's narrow loss in the critical state of New York. Whig journals were certainly convinced that the "Texas candidates" won New York's electoral votes with the help of the Liberty party. The *Ohio State Journal* claimed Birney and other Liberty party leaders would next be seen "hanging about the Executive Offices at Washington, receiving their pay." The fiercest abuse came from Horace Greeley's *New York Tribune,* which moaned, "it is hard that an ultra Slavery candidate should be elected by the abolitionists." Clay's defeat supposedly at the hands of Liberty started a bitter personal and political feud between Birney and Greeley that William Birney said ended only with his father's death.[49]

Whigs had entered the 1844 campaign eager to win back third party defectors, but Clay's heartbreaking loss only inflamed their passions against the small group of Liberty voters. Eventually, Whigs would try again to conciliate third party members, but for now they could not contain their outrage. Greeley's *Tribune* thus cursed Liberty into perdition: "On your *guilty heads shall rest the* curses of unborn generations. Riot in your infamy and rejoice in its triumph, but never ask *us* to unite with you in any thing. . . . You do the dirtiest journey-work of a party which despises you, and who will pay you for their victory *you have gained them,* by trampling on your petitions, and robbing the mails of your papers." Whigs could never let third party voters forget their "responsibility of electing Polk"; the *Ohio State Journal* greeted Birney's 1845 visit to Columbus with the view "a thick cloud darkens his fame."[50] If left to Whig opinion, Liberty party abolitionists appeared primarily responsible for electing Polk and thus helping to precipitate the agonies and ultimate consequences of the war on Mexico.

Aiding the election of a slaveholding annexationist was a serious moral burden that Liberty voters did not dismiss lightly. Considering the aggressiveness of the Southern-dominated Democratic party, some third party leaders began to question the expediency of their political independence. Some pondered the wisdom of an abolitionist party that would adopt positions on other issues and thus become a universal reform party. Still others favored an antislavery party with a broader appeal to Northern voters. For now, however, few sought to abandon the Liberty party. The 1844 campaign convinced most Liberty voters of the essential righteousness of their position as the only party uncorrupted by connection with Southern slaveholders. Most of all, the Garland forgery confirmed their condemnation of the depravity of political partisans whose actions seemed unconcerned with the "morals of the people and of their rulers."

Liberty advocates, who were disconcerted by the 1844 election, eventually regained their equanimity. The campaign turmoil reaffirmed their judgment that the nation's political life had been poisoned by the seeking after office and the protection of narrow political and economic interests to the detriment of national morality. What they had witnessed was not an "excess of democracy," but what they believed was the perversion of the democratic process to suit selfish political needs. When Liberty advocates claimed to speak for the national interest, opponents hurled back the charge of disunionism.[51] When the third party spoke in favor of the ancient morality of the republic, political opponents claimed they sought the nation's destruction in a bloody racial conflict. If this sort of rhetoric breeds

96

civil war, as some historians have alleged, then it was inspired by those who sought political advantage by turning popular fury against the abolitionists, and by those who meant to discredit Liberty through whatever means were necessary.

With James Polk in the White House, Whigs redoubled their efforts to lure Liberty voters back to the party fold. Although the controversy over slavery's expansion eventually divided northwestern Whiggery, initially, it gave antislavery Whigs cause to seek third party support. While still blaming Liberty for Clay's defeat, Whigs sought to conciliate antislavery voters, particularly in northern Ohio and eastern Indiana where the Liberty defection was serious. In these areas Whigs took a firm antislavery posture and continued the older policy of nominating candidates considered friendly to antislavery causes. For the most part, however, Liberty voters rejected these Whig efforts; third party advocates remained committed to political independence from the parties they considered subservient to slavery.[52]

Antislavery Whigs predictably used the 1844 results to prod their party to occupy more advanced antislavery ground. Joshua Giddings hoped Whigs would use their majority control of the Ohio legislature to condemn annexation and repeal "our odious Black Laws." To some extent the 1844 election unnerved Giddings; he advised fellow Reserve Whigs the increasing third party vote might compel an alliance with Liberty to campaign together for Northern rights. By 1846 Giddings had pledged never again to support a slaveholder while urging Whigs and third party voters to form a common effort.[53]

Giddings pressed Whig leaders to call a state antiannexation convention to meet "without distinction of party." Knowing that Democrats would have to oppose such a convention, Giddings expected to win instead "the moderate and thinking portion" of the Liberty party. The Reserve Whig might have been encouraged by the endorsement the *Philanthropist* gave such an anti-Texas convention; editor Bailey advised antislavery voters to unite "irrespective of parties" to oppose annexation. Although Whigs failed to act quickly on this suggestion, the Ohio General Assembly passed resolutions opposing union with the foreign government of Texas as "unconstitutional, unjust, revolutionary and tending to disunion." While the Whig resolves admitted slavery was an institution "peculiar to the States whose laws admit it," they also insisted the free states should be exempt from slavery's "wrongs and charges," which annexation would entail. In both houses opinion on Texas annexation followed strict party lines.[54]

The passage in early March of the joint resolution of Congress clearing the way for Texas annexation further stimulated Whig appeals to the Liberty faithful. With annexation accomplished, the *Ohio State Journal* screamed that the Slave Power had triumphed and trampled the Constitution "under foot!" The state Whig press also chided Ohio's Democratic senators, William Allen and Benjamin Tappan, for ignoring the instructions of the Whig legislature in voting for annexation. Now the *State Journal* joined in the call for an anti-Texas convention, and, when the *Cleveland American* thought such a convention possible, the Whig journal welcomed such a "practical disposition" displayed by a Liberty press. However, the support that the *Philanthropist* initially gave the project had turned to anger when the parties ignored the proposal. Instead, the Cincinnati Liberty leaders were promoting their own project of a great "Southern and Western" Liberty convention to unite slavery's foes. The proposition for an anti-Texas convention, which came too late to win Liberty supporters by now wary of Whig plans, never came off.[55]

Giddings considered the failure to hold a state anti-Texas convention under Whig auspices a tragic mistake. Such a gathering would have "used up" the Liberty party, Giddings thought, for even third party leaders feared it would prove to be "the grave of their party." Now he predicted the third party would rally with its old strength, its aim being to break up the Whig party. Only at their peril could Whig leaders continue to "trifle" with antislavery sentiment, which Giddings believed had been Clay's undoing. He warned that never again would his fellow antislavery Whigs support a presidential candidate "who panders to slavery." Reserve Whigs had other alternatives: "Indeed I regard it as perfectly clear that the Liberty party and that portion of the Whig party which is strongly antislavery *will ultimately unite.*"[56]

Thomas Corwin agreed that the strength of antislavery feeling meant it might be time to "form quietly some community of feeling" between Whigs and Liberty followers. Southern Ohio Whigs like Corwin were eager to win third party voters, but they were not as willing as Giddings to curry favor with the abolitionists. The *Ohio State Journal* reminded third party voters that John Quincy Adams (opposed by Liberty voters in a recent election) and other Whigs had rescinded the House gag on abolitionist petitions. In July an abduction of several Ohio citizens to Virginia in a fugitive slave case gave Whigs still another chance to prove their value as antislavery allies. Insisting this case differed substantially from the Mahan incident, the *Ohio State Journal* denounced the "high-handed outrage" and called for state action. Again Whigs arranged protest meetings "without distinction of party" aimed partly at securing Liberty cooperation. The Whig press also defended C. M. Clay's troubled antislavery activities in Kentucky, denouncing the "overbearing spirit engendered by Slavery" which was so "peculiar to the South."[57]

Ashtabula Whigs implemented Giddings's conciliatory policy by opposing annexation and calling for repeal of the Black Laws or any laws that compelled them to take any responsibility for supporting slavery. Again Whigs did not count on the stubborn independence of third party voters; another round of name-calling resulted when Liberty ballots helped defeat several Whig candidates in the spring local elections. Whigs continued to argue it was not always wrong to vote for a slaveholding candidate, a position pious Liberty voters could not tolerate.[58]

Similar debates raged in Portage County, where Whig congressman Daniel Tilden had narrowly won election in 1843. Late in March the Portage Whig convention called on all who were opposed to the extension of slavery "to cooperate with us in resisting in every lawful mode, the annexation of Texas, and the enlargement of the borders of slavery." As party managers focused on the Liberty element, Tilden caught rank-and-file Whigs by surprise by promising to "make up no issue except upon the great question of slavery." Tilden pledged to persuade the Whig party to "take such high ground that Liberty men could have no excuse for not uniting with them." Tilden's words impressed Liberty advocates, but they remained suspicious when a number of Whigs refused to endorse his position.[59] Again Reserve Whigs failed to take account of antiabolitionist sentiment within their own constituency.

In June the Portage Liberty convention persisted in denouncing both parties as loyal to the Slave Power. Tilden told the Liberty gathering he opposed the expansion of slavery into Texas, but he also held to the Whig creed on currency and tariff issues. For third party voters the sticking point remained his refusal to deny the right of a slaveholder to hold the presidential office. Still, Portage Whigs declared slavery "repugnant to the laws of God and the rights of man," favored its abolition in the District of Columbia and in the territories, supported prohibiting the slave trade between the states, and urged repeal of the Black Laws. For good measure the Whig convention denounced the recent arrest of the Ohioans by the Virginians as "an atrocious trespass upon the rights of our citizens." Within a year Congressman Tilden joined with Giddings and other Whigs to vote against the declaration of war on Mexico. Later he united with still others to support Wilmot's proviso prohibiting slavery in territories wrested from Mexico.[60]

Northern Ohio Whigs thus adopted a more hostile attitude toward slavery partly in response to the third party. To lure Liberty supporters, Whigs wielded a two-edged sword: repeating the old charge that third party votes defeated Clay and thus expedited annexation, while complaining already that Polk's policies promised to shed the nation's blood in an unjust war. Hoping to limit the number of third party defectors, Whigs at the same time urged all the party faithful to visit the polls to overcome "the heavy draft made on our ranks by the Liberty party organization." The Ohio General Assembly remained safely in Whig hands, despite the efforts of the Texas Liberty party (as Whig journals took to calling the third party), which continued to be "an enormous drain" on Reserve Whig sources.[61]

Indiana Whigs also included the Liberty element in their political calculations, expecting that a "successful diversion" would be enough to meet the challenge. As in Ohio, Whigs arranged anti-Texas meetings giving Liberty supporters a prominent part in the proceedings. These gatherings pledged cooperative efforts to halt Democratic schemes to extend "the infamous institution of slavery." The abolition Quaker secession was strongest in Caleb B. Smith's congressional district, where Smith and Liberty leaders Daniel Worth and Matthew Hull addressed several anti-Texas meetings. Smith denounced Texas annexation and the "intrigues and corrupt maneuverings of the friends of the measure." He also hoped his anti-Texas speech in Congress would bring antislavery voters into Whig ranks.[62]

In the Fort Wayne district some third party followers considered supporting the Whig candidate, believing the Democrat to be "one of the most loyal subjects of the overseers of the South." Other Liberty advocates disagreed with this policy. Third party voters in Washington Township, Randolph County, thought little of aiding the Whig candidate, still a member of a proslavery party. Washington Liberty voters elected their candidate for justice of the peace, though Democrats joined with Whigs "to keep out the Abolitionist."[63]

The efforts of Smith and other Indiana Whigs to secure Liberty support ran into determined opposition from the Quaker Liberty paper, the *Free Labor Advocate*. The Liberty press, edited by Benjamin Stanton, a member of the separatist Indiana Meeting of Anti-Slavery Friends, advocated third party independence and adherence to abolitionist principle. Vowing there would be few defectors to Smith and the Whigs in his district, Stanton warned Liberty voters to beware of "specious appearances" or "manifestations of approximation to anti-slavery principles" that might lure them into "the service of either of the pro-slavery parties." There was little danger of Liberty advocates being seduced by the Democrats, Stanton reasoned, but Whigs now found it "expedient to take a pretty decided stand against slavery" to secure Liberty aid. "Be not deceived," Stanton alerted fellow third party members.

Stanton's resolve was endorsed by abolitionists in Wayne, Grant, and Henry counties, among the strongest Liberty counties in the state. In New Castle, Henry County, Anti-Slavery Quaker leader Walter Edgerton directed a resolution with "special benefit" to antislavery Whigs, regretting the proposed coalition with a party still standing as "the guardian of the slave power." The convention adopted Edgerton's resolution unanimously and nominated independent candidates. A Liberty meeting in Economy, Wayne County, echoed Stanton's statement that both parties were "essentially pro-slavery." Liberty voters were warned to exercise "caution and circumspection" as Whigs sought to lure voters with pleas "perfectly deceptive, as every intelligent person knows."[64]

The eventual Liberty candidate in the Fort Wayne district managed to win 3.1 percent of the vote, nearly double the 1.6 percent Birney had polled just a year earlier. In the New Garden district Caleb Smith won reelection, but Liberty candidate Matthew Hull polled 6.4 percent in a district where Birney had won 5.7 percent. These results suggest that Whig efforts to reverse the Liberty defection were largely ineffective. The *Free Labor Advocate* rejoiced that the returns showed the Indiana Whig party "may be considered as defunct."[65]

Northwestern Whigs achieved little in 1845 in attempting to lure third party voters, but as controversy with Mexico intensified and the expansion of slavery even further than Texas became a real possibility, the prospects of cooperation between Whigs and Liberty voters might improve. By questioning the origins and purposes of the Mexican War, Whigs could demonstrate their integrity to antislavery voters, while the whole affair promised to breed dissension in Democratic ranks.[66] When their own party nominated a slaveholder for 1848, however, Whigs realized their miscalculation. In the end they suffered more free-soil defections than northwestern Democrats, losing the entire region in 1848 to Lewis Cass and popular sovereignty.

The declaration of war against Mexico in early May 1846 brought many abolitionists into open battle with the Polk administration. Seeking antislavery support but anxious to escape the fate of the Hartford Convention Federalists, Northern Whigs (along with some Liberty party leaders) adopted the Janus-faced policy of denouncing the purpose and perpetrators of the war while supporting the prosecution of it.[67]

Five Ohio Whigs joined with nine others from the Northeast to cast the fourteen votes in the House of Representatives opposing declaration of war. All five antiwar Whigs from Ohio had reason to notice third party strength. Joshua Giddings probably needed little prodding to oppose this "slaveholders' war," but the Liberty party was exceptionally strong in his northern Ohio district. Daniel Tilden had made overt appeals to Liberty voters to carry his district in 1845. Joseph M. Root's district included the Liberty community at Oberlin and was second only to Giddings's in third party strength. In 1844 Columbus Delano had narrowly carried his Columbus district in a bitterly contested election, claiming to have won the votes of "something like 280 Liberty men."[68] The fifth antiwar vote from Ohio was that of Joseph Vance, who in 1838 was thought to have been denied the governor's chair by abolitionist voters!

No wonder Reserve Whigs such as Edward Paine now led the chorus denouncing the Mexican War as "begun in folly or madness, probably both." Whig sheets in the Lake region endorsed Giddings's view that "the war is aggressive, and without any just cause." Charges that this was an unjust war carried great weight with those of New England heritage; generally, those areas strongest in Yankee origins provided the basis for northwestern antiwar sentiment. Opposition to the war was particularly strong among the very religious bodies that provided Liberty's base of support, chiefly Congregationalists, New School Presbyterians, Free Will Baptists, Wesleyan Methodists, and Quakers.[69]

Benjamin Stanton led Indiana Anti-Slavery Friends in sending a "Memorial and Protest" to Congress and the president expressing their Quaker outrage against an aggressive war "for the purpose of extending and strengthening slavery." While they often condemned the war, third party supporters wisely allowed Whigs to take the political lead. Instead, Liberty advocates expressed their antiwar beliefs primarily through their religious activity. Edward Wade, for example, denounced the "cruel and bloody war" at a Cleveland peace meeting held in the Wesleyan Methodist Chapel.[70]

Whig assaults on the Democratic plot to extend slavery through war were aimed in part at attracting actual or potential third party voters. Some northern Democrats, however, refused to cooperate by themselves opposing slavery's expansion. In August 1846 Pennsylvania Democrat David Wilmot offered an amendment to a House appropriations bill that would have prevented slavery's expansion into all territories won from Mexico. Northwestern Whigs united in supporting Wilmot's proviso, while Democrats split over the issue, seventeen of thirty in the House approving the measure. However, these Democrats' full devotion to stopping slavery might be doubted; most later rejoined party ranks to approve the appropriations bill with the Wilmot amendment excised. Four northwestern Democrats continued to favor the Wilmot principle: Jacob Brinkerhoff of Ohio, Caleb Smith of Indiana, and Joseph Hoge, and "Long John" Wentworth of Illinois. All represented districts where antislavery sentiment and the third party were unusually strong.[71]

Even so, Whigs found their antiwar and antislavery positions failed to encourage the third party to disband; yet another issue was needed to lure antislavery voters. To prove their superiority over prowar, proslavery, and antiblack Democrats, Ohio Whigs decided to push for repeal of the Black Laws in the 1846 gubernatorial campaign. More even than the war that waged to the southwest or the partisan struggle over slavery mounting in Congress, debate over the Black Laws dominated the Ohio campaign. This was also perhaps the first time northwestern votes were asked to vote directly on the issue of civil rights for blacks. As the campaign progressed a party practice more common to national politics emerged. Both Whigs and Democrats found it necessary in Ohio itself to tell audiences to the south something somewhat different from what they said in the north. Once again the Liberty party claimed to be the victim of calculated deception by the major parties.

Northern Ohio Whigs led by Benjamin Wade had been strong opponents of the Black Laws, but antiblack feeling among Whigs in the southern counties and Democrats throughout the state had blocked all efforts for repeal. Democrats remained the fiercest opponents of repeal, as Whigs constantly reminded Liberty voters. Under pressure from Reserve Whigs and to help neutralize third party strength, the Whig candidate for governor, William Bebb, announced he favored (at least at first) a partial repeal of the Black Laws.[72] This was an obvious attempt to lure antislavery support. Ohio's constitution granted the governor little real power; any attempt to repeal the discriminatory laws would have to be undertaken by the legislature.

Bebb's endorsement of repeal may have been influenced by the *Philanthropist*'s refutation of the Whig candidate as a bitter opponent of the Liberty party and "a most decided Anti-Abolitionist." The third party had nominated a popular figure for governor, Samuel Lewis, known throughout the state as an educational reformer. Bebb thus told Reserve gatherings that he not only favored repeal of the black codes, but that he also supported abolition in the federal district and moral efforts against slavery south of Mason and Dixon's line. A Whig convention in Cuyahoga too called for repeal, particularly to provide schools for "all children, without regard to creeds or color." The Whig gathering then declared slavery "wrong and only wrong" and "evil and only evil." With these pledges Whig editors appealed to third party voters for an "undivided front upon the question of slavery."[73]

Throughout the Northwest Liberty supporters rebuked their states' black codes. Most advanced were Michigan Liberty advocates, whose 1845 state platform insisted that the denial of suffrage to taxpayers, "because the almighty wisdom has dictated their color," was "a cringing to slavery, mean and utterly repugnant to republican principles." In late 1846 Wiconsin Liberty voters protested the action of their state constitutional convention denying the suffrage to blacks. To those who claimed blacks constituted a separate and inferior race, the *Freeman* responded that the Bible "distinctly informs us that mankind have a common origin." In early 1847 third party voters thus stood with the minority in support of a public referendum aimed at extending the suffrage to blacks.[74]

Ohio Liberty supporters also opposed their state's racial caste system, yet their inability to win office meant this opposition was limited to resolutions passed at antislavery conventions. Unable to affect even the most minor legal disabilities placed on blacks, Ohio Liberty leaders did not openly advocate granting blacks the suffrage. Moreover, the dedication of third party supporters to racial equality sprang more from religious devotion than practical considerations. Only a few ever had much contact with blacks; Augustus Wattles worked among blacks in southwestern Ohio, while Oberlin accepted black students, though few actually came. Most third party voters lived in regions such as the Western Reserve where blacks were few.[75] Perhaps because it was such an abstract issue to them, Liberty voters refused to support Bebb, though Whigs promised to repeal the odious laws.

As the summer wore on, Whigs regretted their earlier pledges to northern Ohio audiences. The Democratic candidate, David Tod of Trumbull, had adopted a policy of silence on the heated question of repeal. In the meantime, Democratic journals to the south charged that Whig plans to repeal the Black Laws would flood the state with black refugees. These Democratic claims gained some credibility due to a controversial attempt to settle the slaves of John Randolph in Mercer County. The *Cleveland Plain Dealer* used this timely incident to reiterate its support for colonization and to detest the "amalgamation of the races." The Democratic press noted Cuyahoga Whigs adopted the "boiled down quintessence of abolitionism" in their last convention, which had been a "shade darker" than even the regular abolition gathering. Several years earlier Whigs had dropped their representative Leverett Johnson supposedly for saying "a nigger was a man," but, according to the *Plain Dealer,* things had recently changed: "None but a curly head and long heels can go to the Legislature now. Every candidate must have the niggerometer applied to him, and if he has not colored blood enough to raise the abolition mercury, he is no go." Democrats maintained that Whig attempts to repeal the law against black testimony proved "the new born love which whiggery has for the colored race." Now the Democratic state press could document its old charge of a corrupt bargain between Whigs and abolitionists. These demagogic and racist charges notwithstanding, Democrats urged Liberty voters to unite with the Democracy, as "Universal emancipation is the basis of all our efforts."[76]

Like Clay in 1844, the Whig candidate slowly realized his appeals to northern antislavery sentiment threatened even more serious losses among voters to the south. Wary of Whig promises, the *Philanthropist* asked if Bebb would distribute in southern counties the same handbills promising repeal he spread on the Reserve. Liberty voters should not be deceived, Bailey warned, only the sincere Lewis could be trusted to serve the cause of equal justice.[77]

As Bailey predicted, Whigs began to waver in the face of Democratic attacks. First the *Ohio State Journal* insisted Tod should also announce his position, realizing the Democratic candidate was garnering the fruits of silence while Bebb was taking all the heat. Next the Whig press denied the Democratic charge that Bebb promised to place blacks next to whites in the same school "in the same bench" and that he favored "making a negro a *voter.*" Then, just as Whigs feared, Tod suddenly told southern audiences that he stood against repeal. The *Journal* shouted "Fraud! Fraud!" as Tod's reply was printed in southern newspapers too late to reach the Reserve.[78] This amounted to an attempt to steal the election, the *Journal* charged. No doubt Whig complaints would have been even more impassioned had Tod won.

Actually Whigs had little cause to complain since their candidate had also taken advantage of the era's poor communications to tailor his appeal to the prejudices of a particular audience. In Mercer County, where controversy swirled over the Randolph slaves, Bebb suggested that a law to deny blacks the right to hold real estate could prevent a large influx of the unwanted race from coming to the state. Although he admitted he favored repealing some of the discriminatory laws, Bebb told southern gatherings he did not favor "perfect equality" between whites and blacks. This stand,

Liberty journals complained, amounted to reneging on his earlier pledges to Reserve audiences. Even worse than Tod, Bebb made his denials to the south too late in the campaign to influence the result on the Reserve.[79]

Whig denials of these charges rang hollow since they went ever further to prove their reliability on the race issue. Going back to the 1838 campaign when abolitionists had queried candidates, Whigs dredged up Tod's reply, which favored allowing blacks to benefit from the school fund. While this was now also Bebb's position, Whigs claimed they "would not for a moment consent to bring White and Black children together in the same school."[80] But in 1838 Tod was said to have not made this distinction.

Despite Whig backsliding, some abolition voters still might have backed Bebb due to his earlier protestations against slavery and the Black Laws. Nonetheless, the Ohio third party increased its vote to its highest point ever at almost 10,800 ballots (or 4.4 percent), even though candidate Lewis, a loyal Methodist, suffered some defections among Wesleyan Methodist Liberty voters. While the third party vote continued to climb, Bebb won by a slim margin (though larger than Whigs had received in 1844), no doubt aided by Democratic party divisions.[81]

After the election Whigs somewhat halfheartedly attempted to fulfill their pledge to repeal the Black Laws, but their thinly disguised plan to shift responsibility through a public referendum pleased no one, and the idea was allowed to drop. As it turned out, the Black Laws would be partially repealed in 1849 owing to a rather cynical political deal between Democrats and Free Soil leader Salmon P. Chase—cynical because Democrats reversed their long-standing hostility to repeal to win control of the state legislature, while Chase split with his own party to ensure his election as United States senator. Little wonder Liberty advocates were disenchanted when they recalled the 1846 campaign had begun with Whigs professing to stand for equal justice and ended with both parties pledging allegiance to white supremacy.[82]

To restrain the Liberty challenge to their party, northwestern Whigs adopted two rather contradictory approaches. In 1844 they insisted their candidate was much to be preferred to the Democratic annexationist, but at the same time they devised a variety of schemes aiming to neutralize, not conciliate, the third party. At first the Garland forgery and Whig charges that Birney caused Clay's defeat only brought more recriminations. Later Whigs expected their opposition to Texas annexation and their denunciations of the "slaveholders' war" would bring antislavery support. Such Whig efforts, however, were partially undermined by similar Democratic appeals to the latent antislavery sentiments of the region.

In 1846 Ohio Whigs sought to control the Liberty defection through a promise to repeal a part of the state's Black Laws. Although they retreated from even this position, Whigs wondered at the stubborn refusal of third party voters to recognize that their political independence only aided anti-abolition Democrats. Rebuffing such Whig appeals, Liberty followers clung to their independent party and managed to increase their share of the vote, though Whig efforts directed against the third party might have limited its growth.

Both Whigs and Democrats misunderstood the basis of the Liberty protest, which had little to do with conventional political concerns and went far beyond simply stopping slavery's spread to the southwest. Pious third party members insisted on repudiating those parties connected with slavery to the extent of supporting slaveholding candidates. Considering the unwavering religious commitments of Liberty voters, the Whigs' elaborate campaign strategies, including their denunciations of slavery, were for the most part wasted efforts.

At the same time Whigs and Liberty advocates were debating the legitimacy of a slaveholding candidate in 1844, Methodists were dividing over whether their church could tolerate a slaveholding bishop.[83] When Liberty voters refused to accept a political party that tolerated slaveholders, they were only acting with maddening consistency; in their religious affairs, the third party faithful had already declared themselves free of the sin of slavery and those who condoned it.

6

POLITICS OR PRINCIPLES?

War on Mexico brought heated exchanges between North and South over the expansion of slavery, yet, ironically, this controversy did not serve Liberty but rather claimed the party as one of its casualties. Some antislavery leaders questioned whether the abolition party was equal to the vital task of stopping the slave empire's further growth. Internal tensions were always present within the Liberty movement but had seemed minor compared to the hostile opposition the party faced. In the end these latent internal differences helped undermine the party as the election of 1848 approached. While sectionalism intensified, the abolition party nonetheless found itself abandoned by several of its most important leaders, whose desertion left party followers bewildered and powerless to affect events.[1]

Looking to the 1848 contest, leaders of antislavery factions within the major parties investigated the prospect of securing Liberty support should they be compelled to seek new political alliances. Although third party conventions had always rebuffed their overtures, Whigs and Democrats who sought coalition with Liberty discovered a willing ally in Salmon P. Chase. Soon after joining the third party in 1841, Chase emerged as a leading party organizer. Chase, who was respected and dedicated, along with Gamaliel Bailey, nonetheless frequently exasperated other Liberty leaders by activities which seemed to be deflating the party's abolitionist doctrine. Frustrated himself with Liberty party politics by 1847, Chase in effect abandoned the third party by announcing he was willing to support "any honest Wilmot Proviso Democrat." The Cincinnati antislavery leader then sought to merge the abolition party into a larger antislavery coalition dominated by Barnburner Democrats (a New York faction devoted to Martin Van Buren) and Conscience Whigs such as Joshua Giddings. It must be stressed, however, that many of the Liberty party faithful did not share this enthusiasm for antislavery cooperation. Most third party voters—separatists and seceders—instinctively suspected proposals intended to gain widespread popularity by diminishing the moral content of God's message.[2]

The defection of Chase to the Barnburners was not the only sign of Liberty's impending demise. Being always liable to disruption, the third party was torn by competing views and lacked compensating forces for cohesion and continuity. In 1845, for instance, the building housing the Trumbull Whig and Liberty presses burned to the ground. While the major party press was insured, the Liberty paper was not and thus literally perished in the flames. Unlike the major political parties, Liberty had few inducements such as party patronage to compel loyalty. Most of all, third party members in both east and west disagreed among themselves over party policy and especially over their primary mission. In the end the Liberty party never decided whether to pursue politics or promote principles instead.

Politically minded Liberty leaders typically considered the third party a temporary way station to building a more permanent and broader-based antislavery party, one that would seek more conventional political goals including eventual party victory.[3] Religiously minded Liberty advocates believed their party more enduring (after all, the Lord's work is never done) and expected it to go on promoting righteous moral and religious action. Liberty party supporters who had broken from their churches valued the independence the third party gave their abolitionist church bodies. As religious concerns motivated their political independence from the first, pious party members largely opposed the efforts of the politically minded to obfuscate Liberty's abolitionist doctrine and transform the moral-religious protest movement into a more recognizable political organization.

The Liberty party was a poor vehicle for coalition politics. Many of its followers thought politics by nature to be at war with principles. Some believed popularity and righteousness virtually incompatible. Liberty churches restricted membership to those who could prove their conversion to God and their dedication to right principles; a "radical change of heart," not just good intentions, was required of those finally accepted to fellowship. According to Reverend John Keep, "to *do right* is the highest possible expediency." A common Liberty conviction was that "the strength of Liberty men is in their principles, not their numbers"; thus many feared "all compromise of principle" would destroy their influence. Instead of concentrating on winning popularity, many Liberty advocates insisted on guarding their principles and independence from the contagion of party or similar corrupting influences. Gerrit Smith could thus stand the argument between principles and politics on its head: "The Liberty party is feeble not because of its small numbers, but because it misrepresents, is unfaithful to, and stands in the way of the progress and power of its own principles." In seeking to widen the party's appeal, Chase encountered similar sentiments from those who warned of the "danger in putting the work in dishonest hands, who would depress the standard, and thus destroy the cause."[4]

Some form of contention was probably inevitable between Chase and those who did not share his political orientation. Dedicated to antislavery goals, the Cincinnati lawyer nonetheless seldom allowed his thoughts to stray too far from political realities. In 1840 he held back from joining the "premature" third party movement, believing it stood no chance of success. Chase later sought to replace the Liberty standard-bearer with a candidate unassociated with popular fears of abolitionism. Finally reconciled to Birney and convinced he was both "good" and "devoted," Chase still could not help believing that another candidate "would have got more votes." Many Liberty voters held to the evangelical commitment to follow "the straight forward rule of doing right without regard to consequences." S. P. Chase never did anything without first considering the consequences.[5]

Chase (and others who were politically minded) had little in common with those who advised Liberty advocates faced with a difficult decision "to pray over it, and try and find out the will of the Lord in the matter." The Cambridge, Ohio, *Clarion of Freedom* insisted the Liberty voter did not throw his vote away for "it will count in Heaven, if not among men."[6] The sectarian sources of the third party commitment best explain why so many party supporters valued principles over politics, and why they would respond as they did to Chase's efforts to place the party upon what he considered correct political and constitutional ground.

Pious Liberty voters did not abjure political involvement, rather their political activity was designed to serve primarily religious ends.[7] Their religious leaders promised it was their duty to carry their beliefs to the polls. Casting a third party ballot could serve as dramatic proof of conversion, not only to themselves but to their community and their God. Abolitionist political activity often functioned as a unifying force within a self-conscious religious community, showing that, as a body of Christians, they acted unitedly at the polls as well. Moreover, the Liberty party allowed those who had separated from slavery-contaminated religious organizations to deny political fellowship with the sinful institution.

Chase differed from many of the third party faithful by remaining part of a church that did not denounce slavery as sin and that tolerated slaveholders. Some Liberty partisans, who did not share either his political or religious orientation, concluded that Chase sought to compromise the cause to advance his political ambitions. James G. Birney thought Chase "sanguine—perhaps too much so—of speedy success" and wondered if the antislavery cause was not "in some danger from its friends." The Liberty presidential candidate complained that Chase embraced an antislavery approach that was too much "a matter of money policy—so little as a matter of religious duty." Chase's attempt to replace Birney with a more attractive candidate only confirmed suspicions that the Cincinnati lawyer was "ambitious of individual precedence and prominence" and relied too little "on the strength of his principles."[8]

Nonetheless, the conflict within the Liberty party did not pit selfish ambition against uncompromising principle. Most interpreters of Chase have maintained that his career was a complex and ambiguous mixture of political ambition and high ideals. "I desire to be distingushed but I desire more to be useful," Chase confessed to a cousin early in life. Acutely aware of the tension and potential conflict between his desire for advancement and his devotion to principles, Chase worked to reconcile the two. Typically, he coupled recognition of the demands of "sound expediency" with a desire to serve the needs of a "Common Humanity." Chase did not lack principle; his work with fugitive slaves won him the gratitude of Cincinnati's black community. He saw the Free Soil–Republican platform not as an abandonment of principle, but as a way to achieve abolitionist goals while perhaps advancing his own career. The struggle within the Liberty party was not simply a conflict between "political realists" and "religious-minded souls" but reflected more fundamental differences between party members who envisioned the party's mission in quite different ways.[9]

Historians have often overdrawn Chase's power within the northwestern party. Albert Hart considered the Cincinnati lawyer the "leading manager of the Liberty party in the Northwest." Another Chase biographer contends that "almost immediately he assumed a controlling position in the Ohio movement which enabled him to achieve statewide and even national power and influence." (Rather inconsistently, similar claims have been advanced for Gamaliel Bailey. According to one historian, "the Western rank and file would follow only Bailey.") Even former Liberty editors Zebina

Eastman and Theodore Foster later exaggerated Chase's influence within third party ranks.[10] (William Birney did not make this mistake.) Compared to Chase's subsequent prominence as senator, secretary of the treasury, and chief justice, his prestige and power in the 1840s was quite limited.

Salmon P. Chase (or any other individual) should not be considered the "representative man" of the northwestern Liberty movement, a consideration recognized even by Gamaliel Bailey. Moreover, the Cincinnati group of Liberty leaders could never dominate third party ranks as much as they wished. Just as the Liberty party in the East found itself torn by factional disputes and constant wrangling over principles and tactics, the movement in the Northwest was never a harmonious or unified one. Like the major parties, the third party existed mainly at the state level and even then was rent by conflicting views among individuals and regions. This was even true within the so-called Ohio group. Easterners somewhat carelessly referred to the Chase-Bailey group as the "Ohio movement" or the "westerners," but when they were more precise they called it the "Cincinnati clique," which was not without its own factionalism. William Birney suspected Bailey was lowering the Liberty standard his father had so valiantly raised in the Queen City of Mobs. Thomas Morris struggled with Bailey for control of the local party, stirring up opposition based on opposition to the Chase-Bailey constitutional formula. Eventually Bailey won out and bullied Morris into resigning the vice presidential nomination. Morris, who was reinstated by the national convention, died soon after the 1844 election, without position or power.[11]

The record of the Chase group in seeking control of the party needs to be reconsidered. Chase and Bailey's ill-conceived attempts to replace Birney on the ticket had little chance to succeed, especially since their suggested replacements refused to consider a third party nomination. The Cincinnati leaders never brought an Ohio Liberty convention to favor replacing Birney; they merely tried to undercut his support among party leaders. (The closest they ever came to supplanting Birney was at the December 1841 Ohio convention, which called for a future Liberty convention to fill any possible openings in the ticket.) This prompted the wounded candidate to complain their efforts were "singular both in manner and matter." Moreover, the dispute had little to do with sectional differences; Chase and Bailey received some support from easterners, while Birney gained encouragement from some westerners, especially in Michigan.[12]

Emphasis on the influence of the Chase-Bailey group rests primarily on their control of the Ohio third party machinery, particularly the *Philanthropist* and state Liberty conventions. The Cincinnati *Philanthropist*, the unofficial organ of the state party, was considered the foremost antislavery journal in the Northwest but was not able to dictate Liberty party policy. Besides reflecting primarily Bailey's views, the *Philanthropist* could report regularly only party activities in southwestern Ohio. Many Liberty voters continued to read third party papers from the East (especially the *Emancipator*) and the local Liberty press. In 1847 the founding of the *National Era* in the District of Columbia increased the influence of Chase and its editor Bailey, but it also limited coordination between them.[13]

The Cincinnati corps of leaders could usually dominate the state Liberty gatherings, but their control of the Ohio party was far from complete. Their direct influence was limited primarily to southwestern and central Ohio, where the state conventions usually drew delegates. Western Reserve abolitionists usually arranged and attended their own conventions; few northern Ohio Liberty party members journeyed to the state meetings and as a result their actual voting strength within the state party was not represented. The ten Reserve counties cast about one-third of Ohio's third party vote. With a much smaller population, Ashtabula County alone cast more third party ballots than Cincinnati's Hamilton County.[14] The influence of Chase and Bailey over the third party rank and file (including Ohio) should not be exaggerated. As their orientation was always more easterly, few Lake region abolitionists looked to Chase or Cincinnati for inspiration or guidance.

Supposedly, the most distinctive feature of the "Western" Liberty party was its adherence to the Chase constitutional formula, which denied any authority over slavery in the Southern states. Believing the abolitionist attack on slavery in the states "prejudices against us many worthy and sensible people," Chase drafted Liberty platforms that called instead for the national government to separate from all connection with the system of slavery. The Chase formula, intentionally weak as abolitionist doctrine, nevertheless permitted constitutional opposition to slavery and held out the potential to destroy the institution by indirect means.[15]

Some historians have assumed that this constitutional position distinguished the northwestern party from its eastern counterpart. Ohio Liberty addresses often carried the Chase imprimatur, although a state Liberty convention in 1844 went beyond the Chase policy by denouncing slavery in the South. Generally, other northwestern state parties adopted the Chase formula, but his victory was not total. Many Liberty advocates continued to attend antislavery meetings that denounced slavery as sin and called for its immediate abandonment. Chase hardly ever attended these gatherings as he never joined an abolitionist society. The Michigan, Indiana, and Illinois state antislavery societies already had removed from their constitutions the concession saying Congress had no right to legislate for abolition in the South. Northwestern Liberty conventions frequently adopted resolves condemning the sin of slavery. In May 1842, for example, a Western Reserve Liberty convention renounced slavery as a "sin against God." Perhaps to rebuke Chase and Bailey's efforts to supplant Birney, the Reserve gathering predicted Liberty's success would come "not in management" or making "interest with prominent politicians," but by standing "upon the immovable rock of righteous principle."[16]

Inspired by the work of Alvan Stewart, Lysander Spooner, and William Goodell, an abolitionist heresy that slavery was indeed unconstitutional won at least limited support among northwestern abolitionists, primarily in the Lake region of the Northwest. The *Cleveland American* gave qualified endorsement to this view, while the Wisconsin *American Freeman* ran a brief version of Spooner's *Unconstitutionality of Slavery*. In 1846 Illinois Liberty supporters debated a resolution affirming the constitution was indeed antislavery in intention but settled on a compromise resolve instead. Michigan Liberty leaders Guy Beckley and Theodore Foster favored the more radical approach of James Birney and Gerrit Smith, as did Wisconsin's Ichabod Codding and Sherman Booth.[17]

Still, most Liberty followers could accept the Chase-Bailey doctrine by pledging, in Benjamin Franklin's words, to go "to the verge" of the Constitution in opposing slavery. Bailey always insisted that divorcing the national government from the support of slavery would indeed bring the institution's death, and many Southerners in effect endorsed this view. The Chase-Bailey formula promised to isolate slavery in the present states, and "thus insulated, it must fall." If the Liberty party failed to abolish slavery in this manner, Bailey promised, "it will try another." This included constitutional amendments that would "empower Congress in a proper way to interfere for the complete extinction of the evil."[18]

The Chase-Bailey formula, which seemed to identify the Ohio Liberty party, earned the suspicion of some abolitionists who dismissed what they called the Ohio movement as "sham abolitionism."[19] These complaints were apparently confirmed as Chase and Bailey advocated coalition based on common hostility to the expansion of slavery. This political strategy of the Cincinnati leaders also inspired some defections to the small but troublesome Garrisonian element in the Northwest.

Bailey had hoped to maintain the accommodation worked out with Ohio Garrisonians at the founding of the Liberty party. Finally, relations strained to the breaking point, partly due to the compromise of principle Garrisonians thought they saw in Bailey's position. In 1845 and 1846 Garrisonian agents Abby Kelley and Stephen Foster toured the state seeking to undermine the third party. According to one story, Kelley hesitated at the threshold of a Columbiana County Liberty supporter, warning, "I have come to kill the Liberty party." The Quaker abolitionist smiled and replied, "Come in Abby, and we will kill thee with kindness." In attacking the third party, Kelley and Foster received the willing assistance of Joshua Giddings, an apparently unnatural alliance, which Democratic presses were not slow to exploit. Perhaps the Garrisonians' greatest coup was the conversion of the editor and proprietor of the *Ohio American,* the Cleveland Liberty paper. The Quaker Garrisonian *Anti-Slavery Bugle* later condemned Bailey's "exceedingly judicious" course (while establishing the *National Era* in the nation's capital), which the *Bugle* said kept him from being indicted for "incendiarism, fanaticism, and we had almost said abolitionism."[20]

Despite frequent complaints that Chase and Bailey were debasing abolitionism for political advantage, the northwestern Liberty party suffered only minor defections over the issue of the unconstitutionality of slavery. Most Liberty voters probably saw no great threat to their principles in adopting the Chase doctrine as their own. Being more concerned with religious principles than legal ones, they undoubtedly felt Chase expressed their opposition to slavery with appropriate outrage. The Cincinnati lawyer in fact performed useful service in more consistently molding their rather disjointed attacks on the sin of slaveholding. It is still unclear, however, whether most of the Liberty faithful would have gone as far as Chase in denying interference with slavery in the South. Many Liberty advocates insisted on repudiating the Southern institution. In 1848, for example, one Ohio abolitionist advised Chase not to adopt restrictive clauses at Buffalo that would prevent Liberty voters from standing on their own ground even while cooperating in a free-soil campaign.[21]

Another issue dividing Liberty party supporters was fugitive slaves. In 1842 New York abolitionists led by Gerrit Smith adopted an "address to the slaves," urging them to flee and take what they needed along their path to freedom. Chase and the *Philanthropist* decried the radicalism of the address, and some Michigan Liberty advocates agreed. The Indiana *Free Labor Advocate* printed the address and did not dispute its principles but questioned the "propriety of issuing it under existing circumstances." (Perhaps the Anti-Slavery Quakers thought the issue would complicate their struggle with the moderate Quaker majority.) Owen Lovejoy of Illinois supported Smith's appeal, responding to an argument of the New York *Evangelist* that slaveholding was stealing, and runaway slaves were only reclaiming their freedom.[22]

Chase worked to keep the 1843 National Liberty Convention platform from denouncing the fugitive slave provision of the Constitution, but he was overruled by the delegates. His efforts caused Oberlin abolitionists to wonder if some Liberty leaders were giving up their principles; they questioned whether party addresses written by Chase were "antislavery enough." In 1848 Indiana abolitionists denounced fugitive slave laws as wicked, announcing they would pay them no obligation, preferring to "obey God rather than man."[23]

In another respect Chase and his Cincinnati clique were not representative of the northwestern Liberty party. Unlike the majority of third party voters, the Chase group embraced Democratic issues and ideology. Although he was of Whiggish heritage, Chase soured on that party and displayed Democratic loyalties almost as soon as he joined the Liberty movement. The Cincinnati group publicly admitted their Democratic leanings, with Chase insisting the principles of the Democracy were "in exact harmony with the principles of the Liberty men."[24] After the election of 1844, Chase began to urge union with what he called the "True Democracy," and by 1847 he was clearly cooperating with Barnburner Democrats toward that end.

The Democratic sympathies of the Chase group caused ill feelings among Liberty supporters, particularly Western Reserve third party voters who retained their hereditary antipathy toward the Democracy.[25] Year after year Reserve Liberty partisans faced Whig taunts that the abolition party was merely a Locofoco trick to defeat deserving Whig candidates. Some antislavery voters found to be persuasive Whig charges that Liberty votes only helped to elect proslavery, antiabolitionist Democrats. Despite these Whig claims and frauds such as the Garland forgery, Reserve Liberty advocates convinced at least some abolition Whigs to cut their ties with the old party. Chase's efforts sometimes lent further suspicion to Whig charges and undercut the Liberty party in northern Ohio.

Chase largely ignored advice to avoid statements favoring one of the parties. By 1845 he announced that the mission of the Liberty party was "synonymous" with that of the True Democracy. Put on guard, Whiggish Liberty advocates blunted his attempt to endorse this True Democracy at the Cincinnati Southern and Western Liberty Convention in June 1845. Birney referred Chase's address to a committee at which Q. F. Atkins of

Ashtabula moved to strike an offending passage styling the Liberty party as "the True Democracy of the United States."[26]

Chase removed the disputed passage in the printed address, but he permitted another that praised the "maxims of true Democracy" to remain. At once came Atkins's strong protest that Chase had ignored the committee's orders to rescind those passages of "awful squinting" to the Democrats. Atkins charged that Chase had an "overweening desire" to impress his views on the entire Liberty movement. Although he had intended to circulate the address in pamphlet form, Atkins now dared not for fear "our lynx-eyed opponents the Whigs" would use it as they had used other "atrocious falsehoods" to injure the Liberty party.[27]

Chase, though somewhat annoyed, brushed Atkins's charges aside since the address was generally well received. Still, Chase's hopes for an antislavery union with the True Democracy remains one of the more perplexing acts of his political career. Chase and Bailey favored Locofoco financial views, and their antislavery formula leaned close to the radical Democracy's doctrine of limited government and absolute state control of slavery. But one had to look hard to discover antislavery sentiment among the northwestern Democracy. If Chase saw antislavery potential in the Democratic party, he was indeed a rare Liberty man.[28]

To discourage defectors, the Reserve Liberty party insisted on complete independence from the Whig party. Giddings, however, always hoped to win Liberty voters back to the Whig fold and thus "use up" the pesky third party. In 1846 Chase unwittingly became a pawn in these plans by agreeing to a conference and congratulating the Whig congressman on his renomination. When Giddings conveyed these sentiments to a Liberty meeting, third party followers feared Chase meant to abandon the slave to head a "Northern rights party." Q. F. Atkins remarked, "how have the mighty fallen," and noted "how rapidly we are digging the grave of American Liberty." Chase, who was again angry at Atkins, reassured wary Liberty voters he was not in favor of political union unless based "upon the substantial principles & measures of the Liberty men." Willing to surrender separate organizations, the Cincinnati lawyer promised he did not favor abandoning "principle and consistent action both with reference to men & measures in accordance with principle."[29]

Reserve Liberty advocates spurned Giddings's overtures for cooperation, nominating Ed Wade as their candidate. The convention went on to specify their conditions for future political union, including abolition in the District of Columbia and the territories, prohibition of the interstate slave trade, repeal of the fugitive slave law, and the abolition "of all laws in the several States making political or municipal rights dependent on the color of the skin." The Michigan *Signal of Liberty* noted with satisfaction that these resolutions evidently "involved more radicalism than Mr. Giddings could sanction." Still, Chase's intervention in the 1846 campaign might have harmed the Reserve third party. B. F. Hoffman of Warren reproved Chase, saying, "we know Mr. Giddings too well to give him any advantage, by writing him a complimentary letter." "Your letter hurt us, considerably," Hoffman reported.[30]

Since the 1842 special election, Reserve Liberty voters continually refused Giddings's hopes for reunion. As the 1848 election approached, they were no more anxious to reestablish cooperation with rival political forces, certainly not with antiextension Democrats. Indeed, it was Reserve antislavery Whigs who reached out to the third party, particularly when the 1848 Whig presidential nominee promised to produce more antislavery defections. During the 1846 campaign Giddings had pledged never again to support a slaveholding presidential candidate. When his own party nonetheless nominated Louisiana slaveholder Zachary Taylor, Giddings was left in an uncomfortable situation, requiring abolition support for his own defection from Whig ranks. Reserve Whigs quickly established an antislavery press in Cleveland, the *True Democrat* edited by Edward S. Hamlin.[31] When the rush of events in 1847 and 1848 compelled Liberty advocates to seek cooperation, their willingness commonly sprang from the assumption that Whig and Democratic defectors were adopting Liberty principles, not the other way around.

Benjamin Stanton of the Indiana *Free Labor Advocate* certainly was no coalitionist, nor would Chase have considered him much of a political realist. The editor of the New Garden press remained a firm advocate of Liberty party independence right up to the Buffalo Convention. Early in 1847 Stanton warned eastern Indiana Liberty voters that, if they did not make independent nominations, then "I will act by myself, nominate a ticket for myself, and vote it myself. And if I cannot find enough to fill a ticket, whom I believe to be true and devoted men, I will vote for myself!"[32]

In 1847 Indiana Whigs led by Caleb B. Smith again sought third party support by criticizing the Democratic war and slaveholders' schemes to extend slavery. Once again Stanton remained steadfast and ridiculed Whig attempts to win a Liberty endorsement. The Anti-Slavery Quaker editor chaired a Wayne Liberty convention that pronounced it morally wrong to compromise on slavery. The gathering resolved it was the duty of Liberty's friends to vote only for those who "maintain the principle of liberty and are disconnected with either of the pro-slavery parties."[33] Stanton was nonetheless unable to prevent several third party candidates from withdrawing from the 1847 canvass on their own initiative.

Stanton and fellow Anti-Slavery Friends were preoccupied by disputes with the proslavery majority in their local Quaker community. The Liberty party gave dissenting abolition Friends the opportunity to withdraw political fellowship from those who had denied them their religious society. An Indiana antislavery convention made explicit the root of their dedication to independent political activity: "to vote with a pro-slavery party, or to remain in communion with a pro-slavery church, is, in our opinion to give the most effectual support to the institution of slavery." Stanton and other abolitionist churchmen were not primarily concerned with political advance, admitting "we shall not now succeed in electing our ticket—we may never succeed," but at least they could record their "testimony against that system of wickedness which is fast ruining our nation." Recalling that but ten righteous persons would have spared Sodom, the Quaker editor affirmed, "it is our duty to labor on, hoping and praying for Heaven's blessing upon our labors, and leaving the event with God."[34]

Pious Liberty voters represented by Stanton, who were locked in bitter internecine battles with former church members, were most concerned that abolitionist principle remain inviolate. After all, they justified their schism on the basis of righteous principles and never tired of condemning the proslavery corruption of their former coreligionists. Pious third party voters were not interested in political gain for themselves and were only secondarily concerned with party victory, and thus they measured success in different ways than the politically minded. Although hoping to win true converts and perhaps to convince the church majority of its errors, Liberty advocates such as Benjamin Stanton had little desire to cooperate with those who had not first adopted right religious and political principles.

As controversy mounted over the expansion of slavery to the southwest, the Liberty party tore itself apart by arguing over principles and politics. The key to understanding the internal disruption of the party lies in its religious composition. Popular support, not always the leadership, for the party came primarily from religiously minded abolitionists whose church communities had denounced the sin of slavery and renounced all fellowship with those who condoned it. For this reason Chase and his Cincinnati clique—who remained members of religious denominations that tolerated slavery—are poor representatives of the northwestern Liberty party. Chase especially resented the attacks Liberty party abolitionists levelled on the major churches. Eventually, he decided the sectarian Liberty party had outlived its usefulness.

Religiously minded abolitionists did not stop at denouncing slavery as sin and voting for Liberty; they called on others also to withdraw their support for proslavery churches and political parties. The antislavery societies of Michigan, Illinois, and Indiana joined James Birney in declaring churches that did not renounce slavery were "the bulwarks of American slavery." These abolition societies maintained that the "opposition and apathy of the different religious denominations" constituted the greatest barrier to the antislavery cause. Reverend Levi Spencer's Illinois church condemned those churches that failed to bear testimony to the sin of slavery as "false to their consecration vows, hindering truth and strengthening the ungodly." Indiana abolitionists announced that "no Christian or patriot" could consistently vote for proslavery candidates. They then proclaimed it the "duty of every abolitionist, who is a member of any church that does not advocate immediate and unconditional emancipation, if they have no reasonable hopes of that church being reformed, to disown the church without delay."[35]

Salmon P. Chase did not heed the calls of his antislavery brethren. He remained a member of the Episcopal church, which did not define slaveholding as sin or discipline slaveholding members. Chase agreed that the essence of faith was to do good and was distressed at the apathy in his church, but, had he attempted to change its position, he would have found its structure, theology, and Southern membership formidable obstacles. Other Liberty supporters, when faced with similar dilemmas, withdrew from their churches to form the Wesleyan Methodist Connection, the Free Presbyterian church, or the Indiana Yearly Meeting of Anti-Slavery Friends. Chase continued to attend St. Paul's Episcopal Church in Cincinnati.

Chase's membership in what abolitionists considered a proslavery church did not escape notice. Garrisonian agents Abby Kelley and Stephen Foster, who were always glad to embarrass the Liberty party, told antislavery audiences that Chase belonged to the same church as the slaveholder Henry Clay. The *Western Citizen* denounced Bishop Philander Chase for his "bull" against the abolitionists, perhaps not knowing that Salmon Chase had been partly raised by the presiding bishop of the Episcopal church.[36]

Chase's connections to a proslavery church influenced his standing within the Liberty movement. To Lewis Tappan he claimed that some "of

the most ardent, the most determined and the most zealous" of the abolitionists might have gone too far. Their party creed was too narrow, Chase
insisted, requiring others to accept their "faith in the dogma of absolute,
unconditional & immediate Emancipation throughout the United States."
More importantly, Chase complained, pious abolitionists "assumed to act
politically upon ecclesiastical bodies." The loyal Episcopalian considered
this a grievous error for he thought Congress could not abolish slavery in
the states, "nor provide for the government of churches." "And I can see no
reason why political parties . . . should waste energies upon such matters," Chase concluded.[37]

These sometimes bitter religious differences between Chase and pious
third party advocates thus affected to some extent what he thought should
be the proper constitutional and political program of the Liberty party.
Eastern leaders who opposed Chase's efforts to remake Liberty ideology
had long sought abolitionist reformation of the churches. In his *The American Churches: The Bulwarks of American Slavery,* James G. Birney denounced Chase's Episcopal church as among those that gave support to
slavery. Gerrit Smith, who criticized the "sham, half-hearted abolition of
Ohio," also sharply rebuked those who did not see it as a violation of Liberty principles or an insult to the slave "to continue in Church fellowship
with those who are guilty of directly holding him in slavery": "As if they
who have Church fellowship with my oppressors, do not thereby most ef-
fectually endorse my oppression and trample on my rights!"[38]

Not surprisingly, then, Chase regarded the "Liberty League" movement,
led by Smith, Birney, and William Goodell, "and the attempts which are
made to make eccl[esiastical]. connexion a political test in the Lib[erty].
party," as conclusive evidence that a different instrument than the third
party was needed to overthrow slavery.[39] Chase could not cooperate in an
abolitionist campaign not only against slavery in the South, but also
against his own church.

Like Chase, Gamaliel Bailey differed from the bulk of Liberty voters in
his religious connections. In 1838 he had advised abolitionists that they
could not accomplish any more by "drawing off" from their parties than
they could by producing schism within their churches. Reformation of a
church, or a party for that matter, Bailey believed, could progress only "so
long as the reformers continue within it." Only in July 1845 did the Liberty
editor announce his intention to withdraw from the Methodist Protestant
church, citing its "grave delinquency" on slavery. But Bailey also did not
join any other branch of the Christian church, including the comeouter
abolition churches.[40]

Gamaliel Bailey was not a particularly good representative of his fellow northwestern Liberty editors. Guy Beckley of the *Signal of Liberty* and M. R. Hull of the *Clarion of Freedom* were Wesleyan Methodist seceders. Benjamin Stanton of the *Free Labor Advocate* was an Indiana Anti-Slavery Quaker, and Erastus Hussey of the *Michigan Liberty Press* was a Hicksite. Zebina Eastman of the *Western Citizen* withdrew from his Vermilion, Illinois, church, criticizing the majority for failing to take more determined action against the sin of slavery. Like Joshua Leavitt of the *Emancipator,* Ichabod Codding of the Wisconsin *Freeman* was a Congregationalist minister. John Duffey, editor of the short-lived *Columbus Freeman,* was the exception who proved the rule. The rare Irish Catholic antislavery editor believed he suffered from the anti-Catholic bigotry of other abolitionists. When they failed to support his press, he complained it was because his church had not religiously proscribed slaveholders, "or invoked the vengeance of the Deity on the sin of slaveholding."[41]

Bailey also differed from his fellow editors in his treatment of religious issues. While he did report religious news, his emphasis was always more politically oriented and also much more incisive than other Liberty editors. Moreover, he took a more moderate tone in commenting on church positions on slavery and on the abolitionist secessions. Other Liberty presses noted these schisms more approvingly and did not hesitate to vilify what they considered corrupt churches. The *Western Citizen* wondered how Methodists could, without blushing, "gravely declare that their denomination is not pro-slavery!" Guy Beckley's *Signal of Liberty* compared the Methodist church "with the darkest days of Popery." Beckley was put on trial by the Methodist church for "slanders" such as this, but he joined the Wesleyan seceders and carried on his campaign against the mother church from the pages of the *Signal of Liberty.*[42]

Samuel Lewis, the 1846 Ohio Liberty candidate for governor, is often classed with the Chase group. Lewis remained a member of the Methodist Episcopal church, considered by many abolitionists to be a proslavery body. (Still his was a strong antislavery voice within the church, hoping to reform it from within.) In 1841 Lewis presided over the Western Methodist Anti-Slavery Convention in Ohio. This gathering stressed that its attachment to the Methodist church was "strong and unwavering," while arguing it was "manifestly improper for our friends to leave the church of their choice in consequence of opposition from their pro-slavery brethren." Lewis never did join the Wesleyan secession and must have squirmed a bit when an antislavery convention he addressed went on to pass a resolution approving of the secessions from the churches.[43]

The religious connections of the Cincinnati corps of Liberty leaders did not escape the notice of eager Garrisonian critics. While lecturing in eastern Ohio seeking to show the Liberty party's "worthlessness as an anti-slavery instrumentality," G. B. Stebbins told the third party faithful of the corruption of "many of their leaders in Cincinnati" who were still associated with proslavery churches. Parker Pillsbury singled out Samuel Lewis for special criticism, noting that the Liberty candidate belonged to the Methodist Episcopal church, a bulwark of slavery. Pillsbury claimed that the dishonesty of third party leaders in Ohio exceeded that of New England, enough supposedly to convince the Garrisonian agent of the "doctrine of total depravity": "They will do anything to secure votes to the party, except to preach genuine anti-slavery, and some of them (I do not exaggerate) will do even that."[44]

Garrisonians were of course correct about the religious affiliations of the Cincinnati leaders (except that Bailey separated from his church in 1845), but these eastern visitors were wrong in assuming that "the church question has never been thoroughly discussed" in the Northwest. For one thing, easterners failed to appreciate that Yankee churches often took a more advanced position in the Northwest, especially on the slavery issue. In New England, Congregationalists represented the conservative church establishment; in the Northwest they were merely another imported church that appealed to a minority of the region's citizens. Pious abolitionists in the Northwest were all too aware of the church question (for example, the Anti-Slavery Quakers of eastern Indiana), although Garrisonian reminders might have prompted some third party supporters formally to announce their church's repudiation of slavery.[45]

That Garrisonians attacked Lewis for remaining with his proslavery church was to be expected, but Lewis's religious connections also caused troubles within Liberty ranks. Because of his prominence as a loyal anti-slavery Methodist, Wesleyan Methodists regarded him as a prime obstacle to their cause. In his campaign for governor, Lewis thus faced serious opposition from Wesleyan Methodists, usually "a very efficient class of Liberty voters."[46]

The religious motivations and denominational concerns of most Liberty voters provide better insight into the debate over politics and principles within the abolition party. Because of his membership in a proslavery church, Chase found himself in an anomalous position within the Liberty movement. His religious connections separated him from eastern party leaders and the electoral support of the northwestern party. Responding to both political and personal concerns, he sought to make abolition more

123

"respectable" and politically viable by dissociating the goal of abolition from its connection with religious radicals and separatists. The Episcopalian attempted to widen the party's base to keep ecclesiastical connections from becoming a test for membership. But Chase's political goals ran counter to the motivations and needs of religiously minded Liberty followers. The third party gave their churches an independent political voice; fusion with other political elements would mean cooperation with former church members. Insisting instead on the primacy of principles over politics, abolitionist churchmen resisted efforts to turn the Liberty party's religious appeal into a political platform.

As it turned out, politically minded Liberty leaders were generally located where the third party polled relatively few votes. Perhaps this induced them to support some sort of an alliance with other antislavery elements, whom they resembled in many respects. Conversely, opposition to coalition politics was strongest where the party vote was more substantial. In these areas the party drew the support of greater numbers of religiously minded abolitionists, and these larger tallies provided some consolation to the party faithful. Thus, the apparently perverse situation arose in which areas where the party was weak placed greater stress on political advance, while the centers of Liberty party strength insisted instead on adherence to principles over politics.

Although the politically minded were far outnumbered, their eyes were focused on a clear goal. Because they were located in strategic positions, they eventually had their way, even though the opposition they faced in Liberty ranks forced them to seek outside alliances to ensure final victory. In the end, unlike the birth of Liberty in 1840, the Free Soil coalition of 1848 was created by and for politicians, although some thought they saw the hand of God in the work.

7

FROM UNIVERSAL LIBERTY
TO FREE SOIL

"The Liberty party cannot *support"* Martin Van Buren, insisted Liberty party editor Joshua Leavitt, "without deliberately giving the lie to all our declarations for fifteen years past." Historians have often quoted such die-hard statements to show the resistance of eastern Liberty advocates to cooperation with antiextension Democrats in 1848, but scholars should recognize that free-soil fusion encountered opposition in the Northwest as well. Some northwesterners, especially of Democratic heritage, felt the Van Buren nomination was "just the thing for these parts," but others were not so sure. An associate editor of the Chicago *Western Citizen,* Erastus Hussey of the *Michigan Liberty Press,* and Stephen Harding of Indiana later confessed their reluctance to accept Van Buren. The most strident denunciation came from Wisconsin's radical Liberty leaders who pronounced Chase's Ohio Free Territory Convention "an abandonment of the Liberty party." As late as August 30, seventeen Michigan abolitionists proposed a state Liberty convention to nominate presidential electors, believing the proposed union "a violation of the fundamental principles of the Liberty party."[1]

Opposition to the Chase plan surfaced in Ohio as well; even Gamaliel Bailey still harbored doubts about Van Buren. (Recall that prior to the 1840 campaign Bailey had proclaimed that "no consistent, honest-hearted abolitionist" could vote for the New York Democrat.) Some third party supporters outside of southwestern Ohio claimed to prefer "Hale and Liberty," complained of the narrowness of the free-territory platform, and, even after the Buffalo Convention, worked against Whig–Free Soil candidates. Late in the 1848 Free Soil campaign, Edward Wade appealed to Cuyahoga Liberty voters to support "our free soil Whigs." Evidently, many former Liberty voters hesitated to support Whig–Free Soil candidates for fear they were "Taylor men in disguise." Some northern Ohio third party supporters remained unconvinced; in the general election sixty-one Oberlin voters favored Gerrit Smith, the candidate of the abolitionist Liberty League.[2]

By 1848 the Liberty party was well on its way to oblivion before the Buffalo Free Soil Convention performed the formal ceremonies. Salmon Chase has received a great deal of credit for the union achieved at Buffalo, but his role in free-soil fusion has been misunderstood. Because historians have confused Chase's influence within third party ranks, they have also misjudged the significance of the movement for free-soil coalition. Relying on the flawed work of Joseph Rayback, scholars have assumed that the western Liberty party constantly fought eastern ideologues for control of the third party's future. Dominated by Chase, westerners were supposedly less committed to abolitionist doctrine while favoring broader-based antislavery action. Besides exaggerating differences between east and west, this approach also ignores divisions over ideology and tactics within the so-called eastern wing of the party.[3] Scholars who continue to parrot this approach could fail to recognize that its origins lay in the much older (and now largely discredited) practice of construing serious sectional economic and political conflicts between the productive West and the aristocratic East.

Beyond this interpretive failing, the major problem with the usual approach is that the bulk of northwestern third party voters did not share Chase's desire for a new antislavery party. Indeed, until late in the summer of 1848, the Liberty party faithful consistently rejected any alliance with nonabolitionists. Frustrated with the inflexible sectarianism of the religiously minded, Chase determined on his own to help forge a more viable coalition against slavery's political power. He left the religious war on the sin of slaveholding to others.

Because they held a different vision of the third party's mission, pious Liberty advocates insisted their organization remain free of major party contamination. The separatist Liberty party could deliver its message only if it continued independent of society's compromises and corruptions. But as controversy over slavery's expansion promised political advantages to some, those eager to achieve political results promoted union with other antislavery forces. As these events unfolded, religiously minded Liberty voters found themselves confused and in the end outmaneuvered, with few practical choices but to join the Free Soil coalition not of their own making.

Chase sought to postpone the 1847 national Liberty convention until the spring of 1848 to achieve his goal of antislavery cooperation. Evidently, he hoped to take advantage of rising sentiment for the Wilmot Proviso and likely disgruntlement over the major parties' nominations. In this respect Bailey supported his friend's plan, first by trying to bring northwestern editors into line on the question and then by claiming that Liberty newspapers generally favored postponing the convention. Some historians have taken this as evidence for the sectional split they see in the Liberty party, and as a sign of the rising strength of the pro-fusion "Chase wing" of the party.[4]

Actually, northwestern support for delaying the convention was ephemeral at best. In Indiana the *Free Labor Advocate* eventually came out in favor of a later convention but thought the issue "of no great moment." Liberty minister Owen Lovejoy challenged the authority of editors to dictate policy, claiming the *Western Citizen's* endorsement of Hale did not have the approval "of one in a hundred of the Liberty party" in Illinois. Wisconsin Liberty partisans lodged similar complaints about Bailey's policy. Moreover, there was no East-West split among Liberty papers; several eastern presses supported Bailey's view, while the New Lisbon (Ohio) *Aurora* joined the Wisconsin *Freeman* in favoring an early convention. The *Cleveland American* reversed its earlier support for a delayed convention (reported by Bailey's *National Era*), noting that this change "now coincides with all in this region whose views we have gathered, in thinking an early convention desirable, and even imperatively necessary."[5]

Northwestern Liberty supporters did not embrace Chase's proposal for delaying the national convention; Chase himself only claimed that "some of the Liberty men in Ohio" favored a later convention. Interpreted quite correctly as part of an attempt to merge the third party into a free-territory movement, this effort was voted down by the Liberty National Committee by a 7-2 vote. Chase's only support came from Daniel Hoit of New Hampshire, where Liberty partisans had recently cooperated with antislavery Democrats led by John P. Hale.[6]

At the ensuing national Liberty convention in October 1847, Chase again moved to postpone the nominations but once again was defeated, 128-37. Although the breakdown of the vote by states is not known, M. R. Hull, editor of the *Clarion of Freedom* and a delegate to the convention, reported that a *"portion* of the delegates from Ohio, particularly from the Southern part, were for postponement" (emphasis added).[7] Chase's coalitionist strategy did not unite northwestern Liberty followers but instead divided and dismayed third party members who were uncertain how to react to the challenge.

In addition to exaggerating Chase's influence in the third party, historians have overlooked evidence showing that most northwesterners opposed coalition politics until late in 1848. In 1845, for example, Chase helped arrange the Southern and Western Liberty Convention in Cincinnati. The convention was not limited to third party delegates but welcomed those willing to cause the "extinction of Slavery" by reducing it to "its constitutional limits." This convention, which was a sign of Chase's growing influence, should not be overdrawn as a victory for western coalitionists.[8] At this point Chase sought only to attract individual Whig and Democratic converts. Indeed, he suffered a setback when third party supporters of Whiggish heritage rebuffed his effort to endorse the True Democracy in the convention address.

Chase addressed a letter to the Chicago Northwestern Convention in 1846, suggesting the delegates begin a movement for antislavery union. A committee was formed, but nothing came of it, which Theodore Foster attributed to Liberty voters' fears of losing their separate identity. Returning from the Chicago convention, Foster admitted his discouragement with the resistance political experiments received from religiously minded abolitionists: "The ministers in our party, who contribute three fourths of all the public speakers, are mostly opposed to venturing out politically: they will not do it: and they will keep the men with them."[9]

Foster was perturbed by the refusal of party members to support his program of widening the "one idea" of opposition to slavery to include other reform goals. This was the approach of James Birney, Gerrit Smith, and other primarily New York abolitionists who formed the schismatic Liberty League at Macedon Lock in June 1847. Adopting the position that slavery was indeed unconstitutional, this splinter group named Smith and Elihu Burritt to a presidential ticket and then hoped to persuade the regular Liberty convention to adopt their platform and candidates.

Like Chase's free-territory movement, the Liberty League nominations left most northwestern Liberty voters confused and uncertain how to respond. As a result, Smith's northwestern support was limited primarily to Wisconsin and northern and eastern Ohio, areas that also leaned toward the view that slavery was unconstitutional. On his way to the 1847 Liberty convention, M. R. Hull, the Indiana Wesleyan Methodist leader who now edited the eastern Ohio *Clarion of Freedom,* reported that all the Liberty voters he spoke with urged him to vote for Smith at the convention. The support Smith received in Wisconsin was based in part on the high regard Codding and others had for the New York abolitionist, but eventually the *American Freeman* admitted its fear that the Macedon Lock movement was "calculated to distract Liberty ranks."[10]

Although Smith was well respected in both east and west, the Liberty convention instead nominated John P. Hale of New Hampshire, an anti-slavery Democrat who had won third party support in his election to the United States Senate. (On an informal ballot Smith received 44 votes to Hale's 103.) The Hale nomination is sometimes seen as a victory for the Chase wing, but Hale could never have been nominated without critical eastern support. Moreover, some in the Northwest, particularly in Wisconsin, had to be reconciled to Hale's selection. The Congregationalist minister-editor of the *American Freeman* feared the political manipulations in Liberty ranks portended that "we are in danger of overlooking our fundamental principles and forgetting our dependence on God."[11]

According to the usual explanation, the western Liberty party was ripe for coalition because its members were discouraged by the party's poor performance. In fact, such assessments of Liberty's decline after 1844 have been exaggerated. In the 1846 state elections the party increased its share of the total vote in every northwestern state except Michigan, where the third party percentage was still the highest in the region. During the 1847 off-year elections all parties experienced a decline in voter interest; the war in progress might have further depressed voter turnout.[12]

In Ohio the Liberty party did not mount a state campaign in 1847, partly because Bailey's departure to edit the Washington *National Era* meant the *Philanthropist* no longer served as the rallying center for a statewide effort. Nonetheless, Reserve third party supporters early in 1847 made arrangements for "A Great Liberty Convention" and then offered candidates in the fall elections. In Ashtabula County the Liberty candidate for state senator, Uri Seeley, increased the third party total to over 13 percent, from just over 12 percent in 1846. In Lake County poor turnout among major party voters allowed the third party to increase dramatically its share of the vote to 13.7 percent, compared to the just over 8 percent the party won in 1846.[13]

In Illinois the Liberty party remained vigorous right up to the formation of the Free Soil party. From its improved showing in 1846, the Illinois third party nominated local candidates early in 1847 and in April supported candidates in the delegate selection for an upcoming state constitutional convention. In Bureau County, Owen Lovejoy polled over 35 percent of the vote for delegate; in 1846 he had won less than 29 percent of Bureau's vote for Congress. In Cook, De Kalb, Du Page, La Salle, Lee, and Will counties, it was the Whigs who failed to field candidates. In Lake County, where in 1846 the third party ran ahead of the Whigs, the Liberty candidates for delegate actually won election, apparently with Whig help. In the August 1847 local elections, third party voters supported candidates in several northern Illinois counties.[14]

Wisconsin and Illinois provide ideal opportunities to test the extent of Liberty decline prior to the Buffalo Free Soil Convention. Both states held their 1848 state elections earlier in the year; Liberty voters thus went to the polls to vote for regularly nominated third party candidates. Amidst the confusion of the free-territory movement underway in other states, the third party retained much of its voter support. The 1848 Wisconsin Liberty ticket included Charles Durkee for governor, Ichabod Codding for Congress, and James H. Paine (formerly of Painesville, Ohio) as a Liberty presidential elector. In the May elections the Wisconsin third party polled 161 more votes than its candidate for territorial delegate had in 1847, but the third party share of the total vote declined from 4.6 to 3.5 percent. The Illinois state election was held in August, only a few days before the Free Soil Convention met in Buffalo. Despite this distraction, Owen Lovejoy managed to poll 13.5 percent of his district's vote for Congress. In 1846 he had received 16 percent of the vote. In 1850 the Free Soil candidate would poll about 5 percent.[15]

The Chase approach was in fact quite weak outside of southwestern Ohio. In Wisconsin and in northern Illinois and Ohio, the third party vote remained largely intact; Liberty advocates in those areas showed little desire for coalition. Well into 1848 third party supporters in northern Ohio and in Washington County (Marietta) went right on arranging Liberty conventions for the coming presidential election. In July 1847 Ashtabula Liberty supporters had rejected an antiextensionist coalition, reaffirming they would "not abandon our fundamental principle of opposition to slavery itself for the purpose of forming any alliance, based upon its extension merely."[16]

In April 1848 northern Ohio Liberty supporters prepared once again to enter the fall campaign as an independent party, hardly foreseeing, evidently, the formation of a new antislavery coalition. The Liberty convention made arrangements to establish a press, endorsed John P. Hale, and called for a state convention to nominate a candidate for governor. Late in May another Reserve gathering announced the antislavery cause did not end with the Wilmot Proviso but with the end of slavery in the nation.

In Illinois the *Western Citizen* noted that, in any proposed alliance based on opposition to slavery, Liberty voters were prepared "to sacrifice everything but *principle.*" An Elgin Liberty gathering in 1847 had considered enlarging the third party platform (including a provision for free trade) but dismissed the proposal believing "any change in our policy was not only not called for by duty, but would be exceedingly injurious." It was this kind of steadfast dedication to Liberty goals that third party leaders such as Theodore Foster saw as shortsighted stubbornness, and which they believed doomed the party to ineffectiveness, as well as oblivion.[17]

Northwestern Liberty voters could hardly have endorsed Chase's policy of cooperating with Barnburner Democrats because they had so little knowledge of what Chase intended. When the Cincinnati lawyer's private negotiations with Van Buren Democrats began to emerge, skepticism was not limited to the East. At the Buffalo Free Soil Convention, however, Liberty advocates were burdened with a reluctant candidate, by then cooperating more with Chase than other third party leaders. Still, in the balloting for president in the conference committee, the great bulk of Liberty delegates—both from the East and the West—remained firm for John P. Hale, now an unlikely symbol of Liberty party independence. As part of a prior arrangement, however, Chase, Joshua Leavitt, and H. B. Stanton voted instead for Martin Van Buren. The Conscience Whig faction provided Van Buren's margin of victory (244-183), not Chase's western Liberty party.[18]

Historians were simply wrong in assuming that Chase had won most Liberty party advocates to his point of view. Instead, by cooperating with Barnburner Democrats, Chase managed to outmaneuver the Liberty faithful at Buffalo.[19] Indeed, his behind-the-scenes manipulations were necessary precisely because he had failed to win the outright support of the party faithful in both East and West. Proposals for antislavery cooperation had met constant opposition within Liberty ranks prior to the summer of 1848; only an alliance with an outside group brought victory.

Chase's major contributions to Free Soil fusion were arranging free-territory conventions willing to send delegates to Buffalo and persuading key Liberty leaders to acquiesce in the decision of the convention, even though he knew the Barnburners would accept nothing less than the top spot on the ticket. After the convention Liberty leaders Leavitt and Lovejoy did their best to reconcile third party voters to the results, demonstrating that westerners had not been hankering for a wider coalition at too high a price and that opposition to Van Buren and a compromise of principle were not limited to the East.[20]

Benjamin Stanton of the Indiana *Free Labor Advocate* probably would have been content to enter the 1848 contest again as an independent Liberty voter. In April 1848 Stanton moved that the Wayne County convention nominate a full slate of candidates, hoping a respectable ticket would unite the third party's strength and appeal to others as well. Holding no hopes for the other parties, the Quaker editor preferred Liberty advocates continue on their own course, "maintaining the distinctive principles of the Liberty organization" without either "diminishing or adding to them." Liberty partisans like Benjamin Stanton could hardly be considered willing allies in Chase's plans for free-soil fusion. The Indiana Liberty editor, who was initially suspicious of the Wilmot Proviso movement, felt that "no prospect of a gain in numbers can justify a sacrifice of moral principle." But when the Liberty state convention at Indianapolis agreed to cooperate with the free-territory movement, Stanton's eastern Indiana Liberty supporters were forced to reconsider. Hopeful now that a united effort could strike such a blow at slavery as to "cause its death at no distant period," Stanton also hoped antislavery union would spread right principles and produce more Liberty converts. He thus took part in a Wayne County free-territory meeting and accepted appointment as a delegate to the state convention.[21]

Still, Stanton had not foreseen the full implications of Chase's policy of cooperating with Barnburner Democrats. Noting approvingly the address of Chase's free-territory convention at Columbus, the *Free Labor Advocate* at the same time disparaged the Barnburner convention that nominated Van Buren as affording "but little direct aid to the cause of liberty, however it may affect it remotely." Worried now, Stanton wrote to Chase, concerned that the proposed union with the Barnburners would leave the "fundamental principle of the Liberty party untouched." To him the dropping of the "noble Hale" for Van Buren "looks like sacrificing principle to policy"—and that was a bad policy. Chase responded as best he could to Stanton's inquiry that he was rumored to favor Van Buren. (This was difficult since Chase was already committed.) Then conceding the objections Liberty voters held to Van Buren, Chase wondered if the preferred union on Hale was possible under existing circumstances.[22]

Chase's reasoning did not exactly win over Stanton. After the Cincinnati Liberty press claimed third party voters could support Van Buren, Stanton protested, "I can do no such thing." Willing to drop for the time being the Liberty principle of "the entire extinction of slavery," the Quaker editor felt "it is asking a little too much" to expect Liberty's friends to stomach Van Buren. At the upcoming Buffalo Convention, Stanton hoped that "princi-

132

ple, not availability" would be the "primary, the paramount consideration in the choice of candidates." Stanton, who was not appointed an official delegate by the Indiana convention, nonetheless attended the Buffalo gathering and returned a convert to the Free Soil cause. Swayed by the "vast multitudes" there, the former Liberty editor was evidently unaware of Chase's manipulations behind the scenes; the Anti-Slavery Quaker instead believed "an overruling Providence directed the result." His expectation that Van Buren would stand upon the platform drafted by Chase probably eased Stanton's disappointment over Hale's defeat. Still, the veteran Liberty editor closed up his abolitionist press and let others carry the Free Soil banner.[23]

Like eastern Indiana abolitionists, Wisconsin Liberty partisans were eventually forced to bend their wills to mounting Free Soil fusion. All along the Wisconsin third party opposed the Chase plan of a late convention, resisted the nomination of Hale on the third party ticket, and dismissed talk of fusion with other parties on a Wilmot Proviso basis. At first Wisconsin Liberty advocates agreed with Lewis Tappan that the Ohio free-territory movement was "extremely ill-judged," but their state convention in July 1848 noted with approval the movement toward antislavery union underway in Ohio and New York. Still, the state gathering maintained the Liberty party had been organized "for the purpose of abolishing Slavery and protecting the equal rights of all men." Agreeing to send delegates to Buffalo, Wisconsin third party supporters also declared their intention to vote only for candidates "not only pledged against the extension of Slavery, but [who] are also committed to the policy of abolishing it, and of protecting the equal rights of all."[24]

Before the Buffalo Convention convened, Sherman Booth, now editor of the Wisconsin *Freeman,* announced his view that if Hale resigned in favor of "no-Territory" candidates, then the Liberty party "is *dissolved,* and our connection with it is also *dissolved.*" Booth was under pressure to stand firm on abolitionist principle; he admitted his favorite was still Gerrit Smith, whom he voted for on an informal ballot. Booth, later a central figure in a famous case challenging the Fugitive Slave Law of 1850, especially regretted the Free Soil resolution denying authority over slavery in the South. The Wisconsin editor believed slavery to be "unconstitutional every where." The support Smith's Liberty League received in Wisconsin prompted Booth to admit there was "a difference of opinion among Liberty men in this State." Like Benjamin Stanton, however, Booth was forced to retreat from his uncompromising position, admitting days before the convention that the free-territory movement was "daily becoming more and

133

more radical." Nonetheless, the Wisconsin editor affirmed if union took place merely on a Wilmot Proviso basis, "we are out of the Liberty Party in a twinkling." Following Wisconsin's free-territory convention and once the deed was done at Buffalo, Booth came around to support the new coalition, primarily because he believed the platform's pledge to abolish slavery wherever the federal government had constitutional power was "all the Liberty party, as such, ever demanded."[25]

The Buffalo Convention thus performed what Richard P. McCormick suggests was the prime object of such party gatherings: winning the assent of the party faithful to a decision already rendered by party leaders.[26] By bringing together three diverse factions—Barnburner Democrats, Conscience Whigs, and Liberty advocates—Chase's role was particularly crucial. His adroit factional alliances overcame the serious objections most Liberty voters held to a Van Buren nomination, and although he deserted his former party on the presidential question, at least he acquired the privilege of writing the convention's platform. This face-saving gesture played a vital part in securing third party allegiance to the Free Soil coalition. Well-acquainted with the devotion Liberty voters held to their principles, Chase realized he must win a platform most could embrace.

The Free Soil platform, while not a thoroughgoing Liberty document, went beyond simple nonextension by endorsing the Chase doctrine of divorcing the national government from all connections with slavery (though it also renounced all authority over slavery in the Southern states). This concession to Liberty opinion helps answer the obvious question of how so many could so easily forget their earlier hostility to Van Buren. Liberty advocates such as Levi Sutliff of Ohio were concerned not only with Van Buren's proslavery past, but they were dismayed that the former president still did not swear to abolition principles. Sutliff, along with John G. Whittier, believed Van Buren "too old a sinner to hope for his conversion." The *Oberlin Evangelist* was particularly concerned with Van Buren's earlier pledge to veto legislation abolishing slavery in the federal district.[27] Many of the third party faithful were convinced the New Yorker was still unregenerate and thus did not warrant Liberty support.

With assurances that Van Buren would in fact stand upon the Buffalo platform, most third party voters could convince themselves that the other members of the Free Soil coalition were finally adopting Liberty principles. Thus Joshua Leavitt could assure former Liberty supporters that the party was "not dead, but translated" into the Free Soil movement. And Owen Lovejoy could persuade his Illinois followers that the "soul of Liberty" was in the Free Soil party, as the final object—the extinction of slavery—

remained the same. Along with the *Western Citizen,* the *Oberlin Evangelist* now professed to be satisfied with the convention's work, enough even to "ascribe it all to almighty God."[28]

Those who voted for the struggling Liberty party had not promoted free-soil fusion because they had no great fear of political impotence; they were already a self-conceived minority within their churches and northwestern society. Many believed popularity was a crooked road to righteousness. Instead, pious Liberty voters stressed the duty of a righteous minority to reform society. Their churches often maintained highly restrictive requirements for membership. True to their evangelical origins, they accepted to fellowship only the worthy who could demonstrate their conversion and dedication to abolitionist goals. Abolition churches exercised severe discipline over their members; those who failed to measure up to religious and abolitionist principle could be safely excluded. If their larger church body became corrupt, religiously minded abolitionists withdrew to preserve their own purity, though this might lessen their influence with the old group. Once pious Liberty voters separated from their former fellowship, abolitionist principle became the source of their identification and their "tower of strength."

Third party supporters denied religious and political fellowship with corrupt institutions in order to maintain their own integrity. They were not so much interested in the advance of Liberty political power as with the progress of their principles within the churches and society. But because of the Liberty party's failure to achieve political respectability, the politically minded were convinced it had outlived its usefulness. "Not to advance is to recede," Bailey wrote in 1845, "no new and small party can live simply by holding its own." In May 1847 Chase admitted he saw "no prospect of greater future progress, but rather of less." Neither Chase nor Bailey could understand why the party failed to profit from all the public controversy over Texas annexation, the Mexican War, and the Wilmot Proviso. Both failed to see that the Liberty appeal had never been a response to political developments but grew from religious commitment, controversy, and schism, which were only indirectly affected by political or economic events. While many Liberty advocates remained committed to political independence, Chase complained: "As fast as we can bring public sentiment right the other parties will approach our ground, and keep sufficiently close to it to prevent any great accession to our numbers."[29] From the perspective of those who hoped to produce just such a public reformation by guarding their religious and political integrity, this was not really a cause for complaint.

Chase and Bailey were right, however, about the limited political appeal of Liberty; overzealous sectarianism had caused divisions in the party, as Chase was well aware. In 1846 Wesleyan Methodists had complained about Samuel Lewis, a loyal Methodist running as the third party candidate for governor of Ohio. Congregationalist minister Ichabod Codding of the Wisconsin *Freeman* believed himself quite tolerant when he announced he would vote for a "sincere Liberty man," even if he "should believe in the Presbyterian or Episcopalian form of government." Liberty minister John Keep insisted that Congregationalism represented the "spirit of Democracy," while other churches (particularly the Methodist, Episcopal, and Catholic) were "anti-Republican and anti-Democratic." A Wisconsin Liberty convention defeated a resolution that proposed that "sweeping denunciations against religious bodies and benevolent institutions" should not be made before sufficient proof was obtained that they were indeed "chargeable with sin."[30]

Promoting such sectarian views, the Liberty party, not surprisingly, proved of limited appeal to Northerners who belonged to religious denominations that had not defined slavery as sin. (Some church bodies had taken a blatant antiabolitionist stand.) How could church members embrace the abolitionist dogma so closely associated with religious radicals and seceders? Realizing this, Whig leaders told Methodist voters that the Liberty party had denounced their church as "a brotherhood of thieves" (actually a Garrisonian slogan). Whig editors reminded others that the third party disparaged "the character of ministers of the gospel, members of churches, and others of high respectability." To some extent, such claims were part of the Whig effort to associate the Liberty party with Garrisonian radicals, but intense criticism was indeed part of the third party effort to force the churches to recognize their complicity in the sin of slavery.[31]

Whatever their opinions on slavery, most Northern church members found it extremely difficult to support the Liberty party. A moderate antislavery Quaker of eastern Indiana was unlikely to favor a party so closely linked to the radical Quaker abolition schismatics. Loyal Methodists undoubtedly hesitated to support a party openly allied with Wesleyan seceders, fond of denouncing the Methodist church as "the key-stone of the arch that supports American slavery."[32]

Salmon Chase has often been credited with developing a more secular antislavery program. By focusing on the economic and political might of the Slave Power, he provided a more popular basis for Free Soil–Republican coalitions. Still, the Free Soil–Republican appeal was limited to particular cultural-religious groups at the same time that it repelled others.

Thus it might be better to credit Chase with formulating not a more secular appeal, but a more interdenominational and nonsectarian one. Also based on moral opposition to slavery and the South, the Free Soil–Republican message was not limited to comeouter antislavery churches or to those who had denounced slavery as sin. With the Chase doctrine of divorcing the national government from slavery, one could oppose the institution, especially its expansion, without adopting the creed or forms of the abolitionist churchmen. The Free-Soilers and Republicans did not denounce slavery as sin, nor did they call on Christians to reform or withdraw from their churches as many Liberty advocates had.[33] Furthermore, by concentrating on opposition to the expansion of slavery to the western territories, Free-Soilers and Republicans seemed to relieve Northerners from participation in the sin of slavery. The nation was not responsible for slavery—as the Liberty party contended—the South was.[34] Thus, noticeably absent from the Free Soil–Republican campaign speeches and platforms would be the inherent criticism of all American society advanced by pious Liberty advocates.

But the Chase formula was of limited value to abolitionist churchmen. Their churches taught of a sinner's need first to accept responsibility for sin, and then to cast it off. Abolitionism could serve as proof of conversion and membership to a religious society; one could hardly demonstrate a dramatic change of heart by claiming to see the light to abolish slavery "only where we have constitutional power to do so." Still, most Liberty advocates could accept the Chase platform, for it satisfied the least of their demands. As a Northern party, the Free Soil coalition, and later the Republican party, held (virtually) no fellowship with slaveholders or those who used biblical arguments to justify the institution.

Most Liberty supporters thus continued to work within the Free Soil and Republican parties for the triumph of antislavery independence and principle. But perhaps Chase had succeeded too well in widening the antislavery base. In 1858 he echoed an old Liberty complaint against those who sought "to place our cause on the lowest possible ground—to connect with the least possible advocacy of principle; and to seek by means which will make success worse than worthless."[35] By then, however, men and events had conspired to make S. P. Chase the "unavailable" candidate.

The northwestern Liberty party might have differed somewhat from its eastern counterpart, but not in the way historians usually assume. Most westerners were no more sure how the Liberty party could best achieve its holy mission than were third party supporters east of the Alleghenies. Salmon Chase could no more unite or direct the northwestern party than

could the Reverends Owen Lovejoy or John Keep. The Liberty party failed
to survive free-soil fusion in 1848, not because its western wing sought
antislavery coalition, but because the party's internal turmoil and limited
appeal left it unable to respond to the new challenges posed by slavery's
threat to expand following the Mexican War.

Only further research can determine whether the Liberty party's membership varied from East to West. The northeastern party may have attracted more Democrats, particularly considering the relative weakness of
the Yankee Democracy and the absence of those of Southern birth compared to the Northwest. The northwestern Liberty party, particularly in
Ohio, clearly won greater favor from those Whiggish in sentiment, though
the Cincinnati clique touted Democratic principles. Moreover, the ethnoreligious origins of the party need not have been the same in both regions.
For example, the disruption of the Plan of Union between Congregationalists and Presbyterians was not relevant to the New England states, and
Yankees were more likely to be conservative on the slavery issue in their
home region than in the Northwest, where opposition to slavery often distinguished transplanted New Englanders from those of Southern origins.

The northwestern Liberty party differed from its northeastern relative in
one important respect; the third party was not strongest in manufacturing
towns in the Northwest, partly because the region simply had fewer such
centers than the more developed East.[36] Indeed, most third party members
north and west of the Ohio belonged to smaller communities somewhat
isolated from the developments in transportation and manufacturing
sweeping the North. Still, when all is said and done, considering their
common attitudes toward antislavery action and particularly their joint
reluctance to reunite with members of other churches or political parties,
the Liberty party faithful in the East and West were more alike than
different.

Liberty party followers, particularly those connected with abolition
churches, were not willing participants in the process of Free Soil fusion.[37]
(This conclusion should not be startling; most pious abolitionists had hesitated to join the new party of 1840 as well.) With few choices but to go along
with the tide, most of them nonetheless enthusiastically joined the Free Soil
movement to continue their war against slavery. In his emotional address
to the Buffalo Convention, Joshua Leavitt claimed the Liberty party was
not dead, but had been transformed into the Free Soil movement. Like
other third party abolitionists who thought they saw at Buffalo their
visions of antislavery hosts marching in the Lord's path, Leavitt was speaking more rhetorically than with historical accuracy. With their leaders

either confused, preoccupied, or cooperating with other elements, Liberty voters had no control over events at Buffalo; they had to be satisfied with the platform Chase managed to acquire. Some honestly thought this was a sign that Whigs and Democrats were at long last adopting antislavery principles, but such a conclusion was more wishful thinking than careful analysis. Rather than regenerating the Liberty party anew, the rush to Free Soil fusion, like the cultural and economic change swirling about them, merely swamped those Liberty communities who believed themselves islands of righteousness in a sea of proslavery corruption.

CONCLUSION

THE END OF LIBERTY

In the fall of 1848 a Dayton lieutenant of Salmon Chase complained that the local Free Soil organization was "scandalously destitute" of campaign materials to circulate. All that was available, the former Liberty man explained, were some "*old* Abolition documents, which were not very appropriate to the occasion."[1] Minor incidents such as these help illustrate the more important conclusion that political abolition had undergone more than just a transformation in the process of Free Soil fusion; the movement had been fundamentally altered to make it politically competitive. Chase had always sought to separate the Liberty movement from what he considered was the odium of abolitionism. From the third party's inception, Gamaliel Bailey maintained that abolition through federal interference in the slave states was not a legitimate political goal. Thus, in the crucible of the Buffalo Convention, abolitionism was melted away to be replaced by a more resilient alloy, one better able to withstand the pressures of antebellum politics. (A recasting would be necessary in 1854.) In its eight year history, the Liberty party proved that radical religious reform could hardly be achieved through the process in which Americans customarily apportioned political power.

Many historians have concentrated on the considerable continuity between the third party and subsequent antislavery coalitions. One common scholarly approach has been to link the Liberty party with the growing Northern majority against the expansion of slavery. Some have calculated the high correlation between sources of Liberty votes and those for the Free Soil and Republican parties. Such findings, while statistically accurate, can be misleading. Communities once virtually alone in support of the Liberty party were joined in 1848 by others where the third party had been not only weak but also greatly resented. In Ashtabula County, for instance, the Whig party was practically deserted in favor of Giddings's Free Soil creation, which became the majority party in the county. In 1846 the Liberty party had gained just over 12 percent of the county vote, earning support from just a handful of Ashtabula communities. Yet the 1848 Free Soil coalition won all but five of the county's twenty-eight townships.[2]

Other scholars argue that Liberty was indeed dead by 1848.[3] It is true that the connection between the Liberty party and the Free Soil coalition must be drawn with great care; less than one in three of Free Soil voters could ever have cast a Liberty ballot. Many who later joined the Free Soil or Republican parties had bitterly denounced the abolition party in the 1840s. Unlike other antislavery voters, third party advocates had been intensely critical of Northern society, particularly its corrupt political parties and proslavery church bodies.

There can be little doubt that the Liberty party organization was quite moribund once fusion had run its course, although third party voters lived on within the Free Soil and Republican parties, often acting as an antislavery conscience. Their efforts were not always crowned with success, however. As Free Soil blended into Republicanism, former Liberty advocates (including Chase and Bailey) grew more and more dissatisfied with the fruits of coalition. When former Whig congressman Joshua Giddings decried the want of fundamental principle in the wartime Union party, he proved closer to the Liberty mentality than he would have admitted in the 1840s.[4]

In many ways the Free Soil campaign of 1852 was a revival of the old Liberty party, particularly with the passed-over John P. Hale again as the presidential candidate. Many Barnburner Democrats had by then returned to their party, leaving the Free Soil coalition limited to former third party voters and antislavery Whigs, represented on the ticket by George W. Julian. By this time Gamaliel Bailey and Samuel Lewis labored for the most part without the help of Salmon Chase, whose inconstant support for the "Free Democracy" was interspersed with outright alliances with the Democrats.[5]

Still, the continuing (though limited) role of third party members in antislavery politics should not obscure the fact that the Liberty approach to political reformation had been tried and found wanting. Northern society simply would not tolerate an abolitionist party in its political or its religious affairs. Even an enthusiastic and dedicated third party following faced serious obstacles within a relatively stable party system. Liberty appeals had left most voters unmoved, while party politicians used any means to contain the potentially divisive abolition party. Only when events quite beyond the influence of antislavery reformers brought this party system to the verge of collapse was anything like Liberty advocates had wished for within reach.

Although many were unwitting partners in Free Soil fusion, Liberty communities often became the staunchest allies of the new coalition formed to halt slavery's expansion. Oberlin Liberty followers, for example, announced they would support the Free Soil coalition if it would adopt a platform consistent with Liberty principles. In the 1848 contest Van Buren received a majority of Oberlin's tally, while sixty-one ballots were also cast for Liberty Leaguer Gerrit Smith.[6]

Historians have misunderstood how the Liberty party differed fundamentally from its Free Soil and Republican successors. Richard Sewell has correctly argued that scholars have exaggerated the decline in support for black civil rights from Liberty to Free Soil.[7] The two main elements of the Ohio Free Soil coalition, for example, Liberty voters and antislavery Whigs, had been firm opponents of Ohio's Black Laws (though Whigs were less willing to make the issue a party test). The Ohio Free Soil platform called for repeal of the Black Laws, and, with the aid of Chase's manipulations in 1848 and 1849, the laws were partially repealed. At the same time, even for those relatively advanced on the issue, the race question was largely an abstract one. What most distinguished the Liberty party from the Free Soil coalition (and later the Republican party) was not its respective commitments to civil rights or even abolitionism, but that the Liberty appeal was largely limited to abolition religious sects that found so little favor among other Northern church members.

Rather than unite the opponents of slavery, the Liberty party had typically divided (or at least provided a mechanism for latent divisions to become politically manifested) those cultural and religious groups most likely to oppose the institution. Yet with Free Soil fusion, and certainly by the time of Republican victory, many of these cultural-religious groups were reunited in political as well as religious terms. Although several of the abolition sects lingered on, their failure to seriously challenge their parent denominations meant they were destined for irrelevance as controversy over slavery faded and new theological concerns arose. After fending off the abolitionist challenge, Northern churches eventually took more advanced ground against slavery, narrowing the distance between them and the comeouter abolition churches, which had been Liberty's base. Just as the Methodist schism of 1844 allowed moderate Northern church members to stave off further abolitionist defections, the Free Soil and Republican coalitions choked off future important abolitionist political conversions.[8]

The Liberty party was no more successful at bringing a political reformation than a religious one. In certain areas of the Northwest, especially on Ohio's Western Reserve, the third party defection induced some Whig candidates to adopt firmer positions against slavery, the South, and their state's Black Laws. In a more general way, the third party persuaded Whigs in these regions to maintain greater independence of the South, which might have influenced the defection of many antislavery Whigs to the Free Soil coalition in 1848. While these considerations should not be minimized, whatever gains were made among antislavery Whigs were more than offset by the opposite reaction the party encouraged among other Whigs and, especially, northwestern Democrats. These opponents considered the Liberty party an opportunity to prove their antiabolitionist value, both to Northern voters and their Southern allies. Entering politics with third party voters, antiabolitionism defeated the political drive of the abolition movement just as it had already blunted its religious counterpart.[9]

But this was not necessarily the conclusion many Southerners drew of the third party record. Rather than recognizing Liberty's poor performance and being reassured by the major parties' repudiation of abolitionism, Southerners might have seen in the growing Liberty party what they feared the most: the rise of a determined and united abolitionist North led by the likes of Garrison and the Tappans. As the Free Soil and Republican parties replaced Liberty, Southerners might have linked the third party (as historians have) with its distant and less abolitionist relatives. Thus, in an indirect and ironic way, the tiny abolition party might still have hastened slavery's fall. Worried slaveholders who sought to legitimate and extend slavery awakened far more Northern opposition than impassioned Liberty appeals ever could.

The formation of the Liberty party threatened to undermine the practice of party politicians who maintained party unity by adopting deliberately ambiguous positions on controversial matters such as slavery. Whigs were particularly hard-pressed to maintain their Southern alliances without losing too much antislavery support in key Northern states. The third party thus might have contributed to the eventual dissolution of the Whig party, and ultimately, to the onset of political crisis in the 1850s.

In the 1840s, however, party loyalties held firm as Liberty proved unable to crack the political system that protected its national character by discouraging conflicts over sectional issues. When the party system disintegrated in the 1850s, it was due to political party malaise, cultural conflicts, and debates over slavery's expansion that were far removed from the basis of the Liberty protest. Most voters in the 1840s simply refused to place concern for slavery above other political, cultural, and economic issues. Indeed, voters typically viewed the slavery issue in the context of other cultural-religious differences. Thus, as Joel Silbey, William Gienapp, and others have argued, moral outrage over slavery alone could not produce the political reformation abolitionists sought.[10]

The Liberty party failed to become an important political force partly because it represented rather narrow cultural and religious concerns. The third party appealed most to abolitionist churchmen who rebuked those implicated in the sin of slaveholding. Moreover, although the party sought to discourage nativistic views, party members could not help reflecting their cultural prejudices in their political activity, even if just in the common habit of denouncing corrupt activity as popery. The Liberty party also lost support from some elements by endorsing temperance reform, which belied the party's position as a one-idea organization.[11] Such factors weakened Liberty's appeal to nonevangelical voters, but third party advocates also did not win much support from their evangelical brethren, who resented the abolition party's stinging attacks upon their churches and the implication that only Liberty supporters were truly righteous men.

According to Theodore Smith, the Liberty party found it difficult to motivate an "indifferent people" to antislavery action. Actually, the abolition party encountered more than simple indifference; it engendered hostility and even open resistance. Many undoubtedly opposed the party out of fear of the biracial society it seemed to promise, yet American society was flawed by more than its racial ideology, which crippled the young nation's struggle to master its most serious challenge.[12] This society was also torn by serious cultural and religious differences (complicated by coinciding economic conflicts between regions, classes, and interest groups), which hindered it in solving certain issues. Disputes involving race and slavery, which, to some, were merely symbolically important, often pitted one cultural-religious group against another. None of the opposing bodies were willing to compromise or reach accommodation with its counterparts because to do so would mean recognizing and accepting the moral insights of a rival group. Few were willing to make this courageous choice.

The Liberty party certainly did not help bridge these cultural-religious chasms; indeed, it exacerbated tensions involving moral disputes. As pious Liberty advocates sought to free the churches of slavery, they formed still more religious sects. Rather than help obliterate moral or religious differences, these efforts instead intensified denominational identities and cultural loyalties. Of course, this was often their intention; some Congregationalists, for example, sought to disrupt the Plan of Union. Once sectarian conflict mounted, however, accommodation on questions that forced one group or the other to adopt the moral outlook or theological position of its opponent was more than ever unlikely.

Religiously minded party members naturally did not recognize this as the result of their actions. Their aim was to rescue their church bodies from those they believed had led them down the road of corruption, allowing the sin of slavery to continue undisciplined in the church. What appeared necessary was to return their church to the true path. Thus Anti-Slavery Quakers recalled the antislavery labors of John Woolman and Anthony Benezet, while Methodist seceders named their press the *True Wesleyan.*

Liberty party abolitionists failed to achieve their two fundamental objectives. While they managed to preserve their own purity, their independent religious and political stand did little to encourage others to recognize and accept the moral truths they thought were so obvious. Many believed this was not their failing but that of unrighteous men whose moral sense had been debased by the seeking after profit or political office. Since they were untouched by this corruption, pious third party voters regarded themselves worthy enough to recall the moral virtues and original purity of the young nation, which they believed had no intention to become the world's leading slaveholding republic.[13] When their fellow citizens refused to admit this, Liberty supporters were more than ever convinced that American society faced the Lord's judgment, and they did not hesitate to prophesy the nation's impending doom.

Once Liberty was dead, those who scarcely mourned its passing could nonetheless look back with fond memories on the tiny abolition party that had found so few friends while still alive. Despite the party's poor showing, perhaps we should not discount the nostalgic value the "noble and pure" party carried for later advocates of benevolent reform. As they encountered stiff opposition from slavery's defenders, antislavery advocates perhaps harkened back to the third party's memory, which might have provided consolation or inspiration for those torn between the dictates of conscience and the temptations of opportunity that politics often held. If they had actually solicited Liberty's opinion, they would undoubtedly have encountered the sentiments of the Williamsfield, Ohio, "friends of Human Rights," who held that "our strength lies in our integrity and the straight line of integrity is for us the high road to success." These friends of freedom felt only sympathy for those so burdened by "weakness and folly" as to deride Liberty for its meager popular support.[14]

NOTES

INTRODUCTION

1. *Liberty Herald,* April 23, 1845.
2. John R. McKivigan, "The Antislavery 'Comeouter' Sects: A Neglected Dimension of the Abolitionist Movement," *Civil War History* 26 (June 1980): 142–60. Dr. McKivigan kindly provided me a copy of his "Vote as you Pray and Pray as you Vote: Church-Oriented Abolitionism and Antislavery Politics" (Paper delivered at the 1983 convention of the Organization of American Historians, Cincinnati, Ohio).
3. C. C. Goen, "Broken Churches, Broken Nation: Regional Religion and North-South Alienation in Antebellum America," *Church History* 52 (March 1983): 21–35; and *Broken Churches, Broken Nation: Denominational Schisms and the Coming of the American Civil War* (Macon: Mercer University Press, 1985).
4. John R. McKivigan, "Abolitionism and the American Churches, 1830–1865: A Study of Attitudes and Tactics" (Ph.D. diss., Ohio State University, 1977); and *The War Against Proslavery Religion: Abolitionism and the Northern Churches, 1830–1865* (Ithaca, N.Y.: Cornell University Press, 1984).
5. Julian P. Bretz, "The Economic Background of the Liberty Party," *American Historical Review* 34 (January 1929): 250–64; Gilbert Hobbs Barnes, *The Antislavery Impulse, 1830–1844* (1933; reprint, New York: Harcourt, Brace & World, 1964); Richard H. Sewell, *Ballots for Freedom: Antislavery Politics in the United States, 1837–1860* (New York: Oxford University Press, 1976), 106.
6. Two of the most important works include Paul A. Johnson, *A Shopkeeper's Millennium: Society and Revivals in Rochester, New York, 1815–1837* (New York: Hill and Wang, 1978); and Louis S. Gerteis, *Morality and Utility in American Antislavery Reform* (Chapel Hill: University of North Carolina Press, 1987).
7. For covenanted and cumulative communities, see Page Smith, *As a City Upon a Hill: The Town in American History* (New York: Alfred A. Knopf, 1966). Ronald G. Walters notes

the abolitionists' ambivalence toward the North's industrial society in *The Antislavery Appeal: American Abolitionism After 1830* (Baltimore: Johns Hopkins University Press, 1976), 111–28.

8. John Keep, *Congregationalism and Church Action, With the Principles of Christian Union* (New York: S. W. Benedict & Company, 1845), 15–16.

9. Historians have not even agreed on this simple starting point. Ronald P. Formisano, *The Birth of Mass Political Parties: Michigan, 1827–1861* (Princeton: Princeton University Press, 1971), 75, argues that the devotional attitudes of third party members "practically insured their lack of success in a party movement." Yet Sewell, *Ballots for Freedom*, 82, contends it is misleading to consider the Liberty party "more as a religious crusade than as a political party." Alan Kraut argues more persuasively that Liberty supporters sought to "synthesize" religion and politics. "Partisanship and Principles: The Liberty Party in Antebellum Political Culture," in *Crusaders and Compromisers: Essays on the Relationship of the Antislavery Struggle to the Antebellum Party System*, ed. Alan M. Kraut (Westport, Conn.: Greenwood Press, 1983), 71–100. In *Gamaliel Bailey and Antislavery Union* (Kent, Ohio: Kent State University Press, 1986), 36–39, Stanley Harrold maintains that the "Ohio Liberty party" distinguished itself from its eastern counterparts by working to separate morality and politics.

10. Robert Fogel has aptly termed the abolitionists as "mystics" in "Without Consent or Contract" (Paper delivered at 1988 convention of the Organization of American Historians, Reno, Nevada).

11. Chase to George Reber, June 19, 1849, in Edward G. Bourne et al., "Diary and Correspondence of Salmon P. Chase," *Annual Report of the American Historical Association, 1902,* 2 (Washington, D.C.: 1903): 178–79. For Chase's role in the Free Soil coalition, see Frederick J. Blue, *The Free Soilers: Third Party Politics, 1848–54* (Urbana: University of Illinois Press, 1973).

12. Barnes, *Antislavery Impulse*, 176; Aileen S. Kraditor, "The Liberty and Free Soil Parties," in *History of U.S. Political Parties*, vol. 1: *1789–1860, From Factions to Parties*, ed. Arthur M. Schlesinger, Jr. (New York: Chelsea House Publishers, 1973), 741. Although the format did not allow for extensive documentation, Kraditor's analysis was clearly based more on William Lloyd Garrison's *Liberator* than Liberty party sources.

13. Theodore Clark Smith, *The Liberty and Free Soil Parties in the Northwest* (New York: Longmans, Green and Co., 1897). Dissertations on the Liberty party have concentrated on the eastern states: Margaret Louise Plunkett, "A History of the Liberty Party with Emphasis on its Activities in the Northeastern States" (Ph.D. diss., Cornell University, 1930); John R. Hendricks, "The Liberty Party in New York State, 1838–1848" (Ph.D. diss., Fordham University, 1959); Alan Morton Kraut, "The Liberty Men of New York: Political Abolitionism in New York State, 1840–1848" (Ph.D. diss., Cornell University, 1975); Reinhard Oscar Johnson, "The Liberty Party in New England, 1840–1848: The Forgotten Abolitionists" (Ph.D. diss., Syracuse University, 1976).

Reinhard Johnson discusses Liberty's role in Massachusetts politics in "The Liberty Party in Massachusetts, 1840–1848: Antislavery Third Party Politics in the Bay State," *Civil War History* 28 (September 1982): 237–65. See also his "The Liberty Party in New Hampshire, 1840–1848," *Historical New Hampshire* 3 (Spring 1978): 123–66; and "The Liberty Party in Vermont, 1840–1848," *Vermont History* 47 (Fall 1979): 258–75. Alan Kraut studies New York Liberty voters in "The Forgotten Reformers: A Profile of Third Party Abolitionists in Antebellum New York," in *Antislavery Reconsidered: New Perspectives on the Abolitionists,* ed. Lewis Perry and Michael Fellman (Baton Rouge: Louisiana State University Press, 1979), 119–45.

14. *Cincinnati Weekly Herald and Philanthropist,* November 19, 1839; April 19, 1846. The Cincinnati Liberty press underwent several name changes but will be referred to throughout as the *Philanthropist.* For Bailey, see Joel Goldfarb, "The Life of Gamaliel Bailey, Prior to the Founding of the *National Era:* The Orientation of a Practical Abolitionist" (Ph.D. diss., University of California, Los Angeles, 1958); Stanley C. Harrold, Jr., "Gamaliel Bailey, Abolitionist and Free Soiler" (Ph.D. diss., Kent State University, 1975); and *Gamaliel Bailey and Antislavery Union.*

15. Smith, *Liberty and Free Soil,* 54, 66, remarked that the parties dismissed Liberty with a "few contemptuous words." But Dwight L. Dumond claimed the third party "seriously weakened the Whig party" while making it "impossible for Northern Democrats . . . to continue to maintain solidarity with Southern pro-slavery leaders" in *Antislavery: The Crusade for Freedom in America* (New York: W. W. Norton & Co., 1961), 300. Recent scholarship assumes that Liberty tended to damage Whigs more than Democrats; see Lee Benson, *The Concept of Jacksonian Democracy: New York as a Test Case* (Princeton, N.J.: Princeton University Press, 1961), 133–35; Formisano, *Mass Political Parties,* 27–29, 120–21.

16. Gerteis, *Morality and Utility,* 88, argues that reformers adopted independent political action, not to destroy the Whig party, but to overcome its tendency toward expediency on such issues as slavery.

17. Theodore Calvin Pease, ed., *Illinois Election Returns, 1818–1848* (Springfield: Illinois State Historical Library, 1923), 160–62.

18. By the end of the century the major parties had taken definite steps to eliminate such third party challenges. Peter H. Argersinger, " 'A Place on the Ballot': Fusion Politics and Antifusion Laws," *American Historical Review* 85 (April 1980): 287–306.

19. John D. Hicks, "The Third Party Tradition in American Politics," *Mississippi Valley Historical Review* 20 (June 1933): 3–28.

20. Merton L. Dillon, "The Failure of the American Abolitionists," *Journal of Southern History* 25 (May 1959): 159–77; Hugh H. Davis, "The Failure of Political Abolitionism," *Connecticut Review* 6 (1973): 76–86. The Liberty party attracted a relatively small share of the national electorate compared to other nineteenth-century third parties.

21. Smith, *Liberty and Free Soil,* 2; Helen M. Cavenaugh, "Anti-Slavery Sentiment and Politics in the Northwest, 1844–1860" (Ph.D. diss., University of Chicago, 1938), 6–8, 23; Joseph G. Rayback, "The Liberty Party Leaders of Ohio: Exponents of Antislavery Coalition," *Ohio State Archaeological and Historical Quarterly* 57 (April 1948): 165–78; Dumond, *Antislavery Crusade,* 304; Sewell, *Ballots for Freedom,* viii, 3. For a critique of this approach, see Lawrence J. Friedman, "Historical Topics Sometimes Run Dry: The State of Abolitionist Studies," *The Historian* 43 (February 1981): 177–94.

22. Joel Silbey warns against this in "The Civil War Synthesis in American Political History," *Civil War History* 10 (June 1964): 130–40.

23. Racial fears remained strong in these states, even on the verge of slavery's fall. V. Jacque Voegeli, *Free But Not Equal: The Midwest and the Negro during the Civil War* (Chicago: University of Chicago Press, 1967).

24. Dumond, *Antislavery,* 304; Smith, *Liberty and Free Soil,* 2.

25. Louis Filler, *The Crusade Against Slavery, 1830–1850* (1960, reprint, New York: Harper Torchbooks, 1963), 190–91; Sewell, *Ballots for Freedom,* viii, 3. Sewell's phraseology is reminiscent of that of George W. Julian in his *Political Recollection, 1840–1872* (Chicago:

Jansen, McClurg & Co., 1884), 40. For the opposing view, see two articles by Eric Foner, "Politics and Prejudices: The Free Soil Party and the Free Negro, 1849–1852," *Journal of Negro History* 50 (October 1965): 239–56; and "Racial Attitudes of the New York Free Soilers," *New York History* 46 (October 1965): 311–29. Also see Eugene H. Berwanger, *The Frontier Against Slavery: Western Anti-Negro Prejudice and the Slavery Extension Controversy* (Urbana: University of Illinois Press, 1967), 125–36; and Larry Gara, "Slavery and the Slave Power: A Crucial Distinction," *Civil War History* 15 (March 1969): 4–18.

26. Alan Kraut and Reinhard Johnson have examined rank-and-file Liberty voters in the Northeast.

27. In the period 1832–53 Democrats polled an average of 48.9 percent and Whigs 47.3 percent of Ohio's votes. Kenneth John Winkle, "The Politics of Community: Migration and Politics in Antebellum Ohio" (Ph.D. diss., University of Wisconsin, Madison, 1984), 403.

28. Rayback, "Liberty Party Leaders of Ohio." See also Stanley Cooper Harrold, Jr., "Forging an Antislavery Instrument: Gamaliel Bailey and the Foundation of the Ohio Liberty Party," *Old Northwest* 2 (Spring 1976): 371–87. Virtually all authorities have adopted the Rayback approach. See, for example, Sewell, *Ballots for Freedom*, 90–91, 99–101, 107, 115, 121–26.

29. Harrold, *Bailey*, suggests that partly due to his location on the "border" between slavery and freedom, Cincinnati editor Gamaliel Bailey developed a border state perspective that helped set him apart from other abolitionists.

30. For antiblack and antiabolitionist mobs in Cincinnati, see Richard C. Wade, "The Negro in Cincinnati, 1800–1830," *Journal of Negro History* 39 (January 1954): 43–57; Leonard L. Richards, *"Gentlemen of Property and Standing": Anti-Abolition Mobs in Jacksonian America* (New York: Oxford University Press, 1970); and Patrick Allen Folk, " 'The Queen City of Mobs': Riots and Community Reactions in Cincinnati, 1788–1848" (Ph.D. diss., University of Toledo, 1978). For the Lovejoy episode in Alton, see Merton L. Dillon, *Elijah P. Lovejoy: Abolitionist Editor* (Urbana: University of Illinois Press, 1966). For antislavery sentiment in the Oberlin community, see Wilbur Greeley Burroughs, "Oberlin's Part in the Slavery Conflict," *Ohio Archaeological and Historical Society Publications* 20 (April–July 1911): 269–334.

31. In Ohio party positions were an equally strong determinant for voting on the Black Laws. Leonard Erickson, "Politics and Repeal of Ohio's Black Laws, 1837–1849," *Ohio History* 82 (Summer–Autumn 1973): 154–75. For the famous Oberlin-Wellington fugitive slave rescue case, see William C. Cochran, "The Western Reserve and the Fugitive Slave Law," *Western Reserve Historical Society Collections* (1920): 118–204.

32. J. D. DeBow, *The Seventh Census: Report of the Superintendent of the Census for December 1, 1852; to which is appended the Report for December 1, 1851* (Washington, D.C.: Robert Armstrong, 1853), 86–91, 150–52.

CHAPTER 1

1. The proposal was defeated by a 57 to 43 percent margin. Results are in Pease, *Illinois Election Returns*, 27–29. Eugene H. Berwanger cites slightly different figures in *The Frontier Against Slavery: Western Anti-Negro Prejudice and the Slavery Extension Controversy* (Urbana: University of Illinois Press, 1967), 17. See also Norman Dwight Harris, *History of Negro Servitude in Illinois, and of the Slavery Agitation in that State, 1719–1864* (Chicago:

A. C. McClurg, 1904), 6–15, 22–26, 40–48; Calvin T. Pease, *The Frontier State, 1818–1848,* Centennial History of Illinois, ed. C. W. Alvord, vol. 2 (Chicago: A. C. McClurg, 1922), 70–91.

2. Alexis de Tocqueville, *Democracy in America,* trans. George Lawrence, ed. J. P. Mayer (Garden City, N.Y.: Anchor Books, 1969), 343–50, 355–56. On prejudice against blacks, see Leon F. Litwack, *North of Slavery: The Negro in the Free States, 1790–1860* (Chicago: University of Chicago Press, 1961); Berwanger, *Frontier Against Slavery,* 7–59; Richard F. O'Dell, "The Early Anti-Slavery Movement in Ohio" (Ph. D. diss., University of Michigan, 1948), 118–19, 147–53; Henry N. Sherwood, "The Movement in Ohio to Deport the Negro," *Quarterly Publication of the Historical and Philosophical Society of Ohio* 7 (June–September 1912): 53–78; Wade, "Negro in Cincinnati."

3. Berwanger, *Frontier Against Slavery,* 38–51. In 1848 over 70 percent of Illinois voters approved a clause to the state constitution prohibiting black emigration. In 1851 a similar provision was approved by over 83 percent of Indiana voters. In 1850, 71 percent of Michigan voters denied the suffrage to blacks. The 1857 margin in Wisconsin was slightly smaller at 61 percent. Pease, *Illinois Election Returns,* 176–82; Dorothy Riker and Gayle Thornbrough, comps., *Indiana Election Returns, 1816–1851* (Indianapolis: Indiana Historical Bureau, 1960), 388–90; *The Whig Almanac and United States Register for 1851* (1852; reprint, New York: New York Tribune, 1868), 46; Berwanger, *Frontier Against Slavery,* 40–45. (Berwanger gives the wrong figures for Illinois, citing the results for the entire constitution.)

4. Eric Foner, *Free Soil, Free Labor, Free Men: The Ideology of the Republican Party before the Civil War* (London: Oxford University Press, 1970), 262.

5. Smith, *Liberty and Free Soil,* 337.

6. George Rogers Taylor, *The Transportation Revolution, 1815–1860,* vol. 4: *The Economic History of the United States* (1951; reprint, White Plains, N.Y.: M. E. Sharpe, Inc., 1951); *Seventh Census,* 86–91, 150–52.

7. Robert Emmet Chaddock, "Ohio Before 1850: A Study of the Early Influence of Pennsylvania and Southern Populations in Ohio," in *Studies in History, Economics and Public Law,* vol. 31 (New York: Columbia University, 1908), 187–342; Wayne Jordan, "The People of Ohio's First County," *Ohio Archaeological and Historical Quarterly* 49 (January–March 1940): 1–40; Randolph Chandler Downes, *Frontier Ohio, 1788–1803* (Columbus: Ohio State Archaeological and Historical Society, 1935), 55; Jacob W. Myers, "The Beginning of German Immigration in the Middle West," *Journal of the Illinois State Historical Society* 15 (October–January 1922–23): 592–99; Carl Wittke, "Ohio's Germans, 1840–1875," *Ohio Historical Quarterly* 66 (October 1957): 339–54; LaVern J. Rippley, "The Chillicothe Germans," *Ohio History* 75 (Autumn 1966): 212–25; W. J. Orahan, "Irish Settlements in Illinois," *The Catholic World* 33 (May 1881): 157–62; J. P. McGoorty, "Early Irish of Illinois," *Illinois Historical Society Transactions* (1927): 54–64; Elfrieda Lang, "Irishmen in Northern Indiana Before 1850," *Mid-America* 36 (July 1954): 190–98; J. E. Vinyard, "Inland Urban Immigrants: The Detroit Irish, 1850," *Michigan History* 57 (Summer 1973): 121–39.

8. Henry C. Hubbart, *The Older Middle West, 1840–1850* (New York: D. Appleton-Century Co., 1936), 6.

9. Ronald P. Formisano, "The Edge of Caste: Colored Suffrage in Michigan, 1827–1861," *Michigan History* 56 (Spring 1972): 19–41; and "A Case Study in Party Formation; Michigan, 1835," *Mid-America* 50 (April 1968): 83–107. Joel Silbey advances a similar argument for the national level in *The Partisan Imperative: The Dynamics of American Politics Before the Civil War* (New York: Oxford University Press, 1987).

10. Richard Lyle Power, *Planting Corn Belt Culture: The Impress of the Upland*

Notes to Page 4

Southerner and Yankee in the Old Northwest (Indianapolis: Indiana Historical Society, 1953). John D. Barnhart, "Sources of Southern Immigration into the Old Northwest," Mississippi Valley Historical Review 22 (June 1935): 49–62; "The Southern Element in the Leadership of the Old Northwest," Journal of Southern History 1 (May 1935): 186–97; "The Southern Influence in the Formation of Indiana," Indiana Magazine of History 33 (September 1937): 261–76; and Valley of Democracy: The Frontier versus the Plantation in the Ohio Valley, 1775–1818 (Bloomington: Indiana University Press, 1953). But compare with Henry Clyde Hubbart, " 'Pro-Southern' Influences in the Free West, 1840–1865," Mississippi Valley Historical Review 20 (June 1933): 45–62; and Older Middle West, 4–5, 12–13. See also Pease, Frontier State, 7, 18, 173–93; Morton M. Rosenberg and Dennis V. McClure, The Politics of Pro-Slavery Sentiment in Indiana, 1816–1861 (Muncie, Ind.: Ball State University Publications, 1968), 4. Southern influence in southern Ohio might not have been as dominant as in Indiana and Illinois. See Eugene H. Roseboom, "Southern Ohio and the Union in 1863," Mississippi Valley Historical Review 39 (June 1952): 29–44. Some Southerners apparently did make it further north; see Elfrieda Lang, "Southern Migration to Northern Indiana Before 1850," Indiana Magazine of History 50 (December 1954): 349–56.

11. Levi Coffin, Reminiscences of Levi Coffin (1876; reprint, New York: Arno Press, 1968); Harlow Lindley, "The Quakers in the Old Northwest," Proceedings of the Mississippi Valley Historical Association 5 (1911–12): 60–72; Errol T. Elliott, Quakers on the American Frontier (Richmond, Ind.: Friends United Press, 1969); John Rankin, "Life of Reverend John Rankin, Written by Himself in His Eightieth Year," Ohio Historical Society (hereafter referred to as OHS); Paul R. Grim, "The Reverend John Rankin, Early Abolitionist," Ohio State Archaeological and Historical Quarterly 46 (July 1937): 215–56; Larry Gene Willey, "The Reverend John Rankin, Early Ohio Antislavery Leader" (Ph.D. diss., University of Iowa, 1976).

12. Albert G. Riddle, "The Rise of Antislavery Sentiment on the Western Reserve," Magazine of Western History 6 (1887): 151–52. The basic work on New England emigration is Lois K. Mathews, The Expansion of New England (Boston: Houghton Mifflin Co., 1909). See also E. B. Usher, "Puritan Influence in Wisconsin," Proceedings of the Wisconsin Historical Society (1898): 117–28; Charrie P. Kofoid, "Puritan Influences in Illinois Before 1860," Transactions of the Illinois State Historical Society 10 (1905): 315-16; Karl F. Geiser, "The Western Reserve in the Anti-Slavery Movement," Proceedings of the Mississippi Valley Historical Association (1911–12): 77–80; J. Harold Stevens, "The Influence of New England in Michigan," Michigan History 19 (Autumn 1935): 349; Jordan, "Ohio's First County," 1–40; Morris C. Taber, "New England Influences in South Central Michigan," Michigan History 35 (December 1961): 319–23; Kenneth V. Lottich, New England Transplanted (Dallas: Royal Publishing Co., 1964); and two works by David French, "Puritan Conservatism and the Frontier: The Elizur Wright Family and the Connecticut Western Reserve," Old Northwest 1 (March 1975): 85–96; "Elizur Wright, Jr., and the Emergence of Anti-Colonization Sentiments on the Connecticut Western Reserve," Ohio History 85 (Winter 1976): 49–66.

13. Richard L. Power, "Wet Lands and the Hoosier Stereotype," Mississippi Valley Historical Review 22 (June 1935): 33–48; William O. Lynch, "The Flow of Colonists to and from Indiana," Indiana Magazine of History 11 (March 1915): 1–8; Paul W. Gates, "Land Policy and Tenancy in the Prairie Counties of Indiana," Indiana Magazine of History 35 (March 1939): 1–26. But see also Edward H. Rastatter, "Nineteenth Century Public Land Policy: The Case for the Speculator," in Essays in Nineteenth Century Economic History: The Old Northwest, ed. David C. Klingaman and Richard K. Eedder (Athens: Ohio University Press, 1975), 118–37.

14. The Oberlin covenant appears in James H. Fairchild, *Oberlin, the Colony and the College, 1833–1883* (Oberlin: E. J. Goodrich, 1883), 25–27. For Tallmadge, see Lottich, *New England Transplanted,* 51–52. For Yankee colonies in Illinois, see Ella W. Harrison, "A History of the First Congregational Church of Princeton, Illinois, 1831–1924," *Journal of the Illinois State Historical Society* 20 (April 1927): 103–11 (hereafter cited as *JISHS*); Ella Hume Taylor, "A History of the First Congregational Church of Geneseo," *JISHS* 20 (April 1927): 112–27; Anson M. Hubbard, "A Colony Settlement, Geneseo, Illinois, 1836–1837," *JISHS* 29 (January 1937): 403–31; Hermann R. Muelder, *Fighters for Freedom: The History of Antislavery Activities of Men and Women Associated with Knox College* (New York: Columbia University Press, 1959). For a description of a New England colony where abolitionism was weak, see Edward W. Barber, "The Vermontville Colony: Its Genesis and History," *Michigan Historical Collections* 28 (1897): 197–287.

15. Robert H. Nichols, "The Plan of Union in New York," *Church History* 5 (March 1936): 29–51; C. L. Zorbaugh, "The Plan of Union in Ohio," *Church History* 6 (June 1937): 145–64; Frederick I. Kuhns, "The Breakup of the Plan of Union in Michigan," *Michigan History* 32 (June 1948): 157–80; William Warren Sweet, ed., *Religion on the American Frontier, 1783–1850,* vol. 3: *The Congregationalists* (Chicago: University of Chicago Press, 1939), 13–38. For contemporary opinion on the workings of the plan, see James Wood, *Facts and Observations concerning the Organization and State of the Churches in the Three Synods of Western New York and the Synod of Western Reserve* (Saratoga Springs: G. M. Davison, 1837); William S. Kennedy, *The Plan of Union; or, A History of the Presbyterian and Congregational Churches in the Western Reserve* (Hudson, Ohio: Pentagon Steam Press, 1856); J. H. Fairchild, "The Story of Congregationalism on the Western Reserve," *Ohio Church History Society Papers* 5 (Oberlin, 1894): 1–27.

16. Power, *Planting Corn Belt Culture,* 2–10, 30–35, 174. See also *Genius of Liberty,* June 5, 1841; Edward D. Mansfield, *Personal Memories: Social, Political and Literary, with Sketches of Many Noted People, 1803–1843,* (1879; reprint, Freeport, N.Y.: Books for Libraries Press, 1970), 220.

17. Pease, *Illinois Election Returns,* 176–80; Riker and Thornbrough, *Indiana Election Returns,* 388–90; Erickson, "Politics and Ohio's Black Laws"; Godlove S. Orth to Schuyler Colfax, August 16, 1845, in Herman J. Schauinger, ed., "The Letters of Godlove S. Orth, Hoosier Whig," *Indiana Magazine of History* 39 (December 1943): 367; Charles M. Thompson, *The Illinois Whigs Before 1846* (Urbana: University of Illinois Press, 1915); Evarts B. Greene, "Sectional Forces in the History of Illinois," *Transactions of the Illinois State Historical Society* 8 (1903): 75–83. See also Charles Zimmerman, "The Origin and Development of the Republican Party in Indiana," *Indiana Magazine of History* 13 (December 1917): 387–91.

18. See, for example, Edward Wade to Levi Sutliff, January 10, 1842, Sutliff Family Papers, Sutliff Museum, Warren (Ohio) Public Library. See also *Genius of Universal Emancipation,* September 13, 1839; *Western Citizen,* January 20; February 9; June 22, 1843; Julian quoted in Marion C. Miller, "The Antislavery Movement in Indiana" (Ph.D. diss., University of Michigan), 256.

19. Frank J. Heinl, "Jacksonville and Morgan County: An Historical View," *JISHS* 18 (April 1925): 5–14. See also Don Harrison Doyle, *The Social Order of a Frontier Community: Jacksonville, Illinois, 1825–1870* (Urbana: University of Illinois Press, 1978). For Illinois College, see Charles Henry Rammelkamp, *Illinois College: A Centennial History, 1829–1929* (New Haven: Yale University Press, 1928).

20. Formisano, *Mass Political Parties,* 74–76, 120; Benson, *Jacksonian Democracy,* 209–13.

21. For Birney, see William Birney, *James G. Birney and His Times: The Genesis of the Republican Party with Some Account of Abolition Movements in the South Before 1828* (1890; reprint, New York: Negro Universities Press, 1969); and Betty Fladeland, *James Gillespie Birney: From Slaveholder to Abolitionist* (1955; reprint, New York: Greenwood Press, 1969).

22. Virtually every issue of an antislavery paper included a dun to its subscribers; see for example, *Genius of Universal Emancipation*, July 5, 1839. Yet Harrold, *Bailey,* points out that Bailey aroused envy among his fellow antislavery editors by eking out a fair living from his publications.

23. For a discussion of the convention, see Robert Price, "The Ohio Anti-Slavery Convention of 1836," *Ohio State Archaeological and Historical Quarterly* 45 (April 1936): 173–88.

24. Barnes and Dumond, *Weld Letters,* xvi; for Finney's theology, see James E. Johnson, "Charles G. Finney and a Theology of Revivalism," *Church History* 38 (September 1969): 338–58.

25. Barnes and Dumond, *Weld Letters,* xvii.

26. Weld to Birney, September 26; August 19, 1835, in Dumond, *Birney Letters,* vol. 1, 239–40, 246–49.

27. Weld to Birney, December 11, 1834; February 16, 1835, in Dumond, *Birney Letters,* vol. 1, 153–56, 180–82; Weld to Elizur Wright, Jr., March 2, 1835, in Barnes and Dumond, *Weld Letters,* 205–8. Price, "Convention of 1836," incorrectly lists the Paint Valley Society in Portage County. Robert H. Abzug notes that Weld considered West Union "one of the most hopeless places for anti-slavery effort" in *Passionate Liberator: Theodore Dwight Weld and the Dilemma of Reform* (New York: Oxford University Press, 1980), 124.

28. Edward B. Welsh, "Chillicothe: A Distinguished Rural Presbytery," *Journal of the Presbyterian Historical Society* 23 (September 1945): 137–42; Welsh, "Wrestling with Human Values: The Slavery Years," in *They Seek a Country: The American Presbyterians, Some Aspects,* ed. Gaius Jackson Slosser (New York: Macmillan Co., 1955), 210–33; O'Dell, "Antislavery in Ohio," 371.

29. Merton L. Dillon, *Benjamin Lundy and the Struggle for Negro Freedom* (Urbana: University of Illinois Press, 1966), 17–23, 45–47; Ruth Anna Nuermberger, *Charles Osborn in the Anti-Slavery Movement* (Columbus: Ohio Archaeological and Historical Society, 1937); Weld to Birney, August 4, 1835, in Dumond, *Birney Letters,* vol. 1, 227–29.

30. A. O. Fuller, "Early Annals of the Austinburg Church," *Papers of the Ohio Church History Society* 10 (1895): 63–79; Weld to Birney, December 19, 1835, in Dumond, *Birney Letters,* vol. 1, 283–86; Weld to Wright, October 6, 1835, in Barnes and Dumond, *Weld Letters,* vol. 1, 236–40. See also the letters of Charles Stuart, Sereno Streeter, and James A. Thome in *Weld Letters,* vol. 1, 176–77, 256–59, 277–79, 281–86, 315–17; and *Ohio Observer,* October 15, 1835.

Professors and students at Western Reserve College in Hudson, Ohio, began to discuss the evils of slavery before Weld's mission. Indeed, an earlier visit to the college might have sparked Weld's final conversion to immediatism. Wright to Weld, December 7, 1832; September 5, 1833, in Barnes and Dumond, *Weld Letters,* vol. 1, 94–97, 114–17; French, "Wright and Western Reserve"; Jane H. Pease and William H. Pease, *Bound with Them in Chains: A Biographical History of the Antislavery Movement* (Westport, Ct.: Greenwood Press, 1972), 221; Milton C. Sernett, *Abolition's Axe: Beriah Green, Oneida Institute, and the Black Freedom Struggle* (Syracuse: Syracuse University Press, 1986), 21.

31. Riddle, "Reserve Antislavery," 152–53; Fairchild, "Reserve Congregationalism," 11–12; Kennedy, *Plan of Union,* 187, 230.

32. Weld to Lewis Tappan, April 5, 1836, in Barnes and Dumond, *Weld Letters,* vol. 1, 286–89. For the rural origins of evangelical religion and abolitionism, see David M. Ludlum, *Social Ferment in Vermont, 1791–1859* (New York: Columbia University Press, 1939), 146; Whitney R. Cross, *The Burned-Over District: The Social and Intellectual History of Enthusiastic Religion in Western New York, 1800–1850* (New York: Cornell University Press, 1950), 65–75; Charles C. Cole, Jr., *The Social Ideas of the Northern Evangelists, 1826–1860* (New York: Columbia University Press, 1954), 80, 195. For urban middle-class evangelism, see Johnson, *A Shopkeeper's Millennium.*

33. Birney, *Birney,* 169–70; *Genius of Universal Emancipation,* March 29, 1839; James Brewer Stewart, "Evangelicalism and the Radical Strain in Southern Antislavery Thought During the 1820s," *Journal of Southern History* 39 (August 1973): 379–97.

34. Birney, *Birney,* 162–72, 431–35; O'Dell, "Antislavery in Ohio," 390–94. See also Alice Dana Adams, *The Neglected Period of Anti-Slavery in America, 1808–1831* (Boston: Ginn & Co., 1908); James D. Essig, *The Bonds of Wickedness: American Evangelicals against Slavery, 1770–1808* (Philadelphia: Temple University Press, 1982). For the doctrine of immediatism, see David Brion Davis, "The Emergence of Immediatism in British and American Antislavery Thought," *Mississippi Valley Historical Review* 49 (September 1962): 209–30; Anne C. Loveland, "Evangelicalism and 'Immediate Emancipation' in American Antislavery Thought," *Journal of Southern History* 32 (May 1966): 172–88. Dillon, *Lundy,* 64–68, follows the Davis article.

35. Price, "Ohio Convention of 1836," 182–86; *Philanthropist,* March 27, July 31, September 4, 1838; Department of State, *Compendium of Sixth Census* (Washington, D.C.: Thomas Allen, 1841), 78.

36. Barnes, *Antislavery Impulse,* 146–52. The *Emancipator,* February 20, 1840, remarked that Michigan had been "almost self-abolitionized."

37. Ware William Wimberly, "Missionary Reforms in Indiana, 1826–1860: Education, Temperance, Antislavery" (Ph.D. diss., Indiana University, 1977), 227, 236–40, 290; but compare this with Frederick I. Kuhns, *The American Home Missionary Society in Relation to the Antislavery Controversy in the Old Northwest* (Billings, Mont.: 1959); *Free Labor Advocate,* May 5, 1841; Miller, "Antislavery in Indiana," 28–32, 56–66, 68–71; *Emancipator,* October 4, 1838; Bailey to Birney, January 23, 1840, in Dumond, *Birney Letters,* vol. 1, 522. Buffum's progress in Indiana can be followed in the *Emancipator,* February 6, March 12, April 9, December 3, 1840. Birney gives a report of his visit to the 1839 Indiana state convention in Birney to Leavitt, June 11, 1839, in *Emancipator,* June 20, 1839.

38. Kooker, "Antislavery in Michigan," 79–106, facing pp. 138–39, 146–47; Merton L. Dillon, "Elizabeth Margaret Chandler and the Spread of Antislavery Sentiment to Michigan," *Michigan History* 39 (December 1955): 481–94; Maurice D. Ndukwu, "Antislavery in Michigan: A Study of its Origins, Development, and Expression from Territorial Period to 1860" (Ph.D. diss., Michigan State University, 1979), 36, 82–86.

39. Merton L. Dillon examines the "neglected period" of Illinois abolitionism in "The Antislavery Movement in Illinois, 1824–1835," in Harry N. Scheiber, ed., *The Old Northwest: Studies in Regional History, 1787–1910* (Lincoln: University of Nebraska Press), 296–311. See also Dillon's "Abolitionism Comes to Illinois," *JISHS* 53 (Winter 1960): 389–403; Illinois Congregational Association Minutes, November 3, 1836, in Sweet, *Congregationalists,* 177; Pease, *Frontier State,* 420.

40. Edward Beecher, *Narrative of the Riots at Alton* (1838; reprint, Miami: Mnemosyne, 1969); Dillon, *Elijah P. Lovejoy: Abolitionist Editor* (Urbana: University of Illinois Press, 1961), 132–39; Robert Merideth, *The Politics of the Universe: Edward Beecher, Abolition,*

and Orthodoxy (Nashville: Vanderbilt University Press, 1963), 96–97; Hermann R. Muelder, "Galesburg: Hot-Bed of Abolitionism," *JISHS* 35 (September 1942): 216–35.

41. Beecher, *Alton Riots,* 20.

42. Illinois State Anti-Slavery Society Minute Book, October 28, 1837, Chicago Historical Society.

43. Dillon, *Lundy,* 252–62.

44. *Ohio Observer,* August 28, 1834. See also the Ashtabula County Anti-Slavery Society meeting of July 4, 1839, *Ashtabula Sentinel,* July 13, 1839; *Free Labor Advocate,* February, March 8, 1841; Gerald Sorin, "The Historical Theory of Political Radicalism: Michigan Abolitionist Leaders as a Test Case" (Master's thesis, Wayne State University, 1964), 78.

45. Russell B. Nye, *Fettered Freedom: Civil Liberties and the Slavery Controversy, 1830–1860* (1963; reprint, Urbana: University of Illinois Press, 1972); Birney to Gerrit Smith, September 13, 1835, in Dumond, *Birney Letters,* vol. 1, 243.

CHAPTER 2

1. James Brewer Stewart, *Joshua R. Giddings and the Tactics of Radical Politics* (Cleveland: Case Western Reserve University Press, 1970), 17–33.

2. *Liberator,* June 2, 1837; Bailey to Bayle, January 11, 1841, in Alfred A. Thomas, ed., *Correspondence of Thomas Ebenezer Thomas, Mainly Relating to the Anti-Slavery Conflict in Ohio, Especially in the Presbyterian Church* (Dayton: 1909), 32; Barnes, *Antislavery Impulse,* 150–52; Bailey to Birney, May 27, 1837, in Dumond, *Birney Letters,* vol. 1, 385. In "The Economic Background of the Liberty party," Bretz maintains that the abolitionists' complaints about the panic demonstrate their essentially economic motivations. Louis S. Gerteis, "Slavery and Hard Times: Morality and Utility in American Antislavery Reform," *Civil War History* 29 (December 1983): 322, also proposes there was more than "simple opportunism" in the abolitionists' economic arguments.

3. Joshua Leavitt's "The Financial Power of Slavery," *Emancipator,* October 22, 1840; Leavitt to Birney, May 19, June 1, October 1, 1840, in Dumond, *Birney Letters,* vol. 1, 574, 581, 604; Foner, *Free Soil.*

4. See, for example, the controversy over the Illinois and Michigan Canal in Pease, *Frontier State.*

5. *Painesville Telegraph,* September 4, 18, 1835; July 5, November 15, 1838; *Ashtabula Sentinel,* October 24, 1835; February 27, 1836; July 18, 1840.

6. William Warren Sweet, ed., *Religion on the American Frontier,* vol. 2: *The Presbyterians, 1783–1840* (New York: Harper & Brothers, 1936), 99–110. Barnes, *Antislavery Impulse,* has been the leading exponent of the strength of abolitionism among New School Presbyterians.

In 1835 the Synod of Western Reserve declared slavery "a sin against God"; see Victor B. Howard, "The Antislavery Movement in the Presbyterian Church, 1835–1861" (Ph.D. diss., Ohio State University, 1961), 15, 20, 40; *Ohio Observer,* April 14, 1836.

7. Conrad J. Engelder, "The Churches and Slavery: A Study of the Attitudes Toward Slavery of the Major Protestant Denominations" (Ph.D. diss., University of Michigan, 1964), 197–98. The 1818 assembly's position on slavery appears on pp. 291–94.

8. Sweet, *Presbyterians,* 119–25; Engelder, "Churches and Slavery," 207–15.

9. The most forceful advocate of the view that slavery was instrumental in the Presbyterian split is Bruce C. Staiger, "Abolitionism and the Presbyterian Schism of 1837–38," *Mississippi Valley Historical Review* 36 (December 1949): 391–414. Before this, however, William Warren Sweet, *Presbyterians,* 119–25, had stressed the importance of slavery in the division. See also Howard, "Antislavery in the Presbyterian Church," 59, 88. For a summary of the scholarship on the issue, see George M. Marsden, *The Evangelical Mind and the New School Presbyterian Experience: A Case Study of Thought and Theology in Nineteenth Century America* (New Haven: Yale University Press, 1970), 250–51.

10. *Ohio Observer,* July 20, 1837; Howard, "Antislavery in Presbyterian Church," 53–54.

11. *Peoria Register and Northwestern Gazeteer,* December 9, 23, 1837.

12. *Peoria Register,* August 18, 1838. For the Galesburg colony in Illinois abolitionism, see Muelder, *Knox,* 143, 156–57, 162–64; and "Galesburg," 218–27, 234–35.

13. *Peoria Register,* October 27, 1838; *Genius of Liberty,* May 22, 1841.

14. *Peoria Register,* November 3, 17, 1838. The division caused much rearranging of jurisdictional lines; Galesburg, for example, became the heart of the newly formed Knox Presbytery.

15. Lyman Beecher, *Autobiography, Correspondence, Etc. of Lyman Beecher, D.D.,* ed. Charles Beecher, vol. 2 (New York: Harper & Bros., 1866), 428–29; Howard, "Antislavery in Presbyterian Church," 76–77; *Emancipator,* May 3, 1838; J. N. Scott to Chase, January 6, 1845, Salmon P. Chase Papers, Library of Congress (hereafter cited as LC).

16. Leonard L. Richards develops these themes in *"Gentlemen of Property and Standing": Anti-Abolition Mobs in Jacksonian America* (London: Oxford University Press, 1970). The Ohio Colonization Society included many of the state's leading political figures (of both parties). *Ohio State Journal,* February 1, 1839; Carl Wittke, gen. ed., *The History of the State of Ohio,* 6 vols. (Columbus: Ohio State Archaeological and Historical Society, 1941), vol. 3: *The Passing of the Frontier, 1825–1850,* by Francis P. Weisenburger, 365–66; Goldfarb, "Bailey," 137–39. The Painesville Colonization Society was typical in the political and social prestige of its leadership; *Painesville Republican,* July 19, 1838. For antiabolitionist mobs in Cincinnati, see Richards, *Gentlemen of Property and Standing;* and Richard Allen Folk, " 'The Queen City of Mobs': Riots and Community Reactions in Cincinnati, 1788–1848"(Ph.D. diss., University of Toledo, 1978).

17. Nye, *Fettered Freedom; Ohio State Journal,* July 19, 1836; *Painesville Republican,* November 30, 1837; Weld to Birney, September 26, 1835, in Dumond, *Birney Letters,* vol. 1, 246–49; see also letter of October 30, 1835, 251–55.

18. *Ashtabula Sentinel,* July 12, 1834; July 11, 1835; October 10, 1835; July 19, 1837; February 9, July 13, 20, 1839; July 17, 1841. Stewart, *Giddings,* 27, 30.

19. For a Painesville antiabolition meeting in response to a visit by Weld, see *Ohio State Journal,* October 9, 1835. For other such meetings, see *Ashtabula Sentinel,* December 7, 1833; *Ohio Observer,* September 17, 1835; *Ohio State Journal,* October 30, 1835; *Liberator,* February 25, 1837; *Philanthropist,* May 1, 1838; *Painesville Telegraph,* February 28, March 21, 1839. See also Robert Price, "Further Notes on Granville's Anti-Abolition Disturbances," *Ohio State Archaeological and Historical Quarterly* 45 (October 1936): 365–66. An antiabolition lecture in Michigan charged twenty-five cents admission; *Detroit Advertiser,* April 3, 1840.

20. For the Lovejoy episode, see Beecher, *Alton Riots;* and Dillon, *Lovejoy.*

21. Calvin Chapin to Birney, December 18, 1837, in Dumond, *Birney Letters,* vol. 1, 438; *Philanthropist,* March 13, February 20, March 6, 1838.

22. *Ashtabula Sentinel,* January 27, February 3, 1838; *Philanthropist,* January 8, 1836; see also Birney to Lewis Tappan, July 15, 1836, in Dumond, *Birney Letters,* vol. 1, 342–44.

23. Ripley Anti-Slavery Society, August 11, 1836, in Dumond, *Birney Letters,* vol. 2, 635–36. James B. Stewart argues that so-called conservative abolitionists (such as Liberty advocates) insisted that mobs were led by "gentlemen of property and standing" because these abolitionists maintained their faith in the "small" people and refused to recognize the nation's "degeneracy," as Garrisonians did; see "Peaceful Hopes and Violent Experiences: The Evolution of Reforming and Radical Abolitionism, 1831–1837," *Civil War History* 17 (December 1971): 293–309. Stewart's argument might be valid to an extent, but it seems pointless to argue over which group of abolitionists condemned American society more. Pious abolitionists did not shrink from criticizing the nation's moral failings.

24. Beecher, *Alton Riots,* 159.

25. Beecher, *Autobiography,* vol. 2, 430.

26. Sewell, *Ballots for Freedom,* 43, views the growth of political abolition as naturally inevitable. In addition to Birney's fears cited in Birney to Gerrit Smith, September 13, 1835, in Dumond, *Birney Letters,* vol. 1, 243; see also the view of Ohio minister John Keep, *Congregationalism and Church Action,* 137, 140.

27. Barnes, *Antislavery Impulse,* 109–45; James M. McPherson, "The Fight Against the Gag Rule: Joshua Leavitt and the Antislavery Insurgency in the Whig Party, 1839–1842," *Journal of Negro History* 48 (April 1963): 177–95; *Philanthropist,* May 8, 22, June 19, 1838; *Emancipator,* September 20, 1838.

28. *Liberator,* June 2, 1837; *Philanthropist,* April 24, May 29, 1838; *Emancipator,* May 10, September 20, 1838; Sewell, *Ballots for Freedom,* 15–17.

29. *Emancipator,* August 23, 1838.

30. *Philanthropist,* March 13, 27, May 8, 1838; Fladeland, *Birney,* 176; see also Birney to Lewis Tappan, September 26, 1836, and February 3, 1835, in Dumond, *Birney Letters,* vol. 1, 177, 360. Birney, *Birney,* ix, 156, 171–72, claimed his father was an innovator of abolitionist political strategy, citing the statement of Albert G. Riddle that "*He was the first to employ it.*" At this point, however, even Birney did not advocate an independent party. Birney to Chase, June 5, 1837, in Filler, *Crusade Against Slavery,* 141.

31. The executive committee of the Columbiana County Anti-Slavery Society, where Garrisonism was strong, deemed it "inexpedient" to question candidates for office. *Emancipator,* October 11, 1838. Reverend Everton Judson of the Huron County Anti-Slavery Society resigned in protest over the questioning of candidates. *Philanthropist,* April 9, 1839.

32. *Philanthropist,* March 27, June 12, October 2, 30, 1838; *Emancipator,* October 11, 21, 1838; *Painesville Telegraph,* September 20, 1838.

33. *Niles' National Register,* November 3, 1838; *Emancipator,* November 1, 1838; *Liberator,* November 2, 1838; Sewell, *Ballots for Freedom,* 17–18.

34. Benjamin Franklin Morris, *The Life of Thomas Morris: Pioneer and Long a Legislator of Ohio and U.S. Senator from 1833–1839* (Cincinnati: Moore, Wilstach, Keys & Overend, 1856); James B. Swing, "Thomas Morris," *Ohio Archaeological and Historical Society Publications* 10 (1902): 352–60; Smith, *Liberty and Free Soil,* 24–26.

35. Weisenburger, *Passing of Frontier,* 350. As it turned out, Mahan had not been in Kentucky recently and could not be held. The judge's charge to the jury is in *Liberator,* December 7, 1838; see also *Niles' National Register,* December 1, 1838.

In his efforts to see Vance defeated, Bailey went so far as to print 125 extra copies of the *Philanthropist* and to circulate them among the state's major party papers. Bailey to Birney, October 28, 1838, in Dumond, *Birney Letters,* vol. 1, 475; Goldfarb, "Bailey," 147–48.

36. *Whig Almanac for 1839*, 18–19; *Ohio State Journal*, October 12, 16, 23, 1838; *Painesville Telegraph*, October 18, 1838.

37. *Philanthropist*, October 23, 30, 1838; Bailey to Birney, October 28, 1838, in Dumond, *Birney Letters*, vol. 1, 472–76. Bailey could not claim victory in his own congressional district. The Democratic candidate, Alexander Duncan, whose replies to abolitionist questions were less strong, defeated his Whig rival in a close contest. The candidates' replies are in *Emancipator*, October 21, 1838; and *Niles' National Register*, January 5, 1839. See also *Philanthropist*, September 4, October 2, 23, 1838. Duncan was no friend to abolition, but later he did support the reception of their petitions. *Congressional Globe*, 28th Cong., 1st sess., January 6, 1844, 108–10.

38. *Emancipator*, November 1, 1838; *Liberator*, November 2, 1838.

39. *Ohio State Journal and Register*, October 24, 1838. Party presses that cited abolitionism for the Whig defeat included the *Guernsey Times*, *Belmont Chronicle*, and *Akron Balance;* see the *Philanthropist*, October 23, 1838; and *Ohio State Journal*, November 2, 4, 1838. For the Whig editors' warning, see the Cincinnati *Republican* in the *Philanthropist*, November 6, 1838.

40. The strongest claims were made by Smith, *Liberty and Free Soil*, 30–31. Later historians somewhat carelessly repeated each other, while being vague on the role abolitionism played in the Whig defeat. John Bach McMaster stated laconically, "the extradition of Mahan became a political issue, and Governor Vance was defeated." *A History of the People of the United States, From the Revolution to the Civil War*, vol. 6: *1830–1842* (New York: D. Appleton and Co., 1906), 499–500. Others who followed Smith and McMaster include Weisenburger, *Passing of the Frontier*, 348–51; Muelder, *Knox College*, 331; Harrold, *Bailey*, 28–29. For recent acceptance of this view of the election, see Sewell, *Ballots for Freedom*, 18–19; and Lawrence Friedman, *Gregarious Saints: Self and Community in American Abolitionism, 1830–1870* (Cambridge: Cambridge University Press, 1982), 236. Goldfarb, "Bailey," 147–51, 156, at least admits the results were mixed.

41. *Ohio Statesman*, October 5, 30, 1838. The Democratic party organ had not made the Mahan case an abolition issue and estimated only about a third of the state's voters knew of the Mahan case; some Whig papers avoided mentioning the issue for fear of hurting their chances. The *Philanthropist* did not include factors such as Whig lethargy and banking issues in its excerpts. November 6, 1838; *Ohio State Journal*, October 29, November 2, 1838.

42. *Painesville Telegraph*, November 8, 15, 1838. The New York Journal of Commerce, which was hostile to abolitionism, presented a similar analysis of the Ohio result; it was reprinted in the issue of the *Liberator* (November 2, 1838) that was used by some to document the role of abolitionism in the Whig defeat; see McMaster, *History*, 449–50. The *Ohio State Journal*, October 15, 1839, attributed its defeat in 1839 to the failure of Whig voters to go to the polls. Joshua Giddings later blamed Whig neglect at the polls for the 1838 result; see Giddings to Allen, November 15, 1840, in *Painesville Telegraph*, December 10, 1840.

43. *Philanthropist*, August 13, 1839; *Painesville Telegraph*, January 7, March 19, 1840. For Joshua Giddings's replies, see *Painesville Telegraph*, September 27, 1838; and *Ashtabula Sentinel*, September 29, 1838. For others' replies, see *Philanthropist*, October 23, 1838; *Emancipator*, October 11, 1838. In the Ohio senate Benjamin Wade of Ashtabula had presented abolitionists' petitions, supported repeal of the Black Laws, and opposed the annexation of Texas. Seabury Ford of Geauga supported a house bill to make cities and towns liable for the damage done by (antiabolitionist) mobs. *Ohio State Journal*, January 3, 23, February 8, 11, 26, 1838, January 23, February 13, March 29, 1839; *Painesville Telegraph*, January 5, February 2, 1838.

44. *Painesville Telegraph,* October 4, 1838; and *Painesville Telegraph Extra,* October, 1838; R. W. Taylor to Levi Sutliff, September 19, 1838; Giddings to Milton Sutliff, September 10, 1838, Sutliff Family Papers.

45. *Politician's Register, 1839,* 18–19. Recall that the *Cincinnati Gazette* and the *Journal of Commerce* had also claimed the Whig defeat was not the result of abolitionists' efforts. For details about Ashtabula County's election, see *Ashtabula Sentinel,* February 3, October 20, 1838. I examine the overall election returns in greater detail in "The Ohio Election of 1838: A Study in the Historical Method?" *Ohio History* 95 (Summer–Autumn 1986): 85–100.

46. S. B. McCracken, "The Press of Michigan—A Fifty Year View," *Michigan Pioneer Historical Collections* 18 (1891): 382–87. For examples of Whig editors' efforts at blaming the abolitionists, see the Cincinnati *Republican* in the *Philanthropist,* November 6, 1838; and the *Akron Balance* in the *Ohio State Journal,* November 11, 1838. In 1839 some Whigs again blamed their defeat on abolition voters. *Troy Times* and *Wilmington Whig* in *Ohio State Journal,* October 23, 1839.

47. *Ohio Statesman,* November 20, 30, 1838; January 14, 16, February 25, 27, 1839; *Philanthropist,* January 22, 29, 1839; Weisenburger, *Passing of Frontier,* 381–82; *Ohio State Journal,* January 16, 1839; *Painesville Telegraph,* February 7, 1839. Charles B. Galbreath, "Ohio's Fugitive Slave Law [of 1839]," *Ohio Archaeological and Historical Quarterly* 34 (April 1925): 216–40.

48. *Ohio Statesman,* December 21, 1838; January 14, 1839. There was a great deal of debate as to whether or not Tappan held abolition sympathies. *Ohio State Journal,* December 21, 1838; February 26, 1840; *Painesville Telegraph,* January 10, 1839; *Emancipator,* December 27, 1838. Joshua Giddings felt Tappan deserved abolitionist support. Giddings to Flavel Sutliff, November 25, 1838, Giddings Papers, OHS. See also John Jacob Harstine, "Senatorial Career of Benjamin Tappan" (Master's thesis, Ohio State University, 1939). Ohio Democrats took no chances and extracted a pledge from Tappan that he hold to party discipline on the slavery issue. Benjamin to Lewis Tappan, November 21, 1839, Tappan Papers, OHS. See also Benjamin Wade to Milton Sutliff, December 20, 1838, Milton Sutliff Papers, Western Reserve Historical Society (hereafter cited as WRHS). Tappan's correspondence with his brother Lewis left little doubt that the new senator was no abolitionist, though he would later oppose (at first) Texas annexation.

49. *Congressional Globe,* 25th Cong., 3d sess., appendix, 167–75, 237–41, 354–59; Weisenburger, *Passing of Frontier,* 384–85.

50. *Philanthropist,* February 18, 1840. William Birney, *Birney,* 340, claimed Tappan's election was "a compromise by the Democratic party with the anti-slavery sentiment." Tappan's speech is in *Congressional Globe,* 26th Cong., 1st sess., February 4, 1840, 160; and the *Trumbull County Democrat,* March 10, 1840. Nathan Thomas to William Sullivan, June 6, 1839, Thomas Papers, Bentley Historical Library.

51. In Illinois the *Peoria Register,* September 8, 1838, noted "there are several anti-slavery movements in contemplation in this part of the state" and predicted, "we may have some trouble in getting along with them." Ohio Whigs preferred Harrison before the results of the 1838 campaign were known. Thomas Corwin to Allen Trimble, January 22, 1838, Trimble Family Papers, WRHS; Corwin to [?], February 2, 1838, Corwin to Thomas Ewing, March 3, 1838, Thomas Corwin Papers, Vertical File Material, OHS; *Ohio State Journal,* October 31, 1838.

52. It is often said that questioning failed in Ohio in 1838. This is fully correct only if one

accepts the traditional interpretation of the election results. Actually, most abolitionists did not vote for hostile Democratic candidates. On the Reserve, of course, the tactic worked (with important exceptions); supportive Whig candidates were sent to Congress and Columbus.

Oberlin abolitionists extracted a pledge from their Whig legislative candidate, William Andrews, to work for repeal of the Black Laws. Andrews defeated his Democratic rival only to renege and vote for a more severe fugitive slave law. Ellsworth, "Oberlin," 103–4; *Philanthropist*, February 19, May 14, June 18, August 6, 1839.

53. *Liberator*, November 2, 1838; Benson, *Jacksonian Democracy*, 112; Hendricks, "Liberty in New York," 55.

54. Benjamin Wade to Milton Sutliff, December 8, 1838, Sutliff Papers, WRHS; Wade to Samuel Hendry, December 16, 1838, Joel Blakeslee Papers, WRHS. These letters do not mean abolitionists had indeed deserted the Whigs in October.

55. *Painesville Telegraph*, February 28, March 21, September 12, 1839. The pledge was actually a compromise with the Albany immediatist pledge. The Reserve convention and Giddings's Ashtabula Anti-Slavery Society resolved not to be limited by such a strict test. They would consider "the whole moral principles of candidates as constituting fitness for office." *Ashtabula Sentinel*, July 13, August 3, 1839. Giddings spoke at the Fourth of July celebration in Wayne Township.

56. *Ashtabula Sentinel*, September 28, 1839; *Painesville Telegraph*, February 28, March 21, August 6, September 6, 12, 13, 26, October 1, 1839. Wade was not a member of an abolitionist society, but in the Ohio senate he had supported several causes favored by abolitionists. *Ohio State Journal*, January 3, 23, February 26, 1838; January 23, February 13, March 29, 1839.

57. *Painesville Telegraph*, September 20, 1838; September 26, October 1, 8, 1839; *Ashtabula Sentinel*, September 28, October 5, November 30, 1839.

58. Wade managed a small margin in Geauga, but the Ashtabula Union ticket sealed his defeat. *Ashtabula Sentinel*, October 12, 1839; *Painesville Telegraph*, October 15, 1839. The *Ohio State Journal*, October 23, 1839, attributed Wade's defeat to "the uncompromising hostility of the Whigs of these two counties to political abolition." See also *Philanthropist*, May 26, 1840. (A correlation coefficient demonstrates the strength of association between two variables; it does not establish a causal relationship. The statistical measure ranges from $+1.0$, indicating a perfect positive relationship, to -1.0, a negative one.)

59. *Ashtabula Sentinel*, January 18, 1840; Giddings to Milton Sutliff, February 4, April 12, July 22, 1840, M. Sutliff Papers, WRHS. The opposition to Wade in Ashtabula County was centered in rival Conneaut. Giddings to J. A. Giddings, February 8, 13, 1840, Giddings Papers. Wade's biographer mentions his 1839 defeat only briefly and attributes it partly to conservative Whig opposition to Wade's general "independent course," especially on financial issues. Moreover, he does not develop the role Wade's defeat at the hands of antiabolitionists played in the Ohio Republican senator's subsequent career. Hans L. Trefousse, *Benjamin Franklin Wade: Radical Republican from Ohio* (New York: Twayne Publishers, 1963), 41. I examine the implications of Wade's defeat more closely in "Benjamin Wade's Strange Defeat," *Ohio History* 97 (Summer-Autumn 1988): 122–32.

60. Kooker, "Antislavery in Michigan," 293–301; *Emancipator*, November 14, 1839.

61. *Philanthropist*, January 29, 1839. Dumond, *Antislavery*, 282, claimed the Liberty party "came out of the West," but he was referring to western New York. As discussed in the next chapter, independent abolition nominations mostly received opposition in Ohio and apathy elsewhere in the Northwest.

CHAPTER 3

1. Beecher, *Autobiography*, 345. For western New York, see Cross, *Burned-Over District*. Henry B. Stanton recalled that "for many years an influence on behalf of the slave radiated from the central counties of New York which was felt beyond the borders of the state." *Random Recollections*, (New York: Harper & Brothers, 1887), 65. In 1840 the abolition party was known by several names including the Friends of Liberty (or Constitutional Liberty), the Human Rights party, and even the April Fool party (after the Albany convention held on April 1, 1840). The name Liberty party was adopted in 1841 apparently at the suggestion of Gerrit Smith. Whig and Garrisonian opponents preferred the less flattering third party.

2. Historical opinion on the causes of the society's split has varied widely. Barnes and Dumond blamed Garrison's ambition and radical views. Aileen S. Kraditor argues instead that anti-Garrisonians deliberately split the society to rid themselves of Garrison. *Means and Ends in American Abolitionism: Garrison and His Critics on Strategy and Tactics, 1834–1850* (New York: Pantheon Books, 1967). Lewis Perry and Ronald G. Walters stress the similarities between the two groups. Perry, *Radical Abolitionism: Anarchy and the Government of God in Antislavery Thought* (Ithaca, N.Y.: Cornell University Press, 1973); Walters, *The Antislavery Appeal: American Abolitionism After 1830* (Baltimore: Johns Hopkins University Press, 1976). Recent work indicates more than two opposing factions might have been at work. Friedman, *Gregarious Saints;* and Richard O. Curry and Lawrence B. Goodheart, eds., "The Complexities of Factionalism: Letters of Elizur Wright, Jr., on the Abolitionist Schism, 1837–1840," *Civil War History* 29 (September 1983): 245–59. However, Curry and Goodheart's view of a political third faction "increasingly alienated from institutionalized religion" has less relevance for northwestern abolitionism.

Northwesterners took little part in the division of the national society. The "woman question" was less controversial to the west, and few northwestern abolitionists avoided voting as other Garrisonians did. Bailey avoided discussing "the dissensions among our Eastern friends" in the *Philanthropist*. Under his leadership the Ohio Anti-Slavery Society followed a neutral course, breaking with the old society but remaining independent of the new rival organization as well. *Philanthropist*, October 29, 1839; June 30, 1840; Bailey to Birney, October 14, 1837, in Dumond, *Birney Letters*, vol. 1, 428; "Fifth Anniversary of the Ohio State Anti-Slavery Society," in *Philanthropist*, June 9, 1840.

Lewis Tappan announced his support for the Liberty party in 1843. *Western Citizen*, November 9, 1843; Lewis Tappan, *The Life of Arthur Tappan* (New York: Hurd and Houghton, 1870), 301–7; Bertram Wyatt-Brown, *Lewis Tappan and the Evangelical War Against Slavery* (Cleveland: Case Western Reserve University Press, 1969), 198–200. For Weld and the Liberty party, see Weld to Lewis Tappan, December 14, 1841, in Barnes and Dumond, *Weld Letters*, vol. 1, 879–82; Weld to Birney, January 22, May 23, 1842, in Dumond, *Birney Letters*, vol. 2, 662–63, 692–94.

3. Sewell, *Ballots for Freedom*, 54–55. Liberty supporters were later anxious to dispel the appearance that the party had grown from the split in abolitionist ranks. The *Emancipator* insisted the party "never was involved in any portion of that controversy." *Western Citizen*, November 9, 1843. Instead, Holley's role as founder was emphasized, since he died soon after the party was launched. *Emancipator*, February 24, 1847. Theodore Foster also paid homage to Holley but regretted that the formation of the party weakened abolitionists by separating them from "their old friends who still adhered to the other parties" and those of the "old

organization." "Liberty Party," Theodore Foster Papers, Bentley Historical Library (hereafter cited as BHL).

Congressional Globe, 25th Cong. 3d sess., appendix, 354–59; Sewell, *Ballots for Freedom,* 48–49, 55. James Birney felt betrayed by John Quincy Adams's refusal to endorse abolition in the federal district. Joshua Leavitt was outraged by the support antislavery Whigs gave the election of Virginian Robert M. T. Hunter to Speaker of the House. Birney, *Birney,* 343–44, 347; McPherson, "Leavitt and the Gag Rule," 181–82; Bailey to Giddings, February 7, 1839, in Grace J. Clark, "A Letter of Dr. Gam. Bailey to Josh. R. Giddings," *Indiana Magazine of History* 26 (March 1930): 45. Whig papers reprinted Clay's speech with favorable comments. *Painesville Telegraph,* February 21, 1839; *Ohio State Journal,* February 22, 1839. For rebukes of Clay by two local Ohio antislavery societies, see *Philanthropists,* April 16, July 30, 1839.

4. *Emancipator,* April 9, 1840. Another Reserve abolitionist sent a letter advising against the expediency of independent nominations. The proceedings and list of delegates to the Cleveland convention are in *Emancipator,* November 14, 1839. The Albany proceedings are in *Philanthropist,* May 5, 1840. Sewell, *Ballots for Freedom,* 51–71, covers the conventions in greater detail. For Gerrit Smith on abolitionists' political duties, see *Philanthropist,* November 19, 1839. For LeMoyne's refusal and Birney's reluctance and then acceptance, see Dumond, *Birney Letters,* vol. 1, 511–19, 562–74.

5. Richard Carwardine, "Evangelicals, Whigs and the Election of William Henry Harrison" *Journal of American Studies* 17 (April 1983): 47–75.

6. Bailey to Birney, April 18, 1840; November 28, 1839, in Dumond, *Birney Letters,* vol. 1, 556–57, 509–10; *Philanthropist,* April 30, 1839; April 21, 1840. Birney received similar advice from John G. Whittier. Whittier to Birney, April 16, 1840, in Dumond, *Birney Letters,* vol. 1, 555.

7. The *Painesville Telegraph,* May 14, 1840, for example, cited Bailey's opposition to the Albany nominations as part of its effort to dissuade Reserve abolitionists from voting the third party ticket.

8. *Philanthropist,* March 27, 1838; November 19, 26, 1839; June 9, 1840.

9. *Philanthropist,* December 11, 1838; June 11, October 8, November 19, 1839. Bailey believed the Geauga independent ticket was "not expedient," but he urged abolitionists to support Wade for the Ohio senate. For questioning in 1839, see April 23, August 6, July 23, September 3, October 30, November 12, 26, 1839. Bailey advised antislavery voters to withhold their votes if no suitable candidates were presented. For Lorain, see *Oberlin Evangelist,* July 31, September 11, November 6, 1839. For Bailey's response to Leavitt, see Bailey to Birney, February 3, 1840, in Dumond, *Letters,* vol. 1, 524.

10. *Philanthropist,* November 19, 1839; *Emancipator,* November 14, 1839.

11. *Philanthropist,* December 17, 31, 1839; April 21, May 19, June 9, 1840.

12. For a discussion of the pitfalls of political organization, see the "Massachusetts Address" in the *Emancipator,* August 23, 1838. Bailey attempted to keep Garrisonians within the ranks of the Ohio Anti-Slavery Society, but eventually abolitionists in Stark, Clinton, and Columbiana counties organized a separate body auxiliary to Garrison's national society. Brooke to Bailey, January 17, 1842, in *Philanthropist,* March 16, 1842; Abram Brooke to Bailey, December 19, 1842, in *Philanthropist,* January 4, 1843. See also June 22, July 9, August 27, December 14, 1842; C. B. Galbreath, "Anti-Slavery Movement in Columbiana County," *Ohio Archaeological and Historical Society Publications* 30 (1921): 355–95; Cecilia Rosenblum Gross, "Antislavery in Stark County, Ohio, 1831–1856" (Master's thesis, Uni-

versity of Akron, 1962). See also Douglas A. Gamble, "Moral Suasion in the West: Garrisonian Abolitionism, 1831–1861" (Ph.D. diss., Ohio State University, 1973); Gamble, "Garrisonian Abolitionists in the West: Some Suggestions for Study," *Civil War History* 23 (March 1977): 52–68; Gamble, "Joshua Giddings and the Ohio Abolitionists: A Study in Radical Politics," *Ohio History* 88 (Winter 1979): 37–56. Harrold, *Bailey*, 30–31, discusses Bailey's reasons for initially opposing third party organization.

13. *Philanthropist*, November 10, 19, 1839; May 26, 1840; *Emancipator*, June 12, 1840.

14. *Philanthropist*, November 19, December 10, 1839; Harrold, "Bailey," 49; *Emancipator*, May 17, 1838; Sewell, *Ballots for Freedom*, 50–51.

15. Bailey to Birney, May 24, 1838, in Dumond, *Birney Letters*, vol. 1, 457; *Philanthropist*, May 22, 1838. In disputing Stewart's argument, Bailey ironically verged very close to Garrison's view of the Constitution and even the opinion Chief Justice Taney would later present in the *Dred Scott* case. (For example, Bailey insisted black slaves were "in no proper sense parties to the compact" and that the word *persons* did not refer to slaves.)

16. *Philanthropist*, June 12, 1838; Bailey to Birney, June 28, 1838, in Dumond, *Birney Letters*, vol. 1, 463; *Emancipator*, October 4, 1838; *Genius of Liberty*, May 22, 29, July 3, 1841; Miller, "Antislavery in Indiana," 67.

17. *Philanthropist*, December 31, April 30, 1839; July 7, September 8, 1840. For a fuller discussion of Bailey's views, see Stanley Harrold's various works.

18. *Philanthropist*, June 11, 1839. Chase's views have received the bulk of scholarly attention. See, for example, Foner, *Free Soil;* and William M. Wiecek, *The Sources of Antislavery Constitutionalism in America, 1760–1848* (Ithaca: Cornell University Press, 1977). But see also Stanley C. Harrold, Jr., "Forging an Antislavery Instrument: Gamaliel Bailey and the Foundation of the Ohio Liberty Party," *Old Northwest* 2 (Spring 1976): 371–87.

19. *Detroit Free Press*, April 8, 1840; *Emancipator*, February 20, August 6, October 1, 15, 1840; Arthur L. Porter to Seymour Treadwell, April 23, 1840, Treadwell Family Papers, BHL; Kooker, "Antislavery in Michigan," 314; *Philanthropist*, May 26, June 6, 30, 1840; Wade to Bailey, September 14, 1840, in *Philanthropist*, October 13, 1840; King to Bailey, April 20, 1840, in *Philanthropist*, May 5, 1840; Rankin to Thomas, July 31, 1840, and Thomas to Professor J. W. Scott, May 13, July 11, 1840, in Thomas, *Correspondence of Thomas*, 12–13, 17–18. "Address of the Western Reserve Anti-Slavery Convention to the Citizens of the Western Reserve on the Subject of Political Action," in *Painesville Telegraph*, September 26, 1839, and *Philanthropist*, November 19, 1839.

20. *Philanthropist*, August 13, 1839. Henry B. Stanton remarked that "49/50ths of our friends" are Whigs, and "they would wade to their armpits in molten lava to drive Van Buren from power." He also echoed Bailey by reporting that "19/20ths" of Massachusetts abolitionists were "decidedly hostile" to independent nominations. Stanton to Birney, March 21, 1840, in Dumond, *Birney Letters*, vol. 1, 541.

21. Rankin to Bailey, July 16, 1840, in *Philanthropist*, August 4, 1840; June 30, 1840; Rankin to Thomas, July 31, 1840, in Thomas, *Correspondence of Thomas*, 18–19. The Reverend Jonathan Blanchard advanced similar arguments. *Philanthropist*, June 16, 1840; *Emancipator*, July 2, 1840. Whig editors could cite the opposition of prominent abolitionists such as Rankin and Blanchard to deter antislavery defections. *Painesville Telegraph*, July 23, September 3, 1840.

22. *Philanthropist*, March 13, 1838; December 31, 1839; January 28, February 4, March 3, 24, 31, 1840; Bailey to Birney, February 21, March 3, 30, 1840, in Dumond, *Birney Letters*, vol. 1, 531, 536–38, 545–46. Privately, Bailey had received what he considered assurances

from Harrison that he would not oppose abolition in the District of Columbia. Sewell, *Ballots for Freedom,* 64. Bailey might also have initially favored Harrison in recognition of his popularity in Ohio. Bailey to Gerrit Smith, July 21, 1840, quoted in Goldfarb, "Bailey," 201–2.

23. "Report of the Executive Committee of the Ohio State Anti-Slavery Society for 1839–1840," in *Philanthropist,* June 9, 1840. See, for example, the position of the executive committee of the Fayette County Anti-Slavery Society, in *Philanthropist,* July 7, 1840. For the more pragmatic objections of a Zanesville antislavery Whig, see Jonathan Thomas to Nathan Thomas, October 22, 1840, Thomas Papers, BHL.

As part of their effort to pin the abolitionist label on Harrison, Democrats prepared a forgery purporting to show that leading abolitionists were shifting their support from Birney to Harrison. *Ashtabula Sentinel,* November 7, 1840. Amazingly, the Geauga Whig press did not expose the document as a forgery (as the *Sentinel* did), perhaps because it seemed to prove the Whig claim that third party votes "only insured the election of Van Buren." *Geauga Freeman,* November 7, 1840.

24. *Painesville Telegraph,* September 6, 1838; August 15, 1839; September 3, November 12, October 8, 15, 1840; *Ashtabula Sentinel,* January 12, 1838; June 15, 1839; March 14, April 18, July 18, August 22, September 3, 19, 1840; January 9, 1841; *Philanthropist,* July 21, 1840; *Emancipator,* August 6, 1840. Giddings to Lura Maria Giddings, December 12, 1839; Giddings to [?], December 28, 1839; Giddings to Grotius Reed Giddings, June 17, 1840; Benjamin Wade to Giddings, May 3, June 15, 1840, Giddings Papers, OHS; Oren Follett to Thurlow Weed, September 18, 1840, in L. Belle Hamlin, ed., "Selections from the Follett Papers," *Quarterly Publication of the Historical and Philosophical Society of Ohio* 9 (January–April 1914): 22–24; Albert G. Riddle, "B. F. Wade, the Politician—1840," *Magazine of Western History* 3 (April 1886): 593–94. For Corwin and Ewing's reception at Unionville, see *Painesville Telegraph,* August 13, 27, 1840. See also L. D. Butts to Bailey, November 18, 1840, in *Philanthropist,* December 9, 1840.

25. Fenn to Birney, February 17, 1840, in Dumond, *Birney Letters,* vol. 1, 527–31; *Liberty Herald,* February 8, 1844; *Ashtabula Sentinel,* February 29, March 14, April 14, July 18, September 3, 19, 1840; Smith to Bailey, February 21, 1840, in *Philanthropist,* March 10, 1840.

26. *Ashtabula Sentinel,* May 9, October 17, 1840; February 6, May 8, May 29, June 19, September 18, September 25, October 2, 1841; *Philanthropist,* May 26, 1840; George Hezlep to Ephraim Brown, August 18, 1840, Brown Papers, WRHS; *Cincinnati Gazette,* September 22, 1840; John Curtis to *Philanthropist,* October 28, 1840; *Painesville Telegraph,* October 8, 1840. Well into 1841 the third party encountered similar resistance within the Lake County Anti-Slavery Society. *Painesville Telegraph,* January 14, February 11, May 5, 1841.

27. *Philanthropist,* April 14, August 11, 1840; Burgess to Bailey, June 13, 1840, in *Philanthropist,* June 30, 1840; Wattles to Bailey, April 16 and July 13, 1840, in *Philanthropist,* May 26, August 18, 1840.

28. Smith to Weld, July 11, 1840, in Barnes and Dumond, *Weld Letters,* vol. 1, 849–50; Rankin to Thomas, July 31, 1840, in Thomas, *Correspondence of Thomas,* 18–19; *Philanthropist,* June 30, 1840. For Gilliland, see the Hamilton convention in *Philanthropist,* September 8, 1840, and Gilliland to Bailey, September 29, 1840, in *Philanthropist,* October 20, 1840. For Blanchard, see *Emancipator,* July 2, 1840; *Philanthropist,* June 16, 1840; Muelder, *Knox College,* 227–30. Blanchard regretted his support for Harrison and turned to the third party by 1841; Rankin did not immediately change his mind. *Philanthropist,* December 9, 1840. For a view opposite to Rankin, see Reverend James Shaw to Rankin, in *Philanthropist,* October 20, 1840. *Peoria Register,* July 17, 1840; *Genius of Liberty,* February 27, 1841; *Phi-*

lanthropist, June 30, 1840; Muelder, *Knox College*, 162; Smith to Treadwell, March 23, 1840, Treadwell Papers, BHL; Foster, "Antislavery History," Foster Papers, BHL.

29. *Philanthropist*, September 8, 1840. Thomas had determined to withhold his vote instead. Thomas to Scott, July 11, 1840, in Thomas, *Correspondence of Thomas*, 17–18. See also Thomas to Scott, May 13, 1840, 12–13. He favored the 1841 Columbus convention's resolve to adopt prior independent nominations. *Philanthropist*, February 3, 1841.

30. Rankin to Thomas, July 31, 1840, in Thomas, *Correspondence of Thomas*, 18–19; *Philanthropist*, June 16, 1840.

31. *Oberlin Evangelist*, July 31, September 11, November 6, 1839; July 29, September 23, 1840; *Signal of Liberty*, December 19, 1842; *Cincinnati Observer*, August 13, 1840. In September the Lorain County Anti-Slavery Society, meeting during Oberlin's commencement, pledged not to support any presidential candidate who was not in favor of immediate abolition in the District of Columbia and in the territories, nor would they vote for candidates for the state legislature who did not favor the repeal of all laws "founded on a distinction of color." See also Wilbur Greeley Burroughs, "Oberlin's Part in the Slavery Conflict," *Ohio Archaeological and Historical Society Publications* 20 (April–July 1911): 278–80; Fairchild, *Oberlin*, 109; Ellsworth, "Oberlin," 107–10.

32. *Philanthropist*, May 19, September 8, 1840; January 6, 13, 1841.

33. Bretz, "The Economic Background of the Liberty Party," does not appreciate the context of these political and economic arguments. Leavitt to Birney, October 1, 1840, in Dumond, *Birney Letters*, vol. 2, 603–4; Bailey to Bayle, January 11, 1841, in Thomas, *Correspondence of Thomas*, 32; B. F. Hoffman in the *Liberty Herald*, March 14, 1844. See also Leavitt to Birney, May 19, 1840, 574–75. For the convention, see *Philanthropist*, September 8, 1840, and for Leavitt's "Financial Power of Slavery," *Emancipator*, October 8, 22, 1840. William Birney credited Leavitt's presence at Hamilton as "the efficient cause of the success of the 'third party' men." Birney to Birney, in Dumond, *Birney Letters*, vol. 2, 600.

34. Chase expressed disgust with party strife and the servility of both parties shortly after his election to the Cincinnati city council and before he was actually proscribed by the Whig party. Chase to Cleveland, August 29, 1840, Chase Papers, Historical Society of Pennsylvania (hereafter cited as HSP). Ronald Formisano has been an able advocate of the appeal of antipartyism among Whigs and Liberty voters. *Mass Political Parties*, 71–80. Several qualifications to this view are necessary. First, Formisano focused on Michigan where Whigs were usually in the minority. Moreover, the chief obstacle to third party organization in the Northwest was the *strength* of party loyalties among antislavery Whigs. Whig strongholds could hardly be considered sources of antipartyism. Even after the formation of the Liberty party the Whigs rolled up huge majorities on the Reserve. As the preceding chapters indicate, political abolitionists first made every effort to work within the party structure and even hesitated to form the Liberty party long after it was clear the parties would not welcome them nor their antislavery opinions. The emphasis third party members placed on principles over political success partly justified their continued support for a cause that had so little chance of winning popular approval. See also Kraut, "Liberty Party in Antebellum Political Culture."

35. *Philanthropist*, April 21, May 12, June 30, 1840. The Democratic *Detroit Free Press*, July 15, 1840, gave full play to Bailey's conversion. Harrold, *Bailey*, 35, suggests that the editor had dropped his most serious objections to independent nominations as early as May.

36. *Philanthropist*, December 12, 17, 1839; March 3, 24, June 30, July 14, 21, August 11, 1840. When abolitionists faced two unsuitable candidates Bailey had long advocated: "Let them stay at home. No harm can come from this—they violate no duty." For other early supporters to third party action, see, April 28, May 12, 1840.

37. Michael Speer, ed., "Autobiography of Adam Lowry Rankin," *Ohio History* 79 (Winter 1970): 40–42. See also Burgess to Bailey, September 8, 1840, in *Philanthropist,* October 20, 1840. "Proceedings of the State Convention of Abolitionists at Hamilton, September 1, 1840," in *Philanthropist,* September 8, 1840. See also the minority "Protest" and September 22, 1840.

38. The resistance abolition Whigs gave independent nominations meant that an unusually large proportion of third party support in 1840 came from antislavery Democrats, who had reason to protest the repudiation of Morris and the "servility" of Van Buren Democrats. Led by Eli Nichols, some Belmont County abolitionists withdrew from the county society dominated by Whigs and formed a new one more friendly to independent political action. *Philanthropist,* April 14, August 18, 1840; Nichols to Bailey, May 6, 1840, and June 17, 1840, in *Philanthropist,* May 19, 1840, and June 30, 1840; Morris to Eells, January 30, 1840, in *Philanthropist,* August 11, 1840. See also November 25, 1840.

39. Paine to Bailey, August 7, 1840, in *Philanthropist,* August 18, 1840; Atkins to Bailey, September 17, 1840, in *Philanthropist,* October 20, 1840; Edward Wade to Bailey, September 14, 1840, in *Philanthropist,* October 13, 1840. Wade was married to Atkins's daughter. Because he was a leading abolitionist and prominent citizen, General Paine's conversion from Harrison to Birney was of considerable importance in Painesville society and politics. *Painesville Telegraph,* January 14, March 10, April 9, 16, June 18, 25, August 20, 1840. For Belmont County, see *Philanthropist,* August 18, October 13, 20, 28, 1840. For Jefferson County, see David Thomas to Nathan Thomas, December 2, 1840, Nathan Thomas Papers, BHL.

40. *Politician's Register, 1841,* 20–21; L. D. Butts to Bailey, November 18, 1840, in *Philanthropist,* December 9, 1840. Bailey claimed there were fifteen thousand abolition votes in Ohio and hoped the Birney ticket would attract at least five thousand of these. *Philanthropist,* September 8, 15, 1840.

41. Nathan Thomas to William Sullivan, June 6, 1839, Thomas Papers. For early third party efforts in Indiana, see Birney to Leavitt, June 11, 1839, in *Emancipator,* June 20, 1839; (also in Dumond, *Birney Letters,* vol. 1, 492–93); *Emancipator,* August 6, 1840; *Philanthropist,* May 26, July 16, September 8, 15, October 13, 20, 1840; Miller, "Antislavery in Indiana," 78–80; Kooker, "Antislavery in Michigan," 314; Smith to Treadwell, June 30, 1840, Treadwell Papers, BHL; *Politicians' Register, 1841,* 29. Floyd B. Streeter, *Political Parties in Michigan, 1837–1860* (Lansing: Michigan Historical Collections, 1918), 60, gives a slightly different figure.

42. Soon after Lundy's death, in August 1839, the *Genius of Universal Emancipation* ceased publication, and the *Genius of Liberty* did not appear until December 1840. *Genius of Universal Emancipation,* February 26, March 8, 29, June 28, July 5, 12, August 23, September 13, 1839; *Genius of Liberty,* December 19, 1840; January 23, 1841; *Emancipator,* January 25, 1838. See also Calvin DeWolf to James DeWolf, November 7, 1838, DeWolf Papers, Chicago Historical Society; and Eastman, "History of Liberty in Illinois," 138. *Peoria Register,* July 17, 1840; *Emancipator,* August 6, 1840. Smith called this the first third party ticket in the Northwest. *Liberty and Free Soil,* 42–43. Zebina Eastman recalled the 1840 Illinois ticket was formed in Farmington, Fulton County, "by those who had stood by Lovejoy at his death." "History of the Anti-Slavery Agitation, and the Growth of the Liberty and Republican Parties in the State of Illinois," in Rufus Blanchard, ed., *Discovery and Conquests of the Northwest, with the History of Chicago* (Chicago: R. Blanchard and Co., 1900), 138. Members of the Galesburg colony earned the criticism of other abolitionists for their support of the "hard cider" ticket that included a slaveholder. *Genius of Liberty,* February 27, 1841; Muelder, *Knox College,* 143, 157–60, 162. By 1842 Gale became a Liberty supporter and Galesburg a

leading source of Liberty strength. *Peoria Register,* June 17, 1842. Princeton was also notable as a Yankee Congregationalist settlement. Hermann Muelder, "Congregationalists and the Civil War," in *A History of Illinois Congregational and Christian Churches,* Matthew Spinka, ed. (Chicago: Congregational and Christian Conference of Illinois, 1944), 152–53. Sam Willard to Parents, October 31, 1840. Samuel Willard Papers, Illinois State Historical Library; *Politician's Register, 1841,* 28; Smith, *Liberty and Free Soil,* 46–47. Adams County cast forty-two Birney votes, Will sixteen, and Bureau, Knox, and Putnam counties thirteen each. *Genius of Liberty,* December 19, 1840.

43. *Philanthropist,* October 28, November 4, 1840.

44. Birney, *Birney,* 85; Foster, "Antislavery History," Foster Papers, BHL; Bailey to Birney, November 16, 1842, in Dumond, *Birney Letters,* vol. 2, 710; see also *Philanthropist,* January 29, July 23, 1839, January 28, June 9, 1840. Ellsworth, "Oberlin," 51–99. Besides the "fanaticism, hypocrisy, and immorality" that Democrats claimed flourished at Oberlin, the overwhelming Whig sentiment of the colony might have been equally odious to Democrats. *Ohio Statesman,* October 4, 1837. The *Statesman* credited charges contained in a scurrilous anti-Oberlin tract, *Oberlin Unmasked,* written by an embittered former student, Delazon Smith.

45. For a fuller discussion, see my "The Anti-Abolitionist Campaign of 1840," *Civil War History* 32 (December 1986): 325–39. Robert Gunderson mentions abolition briefly in *The Log-Cabin Campaign* (Lexington: University of Kentucky Press, 1957), 72, 224–26. William J. Cooper, Jr., treats slavery and abolition in 1840 in connection with Southern politics. *The South and the Politics of Slavery, 1828–1856* (Baton Rouge: Louisiana State University Press, 1978), 119–48. Daniel Walker Howe, *The Political Culture of the American Whigs* (Chicago: University of Chicago Press, 1979), 78, 90, stresses how Whigs promoted their economic program in 1840. The *Philanthropist,* October 13, 1840, bewailed the campaign of 1840 but blamed both parties for failing to stand for "great fundamental principles." For other examples of contemporary opinion, see Mansfield, *Personal Memories,* 295; Orth to Colfax, August 16, 1845, in Schauinger, "Orth Letters," 367. Julian, *Political Recollections,* 22–29, 64–67, admitted that under the "clatter and nonsense" there was a real issue (slavery), but that it went "unrecognized by both parties." William O. Lynch, "Anti-Slavery Tendencies of the Democratic Party in the Northwest, 1848–1850," *Mississippi Valley Historical Review* 11 (December 1924): 319–31 (hereafter cited as *MVHR*); Henry Clyde Hubbart, " 'Pro-Southern' Influences in the Free West, 1840–1865," *MVHR* 20 (June 1933): 45–62. Weisenburger, *Passing of the Frontier,* 455, conceded abolition was weak among Democrats but insisted the party was sincerely antislavery. See also Edgar Allan Holt, *Party Politics in Ohio, 1840–1850* (Columbus: F. J. Heer Printing Co., 1931). Harold M. Hyman and William M. Wiecek, *Equal Justice Under Law: Constitutional Development, 1835–1875* (New York: Harper & Row, 1982), 9; Leonard L. Richards, "The Jacksonians and Slavery," in Perry and Fellman, *Antislavery Reconsidered,* 99–118; Gerald L. Henig, "The Jacksonian Attitude Toward Abolitionism in the 1830's," *Tennessee Historical Quarterly* 28 (Spring 1969): 42–56; John M. McFaul, "Expediency vs. Morality, Jacksonian Politics and Slavery," *Journal of American History* 57 (June 1975): 24–39.

46. *Trumbull County Democrat,* January 21, April 28, June 30, October 9, 1840; Field, *Race in New York,* 61. Abolitionists were often the same "pietists" or "fanatics" who sought to ban taverns along with the sin of slaveholding. Salmon Chase, Samuel Lewis, and other Liberty advocates joined in the effort to suppress coffeehouses in Cincinnati. *Philanthropist,* March 10, 1841; *Cincinnati Observer,* January 7, 1841; *Watchman of the Valley,* April 1, 15,

1841. Throughout the 1840s competition for foreign-born support raged in the pages of the Democratic *Ohio Statesman* and the Whig *Ohio State Journal.* In Michigan and Illinois party differences over the suffrage of the naturalized citizen were just as severe. *Peoria Register,* December 18, 1840; Formisano, "Party Formation in Michigan."

47. *Trumbull County Democrat,* January 21, 1840; "Democratic State Address," in January 28, 1840, issue. The *Democrat,* April 28, September 8, 1840, continued to harp on this campaign theme. A Portage County Democratic meeting in February echoed the state resolutions against the abolitionists and the intermingling of the white and black races.

48. "Democratic State Address," in *Trumbull County Democrat,* January 28, 1840. For the national party, see "Democratic Address of 1840," in *Proceedings of the National Democratic Convention, Held in the City of Baltimore on the 5th of May, 1840* (Baltimore: Office of the *Republican,* 1840). Also published in *Ohio Statesman,* May 12, 1840. For Illinois, see the letter and circular from S. Dewitt Bloodgood, published in *Old Hickory* and *Sangamo Journal,* in Robert W. Johannsen, ed., *The Letters of Stephen A. Douglas* (Urbana: University of Illinois Press, 1961), 74–80. "To the People of Illinois," June 4, 1840, was published in the *Illinois State Register* on June 12 and is in Johannsen, *Douglas Letters,* 82–96. For antiabolitionism in Michigan, see *Detroit Free Press,* May 8, June 17, July 15, October 14, 1840.

49. *Ohio Statesman,* February 25, 27, March 8, 13, 29, 1839, April 1, 3, 1840; Davis, "Social and Economic Basis of Ohio Whig Party," 266–68.

50. *Ohio Statesman,* May 12, June 24, 30, 1840. The *Painesville Telegraph,* July 30, 1840, denied six blacks were at Ft. Meigs with *Lake County* on their hats, as there were "scarcely six negroes in Lake County," and of the three it knew, only a man and a boy were at the Whig event. (The black man involved reported someone gave him the Lake County badge and told him to wear it.)

51. *Ohio Statesman,* October 16, 1840. Democratic meetings persisted in their charge that "the principles of Federal Whiggery and Abolitionism, are in perfect keeping with each other." *Trumbull County Democrat,* June 9, 1840; see also *Philanthropist,* September 22, 1841, March 16, 1842. *Cincinnati Gazette,* October 28, 1840. See above for the reactions of the *Ashtabula Sentinel* and the *Geauga Freeman.* See also *Painesville Telegraph,* November 19, December 3, 1840.

52. For the Whig dilemma, see James Brewer Stewart, "Abolitionists, Insurgents, and Third Parties; Sectionalism and Partisan Politics in Northern Whiggery, 1836–1844," in Alan M. Kraut, ed., *Crusaders and Compromisers: Essays on the Relationship of the Antislavery Struggle to the Antebellum Party System* (Westport, Ct.: Greenwood Press, 1983), 25–44.

53. *Cincinnati Gazette,* October 7, 1839, September 16, 1840; *Philanthropist,* August 18, 1840. In some cases there was a germ of truth in Whig charges. In 1840, for example, a prominent Reserve abolitionist, Uri Seeley, accepted nomination on a ticket dominated by Democrats, dubbed by Whigs the "Suc-co-tash" ticket. *Painesville Telegraph,* April 2, 1840. V. W. Smith to Follett, July 22, 1843, in Hamlin, "Follett Letters," vol. 5, 6–8. For similar efforts to portray Grangers and Populists as "political bummers" and "chronic office seekers" who sought to harm the Republican party to aid "a defunct Democratic party," see Herbert S. Schell, "The Grange in Dakota Territory," *Agricultural History* 10 (January 1936): 77–78; and Terrence J. Lindell, "South Dakota Populism" (Master's thesis, University of Nebraska, Lincoln, 1982), 70–74. *Ohio State Journal,* June 24, August 19, October 21, 1840. *Peoria Register,* July 17, April 24, 1840; *Detroit Advertiser,* September 11, 12, 1840.

54. *Painesville Telegraph,* October 1, 29, November 5, 1840. The *Telegraph* nonetheless repeated similar charges. In 1840 third party abolitionists generally supported Whig candi-

dates in local and state contests. The *Philanthropist,* December 30, 1840, boasted that Whig congressional candidates Giddings and Andrews received the highest vote of any in the state.

55. *Ohio State Journal,* October 30, 1835, May 22, 1844; Follett to Thurlow Weed, September 18, 1840, in Hamlin, "Follett Letters," 22–24; *Painesville Telegraph,* August 13, 27, 1840; Wade to Giddings, May 3, June 15, September 10, October 8, 1840, Giddings Papers, OHS; Giddings to Milton Sutliff, Sutliff Papers, OHS; Riddle, "Wade and 1840," 593–94. The *Journal* did not take a philosophical view of the growth of abolitionism among the Whigs of the northern counties. From the beginning (October 23, 1839) it recognized abolition as "that rock upon which it is greatly to be feared the Whig party is destined to be shipwrecked." Democrats sought to turn the nomination of antislavery candidates against the Whigs as evidence of their truckling to abolition. *Trumbull County Democrat,* September 8, 1840. One Whig candidate was said to have helped "more than *Three Hundred* negro slaves" escape to Canada. The *Painesville Telegraph,* November 5, 1840, challenged the nation to match the counties of Ashtabula, Lake, Geauga, and Cuyahoga, whose seventy townships all returned Harrison majorities.

56. *Ohio State Journal,* January 18, 29, 1840; *Painesville Telegraph,* February 11, 1840. For Harrison's slavery-related actions, see Dorothy Burne Goebel, *William Henry Harrison: A Political Biography* (Indianapolis: Indiana Library and Historical Department, 1926), 74–78, 222–23, 318, 357–62. This overlooked work mentions slavery's role in the 1840 campaign.

57. James D. Richardson, comp., *A Compilation of the Messages and Papers of the Presidents,* vol. 4 (New York: Bureau of National Literature, 1897), 1868–72. According to Julian, *Political Recollections,* 25, Harrison had planned a more extreme denunciation of the abolitionists, but Clay persuaded him to modify the final address. New York abolition Whig Seth Gates, however, recalled during the 1844 campaign "how we fought to keep Harrison from blowing up abolition in his Inaugural & Mr. Clay would not help an atom." Gates to Giddings, October 2, December 29, 1844, Giddings Papers, OHS. Chase, who was then still a Whig, also advised Harrison to "make no allusions to the subject of slavery." Chase Diary, February 13, April, 8, 9, 1841, Chase Papers, LC; Chase to Harrison, February 13, 1841, quoted in Gruber, "Chase," 91–92. Reserve Whig papers nonetheless approved the general's speech and continued to defend him from third party critics. *Painesville Telegraph,* March 17, 1841; *Ashtabula Sentinel,* March 20, 1841.

58. *Philanthropist,* December 16, 1840; January 13, 1841. The call for the convention was meant to include abolitionists of all parties and not just third party advocates. *Painesville Telegraph,* December 12, 1840.

59. *Philanthropist,* December 16, 1840; January 27, February 3, March 3, June 9, October 20, November 3, December 8, 1841. Bailey insisted that a distinction remain between antislavery societies and the political actions of abolitionists. Thus, at the June meeting of the Ohio Anti-Slavery Society the habit was begun of holding separate antislavery and Liberty party conventions. Often this was a rather thin distinction; typically, antislavery societies merely dissolved and reformed again, this time as a Liberty convention.

60. William G. W. Lewis, *Biography of Samuel Lewis: First Superintendent of Common Schools for the State of Ohio* (Cincinnati: R. P. Thompson, Printer, 1857), 285–86. For a campaign sketch of Lewis, see *Free Labor Advocate,* May 20, 1846.

61. Frederick J. Blue, "From Right to Left: The Political Conversion of Salmon P. Chase" (Paper delivered at Missouri Valley History Conference, Omaha, Nebraska, March 1984); see also William E. Baringer, "The Politics of Abolition: Salmon P. Chase in Cincinnati," *Cincinnati Historical Society Bulletin* 29 (Summer 1971): 79–99; and Fred Blue's new biography,

Salmon P. Chase: A Life in Politics (Kent, Ohio: Kent State University Press, 1987); Chase Diary, July 17, 1840, Chase Papers, LC; Chase to Charles Dexter Cleveland, August 29, 1840, Chase Papers, HSP.

62. Chase Diary, January 4, 5, February 13, 1841, Chase Papers, LC; *Philanthropist*, January 13, 1841; *Genius of Liberty*, February 6, 1841; Chase to William H. Harrison, February 13, 1841, quoted in Robert Henry Gruber, "Salmon P. Chase and the Politics of Reform" (Ph.D. diss., University of Maryland, 1969), 91–92. Following Harrison's death in April, Chase addressed a May 12 Hamilton County antislavery convention on the right of free discussion, the evils of the Black Laws, and the economic effects of slavery on the North. *Philanthropist*, May 5, 19, 1841. Chase had not signed the call for the convention. For his reaction to Harrison's death, see Chase Diary, April 8, 9, 1841. For others, see *Philanthropist*, April 21, 1841; Joseph Thomas to N. M. Thomas, April 23, 1841, Thomas Papers. As late as August Bailey hoped Chase might be selected by the Whigs as a candidate for the state senate. *Philanthropist*, August 11, September 1, 1841. Contributing factors to Chase's failure to win reelection to the city council were his prominence as a temperance advocate and his part in tightening qualifications for Cincinnati voters. See the following items in the Chase LC collection: Chase Diary, May 13, 1840; February 17, 19, March 13, 21, 22, 1841; William Rankin on "Chief Justice Chase as a Bible Student," in *Young People's Paper* (published by the American Sunday School Union); "Minutes of a meeting of the Trustees of the several wards of the city of Cincinnati, held at the office of the City Clerk on Thursday evening, October 8th, 1840." See also, *Watchman of the Valley*, April 1, 15, 1841. Chase's political ambitions have been overemphasized as a factor in his decision to join the Liberty party. (See, for example, Gruber, "Chase," 96–98.) On the contrary, Chase had a choice other than joining the third party; he could have kept his antislavery opinions to himself as other party men did. Joining the tiny third party in 1841 was tantamount to leaving politics for good.

63. Albert Bushnell Hart, *Salmon P. Chase*, American Statesmen Series (Boston: Houghton Mifflin and Co., 1899), 50–51; Chase Diary, June 26, 1843; Chase to Cleveland, October 22, 1841; Chase to Lewis Tappan, March 18, 1847, Chase Papers, LC. Chase often prepared the resolutions and addresses of Liberty party conventions. J. W. Schuckers, *The Life and Public Services of Salmon P. Chase* (New York: D. Appleton and Co., 1874), 47–49. See his Liberty addresses in *Philanthropist*, January 5, March 16, 1842; January 11, 1843; Salmon Portland Chase and Charles Dexter Cleveland, *Anti-Slavery Addresses of 1844 and 1845* (1867; reprint, New York: Negro Universities Press, 1969). Chase to Giddings, December 30, 1841, Giddings Papers, OHS; Chase to Birney, January 21, 1842, in Dumond, *Birney Letters*, vol. 2, 661–62.

CHAPTER 4

1. *Western Citizen*, May 11, 1847; August 11, 1846.
2. Bretz, "Economic Background of the Liberty Party," 250, 252, 254, 259. See also Thomas P. Martin, "The Upper Mississippi Valley in Anglo-American Anti-Slavery and Free Trade Relations, 1837–1842," *Mississippi Valley Historical Review* 15 (September 1928): 204–20. In a recent elaboration of the Bretz approach, Louis S. Gerteis, "Slavery and Hard Times," 319, argues that an economic critique of slavery became increasingly important after 1840, forming the "intellectual core" of the antislavery movement.
3. Giddings was one who faced ruin yet remained a loyal Whig and a fervent opponent of the Liberty party. Stewart, *Giddings*, 16–17.

4. Schuckers, *Chase*, 99; *Philanthropist*, May 19, 1841; Harrold, "Bailey," 200–202; *Genius of Liberty*, July 17, 1841; Ralph Plumb to Levi Sutliff, October 12, 1841, Sutliff Family Papers; *Signal of Liberty*, July 28, 1841; *Genius of Liberty*, May 29, July 10, August 7, 1841; *Western Citizen*, April 20, May 4, 1843; *Trumbull County Democrat*, October 12, 1841. For an antislavery meeting in northern Ohio that protested the Corn Laws as well as the slaveholding interest's war upon the "free laborers of the North," see *Painesville Telegraph*, July 7, 1841. The 1843 national Liberty platform is in Donald Bruce Johnson and Kirk H. Porter, comps., *National Party Platforms, 1840–1972*, 5th ed. (Urbana: University of Illinois Press, 1973), 4–8. Richard H. Bracken to Birney, July 31, 1844, in Dumond, *Birney Letters*, vol. 2, 827–29; *Painesville Telegraph*, September 2, 1846; *Ohio State Journal*, April 4, 1846; *Signal of Liberty*, May 16, 1842; April 24, 1843; *Western Citizen*, April 18, 1844; *American Freeman*, September 15, 1846; Henry W. DePuy to Chase, June 17, 1848, Chase Papers, LC.

5. Samuel Lewis to Chase, December 23, 1841, Chase Papers, HSP; Arnold Buffum, "Lecture Showing the Necessity for a Liberty Party, and Setting Forth Its Principles, Measures and Objects," in *The Antislavery Argument*, eds. William H. Pease and Jane H. Pease (Indianapolis: Bobbs-Merrill Co., 1965), 419–21; *Philanthropist*, December 23, 1840; January 27, May 12, 1841; *Free Labor Advocate*, March 8, 1841; April 30, 1842; *Columbus Daily Freeman*, January 7, 18, 1842; *Declaration of Independence*, April, 1842; Russell Errett to Birney, July 13, August 27, 1844, in Dumond, *Birney Letters*, vol. 2, 820–21, 836–39. Edward C. Reilley, "Politico-Economic Considerations in the Western Reserve's Early Slavery Controversy," *The Ohio State Archaeological and Historical Quarterly* 57 (April 1948): 165–78.

6. *Philanthropist*, January 13, 1841; January 7, 1841; *Free Labor Advocate*, September 3, 1842; *Western Citizen*, February 3, 1843. See also Ichabod Codding in *Western Citizen*, July 30, 1843; and Codding to Brother, January 11, 1843, Codding Papers, Illinois State Historical Library (hereafter cited as ISHL).

7. Foster, "The Liberty Party," Foster Papers; Formisano, *Mass Political Parties*, 74–76.

8. Robert Leslie Jones, *History of Agriculture in Ohio to 1880* (Kent, Ohio: Kent State University Press, 1983), 69–70, 182–91. Contrary to some expectations, the initial effect of the repeal of the Corn Laws in 1846 was to drive down prices for Ohio wheat (some of which was sold in Canada)—or so claimed the Whig *Ohio State Journal*, July 18, August 27, 1846.

9. Trumbull County's agricultural production by townships is in the *Trumbull County Democrat*, January 5, 1841; the township figures from the 1844 presidential contest are in *Liberty Herald*, November 6, 1844.

10. The most important work is Johnson, *Shopkeeper's Millennium*, which argues revivalism (at least in Rochester) was a more urban, middle-class phenomenon than Cross had suggested in *Burned-Over District*. See also Donald Martin Bluestone, "Steamboats, Sewing Machines and Bibles: The Roots of Anti-Slaveryism in Illinois and the Old Northwest, 1818–1860" (Ph.D. diss., University of Wisconsin, Madison, 1973).

11. *Detroit Free Press*, December 1, 1843. For the rural nature of the New York Liberty party, see Benson, *Jacksonian Democracy*, 209–10; Kraut, "Liberty in New York," 217–30; 254, 273. Foster, "Anti-Slavery History," Foster Papers. Gerteis, "Slavery and Hard Times," 323–24, finds some Liberty support among Pittsburgh workingmen's organizations. The third party received about 6 percent of the Cincinnati vote and from 9 to 15 percent of the vote in Chicago. *Ohio Statesman*, October 22, 1845; *Philanthropist*, October 22, 1845; *Western Citizen*, November 14, 1844; August 11, 1846.

12. James Brewer Stewart, *Holy Warriors: The Abolitionists and American Society* (New York: Hill and Wang, 1976), 78–79. Stewart mentions specifically Ashtabula village in Ashtabula County, but the harbor town was not a center of Liberty support.

13. The 1840 figures were taken from the federal census. For the increase in commercial activity in 1844 to 1846, the "Value of Merchants' Capital and Manufacturers' Stock and Moneys and Credits" as entered on the tax duplicates was used as taken from the state auditor's report and printed in the *Ohio State Journal,* September 26, 1846. The *Journal* insisted these figures could be relied upon as "perfectly accurate." Voting returns are for the 1842 and 1846 gubernatorial contests. *Whig Almanac, 1844,* 52; *Ohio State Journal,* December 12, 1846. Comparison of 1844 township and county voting returns with Ohio's "Principal Towns" as listed in the *Compendium of the Sixth Census, 1840,* 78. *Philanthropist,* October 22, 1845; *Cleveland American,* October 7, 1846; *Ohio Statesman,* October 22, 24, 27, 29, 1845; November 4, 11, 1844; *Whig Almanac, 1845,* 49–50.

14. Statistics on the Reserve counties were taken from the Auditor's Report as published in the *Ashtabula Sentinel,* January 5, 1839. "The Footing of the Duplicate of Ashtabula County for 1839" was reproduced in the *Ashtabula Sentinel,* August 31, 1839. For township returns, see October 15, 1842. The value of lands is taken from the official report of the State Board of Equalization as printed in the *Plain Dealer,* November 13, 1846. Township voting returns are from Cleveland *American,* October 22, 1846.

15. Jentz and Magdol follow Bretz in stressing the secular or rational origins of the antislavery appeal. Jentz, "The Antislavery Constituency in Jacksonian New York City," *Civil War History* 27 (June 1981): 101–22; and Magdol, *The Antislavery Rank and File: A Social Profile of the Abolitionists' Constituency* (Westport, Ct.: Greenwood Press, 1986). Kraut, "Forgotten Reformers," contends that the New York Liberty party drew support from society's bone and muscle, but he also suggests that the third party provided a reference point for those undergoing "an important religious transformation." Kraut's "Liberty in New York," 253, did not find a marked preference of Liberty towns for the "abolition churches."

16. Johnson, "Liberty in New England," found a slight relationship between New England Liberty votes and artisans and laborers in manufacturing (though he admits there were many manufacturing centers with few Liberty supporters). He also suggests the northeastern third party won increasing favor among Democrats after 1844. Neither of these conclusions was true for the Northwest, however.

17. Gerteis, *Morality and Utility,* argues persuasively that antislavery thought was characteristic of nineteenth-century utilitarian attitudes concerning social progress. It remains unclear, however, how relevant the ideas of primarily eastern antislavery leaders were to the motivations of rank-and-file third party voters in the Northwest.

18. *Western Citizen,* December 17, 1845; August 11, 1846.

19. Overreliance on "banner" towns or homogeneous areas risks a distortion of the conclusions reached; the sample simply might not hold for the larger population. This is much less a danger in Liberty's case, for such towns represented the most dynamic core of the entire movement.

20. John L. Hammond, "Revival Religion and Antislavery Politics," *American Sociological Review* 39 (April 1974): 175–86; and *The Politics of Benevolence: Revival Religion and American Voting Behavior* (Norwood, N.J.: Ablex, 1979). For Southern evangelicals and slavery, see Donald G. Mathews, *Religion in the Old South* (Chicago: University of Chicago Press, 1977); and David T. Bailey, *Shadow on the Church: Southwestern Evangelical Religion and the Issue of Slavery, 1783–1860* (Ithaca: Cornell University Press, 1985).

21. McKivigan, "Vote as You Pray," and Evans, "Abolitionism in Illinois Churches." There are also numerous studies of slavery and particular denominations, such as Thomas E. Drake, *Quakers and Slavery in America* (1950; reprint, Gloucester, Mass.: Peter Smith, 1965); and Donald G. Mathews, *Slavery and Methodism: A Chapter in American Morality,*

1780–1845 (Princeton: Princeton University Press, 1965). Members of others churches, as well as nonmembers, often joined the Liberty party but in far less proportion than these cited. It is difficult to determine the voting practices of some churches which were more evenly distributed, but we do know where they were *not* strong. For instance, Catholics, Episcopalians, and German Lutherans were comparatively few on the Western Reserve, especially in such rural Liberty strongholds as Hartford or Bloomfield.

22. *Free Labor Advocate,* March 11, 1846; *Ashtabula Sentinel,* May 29, 1845; Foster, "Liberty Party," Foster Papers, BHL; Eastman, "Liberty and Republican Parties in Illinois," 135; Stanton, *Random Recollections,* 279.

23. *Western Citizen,* February 9, 1843; *Free Labor Advocate,* November 16, 1844; see also Spencer's diary in the Illinois State Historical Library.

24. Information on church action against slavery and township voting returns were compiled from the *Western Citizen* for the period 1843–46. Although the First Presbyterian Church of Chicago also rebuked the sin of slavery, it was not included due to the difficulty of determining where its church members cast their ballots among Chicago's four polls. *Western Citizen,* February 23, 1843. Nonetheless, members of this church were prominent among the leadership of the Chicago Liberty party. Evans, "Abolitionism in the Illinois Churches," 201–3.

25. For antislavery and Free Mission Baptists in Illinois and Wisconsin, see *Genius of Liberty,* February 13, June 19, 1841; June 22, July 13, August 24, 1843; November 7, December 26, 1844; *American Freeman,* September 16, 1845; June 11, December 15, 1846; January 20, June 23, 1847. "Minutes of the Meetings of the Congregational Association of Illinois, November 4, 1836," in Sweet, *The Congregationalists,* 177; see also Muelder, "Congregationalists and the Civil War." Evans, "Abolitionism in the Illinois Churches," 134, 220, 269; Heinl, "Jacksonville and Morgan County," 8–14.

26. *Genius of Liberty,* July 10, 1841; March 26, 1842; *Western Citizen,* January 20, 1843.

27. This analysis included the seventy-seven townships in Bureau, De Kalb, Du Page, Kane, Kendall, Lake, Lee, and Whiteside counties. Information on Illinois Congregational churches was obtained from Spinka, *History of Illinois Congregational and Christian Churches,* 350–55. Township returns are from the 1844 and 1846 contests (as available). *Western Citizen,* August 29, November 14, 1844; August 11, 25, 29, 1846.

28. In the 1840 election all thirteen Birney ballots cast in Knox County came from Galesburg. *Peoria Register,* November 13, 1840; see also *Genius of Liberty,* March 6, 1841; Muelder, "Galesburg"; and *Knox College,* 143–58, 250–51.

29. *Genius of Liberty,* May 22, 1841; *Western Citizen,* February 23, May 25, December 7, 1843; December 17, 1845; October 27, 1846; April 20, 1847; Hermann R. Muelder, "Congregationalism and Presbyterians in the Early History of the Galesburg Churches," *Papers in Illinois History and Transactions for the Year 1937* (Springfield: Illinois State Historical Society, 1938), 60–70; and *Knox College,* 379–80. For Blanchard, see Richard Taylor, "Seeking the Kingdom: A Study in the Career of Jonathan Blanchard, 1811–1892" (Ph.D. diss., Northern Illinois University, 1977). Spencer to Eastman, August 31, 1846, in Eastman Papers, Chicago Historical Society.

30. *Genius of Liberty,* September 18, August 14, 1841; *Western Citizen,* December 30, 1842; April 6, 13, November 23, 1843; May 16, 1844; January 30, 1845; May 27, September 8, 1846; for a similar result in Wisconsin, see *American Freeman,* March 22, 1848.

31. *American Freeman,* September 9, 16, 1845; December 8, 1846; January 20, 27, February 3, July 21, 1847; for Codding, see Hannah Maria Preston Codding, "Ichabod Codding," *Proceedings of the State Historical Society of Wisconsin* (1897): 169–96.

32. *American Freeman,* August 4, 1846; June 30, July 7, August 11, 1847; July 12, 26, 1848; see also January 27, June 30, July 7, November 3, December 8, 1847.

33. Giddings was a member of the Jefferson Presbyterian (New School) Church; Jefferson Township polled among the lowest third party totals in Ashtabula County. In 1837 the Democratic *Painesville Republican* had charged that Geauga County was under a church government due to the predominance of Presbyterianism in the local Whig party; see especially the rather muted Whig reply, September 28, October 19, November 9, 1837.

34. See below for township returns. Information on church action against slavery is taken from *Liberty Herald,* October 26, December 28, 1843; January 25, February 8, 15, March 7, May 29, June 19, 1844; March 27, December 20, 1845; *Ashtabula Sentinel,* December 9, 1845; July 1, 1848; *Ohio Observer,* February 23, 1848; Fuller, "Austinburg Church," 73.

35. For the resolves against slavery of three "Calvinistic" Baptist churches in Ashtabula County, see *Liberty Herald,* October 26, 1843; May 29, June 19, 1844. The multiple regression analysis included all 157 townships in eight Reserve counties. Lorain was excluded since full township returns were unavailable. In Lorain, Oberlin's influence would have been great, as Russia township typically polled over 50 percent for the third party. Information on Congregational churches was taken from Kennedy, *Plan of Union,* 132–39. Free Will Baptist and Wesleyan Methodist churches were located through the county histories; and Ira Ford McLeister, *History of the Wesleyan Methodist Church in America* (Syracuse: Wesleyan Methodist Publishing Association, 1934). Township voting returns for 1846 are in *Ashtabula Sentinel,* October 19, 1846; *Painesville Telegraph,* October 21, 1846; *Cleveland American,* October 22, November 4, 11, 1846. For Geauga County the 1844 results were used. *Liberty Herald,* October 26, 1844. Howard, "Antislavery in Presbyterian Church," 15, 53–54. For a description of the Reserve churches in 1837, see Wood, *Churches in the Three Synods of Western New York and the Synod of Western Reserve,* 29–33.

36. The Western Reserve Synod went from 146 churches in 1840 to 127 in 1850. *Oberlin Evangelist,* September 11, 1844; Kennedy, *Plan of Union,* 130–31, 231; *Watchman of the Valley,* August 12, 1841; *Western Citizen,* November 23, 1843; "Chronological List of the Congregational Churches of Ohio," *Papers of the Ohio Church History Society* 9 (1898): 68–70; Keep, *Congregationalism and Church Action,* 10–19, 43–48, 67–78.

37. French, "Wright and Anti-Colonization," 57–59; *Ohio Observer,* September 26, 1849; July 19, October 18, 1848; *Liberty Herald,* September 9, 1845; *Oberlin Evangelist,* July 31, 1839; July 5, 1843; July 3, 1844; July 8, 1846; *Ohio American,* November 14, 1844.

38. *Oberlin Evangelist,* July 29, 1840; *Signal of Liberty,* December 19, 1842; *Ohio Observer,* July 25, 1849; June 7, 1848.

39. Information on Ashtabula churches was taken from Kennedy, *Plan of Union,* 132; "Congregational Churches of Ohio," 68–70; William W. Williams, *History of Ashtabula County, Ohio* (Philadelphia: Williams Bros., 1878), 37. Township election returns are in *Ashtabula Sentinel,* October 19, 1846. The other antislavery churches include the regular Baptist churches cited above. For the entire Western Reserve (excluding Lorain County) Congregational churches, including some who were more conservative both on slavery and theology, correlated at +.19 with the 1846 township Liberty percentages. Churches of strictly Presbyterian form correlated at −.13 with the third party vote.

40. *Ohio Observer,* March 27, 1834; Fuller, "Austinburg Church," 73; *Ashtabula Sentinel,* August 28, 1846; January 25, 1847; February 21, 1848.

41. *Cleveland American,* March 10, 1847; *Liberty Herald,* April 23, July 2, 30, 1845; Keep, *Congregationalism and Church Action,* 10–19, 43–48, 67–78.

42. Keep, *Congregationalism and Church Action; History of Trumbull and Mahoning*

Counties (Cleveland: H. Z. Williams & Bros., 1882), 264-66; Liberty Herald, April 23, 1845.
43. Crisfield Johnson, comp., History of Cuyahoga County, Ohio (Cleveland: D. W. Ensign & Co., 1879), 526; Ohio American, October 22, November 18, 1846; March 10, 1847; History of Medina County and Ohio (Chicago: Baskin & Batley, 1881), 504-5; Oberlin Evangelist, December 4, 1844; January 29, 1845; History of Medina, 535. For antislavery church action in Portage County, see Ohio American, February 10, 1847.
44. Philanthropist, November 19, 1839; Western Citizen, June 23, 1843; Ohio American, March 6, 1845; Liberty Herald, July 17, 1844. For the Free Will Baptist Church, see Norman A. Baxter, History of the Freewill Baptists: A Study in New England Separation (Rochester, NY.: American Baptist Historical Society, 1957). For Michigan, see "History of the Free Will Baptist Church at Cook's Prairie," Michigan Historical Collections 10 (1886): 33-51. For the slavery controversy in a Free Will Baptist conference, see "Records of the Ohio River Yearly Meeting of Free Will Baptists," OHS.
45. McKivigan, "Abolitionism and the American Churches," 166, could not demonstrate Free Will Baptists supported the Liberty party. Formisano, Mass Political Parties, 148-49, found third party voting among church members in Michigan. History of Geauga and Lake Counties, Ohio (Philadelphia: 1878), 100; Liberty Herald, May 9, 1844.
46. Mathews, Slavery and Methodism, 230-32; McLeister, Wesleyan Methodist Church (for Michigan, see 28, 50); see also Signal of Liberty, July 31, 1843; Free Labor Advocate, December 1, 1845. For Indiana, see Philanthropist, December 30, 1840; Free Labor Advocate, September 24, 1841; February 18, March 18, May 6, 1843; February 2, 1844; July 13, August 20, 1845; and Miller, "Antislavery in Indiana," 61-62, 75, 115. For Illinois, see Western Citizen, June 29, July 11, 1843. And for Wisconsin, see American Freeman, August 11, 1846; November 3, 1847; Free Democrat, December 27, 1848. Philanthropist, October 13, 27, 1841; Ohio Statesman, October 11, 1844; Paul H. Boase, "Slavery and the Ohio Circuit Rider," The Ohio Historical Quarterly 64 (April 1955): 199.
47. History of Medina, 278; Liberty Herald, March 28, 1844; Errett to Chase, May 9, 1846, Chase Papers, LC.
48. Adams, Neglected Period, 58-62; O'Dell, "Antislavery in Ohio," 371; Welsh, "Chillicothe Presbytery," 139-41; Philanthropist, October 13, 1841; Charles Augustus Hanna, Historical Collections of Harrison County, Ohio (New York: 1900), 135-37, 149.
49. Cincinnati Observer, July 30, 1840; Genius of Liberty, February 6, 1841; Free Labor Advocate, August 29, 1845; September 26, 1847; Engelder, "Churches and Slavery," 240; Watchman of the Valley, October 23, 1845; Ohio Statesman, November 11, 13, 1844; October 29, 1845; History of Brown County, Ohio (Chicago: W. H. Beers & Co., 1883), 313-14; Clarion of Freedom, February 18, 1848. For the Free Presbyterians, see Welsh, "Wrestling with Human Values," 210-33.
50. Gross, "Antislavery in Stark County," 27-28, Ohio Statesman, November 4, 1844.
51. The Quaker separation is best followed in the pages of the Free Labor Advocate, especially September 17, October 1, 15, 29, December 10, 31, 1842; February 18, 25, 1843. See also Walter Edgerton, A History of the Separation in the Indiana Yearly Meeting of Friends; Which Took Place in the Winter of 1842 and 1843, on the Anti-Slavery Question (Cincinnati: A. Pugh, 1856); and Drake, Quakers and Slavery, 162-66.
52. Coffin, Reminiscences, 230; Osborn to Way and Stanton, December 31, 1842, in Edgerton, Separation of Indiana Friends, 67-69.
53. Free Labor Advocate, March 2, 1842; November 9, December 14, 1844; January 5, February 9, 1846. Miller, "Antislavery in Indiana," 95-99. Election figures for the 1844 presidential contest are in Riker and Thornbrough, Indiana Election Returns, 48-52.
54. Western Citizen, March 30, 1843; see also David W. Blight, "Perceptions of Southern

Intransigence and the Rise of Radical Antislavery Thought, 1816–1830," *Journal of the Early Republic* 3 (Summer 1983): 139–64; and Bailey, *Shadow on the Church.* McKivigan, "Comeouter Sects," 142–60.

55. *Ohio American,* July 17, 1845.

56. Edgerton, *Separation of Indiana Friends,* 39; see also Johnson, "Liberty in New England," 420. Welsh, "Wrestling with Human Values," 229–31. For a similar approach, see James Turner, "Understanding the Populists," *Journal of American History* 67 (September 1980): 354–73. Some years earlier evangelical hostility to slavery was also based on rejection of worldly corruption. Essig, *The Bonds of Wickedness.* Winkle, "Politics of Community," 38, notes the Reserve counties experienced relatively moderate or steady growth during this period. My analysis found little relationship (+.15) between population growth (based on adult white males) in Ashtabula from 1839 to 1847 and the Liberty vote in 1846. See the enumeration of Ashtabula voters in *Ashtabula Sentinel,* June 28, 1847, and October 19, 1846, for voting returns. Poll book analysis similar to that performed by Winkle might find that Liberty communities were stable or dominated by what he calls "persisters" who formed the core community.

Richard S. Taylor, "Beyond Immediate Emancipation: Jonathan Blanchard, Abolitionism, and the Emergence of American Fundamentalism," *Civil War History* 27 (September 1981): 260–74. Perhaps due to their advanced views on race, abolitionists are often considered modernists. Yet a modern political or religious liberal would find little in common with their insistence on a strict definition of good and evil, as well as their literal interpretation (except, ironically, in regards to slavery) of Scripture as revealed truth.

57. Bertram Wyatt-Brown, "Conscience and Career: Young Abolitionists and Missionaries," in *Anti-Slavery, Religion and Reform: Essays in Memory of Roger Anstey,* ed. Christine Bolt and Seymour Drescher (Kent, England: William Dawson & Sons, 1980), 184.

58. *Western Citizen,* June 5, 1845; Goen, "Broken Churches, Broken Nation"; Keep, *Congregationalism and Church Action,* 137, 140.

59. Flavel Bascom, "Piety, the True Source of National Prosperity," *Western Citizen,* August 26, 1842; Owen Lovejoy, "Sermon on Religion and Politics," *Western Citizen,* January 20, 1843; Benjamin Stanton, *Free Labor Advocate,* July 24, 1841; Address of J. W. Rogers to Green County (Wisconsin) Liberty Association, in *American Freeman,* February 7, 1846; *Western Citizen,* December 21, 1843; *Ashtabula Sentinel,* November 23, 1844.

60. An impressive study of reform movements and social status can be found in Nancy A. Hewitt, *Women's Activism and Social Change: Rochester, New York, 1822–1872* (Ithaca: Cornell University Press, 1984). Hewitt's analysis benefits from membership lists of various reform organizations, information largely unavailable for Liberty voters. While it is instructive, Hewitt's study once again points out how the situation varied by region or locality. Her "ultraists" resemble the social groups who supported the northwestern Liberty party, but in Rochester they were found in Garrisonian ranks. It was the more middle-class-oriented "perfectionists" who supported the Liberty party in Rochester. In another case, Magdol, *Antislavery Rank and File,* 49–51, discusses how New York evangelical church members often favored Garrisonian abolitionism, a position somewhat weaker in the Northwest.

CHAPTER 5

1. *Free Labor Advocate,* September 17, 24, October 15, 29, December 10, 1842. Some accounts had Clay responding more angrily by telling Mendenhall to go home and mind his own business. Rariden might have planned the public rebuke of the abolition Quakers, who

had already started to desert the Whig party for Liberty. The Richmond *Palladium* knew of the plan to present the petition to Clay and warned against such an insult to the "distinguished advocate of Liberty." See also Leonard S. Kenworthy, "Henry Clay at Richmond in 1842," *Indiana Magazine of History* 30 (December 1934): 353–59.

2. Gates to Giddings, October 2, 1844, Giddings Papers; Carl Schurz, *Henry Clay,* with an introduction by Glyndon G. Van Deusen, American Statesman Series, gen. ed., Arthur M. Schlesinger, Jr. (1899; reprint, New York: Chelsea House, 1980), vol. 2, 232–33. Julian, *Recollections,* 27–28, also mentioned the Mendenhall incident.

3. And perhaps a third in the Brown, Clermont, and Highland district where the Whig candidate lost by 324 votes while the third party polled 341 ballots. *Whig Almanac, 1844,* 52–53. Ridgway lost by 255 votes in a district in which 370 third party votes were cast.

4. Benjamin Wade thought Clay could not carry Ohio, but "we can carry Scott like a whirlwind." Wade to Giddings, January 2, 1843, Giddings Papers, OHS. The *Ashtabula Sentinel,* September 16, 1843, argued that support for Clay should not be made a test of "Whig orthodoxy." See also J. Burnett to Cincinnati *Gazette* in *Philanthropist,* July 19, 1843.

5. B. F. Hoffman to Ephraim Brown, March 2, 1842, Brown Papers, WRHS: *Ashtabula Sentinel,* October 15, October 29, 1842; *Liberty Herald,* February 22, 1844; *Western Citizen,* January 4, July 11, 1844. Theodore Foster admitted there were more antislavery Whigs. "Antislavery History," Foster Papers, BHL.

6. For this aspect of the Whigs, see Howe *Political Culture of Whigs.*

7. Third party leader J. H. Paine joined the ceremonies in remembrance of the president, but other Liberty supporters continued to recall that the dead general had been "emphatically opposed to the emancipation of slaves." *Painesville Telegraph,* April 14, 1841; *Signal of Liberty,* April 28, 1841. *Ashtabula Sentinel,* February 13, 1841; *Painesville Telegraph,* February 11, 1841. The *Palladium,* which was edited by F. B. Penniman and L. D. Butts, was quickly replaced by Q. F. Atkins's *Declaration of Independence* in December 1841. Reserve third party abolitionists later founded the *Liberty Herald* in Warren and the *Ohio American* in Cleveland. *Painesville Telegraph,* May 5, October 6, 13, 20, 1841; *Ashtabula Sentinel,* September 11, October 28, 1841; Volpe, "Wade's Strange Defeat."

8. *Liberty Herald,* October 19, 1843; Paine to Chase, April 16, 1844, Chase Papers, LC; Riddle, "Antislavery Sentiment on the Western Reserve," 155. For Riddle's view of the Liberty party, see Riddle to Giddings, June 7, 1842, Giddings Papers, OHS; Chase to Giddings, December 30, 1841; Leavitt to Giddings, October 29, 1841; Tappan to Giddings, July 24, 1841, Giddings Papers, OHS; Chase to Giddings, February 15, 1842, George W. Julian Papers, Indiana State Library. Giddings's refusal of Leavitt caused some ill feelings between the two members of the congressional lobby in behalf of the slave. Giddings to Comfort Pease Giddings, January 8, 1843; Giddings to Joseph Addison Giddings, January 12, 1843; Giddings to Wife, December 10, 1843, Giddings Papers. For Giddings's response to Chase, see Giddings to Chase, February 5, 1842, and October 12, 1843. Chase Papers, HSP.

9. The immediate cause of censure was Giddings's introduction of his *Creole* resolutions; see Stewart, *Giddings,* 72–74. For Giddings's defense of the Whig party, see Giddings to Chase, February 19, 1843, Chase Papers, HSP. Gates to Giddings, March 25, April 4, 1842, Giddings Papers, OHS. Giddings always faced conservative opposition within his district, primarily from Conneaut and Cleveland. *Painesville Telegraph,* April 21, 1841; Henry Fassett to Giddings, January 26, 1844; Giddings to J. A. Giddings, January 25, February 15, 1844; Giddings to C. P. Giddings, January 22, 1844, Giddings Papers; Giddings to Follett, July 18, 1843, in Hamlin, "Follett Papers," vol. 10, 11–12.

10. *Painesville Telegraph,* April 6, 13, 1842; *Ohio State Journal,* April 15, 1842; *Philan-*

thropist, April, 6, 13, 27, 1842; Chase to Giddings, May 19, 1842, Giddings Papers. Giddings's margin was substantial but not quite as remarkable as mistakenly printed in Stewart, *Giddings*, 76. The combined result in Ashtabula, Geauga, Lake, and Trumbull counties was 7,469 for Giddings and 3,943 (not 393) for his Democratic opponent. Election returns are in *Painesville Telegraph*, May 4, 1842; *Ashtabula Sentinel*, May 7, 1842; *Ohio State Journal*, May 10, 1842. Chase reckoned Giddings must have received the votes of "a thousand Liberty men." Chase to Giddings, February 9, 1843, Julian Papers, Indiana Historical Library.

11. *Philanthropist*, March 30, May 18, June 29, July 23, August 27, September 16, October 8, 1842. A Medina Liberty meeting endorsed both Giddings and Leicester King, the 1842 Liberty candidate for governor.

12. The *Philanthropist*, July 29, 1843, warned Liberty voters to reject Whig appeals for cooperation as this would "destroy the identity of the Liberty men." Ed Wade was long a Giddings supporter and, as recently as 1842, had addressed a public meeting in his behalf. *Painesville Telegraph*, April 6, 1842. He had also sought Giddings's help in gaining appointments for a friend, his father-in-law, and himself (as district attorney). In July 1842 Wade told Giddings he intended to "go with the Liberty party tooth & nail." Wade to Giddings, April 3, May 24, 1841; January 9, 26, July 7, 1842, Giddings Papers, OHS. *Liberty Herald*, September 14, 21, October 26, 1843; October 9, 1844; *Ashtabula Sentinel*, October 14, 1843. The editor of the *Liberty Herald*, L. L. Rice, had only recently accepted the expediency of the third party. Naturally, this earned him the ridicule of the Whig *Telegraph*, October 11, November 1, 1843, which he had formerly edited.

13. Brown to Giddings, June 3, 1842; Giddings to Brown, June 10, 1842, Brown Papers, WRHS; Giddings to Follett, July 18, 27, August 4, 1843; James A. Briggs to Follett, July 26, 1843; Follett to Briggs, August 9, 1843, in Hamlin, "Follett Papers," vol. 10, 9–13; Stewart, *Giddings*, 56, 84–86; Reilley, "Politico-Economic Considerations in Reserve's Slavery Controversy." Scholars have exaggerated the effectiveness of such Whig economic appeals to Liberty voters. For example, Sewell, *Ballots for Freedom*, 106, uses language similar to that of Giddings but applies the same economic motivation to Liberty advocates as well. See also Gerteis, *Morality and Utility*, 96–97.

14. *Philanthropist*, August 27, 1842; *Declaration of Independence*, August 8, 1842; *Ashtabula Sentinel*, August 13, 1842.

15. *Whig Almanac, 1844*, 53. Charles G. Finney was also said to have supported Hamlin, but H. C. Taylor reported he did not vote. See Taylor to Rice in *Liberty Herald*, November 9, 1843, and also October 26, 1843. The Liberty candidate lost a substantial number of votes. *Philanthropist*, October 25, November 8, 1843. In an embarrassing scandal, Taylor, editor of the *Oberlin Evangelist*, was soon under arrest for embezzlement, seduction, and abortion. See *Liberty Herald*, December 21, 1843. The Democratic victor in the Oberlin district, Henry R. Brinkerhoff, died before taking his seat in Congress. *Painesville Telegraph*, May 15, 1844.

16. Giddings to L. M. Giddings, September 20, 1843, Giddings Papers, OHS; *Ashtabula Sentinel*, October 7, 1843; *Ohio Statesman*, November 13, 1843. Taylor said Giddings failed to sway any Oberlin votes, but voters there "as Liberty men" chose Hamlin because he had "long been an active and independent abolitionist" and was opposed to Clay. *Liberty Herald*, October 12, 19, November 9, 1843. Tilden actually trailed in Trumbull where the Democrats lost only one representative to the Whigs. The Liberty vote, at six hundred, exceeded the slight margin between the parties.

17. Resistance in the southern counties also killed Ben Wade's hopes for the governor's chair. Wade to Calvin Sutliff, November 28, December 13, 1843, M. Sutliff Papers, WRHS. *Cincinnati Republican* in the *Philanthropist*, January 19, 1842; Rankin to Bailey in *Philan-*

thropist, March 9, 1842. The Reverend John Rankin was finally won to the third party cause out of respect for King's "good qualities." King's reputation might also have influenced the defection to the third party of the Columbus *Daily Freeman,* December 29, 1841; January 5, 1842.

18. *Ohio State Journal,* May 21, July 9, October 19, November 2, 1841; Logan *Gazette* quoted in the *Philanthropist,* April 27, 1842; *Ohio State Journal,* March 30, June 15, 1842.

19. *Ohio State Journal,* September 14, 24, 1842. The chief issue of the 1842 campaign was a Democratic plan for reapportionment that prompted Whig protests and resulted in their "absquatulation" (or withdrawal) from the legislature. Weisenburger, *Passing of the Frontier,* 410. Whigs also denounced King as a "HEAVY GAMBLER." The *Philanthropist,* August 20, 1842, denied this, noting Clay was even more notorious as a "duellist, slaveholder and a HEAVY GAMBLER."

20. Stanton to Tappan, July 17, 1842, Tappan Papers, OHS; *Ohio Statesman,* January 29, February 3, June 14, 21, 29, August 5, September 24, October 23, 1842. The *Philanthropist,* September 17, 1842, said a vote for Corwin advanced "the claims of a duellist and slaveholder to the presidency."

21. *Ohio State Journal,* October 12, 14, 15, 17, 19, 28, December 7, 1842. Other factors mentioned were heavy naturalizations and defections produced by the "Tyler interest." Both the *Ashtabula Sentinel,* October 29, 1842, and the *Painesville Telegraph,* November 2, 1842, echoed the *Journal's* charge that the third party was responsible for the Whig defeat. Earlier, however, the *Telegraph,* October 19, November 16, 1842, emphasized the falling off of the Whig vote. This was also the view of the *Cincinnati Gazette* (though it too mentioned King ballots as a factor).

22. *Philanthropist,* October 22, 1842; *Ohio State Journal,* October 19, 21, 1842; *Whig Almanac, 1841,* 52. Initially, the *Painesville Telegraph,* December 21, 1842, placed the Democratic state margin at an even slighter amount (1,792).

23. *Declaration of Independence,* December 16, 1842; November, 1842; *Philanthropist,* October 22, 1842; Corwin to Follett, October 31, November 12, 1842; Follett to Corwin, November 4, 1842, in Hamlin, "Follett Papers," vol. 9, 72–77; Clay to Chase, December 21, 1842, Chase Papers, HSP.

24. *Signal of Liberty,* July 4, 17, November 14, 1842; April 3, 1843; March 18, 1844; Foster, "Antislavery History," Foster Papers, BHL.

25. In addition to collections already cited, see, for example: John A. McClernand, Richard Yates, and Sidney Breese Papers, Illinois State Historical Library; William Woodbridge, Robert M. McClelland, Alpheus Felch Papers, Burton Historical Collection, Detroit Public Library; Joseph A. Wright, Elisha Embree Papers, Indiana State Library.

26. Alan Kraut and Phyllis Field suggest New York party leaders were not above using a public referendum on black suffrage to discredit the third party by revealing Liberty's weakness. "Politics versus Principle: The Partisan Response to 'Bible Politics' in New York State," *Civil War History* 25 (June 1979): 101–18.

27. *Painesville Telegraph,* April 3, 10, 1844; *Ashtabula Sentinel,* March 30, 1844; *Liberty Herald,* May 2, 1844. The *Philanthropist,* April 3, May 1, 1844, claimed Whigs tried to make the Cincinnati Anti-Texas rally "look like a Liberty affair." For similar activities in New England, see David Herbert Donald, *Charles Sumner and the Coming of the Civil War* (1960; reprint, Phoenix Books, 1981), 135–36; Robert F. Dalzell, Jr., *Daniel Webster and the Trial of American Nationalism, 1843–1852* (Boston: Houghton Mifflin Co., 1973), 82–83, 90–91.

28. *Ohio State Journal,* June 6, August 8, 1844; *Philanthropist,* June 5, 1844. The *Journal* printed the protest of Ohio Democrats against the effort to defeat Van Buren. For divisions

among the Democrats on banking issues, see *Painesville Telegraph,* February 21, March 27, 1844; Holt, *Party Politics in Ohio*; Maizlish, *Triumph of Sectionalism;* and Delmer J. Trester, "David Tod and the Gubernatorial Campaign of 1844," *Ohio State Archaeological and Historical Quarterly* 62 (April 1953): 162–78. Walker to McClelland, April 4, 1844, McClelland Papers, Burton Historical Collection; Lucius Lyon to Thomas C. Sheldon, March 13, 1844; Lyon to Cass, April 6, May 2, 1844, in "Letters of Lucius Lyon, 1822–1845," *Michigan Historical Collections* 27 (1896): 571, 574, 578–79. Detroit Democrats held a public meeting in support of Cass. *Detroit Free Press,* June 23, June 28, 1843. The Joseph A. Wright Collection at the Indiana State Library contains numerous letters expressing the opposition of Indiana Democrats to Van Buren on the Texas issue. See, for example, W. P. Sunderland et al. to Howard and Wright, May 13, 1844. For Illinois, see James Shields to Sidney Breese, April 12, 1844; February 19, 1845, Breese Papers, ISHL; Shields to McClernand, December 26, 1844, McClernand Papers, ISHL. The Ohio Democracy had its Cass elements as well. Stanton to Tappan, January 8, 1843; April 28, December 26, 1844; January 10, 1845, Tappan Papers, OHS.

29. For the view that Van Buren and Clay arranged to avoid the Texas issue in the campaign, see James C. N. Paul, *Rift in the Democracy* (1951; reprint, Perpetua, 1961), 36–38. Clay to Gales & Seaton, September 23, 1844, in *Ohio Statesman,* October 4, 1844; *Philanthropist,* September 4, 18, 1844; *Painesville Telegraph,* August 21, 1844; *Ohio State Journal,* October 22, 1844. Clement Eaton believed Clay's missteps were fatal to his chances. *Henry Clay and the Art of American Politics,* Library of American Biography Series, ed. Oscar Handlin (Boston: Little, Brown and Co., 1957), 175. George W. Julian claimed Clay wrote the Alabama letters in a "moment of weakness." Although "inexpressibly disappointed and grieved" by this, Julian still supported Clay, believing it his "clear and unhesitating duty to resist the election of Polk with all my might." *Political Recollections,* 36–38.

30. Orth to Colfax, December 1845, in Schauinger, "Orth Letters," 376–77; *Philanthropist,* May 8, 15, August 9, September 4, 18, 1844; *Ohio State Journal,* January 1, February 8, March 4, July 3, 11, August 6, 8, September 10, 1844. As usual the Liberty reply to Whig complaints was that the Democrats did "not court our votes by professions of anti-slavery principles." *Philanthropist,* August 9, 1844. Whig papers went so far as to quote the *North Star* against the Liberty party. *Painesville Telegraph,* July 3, May 22, August 21, September 4, 1844.

31. *Philanthropist,* March 27, April 3, May 31, June 26, July 3, August 18, 1844. The Liberty platform is in Johnson and Porter, *Party Platforms,* 4–8.

32. *Ohio State Journal,* May 22, September 7, 1844; *Detroit Free Press,* September 6, 1844; *Painesville Telegraph,* September 4, 1844; *Philanthropist,* August 11, September 11, 1844; Foster to Birney, September 12, 1844, in Dumond, *Birney Letters,* vol. 2, 841–42. Benjamin Tappan warned his brother that Cassius was a stool pigeon of Henry Clay, whose aim was to "hoodwink & bamboozle your Liberty party." Later the Democratic senator wondered at the consistency of abolitionists for "almost deifying Cassius M. Clay for talking of Liberty for the black man while he continues to hold them in object bondage." Benjamin to Lewis Tappan, March 9, July 8, 1844, Tappan Papers, OHS. For Wade, see Riddle, "Wade and 1840," 598–99. Riddle, an abolition Whig of the Giddings school, also backed Clay, whose defeat in 1844 depressed him more than even the death of his hero, General Harrison. Wade had earlier been "ripe for rebellion" to prevent Texas annexation. Wade to Giddings, March 23, 1844, Giddings Papers, OHS.

33. C. M. Clay to Colonel J. J. Speed, July 10, 1844, in *Ohio State Journal,* August 22, 1844; Clay to Wickliffe, September 2, 1844, in *Detroit Free Press,* September 13, 1844; H.

Clay to C. M. Clay, September 18, 1844, in *Philanthropist,* October 9, 1844; *Ohio Statesman,* September 9, 25, 30, October 7, 1844; *Detroit Free Press,* August 13, September 13, 1844. See also Sellers, *Polk,* 147–48.

34. Giddings to Follett, January 10, May 12, 1844, in Hamlin, "Follett Papers," vol. 10, 14–16; Giddings to Wife, April 28, 1844; Giddings to Clay, July 6, 1844, Giddings Papers, OHS.

35. State Central Committee of Whigs and Oran Follett to Clay, August 1844, in Hamlin, "Follett Papers," vol. 10, 18–19; Clay to Giddings, September 21, 1844, Julian Papers. For the similar view of the *New York Tribune,* see *Philanthropist,* October 2, 1844.

36. *Philanthropist,* June 26, October 2, 9, 1844; Woolsey Welles to Chase, July 5, 1844, Chase Papers, LC; Sellers, *Polk,* 148. Giddings's efforts in Clay's behalf may have been induced by the opposition in his district to his own renomination. *Painesville Telegraph,* August 7, 14, 1844. For Giddings's confidence in Clay, see Stewart, *Giddings,* 93–94. Hamlin was put forth again in the Oberlin district (the Democratic candidate elected in 1843 had died) and this time was elected. Woolsey Welles to Chase, October 12, 1844, Chase Papers, LC; *Philanthropist,* September 11, 25, October 23, 1844; *Painesville Telegraph,* July 16, 24, 1844; *Ohio State Journal,* July 16, 1844; *Ashtabula Sentinel,* July 6, 1844.

37. *Whig Almanac, 1845,* 49–50; D. T. Disney to Polk, October 28, 1844, Polk Papers, LC; "Whig Central Committee of Greene County, Circular," October 21, 1844, quoted in Maizlish, "Triumph of Sectionalism," 64.

38. Charles Cheney to Chase, October 18, 1844, Chase Papers, LC. Logan Whigs reportedly appointed party followers to visit antislavery voters to win their votes for the Whig ticket. *Philanthropist,* October 30, 1844.

39. *Philanthropist,* October 23, 30, 1844; *Ohio State Journal,* October 5, 22, 23, 1844; *Painesville Telegraph,* October 9, 16, 30, 1844; S. E. Giffen to Chase, October 19, 1844, Chase Papers, LC. On October 1 the *Ohio State Journal* was forced to admit Roorback was "a gross and flagrant imposition" and a "miserable abortion." The *Painesvile Telegraph* exposed the "Roerback [*sic*] Forgery," but in an adjacent column it ran the story of Birney's Saginaw nomination as evidence he was "in the camp of Locofocoism." Northern Ohio Liberty men were especially nervous as they claimed never to have met a Columbus abolitionist whose address Whigs were busy circulating among antislavery voters. *Ohio American,* October 31, 1844; see also Sellers, *Polk,* 149–51.

40. Birney's letters of explanation are in the *Philanthropist,* October 23, 1844; and *Ohio State Journal,* October 15, 1844. See also *Ohio State Journal,* October 5, 12, 22, 23, 1844; *Painesville Telegraph,* October 23, 1844. For the reaction of Michigan Liberty advocates, see Porter to Birney, October 3, 1844, in Dumond, *Birney Letters,* vol. 2, 843–44.

41. The Garland letter is in *Philanthropist,* November 6, 1844. The *Ohio State Journal* released the Garland letter on October 26 and the *Painesville Telegraph* in its October 30 issue. *Painesville Telegraph,* November 6, 1844; *Liberty Herald,* November 20, 1844; *Philanthropist,* November 13, 1844. Fladeland, *Birney,* 241–51, treats the Garland forgery in more detail.

42. *Philanthropist,* November 6, 16, 1844; *Ohio Statesman,* October 23, 28, 30, November 1, 4, 6, 8, 25, 1844; *Detroit Free Press,* October 2, 7, 31, November 1, 1844. The *Statesman's* interest in prolonging Whig embarrassment over the incident lasted until June 1845. See also, *Ohio State Journal,* October 30, 31, November 5, 26, December 10, 29, 30, 1844; *Painesville Telegraph,* November 27, December 18, 1844, January 1, 1845; *Liberty Herald,* November 20, 1844. The *Telegraph* persisted in its claim that Paine was on a Democratic rather than a Liberty mission, noting that after the election a Democratic fife and drum corps stopped at

Paine's house and gave "three cheers for Gen. Paine." Paine dismissed this as another Whig "Roorback."

43. *Ohio American,* October 24, 1844; Welles to Chase, November 4, 1844, Chase Papers, LC.

44. *Whig Almanac, 1845,* 49–50; *Liberty Herald,* October 23, November 6, 20, 1844. Giddings's biographer admits the Clay Whig "exploited it [the forgery] effectively and unscrupulously." Stewart, *Giddings,* 98. Giddings to R. B. Dennis, April 5, 1845, in *Ohio American,* April 24, 1845.

45. Thomas Maxwell to Stanton, November 12, 1844, in *Free Labor Advocate,* December 21, 1844; Miller, "Antislavery in Indiana," 108–9. Fletcher diary, October 28, 31, November 1, 1844, in *The Diary of Calvin Fletcher,* ed. Gayle Thornbrough and Dorothy L. Riker, vol. 3 (Indianapolis: Indiana Historical Society, 1973), 83–84; *Western Citizen,* November 14, 1844.

46. *Detroit Free Press,* October 12, 1843; July 8, 16, September 6, 10, November 1, 2, 13, 1844.

47. *Whig Almanac, 1845,* 49–53; Alexander, "Voter Constancy," 116, may be on safe ground in claiming the Liberty party cost Clay Michigan. (Even so, virtually all 3,632 Liberty ballots would have to have gone to Clay to overcome Polk's 3,466-vote margin.) But the Liberty vote in Indiana (2,106) hardly equaled Polk's margin of victory (2,315). Riker and Thornbrough, *Indiana Election Returns,* 40–52. In Ohio, the Whig margin of victory rose from 1,277 to 5,940, while the Liberty total dropped from 8,411 to 8,050. Stewart, *Giddings,* 98, goes too far in saying Clay carried Ohio on the strength of the Whig fraud. Democratic leader Medary claimed "the cursed abolitionists ruined" Democratic hopes in Ohio. See Medary to Polk, November 10, 1844, quoted in Holt, *Party Politics,* 211.

Birney, *Birney,* 354–55. In some respects William Birney's memory was flawed. Birney had first heard of the forgery at Fairport, Ohio, not in Buffalo where his son said his boat was delayed. *Philanthropist,* November 13, 20, December 4, 1844. Bailey claimed the Liberty vote for governor had actually been several hundred votes higher than the official count. Although this was an old complaint, in this case he was undoubtedly right. The official count lists no third party votes for governor in Cuyahoga County, for example, though Birney received 312 in the presidential election. Township returns published in the *Ohio American* on October 28, 1846, show the Liberty gubernatorial candidate received 334 votes in 1844. Given that this might have been repeated in several other counties, Birney's decline thus would have been more serious than the official returns indicate. See also Smith, *Liberty and Free Soil,* 76.

48. *Philanthropist,* November 27, December 25, 1844; *Ohio State Journal,* November 27, 1844; Foster, "Antislavery History," Foster Papers. While exonerating Birney of the Garland charges, Bailey also believed he had committed "grave errors" in accepting the nomination in the first place. For the denouement of the Garland incident, see *Detroit Free Press,* November–December, 1844; and Fladeland, *Birney,* 247–51.

49. The *Richmond Palladium* claimed that, if Polk carried Indiana, "the responsibility, and it is a heavy one, rests upon the abolitionists." *Free Labor Advocate,* November 9, 1844. Over the years it has often been claimed that if the third party's 15,812 New York votes had gone instead to Clay he might have been able to overturn Polk's slim 5,106-vote margin of victory and thus win New York and the election. Sellers, *Polk,* 159–60, notes that foreign-born voters also contributed to the Whig defeat. (See also Benson, *Jacksonian Democracy,* 258, 261–62, who notes the relative decline of the third party vote over 1843.) The naturalized voter was becoming an issue of great importance in the Northwest as well. Especially after the Philadelphia riots, the *Ohio Statesman, Ohio State Journal,* and *Philanthropist* all claimed to be the special guardians of the immigrant. Illinois Whigs also blamed their defeat on foreign

voters. Thompson, *Illinois Whigs*, 130–31. *New York Tribune* quoted in the *Philanthropist*, November 27, 1844; Birney, *Birney*, 355; *Ohio State Journal*, November 13, 20, 27, December 28, 1844. For similar Whig charges in Massachusetts, see Kinley J. Brauer, *Cotton versus Conscience: Massachusetts Whig Politics and Southwestern Expansion, 1843–1848* (Lexington: University of Kentucky Press, 1967), 96, 98–99. I question the traditional view of the 1844 results in "Did the Liberty Party Elect James K. Polk in 1844?" (Paper delivered at annual meeting of the Society for Historians of the Early American Republic, Charlottesville, Virginia 1989).

50. *New York Tribune* quoted in *Philanthropist*, December 11, 1844; Lewis Tappan to Giddings, December 19, 1845, Giddings Papers; *Ohio State Journal*, June 5, July 19, September 2, 1845; *Philanthropist*, March 4, 11, 1846. Indiana Whig George W. Julian did not blame Liberty voters but New York Democrats for Clay's defeat. *Political Recollections*, 34–35, 40. For Giddings's view, see Giddings to Follett, November 18, 1844, in "Follett Papers," vol. 10, 20–21. Daniel Webster's charges against the Liberty party are in the *Philanthropist*, November 19, 1845.

51. *Oberlin Evangelist*, November 20, 1844; *Philanthropist*, December 4, 1844. See B. F. Hoffman in the *Ohio American*, November 28, 1844. Theodore Smith considered 1844 high tide for Liberty. *Liberty and Free Soil*, 80, 85. (His next chapter is entitled "Discouragement of the Liberty Men.") Perhaps because of the unavailability of sources, Smith's analysis trails off between 1844 and 1848 while he neglects some evidence indicating Liberty's continued strength. (For example, the Ohio Liberty party increased its percentage of the vote from 2.7 in 1844 to 4.4 in 1846.) Sewell, *Ballots for Freedom*, 113–14, also overemphasizes Liberty malaise after 1844. Although it may be true the party had reached its natural limits, party supporters remained obdurate and were not anxious for wider coalition. David Donald, "An Excess of Democracy," in *Lincoln Reconsidered: Essays on the Civil War Era*, 2d ed. (New York: Alfred A. Knopf, 1966), 228–29. According to Donald, "universal democracy made it difficult to deal with issues requiring subtle understanding and delicate handling." Donald's heroes were the conservative statesmen Liberty advocates found most distasteful.

The tour of Garrisonian agents in Ohio in 1845 gave Whigs the opportunity to associate the Liberty party with these so-called disunionists. Bailey rejected Whig charges and sought to distance the Liberty party from the Garrisonian radicals. To this end the Ohio Anti-Slavery Society again reaffirmed its object was neither "the dissolution of the Union, the overthrow of human government, or the destruction of the institutions of religion." *Philanthropist*, July 9, 16, 1845.

52. Liberty supporters in Trumbull county announced the annexation of Texas would not shake them from their third party stand. *Philanthropist*, April 9, 1845.

53. Giddings to Follett, November 14, 1844, in Hamlin, "Follett Papers," vol. 10, 19–20; Giddings to Briggs, June 27, 1845, quoted in Maizlish, "Triumph of Sectionalism," 121; Foster to Birney, August 1, 1846, in Dumond, *Birney Letters*, vol. 2, 1025–26.

54. Giddings to Follett, February 18, 1845, in Hamlin, "Follett Papers," vol. 10, 21–22; *Philanthropist*, February 12, 1845. The senate resolutions were introduced by Reserve Whig William L. Perkins. Their construction was near that of the Chase doctrine of divorcing the federal government from all connection with slavery. *Ohio State Journal*, December 10, 1844; *Painesville Telegraph*, December 18, 1844. For the party vote, see *Philanthropist*, January 1, 1845; Norman E. Tutorow, *Texas Annexation and the Mexican War: A Political Study of the Old Northwest* (Palo Alto, Calif.: Chadwick House Pubs., 1978), 88–89.

55. Whigs used the event to remind third party voters of Birney's campaign statement that Polk was weaker and thus less dangerous than Clay. For Birney's remarks, see *Detroit Free*

Press, October 14, 1844. *Ohio State Journal*, March 3, 4, 6, April 1, 5, 8, 1845; *Philanthropist*, March 19, 26, 1845. Every Whig congressman from Ohio voted against annexation. Efforts to arrange an alliance between Massachusetts Whigs and Liberty voters were equally unsuccessful. Brauer, *Cotton versus Conscience*, 114–26.

56. Giddings to Follett, July 16, 1845, in Hamlin, "Follett Papers," vol. 10, 27–29.

57. Corwin to McLean, September 2, 1845, quoted in Maizlish, "Triumph of Sectionalism," 122; *Ohio State Journal*, December 7, 1844; July 3, 29, August 2, 16, 21, 26, 1845. Earlier Corwin had supported an anti-Texas convention but was "astonished at the apathy so prevalent on the subject of Texas, especially in Ohio." Corwin to Follett, March 13, 1845, in Hamlin, "Follett Papers," vol. 9, 84–85.

58. *Ashtabula Sentinel*, January 10, May 15, 29, 1845; *Ohio State Journal*, April 22, 1845; *Ohio American*, July 3, 1845.

59. *Ohio State Journal*, April 8, 1845; Stephen Baldwin to Tait, April 7, 1845, in *Free Labor Advocate*, May 3, 1845.

60. *Ohio American*, July 10, 1845; *Philanthropist*, October 1, 1845. Whigs in Cuyahoga passed similar resolves. *Ohio State Journal*, October 4, 1845. The effect of such Whig resolutions may have been undermined by similar resolves passed by Portage Democrats. *Congressional Globe*, 29th Cong., 1st sess., 795; Carolyn Barbara Huff, "The Politics of Idealism: The Political Abolitionists of Ohio in Congress, 1840–1866" (Ph.D. diss., University of North Carolina, Chapel Hill, 1969), 53, 59.

61. *Ohio State Journal*, May 3, September 20, 27, October 25, 1845; *Whig Almanac, 1846*, 51. The *Philanthropist*, October 29, November 26, 1845, claimed the Liberty party generally held its own in 1845, while the vote of the other parties fell off. Returns from forty-six counties that cast a total of 6,864 Liberty votes in 1844 showed 7,874 third party votes the following year.

62. Orth to Colfax, August 16, 1845; December 1845; January 27, 1846, in Schauinger, "Orth Letters," 367–68, 378–79; *Free Labor Advocate*, April 19, 26, June 21, 1845. For Smith, see Louis J. Bailey, "Caleb Blood Smith," *Indiana Magazine of History* 29 (September 1933): 213–39. Smith's speech is in *Congressional Globe*, 28th Cong., 2d sess., 78–81. See also Willard H. Smith, "Schuyler Colfax: Whig Editor, 1845–1855," *Indiana Magazine of History* 34 (September 1938): 265–66, 270.

63. *Free Labor Advocate*, April 19, May 5, 1845.

64. *Free Labor Advocate*, May 3, 10, 21, June 21, 28, 1845. Edgerton later wrote a volume on the division of the Indiana meeting of Friends.

65. *Free Labor Advocate*, August 16, 1845. It could be argued that if all 357 Liberty voters had supported the Fort Wayne Whig candidate he could have overcome the Democratic candidate's 355-vote margin. Riker and Thornbrough, *Indiana Election Returns*, 110–13; *Whig Almanac, 1845*, 52.

66. Streeter, *Parties in Michigan*, 66, 69, 83–84; *Ohio State Journal*, October 3, 1846; November 24, 1847. As late as December 1845 Reserve Whigs continued to sponsor anti-Texas meetings. *Painesville Telegraph*, November 26, 1845; *Ashtabula Sentinel*, December 23, 1845.

67. For the House vote on the declaration, see *Congressional Globe*, 29th Cong., 1st sess., 795. For response, see *Ohio State Journal*, May 16, 1846.

68. *Ohio State Journal*, October 12, November 19, 1844; January 17, February 6, 1845. Although reapportionment rearranged district lines, Franklin County (Columbus) had been the heart of the congressional seat Whigs had lost by such a small margin in 1843, due partly to third party voters.

69. Edward Paine speech in Paine Family Papers, Lake County Historical Society; *Painesville Telegraph,* January 20, March 24, 1847. Jeffrey G. Charnley challenges the view that northwestern opposition to the war paled when compared to the Northeast. " 'Swords Into Plowshares,' A Hope Unfulfilled: Michigan Opposition to the Mexican War, 1846–1848," *Old Northwest* 8 (Fall 1982): 199–222. For the antiwar opposition of certain religious groups, see Victor B. Howard, "The Doves of 1847: The Religious Response in Ohio to the Mexican War," *Old Northwest* 5 (Fall 1979): 240–49. See also John H. Schroeder, *Mr. Polk's War: American Opposition and Dissent, 1846–1848* (Madison: University of Wisconsin Press, 1973).

70. *Free Labor Advocate,* June 11, May 27, July 2, 1846. For the *Philanthropist's* view of the war, see June 3, 1846. The Cleveland *Plain Dealer,* June 25, 1846, criticized the antiwar meeting and hinted some in attendance were "in fact English."

71. *Congressional Globe,* 29th Cong., 2d sess., 425, 573; Tutorow, *Texas and Mexican War,* 281–83.

72. Erickson, "Politics and Repeal of Ohio's Black Laws," 155–60, 171, stresses that Democrats were far more united in opposing repeal than Whigs in supporting it. Sectionalism was important only in the sense that what support repeal received was concentrated in the northern counties. See the *Cleveland Herald,* in J. Reuben Scheeler, "The Struggle of the Negro in Ohio for Freedom," *Journal of Negro History* 31 (April 1944): 220. Following Corwin's 1842 defeat (with Liberty help) the *Ohio State Journal,* April 1, 1843, pointed to the strong endorsement of the Democratic *Cincinnati Enquirer* for legislative action to overturn a state supreme court decision recognizing the right of persons of mixed blood (not more than one-half African) to vote. For the 1845 session, see February 17, 1845. Bebb's pledge would not have included granting blacks the suffrage. *Painesville Telegraph,* November 5, December 31, 1845; January 28, February 26, 1846; *Ohio State Journal,* February 2, 5, 1846.

73. *Philanthropist,* February 11, 18, 1846; *Painesville Telegraph,* July 1, October 7, 1846; *Ohio State Journal,* March 5, July 14, 1846; *Plain Dealer,* August 25, 1846. See also *Ashtabula Sentinel,* September 28, 1846.

74. Streeter, *Parties in Michigan,* 58; *American Freeman,* September 22, November 3, 10, December 22, 1846; March 24, November 17, 1847. For referendum results, see April 21, May 11, 1847. The *Western Citizen,* July 27, 1843, reported a meeting of "colored citizens" in Chicago to elect delegates to the 1843 Liberty National Convention in Buffalo. Not all Liberty voters necessarily favored a mixing of the races, as their opponents charged. Indeed, some argued freedom for the slaves would "protect them in their family relations" and thus permit them to transmit "their native African hue . . . in all its pristine gloss and beauty to the latest generations." Evidently, this was to be preferred to Clay's talk of an "150 years bleaching process." *Declaration of Independence,* May 1842.

75. Chase cooperated with Whigs working for repeal in the 1845 session. R. F. Paine to Chase, January 29, February 3, 15, 28, March 10, 1845; Charles Anderson to Chase, February 6, 1845, Chase Papers, LC. See also Chase to Flamen Ball, December 27, 1844. Accepting a commemorative pitcher from Cincinnati blacks (in gratitude for his work with fugitive slaves), Chase affirmed the "exclusion of the colored people as a body from the elective franchise" was "incompatible with true democratic principles." Schuckers, *Chase,* 78–79; *The Address and Reply on the Presentation of a Testimonial to S. P. Chase, by the Colored People of Cincinnati* (Cincinnati; Henry Darby & Co., 1845). See the map in Weisenburger, *Passing of the Frontier,* 46. No relationship existed between Liberty votes in 1846 and the number of blacks listed for Ohio counties in 1850. The two correlated at +.07. *Whig Almanac, 1847,* 51; DeBow, *The Seventh Census,* 817–18.

76. The Democratic Cleveland *Plain Dealer* also noted the *"colored* sympathy of the Bebbites," and compared the "single idea of opposition to banks" within its own party to the so-called fanaticism of the abolitionists. *Ohio State Journal,* February 9, April 2, 1846; *Ohio Statesman,* March 28, 1845; September 9, 30, October 5, 23, 1846; *Plain Dealer,* February 10, March 3, May 5, June 23, July 22, August 4, 25, September 1, 9, 1846. In some cases Reserve Democratic conventions adopted resolves on slavery-related issues similar to those passed at Whig or Liberty meetings, but a Geauga Democratic convention in 1845 decisively rejected resolutions condemning annexation, slavery and the slave trade in the federal district, and a repeal of the Black Laws. *Philanthropist,* October 22, 1845; September 30, 1846. Democrats in Medina and Trumbull were said to favor repeal. *Ohio State Journal,* September 16, October 6, 1846. Hamilton County Democrats said nothing of the Black Laws in their 1846 convention. For the Randolph slaves, see Henry N. Sherwood, "The Settlement of the John Randolph Slaves in Ohio," *Mississippi Valley Historical Association, Proceedings* 5 (1911–12): 39–59.

77. *Philanthropist,* July 8, 15, 1846.

78. *Ohio State Journal,* August 12, 26, September 2, 16, 24. October 6, 7, 8, 14, 21, 1846. Whigs claimed Tod refused to announce his support of the Black Laws due to the known sentiment of the Reserve for repeal. The *Philanthropist,* September 23, 1846, also called on Tod to state his position. The *Ohio Statesman,* October 7, 9, 12, 1846, claimed Tod did in fact announce his opposition to repeal, particularly to two northern gatherings in Portage and Ashland counties. The *Plain Dealer,* October 12, 1846, noted Tod's antirepeal position "will defeat him on the Reserve and elect him in other parts of the State."

79. *Philanthropist,* October 14, November 4, 1846. For the *Ohio State Journal's* explanation, see October 31, November 3, 1846. The *Ohio American,* November 18, 1846, printed documents to substantiate the Liberty charges against Bebb.

80. *Ohio State Journal,* October 3, 1846.

81. Whigs pronounced the third party dead since it did not increase its vote as much as expected. *Ohio State Journal,* October 27, 1846; *Philanthropist,* November 11, 1846. There was also a severe storm that ravaged the Reserve on election day. Election returns are in *Ohio State Journal,* December 12, 1846; and *Whig Almanac, 1847,* 51. (There are some discrepancies between the two sources.) The Whig margin of victory was some 2,300 votes. Democrats continued to disagree over the cause of their defeat. See Benjamin Tappan to Eli Tappan, November 1, 1846, Tappan Papers, OHS; *Plain Dealer,* November 7, 1846; and Maizlish, *Triumph of Sectionalism,* 47–49.

82. For the legislative debate over repeal, see *Ohio State Journal,* January 2, 4, 6, 13, 22, February 2, 4, 5, 1847; *Painesville Telegraph,* January 27, 1847. The contest for the Senate seat in 1849 is best followed in the private collections of Chase (LC) and Joshua Giddings (OHS). See also Erickson, "Politics and Repeal of Ohio's Black Laws," 159–60, 171–75; Blue, *Free Soilers,* 163–68; Gerteis, *Morality and Utility,* 99–105. Maizlish, *Triumph of Sectionalism,* 17, notes Whig vacillation over the race issue, but maintains that, when compared to Democratic racial slurs, theirs was "clearly a bold stand."

83. For the Methodist split, see Mathews, *Slavery and Methodism.*

CHAPTER 6

1. Kraut and Field, "Bible Politics in New York," propose that the Liberty decline was not necessarily due to internal causes but to the efforts of the major parties to destroy a disruptive

political threat. This thesis may hold greater relevance for the New York Liberty party than for its comparatively weaker northwestern relative.

2. Chase to Preston King, July 15, 1847, in Bourne, "Diary and Correspondence of Chase," 120–22; Chase to Benjamin Tappan, March 30, 1848, Tappan Papers, OHS. The arrangements for free-soil coalition can be followed in the papers of both Chase and Giddings. See also Blue, *Free Soilers;* Stewart, *Giddings;* Brauer, *Cotton versus Conscience;* and Donald, *Sumner.* Historians have mistakenly assumed that northwestern Liberty voters generally shared Chase's enthusiasm for coalitionist politics since they were supposedly less concerned with abolitionist principles than easterners. See the discussion below and in the next chapter.

3. Gerteis, *Morality and Utility,* 95, argues that Chase did not see the Liberty party as an end in itself but as a way to lure "Yankee reformers" away from their Whig loyalties. Had Chase announced this as his intention, the Ohio Liberty party would have received even less support.

4. Rankin, *Review of the Statement of the Faculty of Lane Seminary,* 8; Keep, *Congregationalism and Church Action,* 6; *Western Citizen,* February 22, 1844; February 25, 1846; Gerrit Smith "To the Liberty Party," in *Albany Patriot,* reprinted in *Free Labor Advocate,* July 9, 1846; L. L. Rice to Chase, February 26, 1845, Chase Papers, LC.

5. Chase to Birney, January 21, 1842; Russell Errett to Birney, October 4, 1844, in Dumond, *Birney Letters,* vol. 2, 661–62, 844–46; Chase to Lewis Tappan, September 12, 1843, Chase Papers, LC. But see Chase to Cleveland, February 17, 1847, Chase Papers, HSP.

6. *Genius of Liberty,* June 5, 1841; *Clarion of Freedom,* October 8, 1847. Exceptions were Antioch, Illinois, Liberty voters, who insisted the party was not "created and guided by the special direction of God" but was born by "natural means as other political parties are, from the necessity of their existence." *Western Citizen,* September 8, 1846.

7. For a slightly different view, see Ronald P. Formisano, "Political Character, Antipartyism, and the Second Party System," *American Quarterly* 21 (Winter 1969): 704–6; and *Mass Political Parties,* 74–76; see also Kraut, "The Liberty Party in Antebellum Political Culture."

8. Birney Diary, quoted in Gruber, "Chase," 109; and Fladeland, *Birney,* 217; Birney to Chase, February 2, 1842, in Dumond, *Birney Letters,* vol. 2, 670–72.

9. Chase to William H. Collins, February 18, 1846, in Bourne, "Diary and Correspondence of Chase," 107–8; Chase to Cleveland, February 17, 1847, in Chase Papers, HSP; Gruber, "Chase," 2, 27–28, 32, 353; Louis Gerteis, "Salmon P. Chase, Radicalism, and the Politics of Emancipation, 1861–1864," *Journal of American History* 60 (June 1973): 43–44. Blue, *Chase,* also stresses this characteristic of Chase's life. Sewell, *Ballots for Freedom,* 107.

10. Hart, *Chase,* 97; Gruber, "Chase," 112; Goldfarb, "Bailey," 120; see also Harrold, "Bailey," 112–13, Wiecek, *Antislavery Constitutionalism,* 218–20; Sewell, *Ballots for Freedom,* 121–26. Harrold, *Bailey,* 50, notes that Chase rivalled, but never really supplanted, Bailey as a leader of the Ohio Liberty party. Foster, "Antislavery History"; and "The Liberty Party," Foster Papers; Eastman, "Liberty and Republican Parties in Illinois," 125–48; Eastman, *Personal Reminiscences of Ichabod Codding,* quoted in Codding, "Codding," 179; Birney, *Birney,* 364–65; see also Julian, *Political Recollections,* 64–67.

11. Bailey to Birney, November 16, 1842, quoted in Harrold, *Bailey,* 61. See William Birney's letters to his father in Dumond, *Birney Letters,* vol. 2, especially January 12, February 26, March 28, 1844; December 9, 1845; also see Morris to Chase, December 17, 1844, in Chase Papers, LC; Harrold, "Bailey," 169; and *Bailey,* 66–67; Goldfarb, "Bailey," 315–19.

12. *Philanthropist,* January 5, 1842; Chase to Lewis Tappan, September 24, 1842, in Chase Papers, LC. As late as February 1845, the *Ohio American* carried Birney's name at the head of its columns. *Ohio State Journal,* February 20, 1845. After 1844 Birney was no longer a serious

contender for the Liberty nomination, probably to Chase and Bailey's relief. Stewart to Birney, February 19, 1843; Hiram Kellogg to Birney, April 5, 1843; Amnon Gaston to Birney, May 5, 1843; Birney to Charles Stewart and Leavitt, August 7, 1843; Birney to Chase, February 2, 1842, in Dumond, *Birney Letters*, vol. 2, 670–72, 717, 728–30, 738, 754–58; Harrold, "Bailey," 164.

13. Samuel Willard to Julius Willard, September 28, 1840, in Willard Family Papers, ISHS. The availability of the *Philanthropist* in some areas of the Northwest was uncertain. Executive Committee of the Illinois State Anti-Slavery Society, *Genius of Liberty*, December 19, 1840; L. L. Rice to Chase, February 26, 1845, Chase Papers, LC. Harrold, "Bailey," 331–35, 364–66, 374–78.

14. *Philanthropist*, September 8, 1840; January 13, 1841; May 25, August 20, 1842; January 18, 1843; April 23, 1845; *Free Labor Advocate*, February, November 9, 1841; August 27, 1842; September 24, 1844; *Whig Almanac, 1845*, 49–50.

15. Chase to Gerrit Smith, May 14, 1842, quoted in Gruber, "Chase," 101–3. For the Chase doctrine, see the discussions in Foner, *Free Soil*, and Wiecek, *Antislavery Constitutionalism*. Also suggestive is Stanley C. Harrold, Jr., "The Southern Strategy of the Liberty Party," *Ohio History* 87 (Winter 1978): 21–36. Harrold argues that Chase, Bailey, Lewis Tappan, and other Liberty leaders did not give up on persuading Southerners to emancipate their own slaves. Unfortunately, he does not consider adequately the Northern aspects of what he calls their Southern strategy.

16. *Philanthropist*, February 14, 1844; *Signal of Liberty*, January 23, April 6, 1842; February 20, 1843; *Free Labor Advocate*, May 24, 1845; *Genius of Liberty*, April 2, 1842; *Western Citizen*, January 18, 1844; *Declaration of Independence*, June 1842.

17. *Cleveland American*, March 31, 1847; Smith, *Liberty and Free Soil*, 99; Miller, "Antislavery in Indiana," 111–12; *Western Citizen*, April 15, 1846; Wiecek, *Antislavery Constitutionalism*, 256–58.

18. See, for example, *Genius of Liberty*, December 25, 1841; *Western Citizen*, July 26, 1842; *Liberty Advocate*, August 20, 1845; *American Freeman*, September 9, 1845; see also Buffum, "Liberty Party"and Reverend Edward Smith, "Principles, Objects and Measures of the Liberty Party," in *Ohio American*, May 1, 1845. *Philanthropist*, March 16, 25, 1842; January 4, 1843. For the Southern view that slavery must expand to survive, see William L. Barney, *The Road to Secession: A New Perspective on the Old South*, New Perspectives in American History Series, James P. Shenton, ed. (New York: Praeger Publishers, 1972).

19. *Philanthropist*, August 27, 1842; March 1, 1843; Goldfarb, "Bailey," 249.

20. *National Era*, April 29, May 20, 1847; Abby Kelley to Giddings, June 5, 1845, in Giddings Papers, OHS; *Philanthropist*, July 2, November 26, 1845; *Painesville Telegraph*, August 6, 13, 1845. Whig papers commonly used Garrisonism against the third party in two contradictory ways: linking the party with the radical, disunionist, and anticlerical views of the Garrisonians, while quoting Garrisonian complaints that the third party had departed from abolitionist doctrine. *Philanthropist*, December 27, 1843; *Ohio State Journal*, September 2, 1846. Galbreath, "Antislavery in Columbiana," 391–92. The *Plain Dealer* screamed "Treason Openly Avowed—The Ball of Disunion Set in Motion on the Western Reserve" (July 7, 16, 1846). For Giddings's motivation, see Gamble, "Giddings and Radical Politics"; see also Giddings to J. A. Giddings, March 1, 1846, Giddings Papers, OHS. *Ohio American*, August 21, 1845; *Anti-Slavery Bugle*, January 29, 1847, quoted in Harrold, "Bailey," 291. The *Liberator* claimed Bailey's *National Era* could not last a day in the federal district if it were an abolitionist sheet. For Bailey's explanation of why he was *not* mobbed, see Bailey to Eastman, June 11, 1847, Eastman Papers, Chicago Historical Society.

21. See Chase's Liberty address of 1843, *Philanthropist,* January 11, 1843. The Chase-Bailey doctrine was for the most part adopted in the national Liberty platform of 1843. Johnson and Porter, *Party Platforms,* 4–8. Milton Sutliff to Chase, July 25, 1848, Chase Papers, LC. Four years earlier Sutliff had maintained the power of Congress to suppress the domestic slave trade. *Liberty Herald,* November 20, 1844.

22. Chase to Stevens, April 18, 1842, Stevens Papers, LC; *Philanthropist,* October 15, 1842; *Signal of Liberty,* February 23, April 6, 1842; *Free Labor Advocate,* February 23, March 26, 1842.

23. *Signal of Liberty,* April 6, 1842; *Western Citizen,* July 26, 1842; *Philanthropist,* September 27, 1843; Foster, "Antislavery History," Foster Papers, BHL. Zebina Eastman recalled that Ichabod Codding, whom Chase regarded as "the greatest of orators," persuaded the delegates to approve the radical fugitive slave provision. Eastman quoted in Codding, "Codding," 82. H. C. Taylor to Chase, March 24, August 4, 1842, Chase Papers, LC; *Free Labor Advocate,* February 3, 1848.

24. Chase to Giddings, February 9, 1843, Julian Papers, Indiana State Library; Chase to Giddings, August 15, 1846, Chase Papers, LC; *Philanthropist,* August 16, 1843.

25. Bailey's support for Democratic candidates in 1838 had caused hard feelings in northern Ohio and cost him subscribers. Harrold, *Bailey,* 33.

26. Lewis to Chase, December 25, 1841, Chase Papers, LC; Chase to editor of *American Citizen,* April 4, 1845, Chase Papers, HSP; Atkins to Chase, June 25, 1845, Chase Papers, LC; Chase to Atkins, July 2, 1845; Q. F. Atkins Papers, Rutherford B. Hayes Library, Fremont, Ohio.

27. "Address of the Southern and Western Liberty Convention," in Chase and Cleveland, *Anti-Slavery Addresses,* 104; Atkins to Chase, June 25, 1845; J. W. Taylor to Chase, July 11, 1845, Chase Papers, LC.

28. Chase to Atkins, July 2, 1845, Atkins Papers, Hayes Library. *National Era,* January 7, 1847; "The Abolitionists," *The United States Magazine and Democratic Review* 16 (January 1845): 8–9. Of course, Chase would have to be an exception to the view of Gerteis, *Morality and Utility,* 90, that those who deserted the Whigs for Liberty "generally conceived themselves to be independent Whigs." Actually, most of the third party faithful had repudiated the Whig party and considered themselves Liberty men.

29. Giddings to Follett, February 18, July 16, 1845, in Hamlin, "Follett Papers, vol. 11, 21–22, 27–29; Giddings to J. A. Giddings, July 21, 1846, Giddings Papers, OHS. Chase to Giddings, September 4, 23, October 20, 1846, Chase Papers, LC; Stewart, *Giddings,* 117–18; Q. F. Atkins to editor, September 22, 1846, in *Cleveland American,* October 7, 1846; see also Chase to L. L. Rice, October 15, 1846, in *Cleveland American,* October 15, 1846.

30. *Free Labor Advocate,* January 23, 1847; Hoffman to Chase, November 3, 1846, in Chase Papers, LC. Along with John Hutchins, Hoffman himself may have validated Whig charges that the third party was only a Democratic ploy. Both Warren Liberty leaders were law partners of David Tod, the Democratic candidate for governor in 1844 and 1846.

31. Similar to their call for opposition to Texas annexation in 1844 and 1845, Reserve Whigs called for public gatherings in support of the troubled Wilmot Proviso. They also denounced the Taylor nomination as the "total disbandment of the Whig party" and held "anti-Taylor" meetings, reaffirming their refusal to support any man not pledged to oppose the further extension of slavery. *Ashtabula Sentinel,* June 17, July 15, 1848; *Painesville Telegraph,* April 14, 21, 28, 1847; February 16, May 17, June 14, 1848. Many Reserve Whigs had earlier endorsed Thomas Corwin and his pronounced opposition to the Mexican War, but Corwin soon returned to party harness. *Ohio State Journal,* September 23, 1847; Norman A.

Graebner, "Thomas Corwin and the Election of 1848: A Study in Conservative Politics," *Journal of Southern History* 17 (May 1951): 162–79; O. F. Curtis to Codding, July 27, 1847, in *American Freeman*, August 11, 1847.

32. *Free Labor Advocate*, April 1, 29, 1847.

33. *Free Labor Advocate*, June 24, July 1, 8, 17, 22, August 19, September 26, 1847.

34. *Free Labor Advocate*, January 5, July 30, 1846.

35. *Free Labor Advocate*, September 17, 1842; March 11, 1843; November 16, 1844; June 16, August 20, 1846; *Western Citizen*, December 21, 1843; July 24, 1845; *Signal of Liberty*, July 31, 1843.

36. John Husted to Chase, September 29, 1845, Chase Papers, LC; *Western Citizen*, September 15, 1846.

37. Chase to Lewis Tappan, May 21, 1842, in Chase Papers, LC.

38. James Gillespie Birney, *The American Churches, the Bulwarks of American Slavery* (1842; reprint, New York: Arno Press, 1969), 39–44; *Philanthropist*, July 28, 1840; Smith, "To the Liberty Party," *Free Labor Advocate*, July 9, 1846.

39. Chase to John Thomas, June 24, 1847, in Bourne, "Diary and Correspondence of Chase," 118–20.

40. *Philanthropist*, March 27, 1838; July 16, 1845. Harrold, "Bailey," 237–40, claims Bailey's eventual separation from his church was rare for an Ohio Liberty man.

41. Stanley Harrold stresses that Bailey was not a typical abolitionist and is difficult to classify. Indeed, but for his alliance with Chase and his position as an editor "on the border," Bailey might have identified more with the Liberty party comeouters. *Bailey*, 239n. *Genius of Liberty*, September 18, 1841; *Western Citizen*, September 8, 1846; October 27, 1847; Zebina Eastman to Chase, November 10, 1846, Chase Papers, LC; Evans, "Abolitionism in Illinois Churches" 83–84; John Duffey to Chase, February 28, January 29, May 21, August 24, 1842, Chase Papers, LC.

42. *Philanthropist*, January 18, December 13, 1843; October 2, 1844; October 22, 1845; *National Era*, March 18, 1847; *Signal of Liberty*, July 14, 1841; July 31, 1843; *Western Citizen*, December 30, 1842; April 6, 13, November 1843; June 5, 1845; May 27, 1846; *Liberty Advocate*, July 9, 1845; *Clarion of Freedom*, February 18, 1848; McKivigan, "Vote as You Pray," 18–19.

43. *Philanthropist*, October 27, 1841; *Free Labor Advocate*, July 4, 1843; Lewis, *Lewis*, 284, 304–5; Mathews, *Slavery and Methodism*, 219–20.

44. Stebbins to Garrison, July 9, 1845, in *Liberator*, July 25, 1845; Pillsbury to Garrison, July 4, 1846, in *Liberator*, July 17, 1846.

45. The formal denunciations of slavery adopted by many eastern Ohio churches after 1845 might have been partly an attempt to answer the criticism of Garrisonian agents. It must be stressed, however, that separation from proslavery churches was well underway in the Northwest by this late date.

46. Russell Errett to Chase, May 9, 1846; Adams Jewett to Chase, January 4, 1846, L. L. Rice to Chase, April 20, 1846; Woolsey Welles to Chase, April 2, 1844, Chase Papers, LC.

CHAPTER 7

1. Leavitt to Giddings, July 6, 1848, Giddings Papers, OHS. See also Austin Willey to Chase, July 10, 1848, Chase Papers, LC; Sewell, *Ballots for Freedom*, 153. Hale S. Mason to Ed and Will Mason, August 20, 1848, Hale Mason Papers, ISHS; Eli Nichols to *Clarion of*

Freedom, July 7, 1848; French, "Harding," 223; Yvonne Tuchalski, "Erastus Hussey, Battle Creek Antislavery Activist," *Michigan History* 56 (Spring 1972): 13; *Western Citizen*, November 14, 1848; *American Freeman*, June 7, July 26, August 9, 23, 1848.

2. Matthews, Garretson, and Preston to Chase, June 17, 1848; G. N. Ells to Chase, April 8, 1848; H. G. Blake to Chase, September 22, 1848, Chase Papers, LC; *Oberlin Evangelist*, August 30, 1848; *True Democrat*, October 3, 1848; *Ashtabula Sentinel*, October 7, 1848; Ellsworth, "Oberlin," 112–13. For Bailey's doubts about Van Buren, see Harrold, *Bailey*, 256n.

3. Most scholars have followed the approach of Rayback, "Liberty Party Leaders of Ohio." Johnson, "Liberty in New England," stresses divisions within the New England party but adheres to the usual interpretation of east versus west. Friedman's *Gregarious Saints* adopts a better approach toward divisions among eastern abolitionists but does not apply this insight to the northwestern third party. Harrold, *Bailey*, xiii–xiv, 110, 253n, admits that differences between east and west have been exaggerated; he also qualifies the common approach by suggesting that Bailey, and to a lesser extent Chase, were reluctant and inconsistent advocates of coalition. It should be noted, however, that their reluctance referred to coalition with the Whigs earlier in the decade. See also Sewell, *Ballots for Freedom*, 133.

4. Bailey to Eastman, June 11, 1847, Eastman Papers; *National Era*, May 6, July 22, 1847. Adopting the Rayback approach, Sewell, *Ballots for Freedom*, 136, claims that support for delaying the convention was widespread in the West.

5. *Free Labor Advocate*, April 21, June 16, June 24, 1847; *Emancipator*, June 30, 1847; *Cleveland American*, May 26, 1847.

6. Chase to Leavitt, June 16, 1847, in *Emancipator*, June 30, 1847. Chase had reason to believe that some in Ohio favored postponing the convention. Adam Jewett to Chase, June 7, 1847, Chase Papers, LC. Some confusion of the committee vote exists in the secondary literature. A check of the primary sources shows Sewell is most correct in putting the vote at 7–2. (See the *Emancipator* for June 1847. Even the *National Era*, July 22, 1847, put the final count at 7–2.) I was unable to locate the source of Rayback's uncited claim that the result was "by a strict East vs. West vote of seven states to five." "Liberty Party Leaders of Ohio," 176. Naturally, this was a critical piece of evidence for his thesis.

7. *National Era*, November 11, 1847. Theodore Foster evidently voted to postpone nominations. Kephart, "Voice for Freedom," 80; *Clarion of Freedom*, November 5, 1847. See *American Freeman*, June 2, 1847, for opposition to the Chase-Bailey policy in northern Ohio.

8. Wiecek, *Antislavery Constitutionalism*, 218–19, makes this mistake. The call for the convention is in *Philanthropist*, April 23, 1845; and Chase Papers, LC. See also Harrold, "Bailey," 316–17; *Free Labor Advocate*, June 21, 1845.

9. Foster, "Antislavery History," 91, Foster Papers; Russell Errett to Chase, August 31, 1846, in Chase Papers, LC. For the list of committee members, see *Western Citizen*, December 22, 1846. Foster to Birney, August 1, 1846, in Dumond, *Birney Letters*, vol. 1, 1025. The Chicago convention decisively rejected the Foster-Beckley plan to commit the party to a platform of universal (especially financial) reform. See Foster, "Liberty Party," 81–84; Foster Papers, BHL.

10. *Clarion of Freedom*, October 14, 1847; *American Freeman*, June 2, July 14, 21, August 25, September 1, 22, October 13, 1847; see also Smith, *Liberty and Free Soil*, 101–2.

11. *National Era*, November 11, 1847. Smith supporters held a second Liberty convention in Buffalo in June 1848, forming the National Liberty Party in opposition to the Hale nomination. H. B. Stanton to Chase, August 6, 1847, Chase Papers, LC. See Sewell's *Ballots for Freedom*, 134–38; "John P. Hale and the Liberty Party, 1847–1848," *New England Quarterly*

37 (June 1964): 200–223; and *John P. Hale and the Politics of Abolition* (Cambridge: Harvard University Press, 1965); *American Freeman,* October 13, November 10, 1847.

12. Accepting the prevalent notion that Liberty declined after 1844, William Hesseltine added the dubious suggestion that the return of economic prosperity after the 1837 panic refuted the Liberty party's claim (à la Bretz) that slavery and prosperity were incompatible. *The Rise and Fall of Third Parties: From Anti-Masonry to Wallace* (1948; reprint, Gloucester, Mass.: Peter Smith, 1957), 13. Harrold, *Bailey,* 73, notes that by 1846 the Liberty party organization had begun to come apart.

In Ohio a severe storm also dampened turnout in the 1847 election. *Ohio State Journal,* October 12, 1847; *Painesville Telegraph,* October 20, 1847.

13. *Cleveland American,* January 7, February 3, 1847. The Reserve Liberty convention organized the Northern Ohio Liberty Association, attempted to unite the *American* and the *Herald* into one Liberty press, and discussed abolition and the churches. Trumbull County Liberty voters determined to effect a "thorough re-organization of the Liberty party," *Mahoning Index,* February 17, May 3, 1847. *Ashtabula Sentinel,* October 25, 1847; *Painesville Telegraph,* October 20, 1847. The *Telegraph* did not list returns for a Liberty candidate for the 1847 contest for state senator in Geauga County. In Cuyahoga County the Liberty vote declined from almost 17 to 9 percent in a contest complicated by the entrance of the National Reformers into the electoral picture. *True Democrat,* October 19, 1847. For Franklin County, see *Ohio Statesman,* October 16, 1847. One reason little is known of the Liberty party in 1847 is the third party press had virtually ceased to function. The Warren *Liberty Herald* had perished in a fire. Bailey left the *Philanthropist* in late 1846 and began to edit the *National Era* in January 1847. The *Cleveland American* was in disarray, and issues survive only into early 1847. The Cincinnati Liberty press, edited by Stanley Matthews, was still active, and the *Clarion of Freedom* was in service in east-central Ohio.

14. According to one observer, Whigs and Democrats in Princeton decided to cooperate when they saw the Liberty minister running ahead of their candidates. At the same time, Lovejoy evidently won votes from non-Liberty voters. This may have also helped the third party win some city offices in Chicago earlier in the year. *Western Citizen,* March 2, May 4, August 17, 1847, has the township returns. Pease, *Illinois Election Returns,* carries the results by counties. In addition to the Liberty delegate elected from Lake, the Kane County delegation was supposed to contain one Liberty member. *Western Citizen,* April 13, 26, May 4, 1847. Pease does not substantiate this. Liberty candidates also won support in several other counties.

15. *American Freeman,* May 3, 1848. Without considering the relative percentages of the Wisconsin election, Smith considered the third party vote to show an increase. *Liberty and Free Soil,* 136. The 1847 Wisconsin results are in *Whig Almanac, 1848,* 51. The *American Freeman,* November 10, 1847, claimed there were nearly one hundred uncounted third party votes. Pease, *Illinois Election Returns,* 156; Edward Magdol, *Owen Lovejoy: Abolitionist in Congress* (New Brunswick: Rutgers University Press, 1967), 89, 95. Smith thought the Liberty showing in 1848 was "creditable." *Liberty and Free Soil,* 135.

16. *Painesville Telegraph,* April 5, 1848; Philo Matthews, Joel Garretson, E. T. Preston to Chase, June 17, 1848, in Chase Papers, LC; *Ashtabula Sentinel,* July 12, 1847.

17. *Ashtabula Sentinel,* June 3, 1848; *Painesville Telegraph,* April 19, 1848. *Western Citizen,* August 25, 1846; February 16, 1847; Foster, "Liberty Party," Foster Papers, BHL.

18. For eastern opposition, see *Emancipator,* July 12, August 2, 9, 1848; Lewis Tappan to Chase, June 14, 1848, Chase Papers, HSP. Lewis Tappan's letter to the *Emancipator* criticizing Chase's call for an Ohio Free Territory convention is also in *American Freeman,* July 5,

1848. Richard H. Sewell, "Hale and Liberty Party," 200–223; Hale to Chase, June 14, 1848, Chase Papers, HSP; Sewell, *Ballots for Freedom,* 157–59. For Chase and the Buffalo Convention, see Blue, *Free Soilers,* 70–80. The balloting by states is in *Ohio State Journal,* August 21, 1848; see also Charles Sumner to Giddings, June 23, July 5, 1848; Giddings to Seth Gates, July 8, 1848, Giddings Papers. Sumner to Chase, July 7, 1848, Chase Papers, LC; John McLean to Chase, August 2, 1848, Chase Papers, HSP.

19. Chase to Preston King, July 15, 1847, in Bourne, "Diary and Correspondence of Chase," 120–22; Chase to Eli Tappan, August 26, 1847, Chase Papers, LC; Chase to Benjamin Tappan, March 30, 1848, Tappan Papers; Benjamin Tappan to Chase, May 29, 1848, quoted in Gruber, "Chase," 135–38; and Maizlish, "Triumph of Sectionalism" 198–99, 226.

20. Samuel J. Tilden to Chase, July 29, 1848, Chase Papers, LC. The proceedings of the Ohio Free Territory convention are in *Ohio State Journal,* June 22, 23, 1848; and *Painesville Telegraph,* June 28, 1848. Liberty supporters were often given a prominent—but not too prominent—role in these conventions. For example, see the "People's Meeting" for Lake County in *Painesville Telegraph,* June 21, 1848. Leavitt, "To the Liberty Party," and Lovejoy to editors are in *Western Citizen,* August 22, 1848. According to George W. Julian, hesitant antislavery Whigs were reassured by the apparent readiness of "several of the great leaders of the Liberty party" to unite with the Barnburners. *Political Recollections,* 57–61.

21. *Free Labor Advocate,* April 21, June 16, 24, July 7, 14, 1848.

22. Stanton to Chase, July 3, 1848, Chase Papers, LC; Chase to Stanton, July 5, 1848, in *Free Labor Advocate,* July 14, 1848.

23. *Free Labor Advocate,* July 14, 21, August 26, September 15, 1848.

24. *American Freeman,* June 2, September 1, November 10, 1847; June 28, July 5, 26, 1848.

25. *American Freeman,* June 28, July 5, 12, 26, August 2, 9, 23, 1848. The proceedings of the Wisconsin Free Territory convention are in August 9, 1848. The same issue listed "Liberty Principles" adopted at earlier party conventions.

26. Richard P. McCormick, *The Second American Party System: Party Formation in the Jacksonian Era* (Chapel Hill: University of North Carolina Press, 1966), 24–25.

27. Thomas Hudson McKee, *The National Conventions and Platforms of All Political Parties, 1789–1905* (Baltimore: Friedenwald Co., 1906), 66–69; Levi Sutliff, "For the Emancipator," July 24, 1848, Sutliff Family Papers, Sutliff Museum, Warren (Ohio) Public Library. This collection also contains resolutions offered at free-territory meetings held in Hartford and Fowler townships in Trumbull County. *Oberlin Evangelist,* September 13, 1848; Whittier quoted in Sewell, *Ballots for Freedom,* 153.

28. Sewell, *Ballots for Freedom,* 158; Leavitt, "To the Liberty Party," in *Western Citizen,* August 22, 1848; *Oberlin Evangelist,* September 27, 1848.

29. Smith, *Liberty and Free Soil,* 98; Chase to Hale, May 12, 1847, Chase Papers, LC.

30. *Western Citizen,* November 23, 1843; *American Freeman,* September 1, 1846; June 2, 1847; March 22, 1848; Keep, *Congregationalism and Church Action,* 135. See *Western Citizen,* September 8, 1846, for disagreements between pious party voters and free thinkers.

31. *Ashtabula Sentinel,* November 23, 1844.

32. *Western Citizen,* March 30, December 21, 1843; see also *American Freeman,* June 23, 1847.

33. Bretz, "Economic Background of Liberty Party," 260–64; Foner, *Free Soil,* 78–84, 90–102, 115; Formisano, *Mass Political Parties;* McKivigan, "Vote as You Pray," 19; Evans, "Abolitionism in Illinois Churches," 428.

34. Neither did the larger antislavery political coalitions adopt the abolitionist churchmen's position of individual responsibility for the sin of slaveholding. Rather, the Free

Soil–Republican antislavery program resembled more closely the concept of organic sin preferred by such Presbyterians as Edward Beecher (and reflected in his sister's, Harriet Beecher Stowe's, great novel). See Merideth, *Politics of the Universe.*

35. Chase to Sumner, January 18, 1858, in Bourne, "Diary and Correspondence of Chase," 276.

36. Johnson, "Liberty in New England," stresses that the Liberty party in New England appealed increasingly to Democrats and centers of manufacturing.

37. Without this admission, Whig attempts to sow disharmony within the new movement by charging that Liberty voters had been sold out by their leaders at Buffalo appear incomprehensible. *Ohio State Journal,* August 12, 21, 26, 1848.

CONCLUSION

1. Adam Jewett to Chase, October 15, 1848, Chase Papers, LC.

2. Ray M. Shortridge, "Voting for Minor Parties in the Antebellum Midwest," *Indiana Magazine of History* 74 (March 1978): 127–28; see also Thomas A. Flinn, "Continuity and Change in Ohio Politics," *Journal of Politics* 24 (August 1962): 521–44. *Painesville Telegraph,* November 15, 1848. The 1846 Liberty vote correlated at +.45 with that of the Ashtabula Free Soil vote in 1848.

3. Filler, *Crusade Against Slavery,* 190–91.

4. Giddings to Milton Sutliff, April 12, March 27, 1863, M. Sutliff Papers.

5. Miller, "Antislavery in Indiana," 148–49, 202–9; Roger H. Van Bolt, "The Rise of the Republican Party in Indiana, 1840–1860" (Ph.D. diss., University of Chicago, 1950), 104–8; 164–67, Field, *Race in New York,* 84–85; Blue, *Chase,* 85–91.

6. Ellsworth, "Oberlin," 112–13.

7. Sewell, *Ballots for Freedom,* 171–89. Eric Foner has stressed the antiblack sentiments among New York Free-Soilers. Field, *Race in New York,* 61–64, found a lower correlation between the Free Soil vote and support for black suffrage than that of the Liberty vote and such support. Berwanger, *Frontier Against Slavery,* argued race prejudice inspired northwestern opposition to slavery expansion. But John Rozett found high correlations between the Free Soil vote, as well as later the Republican, and that of those who opposed the 1848 Illinois black exclusion provision. "Racism and Republican Emergence in Illinois, 1848–1860: A Reevaluation of Republican Negrophobia," *Civil War History* 22 (June 1976): 109.

8. Welsh, "Wrestling with Human Values"; McLeister, *Wesleyan Methodist Church*; Baxter, *Free Will Baptists.* Even Indiana Quakers eventually healed their breach. Elliott, *Quakers on American Frontier.* Mathews, *Slavery and Methodism.* McKivigan, "Abolitionism and the Churches," stresses the resistance of the churches to the abolition message.

9. See also Formisano, *Mass Political Parties,* 205–7. Gerteis, *Morality and Utility,* 87, 93, suggests that antislavery reformers sought not to rearrange or overcome party loyalties but to advance "liberal tendencies" in both parties. As discussed in the pages above, the Liberty faithful encouraged others to separate from such proslavery bodies as the major political parties. Furthermore, in the 1840s few third party supporters recognized much progress in the position of either political party, especially the northwestern Democracy.

10. Richard Hofstadter, *The Idea of a Party System: The Rise of Legitimate Opposition in the United States, 1780–1840* (Berkeley: University of California Press, 1969); McCormick, *Second Party System,* 12–15; Joel Silbey, *The Shrine of Party: Congressional Voting Behavior, 1841–1852* (Pittsburgh: University of Pittsburgh Press, 1967); William E. Gienapp, *The*

Origins of the Republican Party, 1852–1856 (New York: Oxford University Press, 1987). See also Michael F. Holt, *The Political Crisis of the 1850s* (New York: Wiley & Sons, 1978).

11. Liberty advocates commonly disclaimed any nativist sentiments and made repeated (if unsuccessful) overtures to naturalized voters. See, especially, the *Philanthropist* during the 1844 campaign. For an example of denunciations of the Roman Catholic church, see *Signal of Liberty*, July 14, 1841. The *Oberlin Evangelist*, December 18, 1844, insisted "Catholic emigrants are our brethren," even if they were under the control of a "corrupt priesthood."

In the 1846 Chicago city elections the Whig and Democratic nominees were said to be "rumsellers." The Liberty ticket was the "only ticket made up entirely of temperance men." *Western Citizen*, March 11, 1846; see also *American Freeman*, August 18, 1846; *Signal of Liberty*, August 4, 1841.

12. Smith, *Liberty and Free Soil*, 68; James A. Rawley, *Race and Politics:"Bleeding Kansas" and the Coming of the Civil War* (Philadelphia: J. B. Lippincott, 1969).

13. This was a common theme of Liberty party campaign addresses and literature. See, for example, Chase's Southern and Western Liberty Convention address, Chase and Cleveland, *Anti-Slavery Addresses*, 76–96.

14. Besides the Chase remark quoted in the introduction, see the attitude of George W. Julian (who never joined the third party) in his *Political Recollections*, and the views of Michigan Free-Soiler Isaac P. Christiancy quoted in Ronald E. Seavoy, "The Organization of the Republican Party in Michigan, 1846–1854," *Old Northwest* 6 (Winter 1980–81): 356. *Ashtabula Sentinel*, May 29, 1841. The Williamsfield sentiments should be compared to the concluding statement in Rayback, "Liberty Party Leaders of Ohio," 164.

BIBLIOGRAPHY

PRIMARY SOURCES

MANUSCRIPT COLLECTIONS

Q. F. Atkins Papers, Rutherford B. Hayes Library, Fremont, Ohio.
Joel Blakeslee Papers, Western Reserve Historical Society, Cleveland, Ohio.
Sidney Breese Papers, Illinois State Historical Library, Springfield.
Ephraim Brown Papers, Western Reserve Historical Society.
Salmon P. Chase Papers, History Society of Pennsylvania.
Salmon P. Chase Papers, Library of Congress.
Salmon P. Chase Papers, Ohio Historical Society, Columbus.
Ichabod Codding Papers, Illinois State Historical Library.
Thomas Corwin Papers, Vertical File Material, Ohio Historical Society.
Calvin DeWolf Papers, Chicago Historical Society.
Zebina Eastman Papers, Chicago Historical Society.
Elisha Embree Papers, Indiana State Library, Indianapolis.
Caleb Emerson Family Papers, Western Reserve Historical Society.
Alpheus Felch Papers, Bentley Historical Library, University of Michigan.
Edward H. Fitch Papers, Ohio Historical Society.
Theodore Foster Papers, Bentley Historical Library.
Joshua Giddings Papers, Ohio Historical Society.
Illinois State Anti-Slavery Society, Minute Book, 1837–44, Chicago Historical Society.

George W. Julian Papers, Indiana State Library.
Larwill Family Papers, Ohio Historical Society.
Darius Lyman Papers, Western Reserve Historical Society.
Hales S. Mason Papers, Illinois State Historical Library.
John A. McClernand Papers, Illinois State Historical Library.
Robert M. McClelland Papers, Burton Historical Collection, Detroit Public Library.
Paine Family Papers, Lake County (Ohio) Historical Society.
James K. Polk Papers, Library of Congress.
Pullan Family Papers, Ohio Historical Society.
Records of the Ohio River Yearly Meeting of Free Will Baptists, Ohio Historical Society.
Levi Spencer Diary, Illinois State Historical Library.
Thaddeus Stevens Papers, Library of Congress.
Sutliff Family Papers, Sutliff Museum, Warren (Ohio) Public Library.
Milton Sutliff Papers, Western Reserve Historical Society.
Benjamin Tappan Papers, Ohio Historical Society.
Nathan M. Thomas Papers, Bentley Historical Library.
Richard W. Thompson Papers, Indiana State Library.
Treadwell Family Papers, Bentley Historical Library.
Allen Trimble Family Papers, Western Reserve Historical Society.
Lyman Trumbull Family Papers, Illinois State Historical Library.
Elisha Whittlesey Papers, Western Reserve Historical Society.
Samuel Willard Papers, Illinois State Historical Library.
William Woodbridge Papers, Burton Historical Collection.
Joseph A. Wright Papers, Indiana State Library.
Richard Yates Papers, Illinois State Historical Library.

NEWSPAPERS

American Freeman (Wisconsin)
Ashtabula Sentinel
Cincinnati Gazette
Cincinnati Weekly Herald and Philanthropist
Clarion of Freedom
Cleveland Plain Dealer
Columbus Freeman
Declaration of Independence
Detroit Advertiser
Detroit Free Press
Emancipator

Bibliography

Free Labor Advocate and Anti-Slavery Chronicle
Geauga Freeman
Genius of Liberty
Genius of Universal Emancipation
Indiana Freeman
Liberator
Liberty Courier
Liberty Herald
Mahoning Index
National Era
Niles' National Register
Oberlin Evangelist
Ohio American
Ohio Observer
Ohio State Journal
Ohio Statesman
Painesville Republican
Painesville Telegraph
Palladium of Liberty
Peoria Register and Northwestern Gazeteer
Signal of Liberty
True Democrat
Trumbull County Democrat
Watchman of the Valley
Western Citizen
Western Reserve Chronicle

PUBLISHED DIARIES AND CORRESPONDENCE

Barnes, Gilbert Hobbs, and Dumond, Dwight Lowell, eds. *Letters of Theodore Dwight Weld, Angelina Grimké Weld and Sarah Grimké, 1822–1844.* 2 vols. New York: D. Appleton-Century Co., 1934.
Bourne, Edward G., Frederick W. Moore, Theodore C. Smith, Reuben G. Thwaites, George P. Garrison, Worthington C. Ford, eds. "Diary and Correspondence of Salmon P. Chase," In *Annual Report of the American Historical Association, 1902.* Vol. 2, Washington, D.C., 1903.
Clark, Grace J. "A Letter of Dr. Gam. Bailey to Josh. R. Giddings." *Indiana Magazine of History* 26 (March 1930): 43–46.
Curry, Richard O., and Goodheart, Lawrence B., eds. "The Complexities of Factionalism: Letters of Elizur Wright, Jr. on the Abolitionist Schism, 1837–1840." *Civil War History* 29 (September 1983): 245–59.

Bibliography

Dumond, Dwight L., ed. *Letters of James Gillespie Birney, 1831–1857.* 2 vols. American Historical Association, 1938; Gloucester, Mass.: Peter Smith, 1966.
Hamlin, L. Belle, ed. "Selections from the Follett Papers." *Quarterly Publications of the Historical and Philosophical Society of Ohio* 9 (January–April 1914) through 13 (April–June 1918).
_____, ed. "Selections from the William Greene Papers." *Quarterly Publication of the Historical and Philosophical Society of Ohio* 13 (January–March 1918): 3–28; and 14 (January–March 1919): 3–26.
Johannsen, Robert W., ed. *The Letters of Stephen A. Douglas.* Urbana: University of Illinois Press, 1961.
Schauinger, Herman J., ed. "The Letters of Godlove S. Orth, Hoosier Whig." *Indiana Magazine of History* 39 (December 1943): 365–400.
Speer, Michael, ed. "Autobiography of Adam Lowery Rankin." *Ohio History* 79 (Winter 1970): 18–55.
Thayer, George W., ed. "Life and Letters of Lucious Lyon." *Michigan Pioneer Historical Society Collections* 27 (1896): 404–604.
Thomas, Alfred A., ed. *Correspondence of Thomas Ebenezer Thomas, Mainly Relating to the Anti-Slavery Conflict in Ohio, Especially in the Presbyterian Church.* Dayton: 1909.
Thornbrough, Gayle, and Riker, Dorothy L., eds. *The Diary of Calvin Fletcher.* 9 vols. Indianapolis: Indiana Historical Society, 1973–83.
"Transplanting Free Negroes to Ohio from 1815–1858, Documents." *Journal of Negro History* 1 (July 1916): 302–17.
Vander Velde, L. G. "The Diary of George Duffield." *Mississipi Valley Historical Review* 24 (June 1937): 21–34.
_____, ed. "Notes on the Diary of George Duffield." *Mississippi Valley Historical Review* 24 (June 1937): 53–67.

COUNTY HISTORIES

Hanna, Charles Augustus. *Historical Collections of Harrison County, Ohio.* New York: 1900.
History of Brown County, Ohio. Chicago: W. H. Beers & Co., 1883.
History of Clinton County, Ohio. Chicago: W. H. Beers & Co., 1882.
History of Geauga and Lake Counties, Ohio. Philadelphia: 1878.
History of Medina County and Ohio. Chicago: Baskin & Batley, 1881.
History of Trumbull and Mahoning Counties. Cleveland: H. Z. Williams & Bros., 1882.
Johnson, Crisfield, comp. *History of Cuyahoga County, Ohio.* Cleveland: D. W. Ensign, 1879.
Williams, William W. *History of Ashtabula County, Ohio, With Illustrations and Biographical Sketches of Its Pioneers and Most Prominent Men.* Philadelphia: Williams Bros., 1878.

200

Bibliography

PUBLIC DOCUMENTS

Congressional Globe
Debow, J. D. *The Seventh Census of the United States, 1850.* Washington, D.C.: Robert Armstrong, 1853.
Department of State. *Compendium of the Enumeration of the Inhabitants and Statistics of the United States, Sixth Census.* Washington, D.C.: Thomas Allen, 1841.
Richardson, James D. *A Complilation of the Messages and Papers of the Presidents.* Vol. 4. New York: Bureau of National Literature, 1897.
The Seventh Census: Report of the Superintendent of the Census for December 1, 1852; to which is appended the Report for December 1, 1851. Washington, D.C.: Robert Armstrong, 1853.

ELECTION STATISTICS

Pease, Theodore C., ed. *Illinois Election Returns, 1818–1848.* Springfield: Illinois Historical Collections, 1923.
Petersen, Svend. *A Statistical History of the American Presidential Elections.* New York: Frederick Ungar Publishing Co., 1963.
Riker, Dorothy, and Thornbrough, Gayle, comps. *Indiana Election Returns, 1816–1851.* Indianapolis: Indiana Historical Bureau, 1960.
Whig Almanac, 1839–1848. In *The Tribune Almanac for the Years 1838 to 1868, Inclusive; Comprehending the Politicians's Register and the Whig Almanac.* New York: *New York Tribune,* 1868.

CONTEMPORARY ACCOUNTS

Barber, Edward W. "The Vermontville Colony: Its Genesis and History." *Michigan Historical Collections* 28 (1897): 197–287.
Beecher, Edward. *Narrative of Riots at Alton: In Connection with the Death of Rev. Elijah P. Lovejoy.* Alton, Ill.: George Holton, 1838; Miami: Mnemosyne Publishing, 1969.
Beecher, Lyman. *Autobiography, Correspondence, Etc. of Lyman Beecher, D. D.* Edited by Charles Beecher. New York: Harper & Brothers, 1866.
Birney, James Gillespie. *The American Churches, the Bulwarks of American Slavery.* Newburyport: Charles Whipple, 1842; New York: Arno Press, 1969.
Birney, William. *James G. Birney and His Times: The Genesis of the Republican Party with Some Account of Abolition Movements in the South Before 1828.* D. Appleton and Co., 1890; New York: Negro Universities Press, 1969.

201

Codding, Hannah Maria Preston. "Ichabod Codding." *Proceedings of the State Historical Society of Wisconsin* (1897): 169–96.

Coffin, Levi. *Reminiscences of Levi Coffin.* Cincinnati: Western Tract Society, 1876; New York: Arno Press, 1968.

Eastman, Zebina. "History of the Anti-Slavery Agitation, and the Growth of the Liberty and Republican Parties in the State of Illinois." In *Discovery and Conquests of the Northwest, with the History of Chicago,* 125–48. Edited by Rufus Blanchard. Chicago: R. Blanchard and Co., 1900.

Edgerton, Walter. *A History of the Separation in the Indiana Yearly Meeting of Friends; Which Took Place in the Winter of 1842 and 1843, on the Anti-Slavery Question.* Cincinnati: A. Pugh, 1856.

Fairchild, James H. *Oberlin, the Colony and the College, 1833–1883.* Oberlin, Ohio: E. J. Goodrich, 1883.

————. "The Story of Congregationalism on the Western Reserve." *Ohio Church History Society Papers* 5 (1894): 1–27.

"History of the Free Will Baptist Church at Cook's Prairie." *Michigan Historical Collections* 10 (1886): 33–51.

Howe, Eber D. *Autobiography and Recollections of a Pioneer Printer.* Painesville, Ohio: Telegraph Steam Printing House, 1878.

Howe, Henry. *Historical Collections of Ohio.* Cincinnati: Robert Clarke & Co., 1875.

Hutchins, John. "The Underground Railroad." *Magazine of Western History* 5 (November 1886–April 1887): 672–82.

Julian, George W. *Political Recollections, 1840–1872.* Chicago: Jansen, McClurg & Co., 1884.

Keep, John. *Congregationalism and Church Action, With the Principles of Christian Union.* New York: S. W. Benedict & Co., 1845.

Kennedy, William S. *The Plan of Union; or, A History of the Presbyterian and Congregational Churches in the Western Reserve.* Hudson, Ohio: Pentagon Steam Press, 1856.

Lewis, William G. W. *Biography of Samuel Lewis: First Superintendent of Common Schools for the State of Ohio.* Cincinnati: R. P. Thompson, Printer, 1857.

Mansfield, Edward D. *Personal Memories: Social, Political and Literary, with Sketches of Many Noted People, 1803–1843.* 1879. Reprint. Freeport, N.Y.: Books for Libraries Press, 1970.

May, Samuel. *Some Recollections of Our Antislavery Conflict.* Boston: Fields, Osgood, & Co., 1869.

Morris, Benjamin Franklin. *The Life of Thomas Morris: Pioneer and Long a Legislator of Ohio and U.S. Senator from 1833–1839.* Cincinnati: Moore, Wilstack, Keep & Overend, 1856.

Pease, William H., and Pease, Jane H., eds. *The Anti-Slavery Argument.* Indianapolis: Bobbs-Merrill Co., 1965.

Rankin, John. *An Address to the Churches; In Relation to Slavery.* Medina, Ohio: Anti-Slavery Office, 1836.

Bibliography

————. *Letters on American Slavery, Addressed to Mr. Thomas Rankin, Merchant at Middlebrook, Augusta Co., Va.* Newburyport: Charles Whipple, 1824; Westport, Ct.: Negro Universities Press, 1970.

————. "Life of Reverend John Rankin, Written by Himself in His Eightieth Year." Typescript, Ohio Historical Society.

————. *Review of the Statement of the Faculty of Lane Seminary, In Relation to the Recent Difficulties in that Institution.* Ripley, Ohio: Campbell & Palmer, Printers, 1835.

Riddle, Albert G. "B. F. Wade, the Politician—1840." *Magazine of Western History* 3 (April 1886): 590–600.

————. "The Rise of Antislavery Sentiment on the Western Reserve." *Magazine of Western History* 6 (June 1887): 145–56.

Stanton, Henry B. *Random Recollections.* New York: Harper & Brothers, 1887.

Tappan, Lewis, *The Life of Arthur Tappan.* New York: Hurd and Houghton, 1870.

Tocqueville, Alexis de. *Democracy in America.* Translated by George Lawrence, and edited by J. P. Mayer. Garden City, N.Y.: Anchor Books, 1969.

Wood, James. *Facts and Observations concerning the Organization and State of the Churches in the Three Synods of Western New York and the Synod of Western Reserve.* Saratoga Springs: G. M. Davison, 1837.

OTHER PRIMARY MATERIALS

"The Abolitionists." *United States Magazine and Democratic Review* 16 (January 1845): 3–9.

The Address and Reply on the Presentation to S. P. Chase, by the Colored People of Cincinnati. Cincinnati: Henry Derby & Co., 1845.

Bascom, Flavel. "Piety, the True Source of National Prosperity." *Western Citizen* (August 26, 1842).

Buffum, Arnold. "Lecture Showing the Necessity for a Liberty Party, and Setting Forth Its Principles, Measures, and Objectives." In *The Antislavery Argument,* edited by William H. Pease and Jane H. Pease. Indianapolis: Bobbs-Merrill Co., 1965.

Chase, Salmon Portland, and Cleveland, Charles Dexter. *Anti-Slavery Addresses of 1844 and 1845.* Sampson Low, Son and Marston, 1867; New York: Negro Universities Press, 1969.

Governors' Letterbooks, 1840–1853. Edited by Evarts Boutell Greene and Charles Manfred Thompson. Springfield: Illinois State Historical Library, 1911.

Johnson, Donald Bruce, and Porter, Kirk H., comps. *National Party Platforms, 1840–1972.* 5th ed. Urbana: University of Illinois Press, 1973.

Lovejoy, Owen. "Sermon on Religion and Politics." *Western Citizen* (January 20, 1843).

Bibliography

McKee, Thomas Hudson. *National Conventions and Platforms of All Political Parties: 1789–1900.* Baltimore: Friedenwald Co., 1906.

"Political Portraits with Pen and Pencil Number XIX, Benjamin Tappan, Senator from Ohio." *United States Magazine and Democratic Review* 8 (June–July 1840): 42–51.

"Proceedings of the Democratic National Convention, 1844." *Baltimore Sun* (May 29, 1844).

Proceedings of the National Democratic Convention, Held in the City of Baltimore on the 5th of May, 1840. Baltimore: Office of the *Republican*, 1840.

"The Right of Petition," *United States Magazine and Democratic Review* 7 (April 1840): 326–41.

Smith, Edward. "Principles, Objects & Measures of the Liberty Party." *Ohio American* (May 1, 1845).

Sweet, William Warren, ed. *Religion on the American Frontier, 1783–1850.* Vol. 3, *The Congregationalists.* Chicago: University of Chicago Press, 1939.

SECONDARY SOURCES

BOOKS, ARTICLES, DISSERTATIONS, THESES, AND PAPERS

Abzug, Robert H. *Passionate Liberator: Theodore Dwight Weld and the Dilemma of Reform.* New York: Oxford University Press, 1980.

Adams, Alice Dana. *The Neglected Period of Anti-Slavery in America, 1808–1831.* Boston: Ginn and Co., 1908.

Alexander, Thomas B. "The Dimensions of Voter Partisan Constancy in Presidential Elections from 1840–1860." In *Essays on American Antebellum Politics, 1840–1860.* Edited by Stephen E. Maizlish and John J. Kushma. College Station: Texas A & M University Press, 1982.

Argersinger, Peter H. " 'A Place on the Ballot': Fusion Politics and Antifusion Laws." *American Historical Review* 85 (April 1980): 287–306.

Bailey, David T. *Shadow on the Church: Southwestern Evangelical Religion and the Issue of Slavery, 1783–1860.* Ithaca: Cornell University Press, 1985.

Bailey, Louis J. "Caleb Blood Smith." *Indiana Magazine of History* 29 (September 1933): 213–39.

Baringer, William E. "The Politics of Abolition: Salmon P. Chase in Cincinnati." *Cincinnati Historical Society Bulletin* 29 (Summer 1971): 79–99.

Barker, Anthony J. *Captain Charles Stuart: Anglo-American Abolitionist.* Baton Rouge: Louisana State University Press, 1986.

Barnes, Gilbert Hobbs. *The Antislavery Impulse, 1830–1844.* Introduction by William G. McLoughlin. American Historical Association, 1933; New York: Harcourt, Brace & World, 1964.

Bibliography

Barney, William L. *The Road to Secession: A New Perspective on the Old South.* Foreword by James P. Shenton. New York: Praeger Publishers, 1972.

Barnhart, John D. "Sources of Southern Immigration into the Old Northwest." *Mississippi Valley Historical Review* 22 (June 1935): 49–62.

———. "The Southern Element in the Leadership of the Old Northwest." *Journal of Southern History* 1 (May 1935): 186–97.

———. "The Southern Influence in the Formation of Illinois." *Illinois State Historical Society Journal* 32 (September 1939): 358–78.

———. "The Southern Influence in the Formation of Indiana." *Indiana Magazine of History* 33 (September 1937): 261–76.

———. *Valley of Democracy: The Frontier versus the Plantation in the Ohio Valley, 1775–1818.* Bloomington: Indiana University Press, 1953.

Baughin, William A. "The Development of Nativism in Cincinnati." *Cincinnati Historical Society Bulletin* 22 (October 1964): 240–55.

Baxter, Norman A. *History of the Freewill Baptists: A Study in New England Separation.* Rochester, N.Y.: American Baptist Historical Society, 1957.

Benson, Lee. "An Approach to the Scientific Study of Past Public Opinion." *Public Opinion Quarterly* 31 (Winter 1967): 522–67.

———. *The Concept of Jacksonian Democracy: New York as a Test Case.* Princeton: Princeton University Press, 1961.

Berwanger, Eugene H. *The Frontier Against Slavery: Western Anti-Negro Prejudice and the Slavery Extension Controversy.* Urbana: University of Illinois Press, 1967.

Blight, David W. "Perceptions of Southern Intransigence and the Rise of Radical Antislavery Thought, 1816–1830." *Journal of the Early Republic* 3 (Summer 1983): 139–64.

Blue, Frederick J. *The Free Soilers: Third Party Politics, 1848–54.* Urbana: University of Illinois Press, 1973.

———. "From Right to Left: The Political Conversion of Salmon P. Chase." Paper delivered at Missouri Valley History Conference, Omaha, Nebraska, March 1984.

———. *Salmon P. Chase: A Life in Politics.* Kent, Ohio: Kent State University Press, 1987.

Bluestone, Donald Martin. "Steamboats, Sewing Machines and Bibles: The Roots of Anti-Slaveryism in Illinois and the Old Northwest, 1818–1860." Ph.D. diss., University of Wisconsin, Madison, 1973.

Boase, Paul H. "Slavery and the Ohio Circuit Rider." *The Ohio Historical Quarterly* 64 (April 1955): 195–205.

Bolt, Christine, and Drescher, Seymour, eds. *Anti-Slavery, Religion, and Reform: Essays in Memory of Roger Anstey.* Kent, England: William Dawson & Sons, 1980.

Bourke, Paul F., and Debats, Donald A. "Identifiable Voting in Nineteenth-Century America: Toward a Comparison of Britain and the United States before the Secret Ballot." *Perspectives in American History* 11 (1977–78): 259–88.

Brauer, Kinley J. *Cotton versus Conscience: Massachusetts Whig Politics and Southwestern Expansion, 1843–1848.* Lexington: University of Kentucky Press, 1967.

Bretz, Julian P. "The Economic Background of the Liberty Party." *American Historical Review* 34 (January 1929): 250–64.

Brown, Norman D. *Daniel Webster and the Politics of Availability.* Athens: University of Georgia Press, 1969.

Burroughs, Wilbur Greeley. "Oberlin's Part in the Slavery Conflict." *Ohio Archaeological and Historical Society Publications* 20 (April–July 1911): 269–334.

Cardinal, Eric J. "Antislavery Sentiment and Political Transformation in the 1850s: Portage County, Ohio." *The Old Northwest* 1 (September 1975): 223–38.

––––––. "The Development of an Anti-Slavery Political Majority: Portage County, Ohio, 1830–1856." Master's thesis, Kent State University, 1973.

Carter, Kit Carson, III. "Indiana Voters during the Second American Party System, 1836–1860: A Study in Social, Economic, and Demographic Distinctions and in Voter Constancy." Ph.D. diss., University of Alabama, 1975.

Carwardine, Richard. "Evangelicals, Whigs and the Election of William Henry Harrison." *Journal of American Studies* 17 (April 1983): 47–75.

Cavenaugh, Helen M. "Anti-Slavery Sentiment and Politics in the Northwest, 1844–1860." Ph.D. diss., University of Chicago, 1938.

Chaddock, Robert Emmet. "Ohio Before 1850: A Study of the Early Influence of Pennsylvania and Southern Populations in Ohio." In *Studies in History, Economics and Public Law,* vol. 31. New York: Columbia University, 1908.

Chambers, William N., and Davis, Philip C. "Party, Competition, and Mass Participation: The Case of the Democratizing Party System, 1824–1852." In *The History of American Electoral Behavior.* Edited by Joel M. Silbey, Allan G. Bogue, and William H. Flanigan. Princeton: Princeton University Press, 1978.

Charnley, Jeffrey G. " 'Swords Into Plowshares,' A Hope Unfulfilled: Michigan Opposition to the Mexican War, 1846–1848." *Old Northwest* 8 (Fall 1982): 199–222.

"Chronological List of the Congregational Churches of Ohio." *Papers of the Ohio Church History Society* 9 (1898): 68–70.

Claggett, William. "Turnout and Core Voters in the Nineteenth and Twentieth Centuries: A Reconsideration." *Social Science Quarterly* 62 (September 1981): 443–52. Rejoinder by Ray M. Shortridge.

Clarke, Grace Julian. *George W. Julian.* Indianapolis: Indiana Historical Commission, 1923.

Cole, Charles C., Jr. *The Social Ideas of the Northern Evangelists, 1826–1860.* New York: Columbia University Press, 1954.

Conlin, Mary Lou. *Simon Perkins of the Western Reserve.* Cleveland: Western Reserve Historical Society, 1968.

Cooper, William J., Jr. *The South and the Politics of Slavery, 1828–1856.* Baton Rouge: Louisiana State University Press, 1978.

Bibliography

Cormany, Clayton D. "Ohio's Abolitionist Campaign: A Study in the Rhetoric of Conversion." Ph.D. diss., Ohio State University, 1981.

Cross, Whitney R. *The Burned-Over District: The Social and Intellectual History of Enthusiastic Religion in Western New York, 1800–1850.* New York: Cornell University Press, 1950.

Dalzell, Robert F., Jr. *Daniel Webster and the Trial of American Nationalism, 1843–1852.* Boston: Houghton Mifflin Co., 1973.

Dannenbaum, Jed. "Immigrants and Temperance: A Study of Ethnocultural Conflict in Cincinnati, Ohio, 1845–1860." *Ohio History* 87 (Spring 1978): 125–39.

Davis, David Brion. "The Emergence of Immediatism in British and American Antislavery Thought." *Mississippi Valley Historical Review* 49 (September 1962): 209–30.

Davis, Harold E. "Social and Economic Basis of the Whig Party in Ohio, 1828–1840." Ph.D. diss., Western Reserve University, 1933.

Davis, Hugh H. "The Failure of Political Abolitionism." *Connecticut Review* 6 (1973): 76–86.

Degler, Carl N. *Neither Black Nor White: Slavery and Race Relations in Brazil and the United States.* New York: Macmillan Co., 1971.

Dillon, Merton L. "Abolitionism Comes to Illinois." *Journal of the Illinois State Historical Society* 53 (Winter 1960): 389–403.

————. "The Anti-Slavery Movement in Illinois, 1809–1844." Ph.D. diss., University of Michigan, 1951.

————. "The Antislavery Movement in Illinois: 1824–1835." In *The Old Northwest: Studies in Regional History, 1787–1910.* Edited by Harry N. Scheiber. Lincoln: University of Nebraska Press, 1969.

————. *Benjamin Lundy and the Struggle for Negro Freedom.* Urbana: University of Illinois Press, 1966.

————. *Elijah P. Lovejoy: Abolitionist Editor.* Urbana: University of Illinois Press, 1961.

————. "Elizabeth Margaret Chandler and the Spread of Antislavery Sentiment to Michigan." *Michigan History* 39 (December 1955): 481–94.

————. "The Failure of the American Abolitionists." *Journal of Southern History* 25 (May 1959): 159–77.

Donald, David. *Charles Sumner and the Coming of the Civil War.* Chicago: University of Chicago Press, 1960; New York: Phoenix Books, 1981.

————. "An Excess of Democracy" and "Toward a Reconsideration of Abolitionists." In *Lincoln Reconsidered: Essays on the Civil War Era.* New York: Alfred A. Knopf, 1956.

Dorn, Helen P. "Samuel Medary: Journalist and Politician, 1801–1864." *Ohio State Archaeological and Historical Quarterly* 53 (January–March 1944): 14–38.

Downes, Randolph Chandler. *Frontier Ohio, 1788–1803.* Columbus: Ohio State Archaeological and Historical Society, 1953.

Doyle, Don Harrison. *The Social Order of a Frontier Community: Jacksonville, Illinois, 1825–1870.* Urbana: University of Illinois Press, 1978.

Drake, Thomas. *Quakers and Slavery in America.* New Haven: Yale University Press, 1950; Gloucester, Mass.: Peter Smith, 1965.

Dumond, Dwight Lowell. *Antislavery: The Crusade for Freedom in America.* New York: W. W. Norton & Co., 1961.

Eaton, Clement. *Henry Clay and the Art of American Politics.* Library of American Biography Series. Edited by Oscar Handlin. Boston: Little, Brown and Co., 1957.

Elliott, Errol T. *Quakers on the American Frontier.* Richmond, Ind.: Friends United Press, 1969.

Ellsworth, Clayton S. "Oberlin and the Anti-Slavery Movement up to the Civil War." Ph.D. diss., Cornell University, 1930.

Engelder, Conrad J. "The Churches and Slavery: A Study of the Attitudes Toward Slavery of the Major Protestant Denominations." Ph.D. diss., University of Michigan, 1964.

Erickson, Leonard. "Politics and Repeal of Ohio's Black Laws, 1837–1849." *Ohio History* 82 (Summer–Autumn 1973): 154–75.

Essig, James D. *The Bonds of Wickedness: American Evangelicals against Slavery, 1770–1810.* Philadelphia: Temple University Press, 1982.

Evans, Linda J. "Abolitionism in the Illinois Churches, 1830–1865." Ph.D. diss., Northwestern University, 1981.

Fehrenbacher, Don E. *Chicago Giant, A Biography of "Long John" Wentworth.* Madison: American History Research Center, 1957.

Field, Phyllis F. *The Politics of Race in New York: The Struggle for Black Suffrage in the Civil War Era.* Ithaca: Cornell University Press, 1982.

Filler, Louis. *The Crusade Against Slavery, 1830–1850.* New York: Harper & Brothers, 1960; Harper Torchbooks, 1963.

Fisk, William L., Jr. "The Scotch-Irish in Central Ohio." *Ohio State Archaeological and Historical Quarterly* 57 (April 1948): 111–25.

Fladeland, Betty L. "James G. Birney's Anti-Slavery Activities in Cincinnati." *Bulletin of the Historical and Philosophical Society of Ohio* 9 (October 1951): 251–65.

————. *James Gillespie Birney: Slaveholder to Abolitionist.* Ithaca: Cornell University Press, 1955; Westport, Ct.: Greenwood Press, 1969.

Fletcher, Robert Samuel. *A History of Oberlin College From Its Foundations Through the Civil War.* 2 vols. Oberlin, Ohio: Oberlin College, 1943.

Flinn, Thomas A. "Continuity and Change in Ohio Politics." *Journal of Politics* 24 (August 1962): 521–44.

Fogel, Robert. "Without Consent or Contract." Paper delivered at convention of the Organization of American Historians, Reno, Nevada, 1988.

Folk, Patrick Allen. " 'The Queen City of Mobs': Riots and Community Reactions in Cincinnati, 1788–1848." Ph.D. diss., University of Toledo, 1978.

Foner, Eric. *Free Soil, Free Labor, Free Men: The Ideology of the Republican Party before the Civil War.* London: Oxford University Press, 1970.

―――. "Politics and Prejudice: The Free Soil Party and the Negro, 1849–1852." *Journal of Negro History* 50 (October 1965): 239–56.

―――. "Racial Attitudes of the New York Free Soilers." *New York History* 46 (October 1965): 311–29.

Foraker, J. B. "John A. Bingham," *Ohio Archaeological and Historical Society Publications* 10 (1902): 331–51.

Formisano, Ronald P. *The Birth of Mass Political Parties: Michigan, 1827–1861.* Princeton: Princeton University Press, 1971.

―――. "A Case Study of Party Formation: Michigan, 1835." *Mid-America* 50 (April 1968): 83–107.

―――. "The Edge of Caste: Colored Suffrage in Michigan, 1827–1861." *Michigan History* 56 (Spring 1972): 19–41.

―――. "Political Character, Antipartyism and the Second Party System." *American Quarterly* 21 (Winter 1969): 683–709.

Foster, Charles I. *An Errand of Mercy: The Evangelical United Front, 1790–1837.* Chapel Hill: University of North Carolina Press, 1960.

Fox, Stephen Carey. "The Group Bases of Ohio Political Behavior, 1803–1848." Ph.D. diss., University of Cincinnati, 1973.

―――. "Politicians, Issues and Voter Preference in Jacksonian Ohio: A Critique of an Interpretation." *Ohio History* 86 (Summer 1977): 155–70.

French, David. "Elizur Wright, Jr., and the Emergence of Anti-Colonization Sentiments of the Connecticut Western Reserve." *Ohio History* 85 (Winter 1976): 49–66.

―――. "Puritan Conservatism and the Frontier: The Elizur Wright Family on the Connecticut Western Reserve." *Old Northwest* 1 (March 1975): 85–96.

French, Etta Reeves. "Stephen S. Harding: A Hoosier Abolitionist." *Indiana Magazine of History* 27 (September 1931): 207–29.

Friedman, Lawrence J. "The Gerrit Smith Circle: Abolitionism in the Burned-Over District." *Civil War History* 26 (March 1980): 18–38.

―――. *Gregarious Saints: Self and Community in American Abolitionism, 1830–1870.* Cambridge: Cambridge University Press, 1982.

―――. "Historical Topics Sometimes Run Dry: The State of Abolitionist Studies." *The Historian* 43 (February 1981): 177–94.

Fuller, A. O. "Early Annals of the Austinburg Church." *Papers of the Ohio Church History Society* 10 (1895): 63–79.

Galbreath, Charles B. "Anti-Slavery Movement in Columbiana County." *Ohio Archaeological and Historical Society Publications* 30 (1921): 355–95.

―――. "Ohio's Fugitive Slave Law [of 1839]." *Ohio Archaeological and Historical Quarterly* 34 (April 1925): 216–40.

Gamble, Douglas A. "Garrisonian Abolitionists in the West: Some Suggestions for Study." *Civil War History* 23 (March 1977): 52–68.

_____. "Joshua Giddings and the Ohio Abolitionists: A Study in Radical Politics." *Ohio History* 88 (Winter 1979): 37–56.

_____. "Moral Suasion in the West: Garrisonian Abolitionism, 1831–1861." Ph.D. diss., Ohio State University, 1973.

Gara, Larry. "Slavery and the Slave Power: A Crucial Distinction." *Civil War History* 15 (March 1969): 4–18.

Gates, Paul W. "Land Policy and Tenancy in the Prairie Counties of Indiana." *Indiana Magazine of History* 35 (March 1939): 1–26.

Geiser, Karl F. "The Western Reserve in the Anti-Slavery Movement." *Proceedings of the Mississippi Valley Historical Association* (1911–12): 73–98.

Gerteis, Louis S. *Morality and Utility in American Antislavery Reform.* Chapel Hill: University of North Carolina Press, 1987.

_____. "Salmon P. Chase, Radicalism, and the Politics of Emancipation, 1861–1864." *Journal of American History* 60 (June 1973): 42–62.

_____. "Slavery and Hard Times: Morality and Utility in American Antislavery Reform." *Civil War History* 29 (December 1983): 316–31.

Gienapp, William E. *The Origins of the Republican Party, 1852–1856.* New York: Oxford University Press, 1987.

Glazer, Walter S. "Participation and Power: Voluntary Associations and the Functional Organization of Cincinnati in 1840." *Historical Methods Newsletters* 5 (September 1972): 151–68.

Gleason, Reverend Charles A. "History of Paddy's Run Congregational Church." *Papers of the Ohio Church History Society* 10 (1895): 80–100.

Goen, C. C. *Broken Churches, Broken Nation: Denominational Schisms and the Coming of the American Civil War.* Macon: Mercer University Press, 1985.

_____. "Broken Churches, Broken Nation: Regional Religion and North-South Alienation in Antebellum America." *Church History* 52 (March 1983): 21–35.

Goldfarb, Joel. "The Life of Gamaliel Bailey, Prior to the Founding of the National Era: The Orientation of a Practical Abolitionist." Ph.D. diss., University of California, Los Angeles, 1958.

Graebner, Norman A. "Thomas Corwin and the Election of 1848: A Study in Conservative Politics." *Journal of Southern History* 17 (May 1951): 162–79.

Greene, Evarts B. "Sectional Forces in the History of Illinois." *Transactions of the Illinois State Historical Society* 8 (1903): 75–83.

Griffin, Clifford S. *Their Brothers' Keepers: Moral Stewardship in the United States, 1800–1865.* New Brunswick: Rutgers University Press, 1960.

Grim, Paul R. "The Reverend John Rankin, Early Abolitionist." *The Ohio State Archaeological and Historical Quarterly* 46 (July 1937): 215–56.

Gross, Cecilia Rosenblum. "Antislavery in Stark County, Ohio, 1831–1856." Master's thesis, University of Akron, 1962.

Gruber, Robert Henry. "Salmon P. Chase and the Politics of Reform." Ph.D. diss., University of Maryland, 1969.

Gunderson, Robert Gray. *The Log-Cabin Campaign.* Lexington: University of Kentucky Press, 1957.

————. "Log-Cabin Canvass, Hoosier Style." *Indiana Magazine of History* 53 (September 1957): 245–56.

————. "Thurlow Weed's Network: Whig Party Organization in 1840." *Indiana Magazine of History* 48 (June 1952): 107–18.

Haberkorn, Ruth E. "Owen Lovejoy in Princeton, Illinois." *Journal of the Illinois State Historical Society* 36 (September 1943): 284–315.

Hammond, John L. *The Politics of Benevolence: Revival Religion and American Voting Behavior.* Norwood, N.J.: Ablex, 1979.

————. "Revival Religion and Antislavery Politics." *American Sociological Review* 39 (April 1974): 175–86.

Harris, Norman Dwight. *History of Negro Servitude in Illinois, and of the Slavery Agitation in that State, 1719–1864.* Chicago: A. C. McClurg, 1904.

Harrison, Ella W. "A History of the First Congregational Church of Princeton, Illinois, 1831–1924." *Journal of the Illinois State Historical Society* 20 (April 1927): 103–11.

Harrold, Stanley C., Jr. "Forging an Antislavery Instrument: Gamaliel Bailey and the Foundation of the Ohio Liberty Party." *Old Northwest* 2 (Spring 1976): 371–87.

————. "Gamaliel Bailey, Abolitionist and Free Soiler." Ph.D. diss., Kent State University, 1975.

————. *Gamaliel Bailey and Antislavery Union.* Kent, Ohio: Kent State University Press, 1986.

————. "The Southern Strategy of the Liberty Party." *Ohio History* 87 (Winter 1978): 21–36.

Harstine, John Jacob. "Senatorial Career of Benjamin Tappan." Master's thesis, Ohio State University, 1939.

Hart, Albert Bushnell. *Salmon Portland Chase.* American Statesmen Series. Boston: Houghton, Mifflin and Co., 1899.

Heinl, Frank J. "Jacksonville and Morgan County: An Historical View." *Journal of the Illinois State Historical Society* 18 (April 1925): 5–38.

Hendricks, John R. "The Liberty Party in New York State, 1838–1848." Ph.D. diss., Fordham University, 1959.

Henig, Gerald S. "The Jacksonian Attitude Toward Abolitionism in the 1830's." *Tennessee Historical Quarterly* 28 (Spring 1969): 42–56.

Hesseltine, William B. *The Rise and Fall of Third Parties: From Anti-Masonry to Wallace.* Washington, D.C.: Public Affairs Press, 1948; Gloucester, Mass.: Peter Smith, 1957.

Hewitt, Nancy A. *Women's Activism and Social Change: Rochester, New York, 1822–1872.* Ithaca, Cornell University Press, 1984.

Hicks, John D. "The Third Party Tradition in American Politics." *Mississippi Valley Historical Review* 20 (June 1933): 3–28.

Hightower, Raymond L. "Joshua L. Wilson, Frontier Controversialist." *Church History* 3 (December 1934): 300–316.

Hofstadter, Richard. *The American Political Tradition and the Men Who Made It.*

Bibliography

Foreword by Christopher Lasch. New York: Alfred A. Knopf, 1948; Vintage Books, 1973.

————. *The Idea of a Party System: The Rise of Legitimate Opposition in the United States, 1780–1840.* Berkeley: University of California Press, 1969.

Holt, Edgar Allan. *Party Politics in Ohio, 1840–1850.* Ohio Historical Collections, vol. 1. Columbus: F. J. Heer Printing Co., 1931.

Holt, Michael F. *The Political Crisis of the 1850s.* New York: Wiley & Sons, 1978.

Howard, Victor B. "The Antislavery Movement in the Presbyterian Church, 1835–1861." Ph.D. diss., Ohio State University, 1961.

————. "The Doves of 1847: The Religious Response in Ohio to the Mexican War." *The Old Northwest* 5 (Fall 1979): 237–67.

Howe, Daniel Walker. *The Political Culture of the American Whigs.* Chicago: University of Chicago Press, 1979.

Hubbard, Anson M. "A Colony Settlement, Geneseo, Illinois, 1836–1837." *Journal of the Illinois State Historical Society* 29 (January 1937): 403–31.

Hubbart, Henry C. *The Older Middle West, 1840–1880.* New York: D. Appleton-Century Co., 1936.

————. " 'Pro-Southern' Influences in the Free West, 1840–1865." *Mississippi Valley Historical Review* 20 (June 1933): 45–62.

Huff, Carolyn Barbara. "The Politics of Idealism: The Political Abolitionists of Ohio in Congress, 1840–1866." Ph.D. diss., University of North Carolina, 1969.

Hunter, W. H. "The Pathfinders of Jefferson County." *Ohio Archaeological and Historical Society Publications* 6 (1898): 94–313.

Hyman, Harold M., and Wiecek, William M. *Equal Justice Under Law: Constitutional Development, 1835–1875.* New York: Harper & Row, 1982.

Jensen, Richard J. *Illinois: A Bicentennial History.* New York: W. W. Norton & Co., 1978.

Jentz, John. "The Antislavery Constituency in Jacksonian New York City. " *Civil War History* 27 (June 1981): 101–22.

Johnson, James E. "Charles G. Finney and a Theology of Revivalism." *Church History* 38 (September 1969): 338–58.

Johnson, Paul E. *A Shopkeeper's Millennium: Society and Revivals in Rochester, New York, 1815–1837.* New York: Hill and Wang, 1978.

Johnson, Reinhard O. "The Liberty Party in Massachusetts, 1840–1848: Antislavery Third Party Politics in the Bay State." *Civil War History* 28 (September 1982): 237–65.

————. "The Liberty Party in New England, 1840–1848: The Forgotten Abolitionists." Ph.D. diss., Syracuse University, 1976.

Jones, Robert L. *The History of Agriculture in Ohio to 1880.* Kent, Ohio: Kent State University Press, 1983.

Jordan, Wayne. "The People of Ohio's First County." *The Ohio State Archaeological and Historical Quarterly* 49 (January–March 1940): 1–40.

Kenworthy, Leonard S. "Henry Clay at Richmond in 1842." *Indiana Magazine of History* 30 (December 1934): 353–59.

Bibliography

Kephart, John E. "A Pioneer Michigan Abolitionist." *Michigan History* 45 (March 1961): 34–42.

———. " 'A Voice for Freedom': *The Signal of Liberty,* 1841–1848." Ph.D. diss., University of Michigan, 1960.

Kindig, Everett William, II. "Western Opposition to Jackson's 'Democracy': The Ohio Valley as a Case Study, 1827–1836." Ph.D. diss., Stanford University, 1975.

Kleppner, Paul. *The Cross of Culture: A Social Analysis of Midwestern Politics, 1850–1900.* New York: Free Press, 1970.

———. *The Third Electoral System, 1853–1892: Parties, Voters and Political Cultures.* Chapel Hill: University of North Carolina Press, 1979.

Klingaman, David C., and Eedder, Richard K., eds. *Essays in Nineteenth Century Economic History: The Old Northwest.* Athens: Ohio University Press, 1975.

Kofoid, Charrie P. "Puritan Influences in Illinois Before 1860." *Transactions of the Illinois State Historical Society* 10 (1905): 261–338.

Kooker, Arthur Raymond. "The Anti-Slavery Movement in Michigan, 1796–1840: A Study in Humanitarianism on an American Frontier." Ph.D. diss., University of Michigan, 1941.

Kraditor, Aileen S. "The Liberty and Free Soil Parties." In *History of U.S. Political Parties.* Vol. 1, *1789–1860, From Factions to Parties.* General editor Arthur M. Schlesinger, Jr. New York: Chelsea House Publishers, 1973.

———. *Means and Ends in American Abolitionism: Garrison and His Critics on Strategy and Tactics, 1834–1850.* New York: Pantheon Books, 1967.

Kraut, Alan Morton. "The Forgotten Reformers: A Profile of Third Party Abolitionists in Antebellum New York." In *Antislavery Reconsidered: New Perspectives on the Abolitionists.* Edited by Lewis Perry and Michael Fellman. Baton Rouge: Louisiana University Press, 1979.

———. "The Liberty Men of New York: Political Abolitionism in New York State, 1840–1848." Ph.D. diss., Cornell University, 1975.

———. "Partisanship and Principles: The Liberty Party in Antebellum Political Culture." In *Crusaders and Compromisers: Essays on the Relationship of the Antislavery Struggle to the Antebellum Party System.* Edited by Alan M. Kraut. Westport, Ct.: Greenwood Press, 1983.

Kraut, Alan M., and Field, Phyllis. "Politics versus Principles: The Partisan Response to 'Bible Politics' in New York State." *Civil War History* 25 (June 1979): 101–18.

Krug, Mark M. *Lyman Trumbull: Conservative Radical.* New York: A. S. Barnes and Co., 1965.

Kuhns, Frederick I. *The American Home Missionary Society in Relation to the Antislavery Controversy in the Old Northwest.* Billings, Mont.: 1959.

———. "The Breakup of the Plan of Union in Michigan." *Michigan History* 32 (June 1948): 157–80.

Lang, Elfrieda. "Irishmen in Northern Indiana Before 1850." *Mid-America* 36 (July 1954): 190–98.

Bibliography

_____. "Southern Migration to Northern Indiana before 1850." *Indiana Magazine of History* 50 (December 1954): 349–56.

Lawlis, Chelsea L. "Prosperity and Hard Times in the Whitewater Valley, 1830–1840." *Indiana Magazine of History* 43 (December 1947): 363–78.

Lindell, Terrence J. "South Dakota Populism." Master's thesis, University of Nebraska, Lincoln, 1982.

Lindley, Harlow. "The Quakers in the Old Northwest." *Proceedings of the Mississippi Valley Historical Association* 5 (1911–12): 60–72.

Litwack, Leon F. *North of Slavery: The Negro in the Free States, 1790–1860.* Chicago: University of Chicago Press, 1961.

Locke, Mary Stoughton Locke. *Anti-Slavery in America, From the Introduction of African Slaves to the Prohibition of the Slave Trade, 1619–1808.* Boston: Ginn & Co., 1901.

Loomis, Willard D. "The Anti-Slavery Movement in Ashtabula County, Ohio, 1834–1854." Master's thesis, Western Reserve University, 1936.

Lottich, Kenneth V. "Culture Transplantation on the Connecticut Reserve." *Historical and Philosophical Society of Ohio Bulletin* 17 (July 1959): 154–66.

_____. *New England Transplanted.* Dallas: Royal Publishing Co., 1964.

_____. "The Western Reserve and the Frontier Thesis." *The Ohio Historical Quarterly* 70 (January 1961): 45–57.

Loveland, Anne C. "Evangelicalism and 'Immediate Emancipation' in American Antislavery Thought." *Journal of Southern History* 32 (May 1966): 172–88.

Ludlum, David M. *Social Ferment in Vermont, 1791–1850.* New York: Columbia University Press, 1939.

Lupold, Harry Forrest, "Antislavery Activities in a Western Reserve County, 1820–1860." *Negro History Bulletin* 38 (1975): 468–69.

Lynch, William O. "Anti-Slavery Tendencies of the Democratic Party in the Northwest, 1848–1850." *Mississippi Valley Historical Review* 11 (December 1924): 319–31.

_____. "The Flow of Colonists to and from Indiana." *Indiana Magazine of History* 11 (March 1915): 1–8.

Mabry, William A. "Ante-Bellum Cincinnati and its Southern Trade." In *American Studies in Honor of William Kenneth Boyd.* Edited by David K. Jackson. Durham: Duke University Press, 1940; Freeport, N.Y.: Books for Libraries Press, 1968.

McCormick, Richard P. *The Second American Party System: Party Formation in the Jacksonian Era.* Chapel Hill: University of North Carolina Press, 1966.

McCracken, S. B. "The Press of Michigan—A Fifty Year View." *Michigan Pioneer Historical Collections* 18 (1891): 302–97.

McFaul, John M. "Expediency vs. Morality, Jacksonian Politics and Slavery." *Journal of American History* 57 (June 1975): 24–39.

McGoorty, J. P. "Early Irish of Illinois." *Illinois State Historical Society Transactions* 34 (1927): 54–64.

Bibliography

McKivigan, John R. "Abolitionism and the American Churches, 1830–1865: A Study of Attitudes and Tactics." Ph.D. diss., Ohio State University, 1977.

———. "The Antislavery 'Comeouter' Sects: A Neglected Dimension of Abolitionist Movement." *Civil War History* 26 (June 1980): 142–60.

———. "The Christian Anti-Slavery Convention Movement of the Northwest." *The Old Northwest* 5 (Winter 1979–80): 345–66.

———. "Vote as you Pray and Pray as you Vote: Church-Oriented Abolitionism and Antislavery Politics." Paper delivered at convention of Organization of American Historians, Cincinnati, Ohio, 1983.

———. *The War Against Proslavery Religion: Abolitionism and the Northern Churches.* Ithaca: Cornell University Press, 1984.

McLeister, Ira Ford. *History of the Wesleyan Methodist Church in America.* Syracuse: Wesleyan Methodist Publishing Association, 1934.

McMaster, John Bach. *A History of the People of the United States, From the Revolution to the Civil War.* Vol. 6, *1830–1842.* New York: D. Appleton and Co., 1906.

McPherson, James M. "The Fight Against the Gag Rule: Joshua Leavitt and the Antislavery Insurgency in the Whig Party, 1839–1842." *Journal of Negro History* 48 (April 1963): 177–95.

Magdol, Edward. *The Antislavery Rank and File: A Social Profile of the Abolitionists' Constituency.* Westport, Ct.: Greenwood Press, 1986.

———. *Owen Lovejoy: Abolitionist in Congress.* New Brunswick: Rutgers University Press, 1967.

Maizlish, Stephen E. "The Triumph of Sectionalism: The Transformation of Politics in the Antebellum North, Ohio, 1844–1860." Ph.D. diss., University of California, Berkeley, 1978.

———. *The Triumph of Sectionalism: The Transformation of Ohio Politics, 1844–1856.* Kent, Ohio: Kent State University Press, 1983.

Maizlish, Stephen E., and Kushma, John J., eds. *Essays on American Antebellum Politics, 1840–1860.* College Station: Texas A & M University Press, 1982.

Marsden, George M. *The Evangelical Mind and the New School Presbyterian Experience: A Case Study of Thought and Theology in Nineteenth-Century America.* New Haven: Yale University Press, 1970.

Martin, Thomas P. "The Upper Mississippi Valley in Anglo-American Anti-Slavery and Free Trade Relations, 1837–1842." *Mississippi Valley Historical Review* 15 (September 1928): 204–20.

Mathews, Donald G. *Religion in the Old South.* Chicago: University of Chicago Press, 1977.

———. *Slavery and Methodism: A Chapter in American Morality, 1780–1845.* Princeton: Princeton University Press, 1965.

Mathews, Lois. *The Expansion of New England.* Boston: Houghton Mifflin Co., 1909.

Mayfield, John. *Rehearsal for Republicanism: Free Soil and the Politics of Antislavery.* Port Washington, N.Y.: Kennikat Press, 1980.

Bibliography

Mead, Sidney Earl. *Nathaniel William Taylor, 1786–1856: A Connecticut Liberal.* Chicago: University of Chicago Press, 1942; Hamden, Ct.: Archon Books, 1967.

Merideth, Robert. *The Politics of the Universe: Edward Beecher, Abolition and Orthodoxy.* Nashville: Vanderbilt University Press, 1968.

Miller, Marion C. "The Antislavery Movement in Indiana." Ph.D. diss., University of Michigan, 1938.

Miyakawa, T. Scott. *Protestants and Pioneers: Individualism and Conformity on the American Frontier.* Chicago: University of Chicago Press, 1964.

Muelder, Hermann R. "Congregationalism and Presbyterians in the Early History of the Galesburg Churches." *Papers in Illinois History and Transactions for the Year 1937.* Springfield: Illinois State Historical Society, 1938.

_____. "Congregationalists and the Civil War." In *A History of Illinois Congregational and Christian Churches.* Edited by Matthew Spinka. Chicago: Congregational and Christian Conference of Illinois, 1944.

_____. *Fighters for Freedom: The History of Antislavery Activities of Men and Women Associated with Knox College.* New York: Columbia University Press, 1959.

_____. "Galesburg: Hot-Bed of Abolitionism." *Journal of the Illinois State Historical Society* 35 (September 1942): 216–35.

Myers, Jacob W. "The Beginning of German Immigration in the Middle West." *Journal of the Illinois State Historical Society* 15 (October–January 1922–23): 592–99.

Ndukwu, Maurice D. "Antislavery in Michigan: A Study of its Origin, Development, and Expression from Territorial Period to 1860." Ph.D. diss., Michigan State University, 1979.

Nichols, Robert H. "The Plan of Union in New York." *Church History* 5 (March 1936): 29–51.

Nordquist, Philip A. "The Ecology of Religious Denominational Preference in the United States: 1850." Ph.D. diss., University of Washington, 1964.

Nuermburger, Ruth Anna. *Charles Osborn in The Anti-Slavery Movement.* Columbus: Ohio Archaeological and Historical Society, 1937.

Nye, Russel B. *Fettered Freedom: Civil Liberties and the Slavery Controversy, 1830–1860.* Urbana: University of Illinois Press, 1963.

O'Dell, Richard F. "The Early Anti-Slavery Movement in Ohio." Ph.D. diss., University of Michigan. 1948.

Orahan, W. J. "Irish Settlements in Illinois." *The Catholic World* 33 (May 1881): 157–62.

Paul, James C. N. *Rift in the Democracy.* New York: A. S. Barnes & Co., 1951; Perpetua, 1961.

Pearson, Samuel C. "From Church to Denomination: American Congregationalism in the Nineteenth Century." *Church History* 38 (March 1969): 67–87.

Pease, Calvin J. *The Frontier State, 1818–1848.* Edited by C. W. Alvord. Vol. 1,

Centennial History of Illinois. Chicago: A. C. McClurg, 1904.

Pease, Jane H., and Pease, William H. *Bound with Them in Chains: A Biographical History of the Antislavery Movement.* Westport, Ct.: Greenwood Press, 1972.

Perry, Lewis. *Radical Abolitionism: Anarchy and the Government of God in Antislavery Thought.* Ithaca: Cornell University Press, 1973.

Plunkett, Margaret Louise. "A History of the Liberty Party with Emphasis on its Activities in the Northeastern States." Ph.D. diss., Cornell University, 1930.

Powell, Milton Bryan. *The Abolitionist Controversy in the Methodist Episcopal Church, 1840–1864.* Ph.D. diss., University of Iowa, 1963.

Power, Richard Lyle. *Planting Corn Belt Culture: The Impress of the Upland Southerner and Yankee in the Old Northwest.* Indianapolis: Indiana Historical Society, 1953.

———. "Wet Lands and the Hoosier Stereotype." *Mississippi Valley Historical Review* 22 (June 1953): 33–48.

Price, Robert. "Further Notes on Granville's Anti-Abolition Disturbances." *Ohio State Archaeological and Historical Quarterly* 45 (October 1936): 365–66.

———. "The Ohio Anti-Slavery Convention of 1836." *Ohio State Archaeological and Historical Quarterly* 45 (April 1936): 173–88.

Rammelkamp, Charles Henry. *Illinois College: A Centennial History, 1829–1929.* New Haven: Yale University Press, 1928.

Rastatter, Edward H. "Nineteenth Century Public Land Policy: The Case for the Speculator." In *Essays in Nineteenth Century Economic History: The Old Northwest.* Edited by David C. Klingaman and Richard K. Eedder. Athens: Ohio University Press, 1975.

Ratcliffe, Donald J. "Antimasonry in Lake County, Ohio, 1827–1834." *Lake County Historical Quarterly* 22 (March 1980): 1–6.

———. "Politics in Jacksonian Ohio: Reflections on the Ethnocultural Interpretation." *Ohio History* 88 (Winter 1979): 5–36.

———. "The Role of Voters and Issues in Party Formation: Ohio, 1824." *Journal of American History* 59 (March 1973): 847–70.

Rawley, James A. *Race and Politics: "Bleeding Kansas" and the Coming of the Civil War.* Philadelphia: J. B. Lippincott, 1969.

Rayback, Joseph. "The Liberty Party Leaders of Ohio: Exponents of Antislavery Coalition." *The Ohio State Archaeological and Historical Quarterly* 57 (April 1948): 165–78.

Reilley, Edward C. "Politico-Economic Considerations in the Western Reserve's Early Slavery Controversy." *The Ohio State Archaeological and Historical Quarterly* 52 (April–June 1943): 141–57.

Rice, Madeleine Hooke. *American Catholic Opinion in the Slavery Controversy.* New York: Columbia University Press, 1944.

Richards, Leonard L. *"Gentlemen of Property and Standing": Anti-Abolition Mobs in Jacksonian America.* New York: Oxford University Press, 1970.

Bibliography

————. "The Jacksonians and Slavery." In *Antislavery Reconsidered: New Perspectives on the Abolitionists*. Edited by Lewis Perry and Michael Fellman. Baton Rouge: Louisiana State University Press, 1979.

————. *The Life and Times of Congressman John Quincy Adams*. New York: Oxford University Press, 1986.

Rippley, LaVern J. "The Chillicothe Germans." *Ohio History* 75 (Autumn 1966): 212–25.

Roseboom, Eugene H. "Southern Ohio and the Union in 1863." *Mississippi Valley Historical Review* 39 (June 1952): 29–44.

Rosenberg, Morton M., and McClurg, Dennis V. *The Politics of Pro-Slavery Sentiment in Indiana, 1816–1861*. Muncie, Ind.: Ball State University Publications, 1968.

Rozett, John. "Racism and Republican Emergence in Illinois, 1848–1860: A Reevaluation of Republican Negrophobia." *Civil War History* 22 (June 1976): 101–15.

————. "The Social Bases of Party Conflict in the Age of Jackson: Individual Voting Behavior in Green County, Illinois, 1838–1848." Ph.D. diss., University of Michigan, 1974.

Rudolph, L. C. *Hoosier Zion: The Presbyterians in Early Indiana*. New Haven: Yale University Press, 1963.

Scheeler, J. Reuben. "The Struggle of the Negro in Ohio for Freedom." *Journal of Negro History* 31 (April 1946): 208–26.

Scheiber, Harry N. *The Old Northwest: Studies in Regional History, 1787–1910*. Lincoln: University of Nebraska Press, 1969.

————. "Urban Rivalry and Internal Improvements in the Old Northwest, 1820–1860." *Ohio History* 71 (October 1962): 227–39.

Schell, Herbert S. "The Grange in Dakota Territory." *Agricultural History* 10 (January 1936): 77–78.

Schroeder, John H. *Mr. Polk's War: American Opposition and Dissent, 1846–1848*. Madison: University of Wisconsin Press, 1973.

Schuckers, J. W. *The Life and Public Services of Salmon Portland Chase*. New York: D. Appleton and Co., 1874.

Seavoy, Ronald E. "The Organization of the Republican Party in Michigan, 1846–1854." *The Old Northwest* 6 (Winter 1980–81): 343–76.

Selby, Paul. "The Genesis of the Republican Party in Illinois." *Transactions of the Illinois State Historical Society* 11 (1906): 270–83.

Seldon, Mary Elisabeth. "George W. Julian: A Political Independent." In *Gentlemen from Indiana: National Party Candidates, 1836–1940*. Edited by Ralph D. Gray. Indianapolis: Indiana Historical Bureau, 1977.

Sellers, Charles G. "Election of 1844." In *History of American Presidential Elections, 1789–1968*. Edited by Arthur M. Schlesinger, Jr., and Fred L. Israel. Vol. 2. New York: Chelsea House Publishers, 1985.

————. *James K. Polk, Continentalist*. Princeton: Princeton University Press, 1966.

Sernett, Milton C. *Abolition's Axe: Beriah Green, Oneida Institute, and the Black Freedom Struggle*. Syracuse: Syracuse University Press, 1986.

Sewell, Richard H. *Ballots for Freedom: Antislavery Politics in the United States, 1837–1860*. New York: Oxford University Press, 1976; W. W. Norton & Co., 1980.

———. "John P. Hale and the Liberty Party, 1847–1848." *New England Quarterly* 37 (June 1964): 200–223.

———. *John P. Hale and the Politics of Abolition*. Cambridge: Harvard University Press, 1965.

Sharp, James Roger. *The Jacksonians versus the Banks*. New York: Columbia University Press, 1970.

Sherwood, Henry N. "Movement in Ohio to Deport the Negro." *Quarterly Publication of the Historical and Philosophical Society of Ohio* 7 (June–September 1912): 53–78.

———. "The Settlement of the John Randolph Slaves in Ohio." *Mississippi Valley Historical Association, Proceedings* 5 (1911–12): 39–59.

Shilling, David C. "Relation of Southern Ohio to the South During the Decade Preceding the Civil War." *Quarterly Publication of the Historical and Philosophical Society of Ohio* 8 (January–March 1913): 3–38.

Shortridge, Ray M. "Democracy's Golden Age?: Voter Turnout in the Midwest, 1840–1872." *Social Science Quarterly* 60 (March 1980): 617–29.

———. "The Voter Realignment in the Midwest during the 1850s." *American Political Quarterly* 4 (April 1976): 193–222.

———. "Voting for Minor Parties in the Antebellum Midwest." *Indiana Magazine of History* 74 (March 1978): 117–34.

———. "Voting Patterns in the American Midwest, 1840–1872." Ph.D. diss., University of Michigan, 1974.

Silbey, Joel H. "The Civil War Synthesis in American Political History." *Civil War History* 10 (June 1964): 130–40.

———. *The Partisan Imperative: The Dynamics of American Politics Before the Civil War*. New York: Oxford University Press, 1987.

———. *The Shrine of Party: Congressional Voting Behavior, 1841–1852*. Pittsburgh: University of Pittsburgh Press, 1967.

———. "The Slavery-Extension Controversy and Illinois Congressmen, 1846–1850." *Journal of the Illinois State Historical Society* 58 (Winter 1965): 378–95.

Skotheim, Robert A. "A Note on Historical Method: David Donald's 'Toward a Reconsideration of Abolitionists'." *Journal of Southern History* 25 (August 1959): 356–65.

Slosser, Gaius, ed. *They Seek a Country: The American Presbyterians, Some Aspects*. New York: Macmillan Co., 1955.

Smith, Page. *As a City Upon a Hill: The Town in American History*. New York: Alfred A. Knopf, 1966.

Smith, Theodore Clarke. "The Free Soil Party in Wisconsin." *Wisconsin State Historical Society Publications* 42 (December 1894): 97–162.

Bibliography

_____. *The Liberty and Free Soil Parties in the Northwest*. New York: Longmans, Green, and Co., 1897.

Smith, Willard H. "Schuyler Colfax: Whig Editor, 1845–1855." *Indiana Magazine of History* 34 (September 1938): 262–82.

Sorin, Gerald. "The Historical Theory of Political Radicalism: Michigan Abolitionist Leaders as a Test Case." Master's thesis, Wayne State University, 1964.

Spinka, Matthew, ed. *A History of Illinois Congregational and Christian Churches*. Chicago: Congregational and Christian Conference of Illinois, 1944.

Staiger, C. Bruce. "Abolitionism and the Presbyterian Schism of 1837–38." *Mississippi Valley Historical Review* 36 (December 1949): 391–414.

Stanley, John L. "Majority Tyranny in Tocqueville's America: The Failure of Negro Suffrage in 1846." *Political Science Quarterly* 84 (September 1969): 412–35.

Stevens, J. Harold. "The Influence of New England in Michigan," *Michigan History* 19 (Autumn 1935): 321–53.

Stewart, James Brewer. "Evangelicalism and the Radical Strain in Southern Antislavery Thought During the 1820s." *Journal of Southern History* 39 (August 1973): 379–96.

_____. *Joshua R. Giddings and the Tactics of Radical Politics*. Cleveland: Case Western Reserve University, 1970.

_____. *Holy Warriors: The Abolitionists and American Society*. New York: Hill and Wang, 1976.

Streeter, Floyd B. *Political Parties in Michigan, 1837–1860*. Lansing: Michigan Historical Collections, 1918.

Sweet, William Warren, ed. *Religion on the American Frontier*. Vol. 2, *The Presbyterians, 1783–1840*. New York: Harper & Brothers, 1936.

Swing, James B. "Thomas Morris." *Ohio Archaeological and Historical Society Publications* 10 (1902): 352–60.

Taber, Morris C. "New England Influences in South Central Michigan." *Michigan History* 35 (December 1961): 305–36.

Taylor, Ella Hume. "A History of the First Congregational Church of Geneseo." *Journal of the Illinois State Historical Society* 20 (April 1927): 112–27.

Taylor, George Rogers. *The Transportation Revolution, 1815–1860*. Vol. 4, *The Economic History of the United States*. New York: Holt, Rinehart and Winston, 1951; White Plains, N.Y.: M. E. Sharpe, 1951.

Taylor, Richard S. "Beyond Immediate Emancipation: Jonathan Blanchard, Abolitionism, and the Emergence of American Fundamentalism." *Civil War History* 27 (September 1981): 260–74.

_____. "Seeking the Kingdom: A Study in the Career of Jonathan Blanchard, 1811–1892." Ph.D. diss., Northern Illinois University, 1977.

Thomas, Benjamin. *Theodore Weld: Crusader for Freedom*. New Brunswick: Rutgers University Press, 1950.

Thompson, Charles M. *The Illinois Whigs Before 1846*. Urbana: Illinois University Press, 1915.

Bibliography

Trefousse, Hans L. *Benjamin Franklin Wade: Radical Republican from Ohio.* New York: Twayne Publishers, 1963.

Trester, Delmer J. "David Tod and the Gubernatorial Campaign of 1844." *The Ohio State Archaeological and Historical Quarterly* 62 (April 1953): 162–78.

Tuchalski, Yvonne. "Erasmus Hussey, Battle Creek Antislavery Activist." *Michigan History* 56 (Spring 1972): 1–18.

Turner, James. "Understanding the Populists." *Journal of American History* 67 (September 1980): 354–73.

Tutorow, Norman E. *Texas Annexation and the Mexican War: A Political Study of the Old Northwest.* Palo Alto: Chadwick House Pubs., 1978.

Usher, E. B. "Puritan Influence in Wisconsin." *Proceedings of the Wisconsin Historical Society* (1898): 117–28.

Van Bolt, Roger H. "The Rise of the Republican Party in Indiana, 1840–1860." Ph.D. diss., University of Chicago, 1950.

Vandermeer, Philip R. "Religion, Society, and Politics: A Classification of American Religious Groups." *Social Science History* 5 (Winter 1981): 3–24.

Vander Velde, L. G. "The Synod of Michigan and Movements for Social Reform, 1834–1869." *Church History* 5 (March 1936): 52–70.

Vinyard, Jo Ellen. "Inland Urban Immigrants. The Detroit Irish, 1850." *Michigan History* 57 (Summer 1973): 121–39.

Voegeli, V. Jacque. *Free But Not Equal: The Midwest and the Negro during the Civil War.* 1967. Reprint. Chicago: University of Chicago Press, 1970.

Volpe, Vernon L. "The Anti-Abolitionist Campaign of 1840." *Civil War History* 32 (December 1986): 325–39.

———. "Benjamin Wade's Strange Defeat." *Ohio History* 97 (Summer–Autumn 1988): 122–32.

———. "Did the Liberty Party Elect James K. Polk in 1844?" Paper delivered at annual meeting of the Society for Historians of the Early American Republic, Charlottesville, Virginia, 1989.

———. "The Ohio Election of 1838: A Study in the Historical Method?" *Ohio History* 95 (Summer–Autumn 1986): 85–100.

Wade, Richard C. "The Negro in Cincinnati, 1800–1830." *Journal of Negro History* 39 (January 1954): 43–57.

Walters, Ronald G. *The Antislavery Appeal: American Abolitionism After 1830.* Baltimore: Johns Hopkins University Press, 1976.

Warden, Robert B. *An Account of the Private Life and Public Services of Salmon Portland Chase.* Cincinnati: Westach, Baldwin & Co., 1874.

Watson, Robert Meredith, Jr. "The Anatomy of a Crusade: A Western Reserve Township and the War Against the Slaveholders, 1831–1865." Ph.D. diss., Memphis State University, 1978.

Weisenburger, Francis P. "A Life of Charles Hammond." *The Ohio State Archaeological and Historical Quarterly* 43 (October 1934): 337–427.

———. *The Passing of the Frontier.* Vol. 3, *The History of the State of Ohio.*

221

Edited by Carl Wittke. Columbus: Ohio State Archaeological and Historical Society, 1941.

Welsh, Edward B. "Chillicothe: A Distinguished Rural Presbytery." *Journal of the Presbyterian Historical Society* 23 (September 1945): 137–42.

_____. "Wrestling with Human Values: The Slavery Years." in *They Seek a Country: The American Presbyterians, Some Aspects.* Edited by Gaius Jackson Slosser. New York: Macmillan Co., 1955.

Wendler, Marilyn V. "Antislavery Sentiment and the Underground Railroad in the Lower Maumee Valley." *Northwest Ohio Quarterly* 52 (Spring 1980): 193–208.

Wiecek, William M. *The Sources of Antislavery Constitutionalism in America, 1760–1848.* Ithaca: Cornell University Press, 1977.

Willey, Larry Gene. "The Reverend John Rankin: Early Ohio Antislavery Leader." Ph.D. diss., University of Iowa, 1976.

Wimberly, Ware William. "Missionary Reforms in Indiana, 1826–1860: Education, Temperance, Antislavery." Ph.D. diss., Indiana University, 1977.

Winkle, Kenneth J. "The Politics of Community: Migration and Politics in Antebellum Ohio." Ph.D. diss., University of Wisconsin, Madison, 1984.

_____. "A Social Analysis of Voter Turnout in Ohio, 1850–1860." *Journal of Interdisciplinary History* 13 (Winter 1983): 411–35.

Wittke, Carl. "Ohio's Germans, 1840–1875." *The Ohio Historical Quarterly* 66 (October 1957): 339–54.

Wyatt-Brown, Bertram. "Conscience and Career: Young Abolitionists and Missionaries." In *Anti-Slavery, Religion and Reform: Essays in Memory of Roger Anstey.* Edited by Christine Bolt and Seymour Drescher. Kent, England: William Dawson & Sons, 1980.

_____. *Lewis Tappan and the Evangelical War Against Slavery.* Cleveland: Case Western Reserve University Press, 1969.

Zimmerman, Charles. "The Origin and Development of the Republican Party in Indiana." *Indiana Magazine of History* 13 (September 1917): 211–69; (December 1917): 349–412.

Zorbaugh, C. L. "The Plan of Union in Ohio." *Church History* 6 (June 1937): 145–64.

INDEX

Index

Ashtabula Anti-Slavery Society (cont.)
161n.55; opposes formation of Liberty
party, 42
Ashtabula Colonization Society, 22
Ashtabula Consociation, 72
Ashtabula County, Ohio: Congregationalists in, 72; 1838 election in, 28; divisions
over abolitionism, 22; 1839 election in,
31–33, 161n.58; 1845 election in, 99;
1847 election in, 129; and free-soil fusion, 141; and Liberty party, 41, 42, 62,
70, 83, 113, 172n.12; and Whig party, 41
Ashtabula Sentinel, 41, 52, 84
Atkins, Q. F.: dispute with Chase, 116–17;
supports Liberty party, 47
Austinburg, Ohio: church denounces sin of
slavery, 72; debate over Liberty party,
42; Liberty party vote in, 72

Bailey, Gamaliel: attempt to replace Birney, 114, 189n.12; "border state perspective" of, 150n.29, 191n.41; and coalition
strategy, 192n.3; constitutional views
of, 38–39, 54, 114, 140, 164n.15, 170n.59,
189n.15, 190n.21; and Democratic party,
33, 49, 116–17; dispute with Morris, 112;
and division of American Anti-Slavery
Society, 162n.2; economic views of, 57–
58; edits *National Era,* 113; edits *Philanthropist,* xix, 7, 113, 154n.22, 193n.13;
and 1838 Ohio election, 26–28, 30,
159n.37, 190n.25; and 1839 Ohio election, 163n.9; and 1840 election, 48; and
1840 Hamilton convention, 46; and 1841
Columbus convention, 53; and 1842 Ohio
election, 86; and 1846 Ohio election, 105;
and 1852 election, 141; and free-soil fusion, 127, 141; and Garrisonians, 115,
163n.12, 184n.51, 189n.20; initial opposition to Liberty party, 36–39, 44; and
Mahan case, 27, 158n.35; and Oregon,
90; political views of, 22, 43; religious
views of, 36–37, 121–22, 191n.40; role in
Liberty party, 111–14, 188n.10; supports
Giddings, 83; supports Harrison, 40–41,
44, 46, 48, 164n.22; supports Liberty

party, 39, 46–47, 53, 166n.35, 167n.40;
and Texas issue, 90; view of Chase, 112;
view of Liberty party, xv, 135–36; view
of Van Buren, 40, 125; viewed by William
Birney, 112
Baptists, 70. *See also* Free Will Baptists
Barnburner Democrats, 109, 141. *See also*
Democrats
Barnes, Gilbert Hobbs: view of antislavery
movement, xiii, 8; view of Garrison,
162n.2; Liberty party, xv, 65; view of
Weld's importance, 8–9
Bartley, Mordecai, 92
Batavia, Geauga County, Ohio, 31
Beard, Charles, 56
Bebb, William, 103, 105–6
Beckley, Guy: constitutional views of, 114;
and Liberty party, 74; and Methodist
church, 122; reform program of, 192n.9;
mentioned, 47
Beecher, Edward: and Illinois antislavery
movement, 13–14; and Presbyterian
church, 14, 20; response to Lovejoy's
death, 24; mentioned, 68
Beecher, Lyman: view of abolitionists'
origins, 34; view of Presbyterian division, 21
Bellefontaine (Ohio) Anti-Slavery Society, 42
Belmont County, Ohio, 47, 86
Benezet, Anthony, 145
Birney, James G.: and Chase, 111, 116; and
churches, 21, 26, 120–21; constitutional
views of, 114; and 1840 election, xi,
35–36, 46, 51; and 1844 election, 90, 93,
95; feud with Greeley, 95; and formation
of Liberty party, 35; founds *Philanthropist,* 7; and Garland forgery, 94–95,
183n.47; and Liberty League, 121, 128;
opposed by Chase and Bailey, 55, 110,
114, 188n.12; pessimism of, 15; political
strategy of, 7, 25–26, 158n.30; and Riddle, 158n.30; support in Ohio, 47; visit to
Columbus, 96; and Weld, 8–9; mentioned, 6, 8, 12, 25, 188n.12
Birney, William: father's feud with Greeley, 95; view of Bailey, 112; view of immediate abolition, 12

224

Index

Index

Leavitt, Joshua (cont.)
critique of slavery, 45, 57; 1840 visit to Ohio, 42, 45; and Free Soil party, xviii, 131, 134, 138; part in Democratic forgery, 51; view of Van Buren, 125; mentioned, 122
Lee County, Illinois, 68, 130
LeMoyne, Francis, 35
Lenawee, Michigan, 13
Letters on American Slavery, 9
Lewis, Samuel: criticized by Pillsbury, 123; and 1846 Ohio election, 103, 105–6, 123; and 1852 election, 141; and Liberty party, 54; religious views of, 122; and Wesleyan Methodists, 123, 136; mentioned, 168 n. 46
Liberator, 27
Liberty Hall, 24
Liberty Herald, 83, 85, 193 n. 13
Liberty League, 121, 126, 128
Liberty party: and American Anti-Slavery Society, 162 n. 3; and black civil rights, 2, 56, 104–5, 118, 186 n. 74; community origins of, xii, xiii, 57, 61–62, 64–65, 77–78, 173 n. 19, 177 n. 56; and Congregationalists, xii, 44, 66–70, 72, 175 n. 39; constitutional doctrine of, 39, 114–15, 134, 137; and Democratic party, xvii, 4, 36, 48, 92–95, 167 n. 38, 170 n. 55; and economic interpretation of, 59–62; and economic issues, 58–59, 63, 84, 172 n. 4, 179 n. 13, 193 n. 12; effectiveness of, xvii, 149 n. 20; and 1840 election, 34–53, 168 n. 42, 169–70 n. 54; and 1841 Ohio election, 54; and 1842 Ohio election, 72, 83–87, 180 n. 17; and 1843 Ohio election, 81, 83–85, 179 n. 16; and 1844 election, 82, 88–96; and 1845 Indiana election, 100–101; and 1845 Ohio election, 97–100, 185 n. 61; and 1846 Ohio election, 103–7, 187 n. 81; and 1847 Indiana election, 117–18; and 1847 national convention, 116, 127; and 1847 Ohio election, 129; and 1848 elections, 126, 129–31; and election of Polk, 96; and Free Presbyterians, xii, 66, 74–75; and free-soil fusion, 128, 130–32, 135, 138–42; and Free Soil party, 125–26, 140–41, 194–95 n. 34, 195 nn. 7, 9; and Free Will Baptists, xii,

66, 70, 74, 176 n. 45; and fugitive slaves, 115–16, 118; and fundamentalism, 177 n. 56; and Garland forgery, 92–96; and Garrisonians, 114–15, 120, 136, 184 n. 51, 189 n. 20; in Illinois, xvi, 40, 48, 53, 56, 58, 60–61, 65, 67–69, 129–30, 168 n. 42, 174 n. 24; in Indiana, 40, 53, 60, 63–64, 76, 97, 118, 132, 183 n. 47; and Mexican War, 99, 102, 108; in Michigan, 39, 47, 53, 59–61, 88, 112, 125, 183 n. 47; and New England culture, 6–7; in New York, 93–95, 177 n. 60, 180 n. 26, 183 n. 49, 187 n. 1; in Ohio, xi, xix–xx, 37, 39, 40, 46–47, 53–54, 59–60, 62, 70–75, 81–88, 94, 97, 106, 113, 183 n. 47, 185 nn. 61, 68; origins of, 24, 33–35, 162 n. 1; and partisan loyalties, 40, 42, 45, 47, 142–44, 148 n. 9, 166 n. 34; political divisions in, xx–xxi, 43, 45, 108–12, 115, 119, 123–24, 126–28, 142; political strategy of, xx; and racism in Old Northwest, 2; religious origins of, xi–xii, xiv–xv, 7, 42–43, 55, 66–67, 70–78, 119, 123–24, 135, 137, 145, 174 nn. 21, 24, 177 n. 56, 188 n. 6, 191 n. 45; and Republican party, xix, 140–41, 194 n. 34, 195 n. 7; rural origins of, 61; sectarianism of, xvi, 120–21, 141, 144–45; sectional division in, 192 nn. 3, 4, 6, 125–27, 129, 137–38; social origins of, 63, 79; and Southerners, xvii, 143; and Texas issue, 89–90; urban vote of, 62, 172 nn. 4, 11; on Western Reserve, xix, 37, 41, 61–62, 70, 72–73, 81–84, 94, 97–99, 105–6, 113–14, 129–30, 172 n. 12, 175 n. 39, 179 n. 16, 183 n. 47, 193 n. 13; and Whig party, xvi–xvii, 35–36, 40, 48–49, 51–52, 81–88, 92–107, 118, 136, 143, 169 n. 54, 170 n. 55, 180 n. 19, 181 n. 30, 182 n. 39, 183 n. 49, 184 n. 55, 187 n. 81, 189 n. 20, 190 n. 28, 195 n. 37; in Wisconsin, 69–70, 125, 130, 193 n. 15
Litchfield, Ohio, 73
Livonia, Michigan, 61
Lorain County, Ohio, 61, 94, 166 n. 31
Lorain County Anti-Slavery Society, 166 n. 31
Lovejoy, Elijah: anti-Catholicism of, 23; death of, 14, 16, 20, 23–24, 48; edits *Ob-*

Index